A COMPLETE HISTORY OF
U.S. Combat Aircraft
Fly-Off Competitions

Erik Simonsen

Winners, Losers, and What Might Have Been

Specialty Press
838 Lake Street South
Forest Lake, MN 55025
Phone: 651-277-1400 or 800-895-4585
Fax: 651-277-1203
www.specialtypress.com

Edit by Mike Machat
Layout by Monica Seiberlich

ISBN 978-1-58007-227-4
Item No. SP227

Library of Congress Cataloging-in-Publication Data Available

Written, edited, and designed in the U.S.A.
Printed in China
10 9 8 7 6 5 4 3 2 1

Front Cover:
Chance Vought's impressive F8U-3 Super Crusader launches into the evening sky. (Photo illustration by Erik Simonsen)

Front Flap:
North American Aviation's Mach 2 F-107A. (Boeing Archives)

Front End Paper:
Winner of the first post–World War II U.S. military fly-off competition, Boeing's revolutionary B-47 Stratojet makes a RATO takeoff. (USAF)

Title Page:
Final U.S. variant of the venerable McDonnell Phantom II was this F-4G Wild Weasel. The Phantom II was one of the greatest multi-role fighters ever built. (Photo illustration by Erik Simonsen)

Contents Page:
A Martin XB-51 tri-jet bomber is shown taking off from the company's Baltimore facility. (USAF)

Back End Paper:
Winner of the most recent U.S. military fly-off competition is the Lockheed Martin X-35 Lightning II Joint Strike Fighter. This USMC F-35B STOVL version is hovering. (Erik Simonsen)

Back Cover Photo:
Fly-off competition for a penetration fighter was held with three very different designs. From top, the North American YF-93A, McDonnell's XF-88, and the Lockheed XF-90. (Photo illustration by Erik Simonsen)

Distributed in the UK and Europe by

Crécy Publishing Ltd
1a Ringway Trading Estate
Shadowmoss Road
Manchester M22 5LH England
Tel: 44 161 499 0024
Fax : 44 161 499 0298
www.crecy.co.uk
enquiries@crecy.co.uk

TABLE OF CONTENTS

*by **Richard P. Hallion,*** USAF historian, author and lecturer

FOREWORD

In an era of development programs taking a quarter-century or even longer, it is refreshing, if sobering, to reflect on an earlier era when the successors to aircraft just entering service were already progressing across the drafting boards of the nation's leading aviation manufacturers.

Likewise, it is startling to realize how many of the manufacturers who were competing for advanced fighter and bomber contracts in the post–World War II era are no longer with us, at least not as independent entities. Republic, Fairchild, McDonnell, Douglas, Vought, Martin, Grumman, Convair, and North American were legendary manufacturers. They built such diverse aircraft as the P-47 Thunderbolt and F-105 Thunderchief, the P-51 Mustang and F-86 Sabre, the F2H Banshee and F4H (later F-4) Phantom II, the F4U Corsair and F8U (later F-8) Crusader, the F6F Hellcat and F-14 Tomcat, the B-58 Hustler and F-106 Delta Dart, and the C-123 Provider and A-10 Thunderbolt II. All those companies are now bygone memories, legacy firms incorporated, in great measure, by the large aerospace conglomerations that have absorbed them: Boeing, Lockheed Martin, and Northrop Grumman.

What is astonishing by recent standards is the tremendous vibrancy that was embodied in the aviation and, after 1957, aerospace industry of the United States during the Cold War, which is now remembered almost with a quaint nostalgia for its seeming predictability and normalcy. While much of this development was government supported, it also reflected the individual initiative of companies that risked their futures on a technological bet, on the promise that some new development, some new revolutionary path, would transform aeronautics, reshaping the airplane for a new era.

Boeing staked its future on the swept wing and the podded jet engine, thereby producing not only the B-47 and B-52—which revolutionized America's postwar global strategy—but the 707 and its successors, up to the modern 787. Those passenger jets have proven to be America's most enduring and profitable international export products, extending the nation's civil air dominance that dated to the earlier invention of the Douglas DC-2 and DC-3 of the 1930s.

Lockheed took an obscure paper by a Russian scientist, combined it with advances in computer-aided prediction, envisioned applying the resulting shape to a new design crafted of advanced materials and governed by electronic flight controls, and thereby generated Have Blue, predecessor to the F-117A stealth fighter that single-handedly demolished the heart of Iraq's integrated air-defense network on opening night of the First Gulf War in January 1991.

Readers who know Erik Simonsen's previous works will not be surprised at the attention to detail, the thorough analysis, and the imaginative graphics that are contained in this book. Those who do not are in for a treat.

To place it in context, I think, one must go back to the "Machina" art books of the Renaissance, the speculative books of technology and art that were created for the great patrons of imaginative engineer-artisans such as (and foremost of all) Leonardo da Vinci. But there is an important difference: whereas Leonardo gave us images of the fanciful and what might *be*, Erik Simonsen gives us images and a sense of what might have *been*.

Simonsen shows what in different circumstances might have been a very different aerospace world. In this world, Strategic Air Command might have exchanged its B-36 Peacemakers for B-60 Peacemaker IIs; John F. Kennedy and his advisors might have looked at images of Soviet missiles in Cuba brought back by F8U-3P Crusader III reconnaissance planes; Green Berets defending hamlets in South Vietnam's highlands might have relied upon on-call support from Martin B-51 light bombers; "Going Downtown" deep in Pac Six might have seen F-107s battling MiG-17s and MiG-21s; Soviet generals contemplating war across the Fulda Gap might have worried about Northrop A-9A attack aircraft; and today, Air Force, Marine, Navy, and alliance partners would be transitioning into the Boeing F-32 Joint Strike Fighter and practicing joint tactics with Northrop Grumman YF-23s.

Explorations of "what might mave been" are a too-little-appreciated way of assessing the past and its impact upon the present. Certainly, as a thought experiment such an approach offers a useful means of assessing critical nodal paths in aerospace development and the impact of certain technological developments, industrial approaches, and decision- and policy-making.

But enough of the serious stuff! Time now to sit back and explore the world of Erik Simonsen, a world of vibrant images and exciting projects, all underpinned by an authoritative and provocative text. Enjoy!

ACKNOWLEDGMENTS

The primary goal of this book was to portray aviation history in a creative way. This called for precise imagery presented in conjunction with historic documentation. In particular, this required never-before-seen views of hypothetical aircraft in dramatic color, when existing photography was primarily black and white. This documentation, and its unique visual presentation, was guided by the expert assistance of several individuals. A special acknowledgment goes to my wife, Sharon, whose digital magic turned our three-dimensional aircraft concepts into credible-looking flying machines, bringing to life numerous "what might have been" aircraft. I would also like to thank Dr. Richard P. Hallion, USAF historian, author, and lecturer, for bringing his expertise to the foreword; Dr. Henry Brownlee Jr., aviation historian at the Boeing Archives; Robert F. Dorr, author and aviation historian; Eric Hehs, editor, *Code One* magazine, Lockheed Martin Aeronautics Company; Tony Landis, aviation photographer and author, for providing historic fighter images; Michael J. Lombardi, aviation historian at the Boeing Archives; Mike Machat, aviation artist, for his visionary publishing expertise; William J. Simone, aviation author and historian, for his expert assistance on the history of the North American Aviation F-107A; and Bill Yenne, aviation author and historian.

INTRODUCTION

There are numerous motivations for researching and writing about aircraft competitions. This has been done many times before, but as the decades pass the military procurement process has become increasingly complex and influenced by numerous variables. *A Complete History of U.S. Combat Aircraft Fly-Off Competitions* examines 10 aircraft competitions and at the same time presents a distinctive visual experience. Despite the complexities, the Department of Defense (DoD) competitive process continues as the best solution. However, there are always many unanswered questions following a major down-select. Currently, with so few major new-start programs, is the winner-take-all solution the best way to proceed?

In the 1980s, during the initial Advanced Tactical Fighter (ATF) competition, there were seven prime contractors capable of mass-producing a fighter or bomber. The ensuing years took a toll. In July 1993, what was dubbed the Last Supper was held at the Pentagon. Secretary of Defense Les Aspin and Deputy Secretary of Defense Dr. William Perry presented the CEOs of the top defense contractors with a blunt prediction: "All of you will not be around in a few years." This led to a series of companies extricating themselves from the defense-related business, with others consolidating or merging. Currently there are only three prime airframe contractors left in the United States. In an attempt to prevent any further whittling-down of America's industrial base, the Pentagon is now discouraging major mergers. Yet, dispersing aerospace contract work is difficult with very few major new-starts on the horizon. The contractors have a valid point, especially in light of so many recently contested winner-take-all awards. Substantial contracts, such as the 23 April 1991 Joint Strike Fighter (JSF) award to Lockheed Martin and the 27 October 2015 Long Range Strike-Bomber (LRS-B) award to Northrop Grumman, left the losing competitor with limited options.

The other procurement anomaly is the predictable tendency to reduce the original contracted production number. Gradually reducing the B-2A Stealth bomber fleet from 132 down to only 21, and the reduction and final capping of the F-22 Raptor fleet from an original 750 to 187 fighters, have caused unit costs to soar. Subsequently, the DoD has faced never-ending media criticism. At the end of the Cold War in 1991, there was a rationale to reduce U.S. defense spending. But, as history so often attempts to teach us, world events are cyclical and an overreaction is not prudent. What may be perceived as a relaxation in hostilities will most certainly be temporary. Decisions of this magnitude cannot be corrected. Today we witness China's military buildup and challenge in the Pacific region and the reemergence of Russia's military adventurism.

This book points out within several chapters the importance of multifaceted communications to ensure that the three-way flow keeps contractors, the Pentagon, and Congress properly informed. On 6 April 2009, Sec. of Defense Robert M. Gates announced a massive defense-spending cut that canceled a host of major DoD programs. One of the programs swept up in the cuts was the airborne laser (ABL). Actual ABL performance data and the facts related in Secretary Gates's book, *Duty: Memoirs of a Secretary at War* (2014), seemed at odds with each other. Critical program communications with DoD seemed to be lacking regarding the actual ABL mission operations. As a result, the ABL's performance data was diminished, and the costs were overestimated. Now the United States is without a missile defense system capability to attack during an enemy missile's vulnerable boost phase.

Seeking to improve the procurement process extends beyond aircraft and into the civilian U.S. space program. Long before the Space Shuttle's premature retirement, a NASA X-33 reusable launch vehicle (RLV) competition was held. The X-33 technology demonstrator would present a 50-percent scale RLV. The goal was to quickly develop an unmanned reusable space vehicle to place NASA, military, and emerging commercial payloads into low Earth orbit; if required, a manned capability could be added later. Lockheed and Rockwell International submitted their final X-33 RLV proposals for a spacecraft that could eventually replace the shuttle. Rockwell's proposal was based on proven low-risk shuttle technologies. On 2 July 1996, in front of NASA's Jet Propulsion Laboratory (JPL), NASA Administrator Dan Golden and Vice President Al Gore lifted a scale model of the winning X-33 RLV design out of its box. It was the Lockheed Martin wedge-shaped X-33, named VentureStar. Instead of a rapid development program, NASA elected to take a high-risk path with both the space vehicle and the unproven J-2S linear Aerospike rocket engine. This concept would have been feasible if NASA had an unlimited budget and a decade of development time. The result was a disaster. Beset by technical problems, in 2001 the X-33 program was canceled. Instead of having a Space Shuttle replacement operating by the year 2000, there was nothing.

Despite delays in the NASA Constellation program to develop a new human-rated spacecraft, the retirement process for the shuttle continued. At anytime during the George W. Bush or Barack H. Obama administrations, the impending retirement could have been reversed, but it wasn't. Former Martin Marietta CEO Norman R. Augustine convened a Human Spaceflight Plans Committee to study the situation. At its conclusion, neither the U.S. Congress nor the Obama administration requested additional NASA funding, and the Space Shuttle retirement was complete.

Whether it's an aircraft or spacecraft, the prudent path is to have a new system ready prior to retiring the operational system. This process was not followed and the United States lost its capability to place humans into low Earth orbit. The United States now relies on Russian Soyuz spacecraft to reach the International Space Station, in which billions of U.S. dollars have been invested. Just prior to the Space Shuttle being retired in 2011, the cost was $22 million for a single seat on the Soyuz. By mid-2015 Russia had more than tripled the cost to $76 million for a U.S. astronaut to ride into orbit. During 2014 alone, NASA paid the Russians $400 million in fees. As of late 2015, the United States was still more than 8 years away from having a human-capable space vehicle.

That's 13 years since the Space Shuttle was retired. Experts agree that international cooperation in space exploration is a worthwhile endeavor. However, cooperation is far different from being left vulnerable and dependent on another country to support your entire human spaceflight program. That is placing too much trust in international politics remaining stable. With plenty of blame to go around, this period in the history of the U.S. human spaceflight program will go down as a time of unfortunate and costly decisions.

The high-technology competitions of today's aircraft and space industries offer a bright future. However, for the United States to remain a technology leader in the world, we must make sure we have competent leaders that are not only properly informed, but can apply the lessons of history. During the journey through the 10 chapters of this book, a unique historical and visual experience awaits.

The Photo Illustrations of Erik Simonsen

Over the years I have developed a technique for integrating 3D models and actual aircraft with aerial photography backgrounds. This allows for aircraft concepts that have never flown or entered operational service to be depicted in a realistic inflight scenario. With critical control of lighting, actual aircraft can also be portrayed in dramatic situations that would be difficult to create with air-to-air photography. These images are credited as "Author Photo/Illustration" in contrast to my photographs, which are credited as "Author."

EARLY TECHNOLOGY SHAPES THE FUTURE
JET ENGINES AND SWEPT WINGS

Going vertical in a hypothetical dogfight between USMC Maj. John Glenn's F-86F Sabre Jet, with "MiG Mad Marine" artwork on the fuselage, and a North Korean MiG-15. Maj. Glenn shot down three MiG-15s during his combat tour. Throughout the Korean War the F-86 achieved a 10 to 1 kill ratio over the Soviet-built MiG-15 fighter. However, air-to-air combat during the Korean War demonstrated distinct superior qualities of both the swept-wing designs. The U.S. and the Soviet Union both incorporated captured German aeronautical technology into their new jet fighters. (Author Photo/Illustration)

Throughout World War II, the United States and its allies consistently tracked and documented the significant advances achieved by German aerodynamicists and rocket scientists. Yet they were not doing an adequate job of analysis or replicating the technology. Overall, the consensus was that it was vital that the Allies capture as much aeronautical and scientific data before Germany, or its Axis-ally Japan, could fully exploit the technology.

A Leading Edge

Late in the war, three first-of-a-kind advanced aircraft were fielded by the Luftwaffe. Achieving flight on 18 July 1942, the first operational twinjet Messerschmitt Me 262 Schwalbe[1] (Swallow) fighters appeared near the end of the war. Over Munich, Germany, on 25 July 1944, a Royal Air Force (RAF) Mosquito reconnaissance aircraft was attacked by an Me 262, marking the first combat sortie by a jet fighter. During the next few months, startled gunners aboard United States Army Air Forces (USAAF) Boeing B-17s and Consolidated B-24s found it nearly impossible to track the fast-moving jets.

Only 300 of the 1,400 Me 262s produced ever entered combat. Had the Luftwaffe been able to field the jet interceptor in greater numbers, it could have been disastrous for the Allied bombing campaign. Piston-powered USAAF P-51, P-47, and P-38 escort fighters had to confront the Luftwaffe jets. At 437 mph combat speed, the P-51 was the fastest AAF fighter; the Luftwaffe Me 262 was about 100 mph faster. With better performance plus experience, P-51 pilots capitalized on several Me 262 operational weaknesses. Under certain conditions with precise maneuvering, the P-51 could outturn the Me 262, thus increasing the odds of a firing solution.

In aerial combat, both the Republic P-47 Thunderbolt and Lockheed P-38 Lightning utilized increased speed during a dive to gain the advantage. With the slow spool-up in power of early jet engines, the Me 262 was sluggish during takeoff. Engine responsiveness and the mild sweep of the wings resulted in poor low-speed handling. Additionally, the Me 262 was particularly vulnerable during landing, and AAF pilots established a routine of loitering just out of sight near Luftwaffe Me 262 airbases.

Although the liquid-fuel rocket-powered Messerschmitt Me 163B Komet[2] first flew on 1 September 1941, it was not ready for combat operations until July 1944. (The unstable liquid fuel for the Komet's Walter HWK 509A-2 rocket engine proved extremely hazardous during transport and fueling operations.) The Me 163B attained a

The Messerschmitt Me 262 Swalble (Swallow), was the first jet fighter to see combat during World War II. Equipped with twin-engines, the Me 262 had a top speed of 540 mph. First flown on 18 July 1942, it featured a slight 18.5-degee wing sweep on the outer wing panel, with a straight center-wing section. The Messerschmitt design also incorporated the first leading-edge slats to negate instability tendencies at low speeds. (Author Photo/Illustration)

The NAA P-51B/D Mustang changed the course of the war in Europe, once it was able to escort allied bombers deep into Germany and back. Under the direction of NAA engineer Edgar Schmued, an 85-gallon fuel tank was installed aft of the P-51B's cockpit armor plate. This extra tank, combined with internal fuel and drop tanks, increased endurance from 4.75 hours to 7.5 hours. Additionally, Schmued's team solved problems associated with the altered aircraft center-of-gravity, and the P-51s were ready to go. (Author Photo/Illustration)

With its unique liquid fuel rocket engine, the Messerschmitt Me 163B Komet saw limited Luftwaffe service during World War II. The Me 163B could reach approximately 600 mph with a 7.5 second fuel-burn time, which allowed for only one or two intercept passes. With its rocket fuel expended, the aircraft would glide back to its base. Although the Komet was a difficult target for gunners aboard allied bombers, the high speed also hindered the Me 163B pilot from achieving a firing solution. The rocket plane did manage at least nine confirmed bomber kills. (Author Photo/Illustration)

top speed of 600 mph, but had a very limited engine burn time of approximately 7.5 minutes. This required the Komet to take off near the bombers' predicted route and just prior to their arrival overhead. The Me 163B accelerated to an altitude well above the bomber formations and then, in idle power, dove firing its two 30mm cannons. With its rocket fuel expended, the mission culminated with a glide back to base. These mission tactics relegated the Me 163B to a rather limited role, although its technology held promise. Only 279 Me 163Bs were delivered, and the JG 400 Komet Group was credited with shooting down nine bombers during their combat service.

An inflight view of the first U.S. jet fighter, the Bell YP-59A Airacomet. It was during World War II, on 1 October 1942, when the aircraft took flight. Powered by two GE-1A engines that produced only 1,200 pounds of thrust each, the Airacomet was underpowered. This image depicts a YP-59A prototype (t/n 2108772). Eventually 20 P-59As and 30 P-59Bs were produced by Bell Aircraft. Although the P-59 never saw combat, the new jet engine technology ushered jet fighters into the U.S. arsenal. (Author Photo/Illustration)

Although only three prototypes of the Curtiss XP-55 Ascender were built, this view depicts a conceptual operational P-55 attack aircraft. The swept-wing/forward canard, and pusher-propeller design of the Curtiss XP-55 is reminiscent of the Burt Rutan VariEze configuration first flown many decades later, in May 1975. The XP-55 made its first flight on 19 July 1943, which was two years prior to the U.S. obtaining captured German swept-wing technology. Beginning in November 1939, United States Army Air Corps (USAAC) planners were hoping for improved speed with the incorporation of a swept-wing on a light-attack aircraft. However, aerodynamicists were unaware of severe instability encountered in certain flight regimes. The first XP-55 prototype flown by Curtiss test pilot Harvey Gray was lost when the aircraft entered an uncontrollable inverted flat spin. Gray was able to bail out and survived. Several aerodynamic modifications were ordered for the remaining two prototypes, but the XP-55 never entered production. (Author Photo/Illustration)

First flown on 15 June 1943, and entering service during World War II, the Luftwaffe Arado Ar 234B "Blitz" light bomber/reconnaissance was the first multi-jet bomber, and the first to incorporate engines in sleek nacelles under the wings. The Ar 234B also used a Rocket Assisted Takeoff (RATO) system mounted under the wings, and drop tanks mounted on the nacelles. Developed after the war, the Soviet Ilyushin IL-28 Beagle light bomber also featured a similar nacelle configuration. Only the Boeing XB-47 located engines within nacelles mounted on struts below its swept wing. Later, both the XB-47 and XB-45 used RATO, and the XB-45 incorporated drop tanks mounted under the nacelles. (Author Photo/Illustration)

Although capable of outturning U.S. fighters while under power, during the glide phase of the mission, the Me 163B was susceptible to intercepts and many were destroyed on the ground by strafing U.S. fighters.

In Autumn 1944, Germany also deployed the first multiengine jet bomber/reconnaissance aircraft. The Arado Ar 234B Blitz (Lightning) was a single-seat twin-engine light bomber/reconnaissance aircraft. Capable of reaching 461 mph and 32,800 feet altitude, the unique aircraft incorporated its jet engines in wing-mounted nacelles, a configuration that was later emulated. The Ar 234B had its share of engine problems, however, and was predominantly assigned to reconnaissance missions. On 2 August 1944, a Luftwaffe Ar 234B flew a reconnaissance sortie over Normandy Beach, France, the first recce mission by a jet aircraft. In September, reconnaissance sorties were flown over Great Britain, and in late 1944, Ar 234Bs were used in combat during the Battle of the Bulge.

As a follow-on to the Me 262, the single-engine Heinkel He 162A-2 Spatz (Sparrow) went into production very late in the war. In a remarkable 38-day evolution from drawing board to prototype, the He 162 flew on 6 December 1944. Because of diminishing strategic materials due to Allied bombing the aircraft was primarily constructed with wood, with the exception of necessary metal parts. A planned production run of 4,000 He 162s could have overwhelmed Allied bombers and fighters. With a top speed of 559 mph, the He 162 proved to be the fastest jet in the Luftwaffe inventory. Fortuitously for the Allies, several contributing factors not related to advanced technology enabled the defeat of the Luftwaffe.

An overriding cause was the ill-advised military tactical/strategic decisions of Nazi dictator Adolf Hitler, which included an order to deploy the Me 262 as a bomber rather than a fighter/interceptor. This severely hampered the jet's introduction into the war, and it was never deployed as a bomber. Additionally, Germany's senior command failed to adequately fund and promptly field these innovative technologies.

Another factor was the introduction of long-range P-51B fighter escorts throughout Allied bombing missions. NAA had modified the Merlin-powered P-51B Mustang to extend its range, resulting in a dramatic increase in successful bombing results. Even more aggressive tactics were initiated by the commander of the Eighth Air Force, Gen. Jimmy Doolittle,[3] who ordered escorting P-51s to push ahead of the bomber force and intercept Luftwaffe fighters.

Check your six! A Luftwaffe Me 262 presenting its sleek head-on profile, a situation that allied pilots trained hard to avoid. (Author Photo/Illustration)

Gen. Jimmy Doolittle considered the P-51's performance superior to the P-38. Gen. Doolittle gradually increased P-51 numbers for bomber escort duty and assigned the P-38 to reconnaissance sorties. Hence, with more bombers getting through, the vastly improved bombing of vital military industrial and aircraft manufacturing plants took its toll. With a lack of war materials and the continued destruction of factories, German industry was unable to produce the needed numbers of aircraft and ancillary equipment. In retrospect, the advanced Luftwaffe jet fighters still represented a quantum leap in technology, placing them in a category vastly superior to Allied aircraft. Had the Luftwaffe properly fielded this new technology, World War II might have lasted much longer.

Operation LUSTY

If it weren't for the quick action taken by several astute AAF planners and strategists, the famed Boeing B-47 Stratojet and NAA F-86 Sabre Jet configurations may have evolved much differently. In fact, the path and duration of the Cold War might have been altered without the United States having acquired German rocket technology. By early 1945, U.S. military intelligence was formulating various strategies to safely secure advanced German technology when the war reached a conclusion. If possible, the United States and its close allies needed to collect various critical technologies before they were destroyed by German scientists or captured by Soviet forces. Even though the Soviet Union was an ally in the fight against Germany, there were clear signals from Russian dictator and General Secretary Joseph Stalin that he had his own post-war plans for Soviet expansion. This affected large sections of Eastern Europe well after the war. On the outside we celebrated victory, but the bond of trust customary within allied warriors was evaporating.

Per orders from Gen. Carl Spaatz, Commander, Strategic Air Forces in Europe, a plan code-named LUSTY (Luftwaffe Secret Technology) was initiated. Operation LUSTY would enable the exploitation of Luftwaffe technology by retrieving as much data and equipment as possible from various German scientific centers and Luftwaffe facilities. This included actual intact aircraft and missiles. Concurrently, Operation Overcast, later known as Operation Paperclip, was established to secure German scientists and technicians and process them for relocation to the United States.

The P-51D Mustang entered combat service in early June 1944, just in time for the Allied 6 June D-Day invasion. The "D" model featured a 360-degree bubble canopy, six .50-cal. wing-mounted guns, and superior range that encompassed all of Europe. The P-51 accounted for almost half of all enemy aircraft destroyed in Europe, 4,950 aerial victories and 4,131 destroyed on the ground. (Author Photo/Illustration)

This view depicts a conceptual evolved version of a Luftwaffe Focke-Wulf Ta 183 Huckebein. During World War II, aircraft designer Kurt Tank designed the swept-wing t-tail jet fighter, but it never went into production. The November 1950 appearance of the similarly shaped MiG-15 "Fagot" during the Korean War, confirmed that the Soviet Union had also collected sophisticated German aeronautical data immediately after the war. After the war, Kurt Tank helped develop a similar aircraft for Argentine Air Force, the Pulga II, which served in the Fuerza Aerea Argentina until 1960. (Author Photo/Illustration)

A year after World War II ended in Europe, on 17 May 1946, the USAAF's first multi-jet engine bomber made its initial flight. The Douglas XB-43 Jetmaster, with J35 jet engines located in the fuselage, evolved from the XB-42 Mixmaster, an unusual counter-rotating pusher-prop design. The XB-43 retained straight-wings and only two prototypes were produced. The light bomber which also featured unusual separate side by side blister canopies, was not ordered into production. The USAAF considered the XB-43 more of a testbed for multi-engine configurations. (National Museum of the USAF)

The operations were vital to continued prosecution of the ongoing war against Japan in the Pacific Theater. Critical questions lingered. Did Germany transfer jet engines, ballistic rocket technology, and nuclear materials/data to the Japanese military? Examination of documents and/or interviewing German scientists could provide the answers.

Secrets Hidden Right Before Your Eyes

On 13 April 1945, the Hermann Goering Aeronautical Research Center,[4] also referred to as the Luftfahrtforschungsanstalt (LFA), at Volkenrode, near the western part of Braunschweig, Germany, was captured by American forces. Within nine days Col. Donald Putt set up a command center, commencing Operation LUSTY. As one of the first military transport aircraft landed at the austere airfield, newly arriving intelligence officials peered out the windows and wondered where the huge aeronautical facility was. Later they learned it was actually adjacent to the airfield, but extensively camouflaged.

Aerial views portrayed an innocuous scene of innocent farms with planted gardens and stork nests on rooftops. In reality, various buildings were covered by separate layers of thick cement, which in turn were covered with several feet of soil that included plants and trees.[5] Due to the elaborate concealment effort, Allied reconnaissance flights had completely missed the facility. Unknown to the Allies, the location was a facility consisting of 76 buildings that included munitions storage, laboratories, and seven wind tunnels, including an 8-meter tunnel.

German aerodynamicist Dr. Theodore Zobel, who assisted Col. Putt's team at the site, had invented a technique for using interferometry to make wind-tunnel airflow visible as it passed over a model. His method employed mirrors and special optics. Dr. Zobel's equipment was quickly shipped to Wright Field, Ohio.[6] Another massive wind-tunnel facility not too far from Peenemunde accommodated wind-tunnel models for testing up to Mach 7 (5,328.4 mph). It was at this location that models of the V-1 Buzz Bomb and V-2 ballistic rocket were tested.

Col. Putt arranged for debriefings of onsite scientists detained by U.S. soldiers. The majority were cooperative and even led investigators to their homes to retrieve documents they were saving for later research or industrial use. Detailed data buried in tin cans in backyards revealed rocket-fuel formulas. Nearly 5,000 documents were retrieved in this manner. Numerous wind-tunnel documents included work on swept-wing aircraft in the Mach .8 (608.9 mph) to Mach 1.2 (913.4 mph) range. Additional Volkenrode wind tunnels were capable of higher Mach regimes and were linked to aircraft concepts such as the Me 262 HG III (Stage II) with a 35-degree sweep and the Me 262 HG III (Stage III) with a more advanced 45-degree sweep. These advanced designs came about too late in the war for the Luftwaffe.

Professor Dr. Adolf Busemann,[7] who had directed aerodynamic model testing in the wind tunnels, remained onsite and assisted the Americans. Busemann, a German aerospace engineer, had presented the first research paper on the concept of swept wings at the Volta Conference in Rome in 1935. Under the auspices of Operation Paperclip, Busemann would eventually emigrate to the United States in 1947. Col. Putt decided that Dr. Theodore von Karman[8] should visit Volkenrode and speak with Dr. Busemann. In 1944, at the urging of Gen. "Hap" Arnold, von Karman had left the California Institute of Technology to become head of the AAF Scientific Advisory Board. (During von Karman's illustrious career he received numerous prestigious scientific awards; in his honor, each year Caltech presents the International Von Karman Wings Award to a selected individual.)

One meeting was also attended by Boeing chief aerodynamicist George Schairer,[9] also onsite at Volkenrode primarily as a member of the AAF Scientific Advisory Board. At the meeting, von Karman asked Dr. Busemann to explain in basic terms the advantage of swept wings. Busemann replied, "By sweeping the wings you fooled the air into thinking that it was not going as fast as it really was, or not so fast as the airplane itself was moving through the atmosphere.

Therefore you delayed the onset of compressibility drag." Busemann continued, "When you get close to the speed of sound drag just takes off, but by sweeping the wings and fooling the molecules in the air you delay that great rise in drag curve."[10]

Schairer could read German and was able to absorb the technical materials quickly. Of course, he was there as a government agent and not as a Boeing employee; the government eventually shared the recovered data with all U.S. aircraft manufacturers. Schairer was intrigued by the swept wing. He knew that work was underway on the XB-47 with a straight-wing configuration, and that Boeing had heavily invested time and money in the design. Schairer was also aware that testing had indicated that the current configuration would not produce performance that could beat the competing designs from Consolidated-Vultee (Convair), Martin, and North American Aviation (NAA). He felt so strongly about the swept-wing revelations that he quickly notified his design team to hold up work.

Mounting the engines on struts below the wing instead of being integral with the wing had two advantages: The wing could be swept and the struts holding the engines mated at the correct airflow angle. This meant that redesigning integrated wing engines would be much more difficult. Also, in the event of an engine fire, the new design would allow the engine to drop away, therefore not compromising the wing and causing catastrophic damage.

Schairer quickly sent a letter[11] to his Boeing team that contained additional details. (The original letter referring to the German wind-tunnel data written by George Schairer no longer exists, but a replica resides in the Boeing archives.) He misled the censors by pre-signing the mailing envelope as a team member and printing out the word CENSORED. Back at Boeing, Schairer's notes did not immediately convince everyone that a design change was in order. Initially, the AAF Program Office also concurred that it would be foolish to modify the XB-47, and many Boeing engineers agreed.[12] However, after additional wind-tunnel testing, the Boeing team concurred with Schairer and quickly received AAF approval for a configuration change. It was a critical decision that literally changed history.

Wind "Tunnel Vision"

During the 1940s, Boeing began to pursue the idea of constructing their own wind-tunnel facility. Along with several major aircraft contractors, Seattle-based Boeing had been renting time at Caltech's 10-foot wind tunnel in Pasadena, California.[13] Prior to and during World War II, several aircraft wind-tunnel models, including the AT-6, B-25, B-17, B-24, B-29, P-38, and P-51, had been tested there. Rumors that Douglas had acquired confidential data on the Boeing Model 247 through security leaks at that facility provided further impetus. Boeing proceeded with an eye on future aviation technology and the protection of their industrial secrets. The total cost of an advanced wind tunnel would be approximately $1 million, a huge sum at the time.

Consulting wind-tunnel experts Theodore von Karman and John Markham convinced Boeing president Bill Allen that the new Grand Coulee Dam in the northwest part of the country would generate cheaper electricity to run the tunnel facility. Both consultants were also familiar with recent jet-engine technology developments that would guide the future of aviation design. Allen urged the Boeing board to authorize an initial kick-start amount of $25,000. Funding was reluctantly approved, and the wind-tunnel construction was initiated. It would feature an advanced 24-foot-diameter fan capable of testing models to just under the speed of sound (Mach 1 = 761.2 mph).[14]

It was during construction, in March 1943, that all doubts regarding the project dissolved. That month, Allen attended the secret AAF-sponsored aircraft contractor's meeting at Muroc Army Air Field. The visit included an exclusive aerial demonstration of the Bell XP-59A Airacomet, the United States' first jet fighter. Presidents of all the major U.S. companies were also briefed on the status of jet-engine technology. This event confirmed that Allen had made the correct decision. Boeing's wind tunnel began operations during February 1944, an investment that would pay dividends for decades.

The evolution of the XB-47 is depicted in the wind tunnel models from the upper left; straight-wing Model 424 that was similar to the competing medium bombers; model with engines located in the upper fuselage, deemed unsafe by the AAF program office; final XB-47 configuration with 35-degree swept-wing with engines mounted below the wings. (Boeing Archives)

Furys, Tornados, and Sabres

It was September 1945 and the war in the Pacific Theater had ended. NAA was anxious to greatly expand its business in the jet aircraft market. As a result of the post-war drawdowns, NAA's employee count went from 87,000 to approximately 5,000 practically overnight. President and Chairman Dutch Kindelberger had to carefully plan for the retention of his engineering teams. Concurrently, hundreds of aircraft orders on the books were canceled. Additionally, NAA was in the process of tooling-up to build Lockheed's P-80 fighter jet under license when its Kansas City Plant[19] was closed. (During World War II, NAA's Kansas City Plant had turned out thousands of B-25 Mitchell bombers and P-51 Mustang fighters.) To turn things around, NAA had a multipronged effort underway to pursue an AAF medium bomber contract and produce jet fighters for both the AAF and Navy.

The XFJ-1 being developed for the Navy was a straight-wing configuration, reminiscent of previous World War II aircraft, only jet-powered. The contract for three XFJ-1 (NA-134) prototypes was signed on 1 January 1945, prior to the end of World War II. The following

Flight-Testing Luftwaffe Aircraft

Another AAF team, known as "Watson's Whizzers" operated under the command of Col. Harold Watson.[15] They were responsible for acquiring various Luftwaffe aircraft types in flyable condition, if possible. The Whizzers also managed to train volunteer AAF pilots to test fly the Me 262 and the He 162A-2 in Germany. Many types of Luftwaffe aircraft (flyable and nonflyable) were acquired, including at least 15 Me 262s.[16, 17] Although examples of the Me 163B Komet were captured, its rocket engine was considered too dangerous to ignite. It was flight-tested in the glide mode only. NAA engineers were able to examine a captured Me 262 and replicate its leading edge slats.

Some Me 262s were flown to France and others were transported by truck. All were cocooned for weather protection and transported by ship to the United States and eventually to Wright Field (Wright Field was renamed Wright-Patterson AFB on 13 January 1948).

An AAF B-17 and B-24 were dedicated to Col. Putt for transporting documents to Wright Field[18] and then quickly returning for additional materials. The Whizzers moved with haste, mostly at night, as this section of Germany was located in the British sector. Ownership complications and delays could have ensued if arriving British commanders figured out what was going on.

NAA opted to incorporate swept-wing data into their XP-86 fighter. The performance proved exceptional, and in turn led to the evolution of one of the top air-to-air combat fighters. This plan view illustrates the similarities and differences of a NAA F-86F Sabre Jet and Soviet Mikoyan MiG-15 "Fagot," both evolving from post–World War II technology. (Author)

Chapter 1

THE QUEST FOR A MEDIUM JET BOMBER

NAA XB-45, CONVAIR XB-46, BOEING XB-47, MARTIN XB-48

A USAF B-45C Tornado (t/n 8010) from the 47th Bomb Wing begins a night sortie. This particular B-45C is currently on display at the National Museum of the United States Air Force. (Author Photo/Illustration)

The USAAF pursuit for the first jet-powered medium bomber is a story of competition and expediency. Although the jet engine was in its developmental infancy, the United States was confident that the technology would mature rapidly. Not knowing at the time when Germany could be defeated, the U.S. and its allies were under tremendous pressure to increase the effectiveness of its strategic bombing program. Moreover, the Allies had to wonder if Germany had any additional technical surprises ready to be unleashed. As a result, the USAAF pursuit of a new jet-powered medium bomber would be a rapid-paced competition.

The official U.S. shift to recognize the potential of jet engines began in April 1941, when the Commander of the USAAF, Gen. Henry "Hap" Arnold, witnessed a ground taxi demonstration of Great Britain's first jet-powered fighter, the Gloster E.28/39 Meteor. During the visit the U.S. military delegation was also provided with detailed design plans for the British centrifugal turbojet. Two brilliant engineers who changed history share the invention of the jet engine. In Great Britain Frank Whittle, a Royal Air Force officer and engineer, patented his design for a centrifugal turbojet in 1930; his first prototype was ground tested in 1937. At nearly the same time while working independently in Germany, Dr. Hans von Ohain invented a 992-pound-thrust jet engine that powered Germany's first jet fighter, the Heinkel He 178. It first flew on 27 August 1939. Whittle's 1,700-pound-thrust engine powered the British Gloster Meteor, on its first flight on 15 May 1941. Despite problems with reliability and generating adequate thrust, the potential for the new type of engine was significant.

The summer of 1941 was a critical time for U.S. jet-engine technology. Per orders from Gen. Arnold, General Electric[1] was contracted under license to develop an improved variant of the British TG-100 engine. Additionally, during August of that year, Gen. Arnold held a secret briefing for Bell Aircraft president Lawrence Bell regarding the new propulsion technology; he also discussed the possibility of designing a new jet-powered fighter. At the direction of the AAF, General Electric was developing the GE-1A engine under license—it was a U.S. version of the British engine. With extremely tight security, Bell Aircraft proceeded and America's first jet fighter was born. Powered by two GE-1A centrifugal-flow engines generating 1,200 pounds of thrust each, the Bell XP-59A Airacomet made its first flight on 1 October 1942.

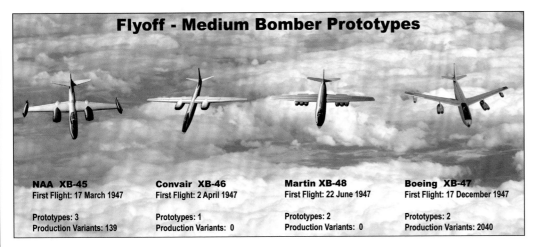

Flyoff - Medium Bomber Prototypes

NAA XB-45
First Flight: 17 March 1947

Prototypes: 3
Production Variants: 139

Convair XB-46
First Flight: 2 April 1947

Prototypes: 1
Production Variants: 0

Martin XB-48
First Flight: 22 June 1947

Prototypes: 2
Production Variants: 0

Boeing XB-47
First Flight: 17 December 1947

Prototypes: 2
Production Variants: 2040

Bomber prototype diagram. (Author Photo/Illustration)

(Convair),[5] Glenn L. Martin Company, and NAA. Lockheed deferred on this competition and focused its resources on a new jet fighter. Northrop also declined to compete and continued to invest in heavy-bomber designs with a flying-wing configuration. Subsequently, the following aircraft designations were assigned: Boeing XB-47, Convair XB-46, Martin XB-48, and NAA XB-45.

North American Aviation XB-45 Tornado: Preplanning Expertise

Business-savvy NAA Chairman and President Dutch Kindelberger was cognizant of how eager the AAF was to have a jet-powered bomber in service as soon as possible. His passion and attitude prevailed, and this had a tremendous impact on the development of NAA's next aircraft. Precisely when the war ended was not a factor, since Kindelberger was confident that jet-powered aircraft were the future for NAA. Essentially, NAA had been working on new bomber-design studies since 1943. By January 1944, Kindelberger had actually discussed progress on future concepts with the AAF. NAA had developed the piston-powered XB-28 (NA-63), which was a larger and more-advanced follow-on to the famed B-25 Mitchell medium bomber. The XB-28 was not authorized for production, and only two prototypes were built and tested. Nevertheless, demonstrating the basic design proved useful, and the propulsion could be switched to jets. In turn, the AAF's leadership was well aware of NAA's dependable reputation for aircraft production rates and innovative assembly processes that were supporting the war effort.

Let the Planes Begin

An informal AAF request issued to aircraft manufacturers in June 1943 set the groundwork for the development of a large multi-jet-engine bomber. After reviewing the responses, the Air Materiel Command (AMC), with increased confidence, issued more specific prerequisites on 17 November 1944.[2] Post–World War II requirements for the medium bomber called for a minimum of four engines, an aircraft weight between 80,000 and 200,000 pounds, and a bomb load of 8,000 to 22,000 pounds,[3] depending on mission combat radius. Additionally, a cruising speed of 450 mph, a top speed of 550 mph, a range of 3,500 miles, and a service ceiling of 45,000 feet were stipulated.[4] Based on the performance of interceptors at the time, the defensive armament would consist of Emerson Electric radar-directed twin .50-cal. machine guns or 20mm cannons mounted in the tail. The AAF concluded that because of its speed, the new jet bomber could only be intercepted from its six-o'clock position.

Four major aircraft contractors responded with their respective aircraft configurations: the Boeing Company, Consolidated-Vultee

NAA's number-one XB-45 prototype (t/n 559479) shows off its clean lines with a low-level pass over the runway at Muroc Army Air Field. (National Museum of the USAF)

The first NAA XB-45 (t/n 559479) prototype taking off at Muroc using Rocket-Assisted TakeOff (RATO). Other than the Boeing XB-47, the XB-45 was the only medium-bomber competitor to employ a RATO system. (National Museum of the USAF)

Trailing black smoke from early jet engines, a B-45A Tornado (t/n 7073) begins a test flight. (USAF)

Under the direct leadership of NAA vice president Lee Atwood, design work on a new medium bomber commenced. The new configuration eventually evolved into Model NA-130 and incorporated some of the basic structural configuration of the XB-28, but with aerodynamically designed nacelles each housing two jet engines. By July 1943, the mockup was approved and the XB-45 moved into detailed production design.

Tornado: A Twist of Fate

An unusual twist in the medium-bomber competition took place when AAF evaluation officers reached several early decisions, prior to any of the competing prototypes being flown. Their studies concluded that the four-engine Convair XB-46 was inferior to the NAA four-engine XB-45, mainly due to its increased weight combined with the thrust limits of current jet engines. However, a single XB-46 prototype was permitted to be completed for flight-testing. Convair elected to defer its funding for a second XB-46 prototype to initiate other concept studies. Meanwhile, the six-engine competitors, the Boeing XB-47 and Martin XB-48, would proceed with assembly of their prototypes. Additionally, because of its extensive prelimi-

A USAF B-45A Tornado (t/n 7038) prepares for a sortie. Note the B-45's configuration of the engine intakes positioned well ahead of the leading edge of the wing and directly in the cockpit's left and right field of view. Both the prototypes and production aircraft received flat black antiglare paint on the nacelles. (USAF)

A look-down view of a B-45A (t/n 7093) flying over the Grand Canyon. The radar-directed tail guns slated for the B-45B proved to be unsuccessful, and NAA quickly moved to the C variant with a manned tail-gunner's position. (Photo of Aircraft, USAF; Photo of Background, Author)

nary work, NAA was awarded a contract for three XB-45 experimental prototypes on 5 February 1946. With the Cold War heating up, critical procurement decisions were accelerated, and on 30 October 1946 NAA, was awarded a production contract for 96 B-45A Tornados (NA-147). The AAF[6] required a medium jet bomber quickly, and NAA was the contractor in the best position to expedite the job.

NAA's design featured four engines mounted integral with and below the wings. Each Allison-built GE J35 provided 4,000 pounds of thrust. This configuration was a basic laminar-flow straight-wing design with a span of 89 feet. The landing gear had a traditional tricycle arrangement, consisting of a nose wheel and main landing gear which retracted into the engine nacelles. Engineers increased the dihedral of the horizontal stabilizer to keep its leading-edge surfaces out of the hot engine exhaust. The XB-45's wings were thick enough to allow for internal self-sealing fuel tanks capable of holding 3,400 gallons. The B-45 design also provided for 600-gallon wingtip tanks, plus drop tanks mounted below the engine nacelles to further increase range beyond its average of 1,800 miles.

The XB-45 was manned by a crew of three in a pressurized environment with the pilot and copilot's cockpit located under a clear, fixed canopy. NAA opted for this configuration to simplify the pressurization system. The navigator/bombardier was located in the lower forward fuselage. Similar to the Boeing B-29's arrangement, the bomb bay and aft section were not pressurized. In the operational

Parked B-45As from the 47th Bomb Wing on the Langley AFB, Virginia, flight line in July 1952, prior to the 47th departing for RAF Sculthorpe, England. (USAF)

attention of the engineering team was the sluggish hydraulic flight controls. The good news for NAA was that none of these issues were showstoppers, and basically the XB-45 flew very well.

By mid-April 1948, XB-45 number one had accumulated 120 flights, attaining a top speed of 516 mph. After making a total of 135 flights, the number-one aircraft was flown to the Douglas plant in Long Beach, California, and temporarily stored. On 3 August, it was flown to Muroc for installation of the uprated General Electric J47 engines, each capable of delivering 5,200 pounds of thrust. After additional flight-testing with J47s by both NAA and Air Force pilots, the first prototype was accepted by the USAF[9] on 30 April 1948. In a long line of NAA firsts, the B-45[10] became the first operational multi-engine jet bomber in the USAF. The second prototype (t/n 559480) had initiated test flights on 10 December 1947. After completion of 44 flight hours, and a J47 retrofit, the second prototype was also accepted by the USAF[11] on 27 July 1948.[12]

bomber, the tail gunner's compartment for the fourth crewman was pressurized. The B-45B was designed with a radar-directed tail-gun assembly operated from the forward section. The system proved unsuccessful, however, and the manned tail-gunner's station was retained. An abundant amount of captured World War II swept-wing aeronautical data, collected under Operation LUSTY, was translated and studied by NAA engineers. However, the engineering team concluded that the XB-45 was too far along in development to make the switch to a new configuration. NAA executives had determined that keeping the XB-45 on schedule was paramount, and the new swept-wing data would be directed toward NAA's XP-86. Since work on the XP-86 jet-fighter program was under way at NAA's Englewood facility, only the three XB-45 experimental prototypes would be built there. Additional factory space at Douglas Aircraft in Long Beach, California, was leased for B-45A production.

Tragedy at Muroc

On 20 September 1948, during a test flight of the number-one prototype at Muroc, George Krebs initiated a high-speed diving maneuver to test the load factor of the aircraft. As the aircraft accelerated, a sudden explosive force ripped off the right nacelle. The debris entered the slipstream and part of the horizontal stabilizer was hit and separated from the aircraft. As the XB-45 departed

The Tornado Flies First

To avoid the XB-45 being viewed from the adjacent Los Angeles Airport, the number-one XB-45 prototype (t/n 559479) was disassembled and transported overland 105 miles to Muroc for its first flight. On 17 March 1947, the XB-45 took to the air with engineering test pilots George Krebs and copilot Paul Brewer aboard.[7] Because of previously known landing-gear-door lock problems, the gear was not retracted during the flight. This required speed to be limited to no more than 230 mph. The rationale for this was that even though new landing-gear-door locks were available, they had not yet been installed on the prototype. NAA felt that keeping the first flight on schedule was more important than achieving a higher speed on that flight. The speed objective could be easily reached later.[8]

During the flight debrief, the pilots reported a smooth-flying aircraft with no major anomalies. There were several squawks, including a problematic pressurization system that required the crew to wear oxygen masks even though the primary reason for the fixed canopy was to improve cockpit pressurization. Another item brought to the

NAA B-45A (t/n 7011) during a test sortie near Muroc, with a clear view of the blister-enclosed bombardier position and tail-gunner's station. (USAF)

controlled flight, the wings sheared off, and George Krebs and Nick Piccard were killed in the resulting crash. The accident investigation team determined that an insulation lining inside the engine nacelle was frayed and had loosened during the recent J47 engine installation. Gradually, as flight time was accumulated, the insulation near the exhaust nozzle became flammable, and a minor fuel leak ignited it.[13] The investigation also brought to light a design problem with having a fixed canopy instead of a movable canopy with cockpit ejection seats. The fixed canopy simplified the pressurization system, but proved disastrous for quick egress during an in-flight emergency. Under high G-forces, the crew was unable to move quickly enough to lower the escape hatch to bail out.

Design engineers redesigned the fixed canopy to an aft-moving canopy. The pilot and copilot were also equipped with ejection seats in the remaining two prototypes. Subsequent B-45A production models included ejection seats, a redesigned nose panel, increased horizontal-stabilizer area, bomb bay modifications to carry three types of nuclear weapons or auxiliary fuel tanks, and drop-tank hardpoints under the engine nacelles. The single large nose wheel was replaced with smaller dual wheels.

*The RB-45C variant was introduced in June 1950. **Inset**: A close-up of the modified nose section of an RB-45C reconnaissance variant. The variant's nose housed five camera ports, and the bomb bay was converted to hold seven cameras. (USAF)*

Photographed in 1949, the ground crew prepares the number-one B-45C (t/n 8001) for a test flight at Edwards AFB, California. The C variant made its first flight on 3 May 1949, was equipped for aerial refueling, and was modified to carry 1,200-gallon wingtip tanks. The fuel tanks increased the wingspan from 89 to 96 feet. (USAF)

Lesson Number One: Maintain a Strong Defense

A B-45A Tornado participated in the politically significant Congressional Air Show at Andrews AFB, Maryland, held on 15 February 1949. President Harry S. Truman attended and personally toured the latest USAF fighters and bombers. Aerial demonstrations were also conducted for the VIP audience. Although the flight line was impressive, in reality the USAF had no depth.[14] Post–World War II draconian budget cuts were ongoing, and the number of up-to-date aircraft in the inventory was dismal. At the time, no one could have imagined that just over a year later, the RB-45C[15] would be pressed into a combat-reconnaissance role in the Korean War.

Evidently, the Pentagon's negative-flow budget activity was being closely monitored by the Soviet Union and China. They were keenly aware of the drastic drawdowns conducted by the United States and its European allies following World War II. Its continued slide fit nicely with planned Communist global ambitions. This implied that U.S. strategic weakness was an open door. With backing from the Soviet Union and China, their surrogate North Korea was unleashed. On 25 June 1950, hostilities broke out on the Korean peninsula as North Korea invaded South Korea. When North Korea needed further assistance, China intervened with its own army. Our former World War II ally, the Soviet Union, assisted with advisors and military hardware, including the latest MiG-15 jet fighters, many flown by Soviet pilots. The United States and its allies were completely caught by surprise.

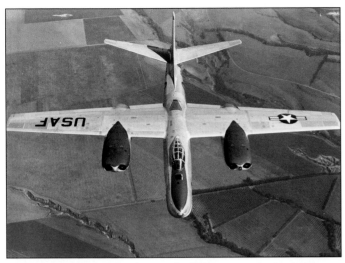

The nose port for the forward oblique camera is visible on this RB-45C variant, as well as the air-to-air refueling receptacle aft of the cockpit. (USAF)

A USAF/NAA RB-45C Tornado reconnaissance variant being refueled by a KB-29P tanker. Modified from a B-29 bomber, the Boeing-developed tanker was critical in extending the range of the B-45C/RB-45C fleet. In 1952, an RB-45C flew from Elmendorf AFB, Alaska, to Yokota AB, Japan, with two air-to-air refuelings. The nonstop transpacific 4,000-mile flight earned the RB-45C the 1952 Mackay Trophy for "most meritorious flight." (Author Photo/Illustration)

Once again, a long-standing lesson to maintain a top intelligence system and a strong military had been ignored. Unfortunately, mistakes of this nature cost lives. The Korean War evolved into a United Nations effort to repel the North Koreans and Chinese troops from the south. To bolster the situational awareness of the United Nations and its allies, in September 1950 three RB-45C reconnaissance variants were deployed to Yokota AB, Japan. From there they carried out optical/radar photographic missions over the Korean peninsula, Manchuria, and Chinese coastal areas.[16]

A USAF RB-45C (t/n 8027) painted flat black in an attempt to foil more powerful searchlights being employed by North Korean anti-aircraft sites. If contrails appeared during daylight sorties, an abort was called. During night-reconnaissance missions over denied airspace, standard RB-45Cs were being tracked by the searchlights with or without contrails. (Author Photo/Illustration)

Mission Possible

The aerial refueling boom Boeing developed in 1948 was a critical enhancement for the new jet bombers and fighters. In 1949, the first aerial tankers introduced were B-29 bombers modified into a KB-29M variant, followed by the KB-29P with a rigid support mount above the boom. Subsequently, B-45s and RB-45Cs in service were equipped with receptacles to receive fuel from the new flying boom. By the end of 1950, there were 129 KB-29P[17] tankers in service. During Korean War reconnaissance sorties, RB-45Cs were harassed by MiG-15s, with one aircraft shot down on 4 December 1950 and another seriously damaged the following spring. The RB-45Cs were temporally withdrawn from flying daylight missions: With all-black paint schemes, and their contrails hopefully obscured by the dark sky, RB-45Cs returned to flying night sorties[18] from December 1952 to April 1953. They successfully obtained radar images of numerous Chinese targets.[19]

The RB-45C also conducted classified missions over Soviet territory to collect intelligence during the Cold War. Great Britain was extremely worried about increasing Communist aggression worldwide. In 1951, President Harry S. Truman and British prime minister Clement Attlee[20] reached an agreement to have RB-45Cs operate from an RAF base. In March 1952, four RB-45Cs from the 91st Strategic Reconnaissance Wing (SRW) were transferred to RAF Sculthorpe at Norfolk in eastern England; the aircraft were subsequently painted in RAF markings. With in-flight refueling, this location brought Soviet targets of interest within range. These special high-altitude missions were flown by RAF aircrews that had been trained in the United States. On 17 to 18 April 1952, two RB-45Cs entered denied airspace near Murmansk, Belorussia, flying toward Moscow, and a third flew in on a southern route over the Ukraine.

A rare RB-45C Tornado reconnaissance aircraft in RAF markings. After approval by U.S. President Harry Truman and British Prime Minister Clement Attlee, a covert overflight of the Soviet Union, dubbed Special Duty Flight, was launched. In early 1952, four USAF RB-45Cs were transferred to RAF Sculthorpe and painted in RAF markings. In the preceding months, British aircrews had been trained in the United States to fly the Tornado. On 17 to 18 April 1952, three RB-45Cs departed to perform covert high-altitude missions over three separate Soviet targets simultaneously. Note the nose camera port, on which several aircraft crews marked their RB-45Cs with a painted eyeball on the glass perimeter. (Author Photo/Illustration)

All three aircraft obtained radar imagery of key targets and managed to escape anti-aircraft fire and interceptors.[21] As a bonus, the extensive electronic ears of U.S. Signal Intelligence (SIGINT) installations recorded the Soviet defensive response for future war planning.

Subsequently, as the more advanced B-47 was phased into the SAC fleet, B-45s were gradually relegated to ancillary tasks, such as target towing (TB-45C), and use as in-flight engine testbeds. Although the B-45C bomber variant never dropped a conventional bomb during a conflict, it was the first multi-engine jet to airdrop a nuclear device during testing. In all, a total of 143 Tornados were built. This included the B-45A, the longer-range B-45C, and 33 RB-45Cs, the workhorse of strategic reconnaissance. The B-45 served with the USAF until its retirement in 1972.

Consolidated-Vultee (Convair) XB-46

The AAF awarded a contract to Convair to design and build the XB-46 (Model 109) prototype on 17 January 1945. The XB-46 would be the second four-engine competitor. The first document covered preliminary engineering, wind-tunnel tests, and a mockup. A supplemental contract issued the following February called for three prototypes. In the fall of 1945, per direction of the AAF Program Office, part of the XB-46 funding was diverted to a new Convair jet-powered attack aircraft, the XA-44.[22] Funding was being stretched, but Convair was permitted to complete one basic flight-worthy XB-46 for testing. The program office felt that the XB-46 should proceed if the XB-45 faltered. Convair engineers were also privy to the German swept-wing wind-tunnel test data, but chose not to alter the design of their single prototype, preferring to keep their aircraft on schedule. The XB-46 would remain a straight-wing configuration with its aesthetically pleasing engine nacelles perfectly integrated below the wings. In all, Convair followed a standard design procedure that was comparable to technology at the time. The four-engine aircraft had a maximum gross weight of 94,400 pounds and an empty weight of 48,000 pounds.

Graceful Design Takes Flight

The XB-46 medium bomber taxied out to the Lindbergh Field[23] runway on 2 April 1947. The airfield was adjacent to the Convair factory in San Diego, California, which had a single 8,750-foot runway. Because of the surrounding hills, the airport perimeter offered great views of the unusual aircraft that operated there. Convair test pilots E. D. "Sam" Shannon[24] and copilot Bill Martin were seated in tandem in the pressurized XB-46 (t/n 5.59582), awaiting takeoff clearance from the tower. The sleek fighter-type canopy was designed to slide aft to open and was also jettisonable in an emergency.[25] Shannon pushed the throttles forward, and the takeoff proceeded uneventfully; Convair's prototype used 4,100 feet of runway. Shannon retracted the landing gear at approximately 300 feet altitude. Powered by four Allison 3,820-pound-thrust J35-C-3 turbojet engines, the graceful XB-46 took to the air with its metallic

Had the USAF/Convair XB-46 made the final cut, this could represent the operational B-46A flying high over the Gulf of Mexico on approach to Eglin AFB, Florida. (Author Photo/Illustration)

The Convair XB-46 prototype taxiing at Lindbergh Field adjacent to the Consolidated-Vultee (Convair) plant. Note the overlooking homes on the hillside in the background. (National Museum of the USAF)

The Convair XB-46 prototype (t/n 5 59582) over the Mojave Desert near Muroc. The aesthetically pleasing design did not offer improved performance, mainly due to the thrust limitations of the jet engines at the time. (USAF)

finish glistening. Observations of the aircraft from the ground presented an aesthetically pleasing view of its thin high-aspect-ratio wings that spanned 113 feet. During the one-and-a-half-hour ferry flight to Muroc Army Air Field in the Mojave Desert, stability, handling characteristics, stalls, and minor speed variations were tested. Shannon reported that there was ample stall warning via buffeting from the tail.[26]

Further flight-testing commenced at Muroc with Shannon at the controls. The X-46's second flight lasted more than two hours, testing handling at varying speeds from 98 to 405 mph. Everything looked good thus far, with an added comment that the braking system was excellent. The third flight was a different story. As the XB-46 was put into a gentle dive from 25,000 feet, the streamlined aircraft quickly increased its speed as it passed through 17,000 feet. Suddenly the aircraft began to vibrate violently. A resonating wing aileron/spoiler caused vibrations that literally flapped the outer wings for up to 30 seconds.[27] Attempting to bring the aircraft back under control at excessive speed, 30 seconds felt like an eternity. Shannon was able to slow the aircraft and land safely.

Fortunately, the test pilots of the day were outstanding airmen, referred to as extremely competent stick-and-rudder pilots. Some minor structural damage was found, caused by exceeding the design loads. A fix was installed that involved placing a cap strip on the wing aileron/spoiler blades and adjusting the cable tension. However, flight number four encountered the same problem at high

The streamlined Convair XB-46 engine nacelles were effectively integrated with the high-aspect-ratio wing that spanned 113 feet. (USAF)

speed. An investigation discovered that the spoilers were overbalanced. Although they operated very well at slow speed, at higher speeds the cap strip would not hold down the ailerons/spoilers. This anomaly was never fully solved.

Except for the aileron/spoiler and some engine problems, company test pilots rated the XB-46 favorably. Overall, the XB-46 was stable and flew very well. Pilots also praised the power-operated pneumatic braking system and bomb bay doors. By functioning rapidly and producing minimum drag, the operation of the bomb bay doors were noted as an improvement over current technology. A bomb load of up to 20,000 pounds would have been carried. Convair flight-testing, concluded in September 1947, accumulated 26 hours of flight time in 16 flights. Speeds of 491 mph at sea level, and 505 mph at 23,000 feet, were achieved.

Although appearing aerodynamically sleek, a final USAF report was issued regarding the reduced diameter of the fuselage. Operational radar equipment would have been difficult to install. In addition, although the bomb bay and its doors drew praise, its dimensions did not match the current gravity nuclear bombs in the USAF inventory. The potential cost and negative aerodynamic effects on airspeed precluded any fuselage/bomb bay widening or modifications. Once in service during the height of the Cold War, a SAC medium bomber would certainly be assigned a nuclear mission, with specified ordnance size requirements. Convair met the original criteria that the aircraft was safe for experimental flight-testing. However, the XB-46 program was technically canceled at this point. Despite its cancellation, the XB-46 was delivered to the USAF, and test pilots flew the prototype for 46 flights, accruing an additional 101 hours. During the USAF flight-test phase, the XB-46 was flown by Capt. Glen Edwards, who was later killed in a Northrop YB-49A Flying Wing accident on 5 June 1948. Muroc Air Force Base was renamed Edwards Air Force Base on 8 December 1949 in honor of Capt. Edwards.

Flight-test activities were eventually transferred to Palm Beach AFB, Florida, where additional stability and control tests were

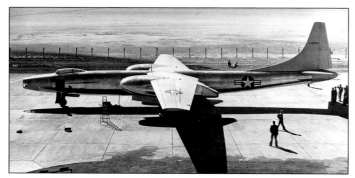

The XB-46 prototype being readied for a test flight at Muroc. AAF evaluators gave high marks to the XB-46's cockpit design and the smooth operation of the bomb bay doors. (National Museum of the USAF)

A conceptual view of an operational USAF Strategic Air Command B-46A medium bomber with added external wing tanks. (Author Photo/Illustration)

carried out. After approximately 44 flight hours, additional flying proved difficult because of increasing technical problems exasperated by the lack of spares. In a final transfer, the aircraft's systems were cold-weather tested in the climatic chamber at Eglin AFB, Florida, from June to November 1950. This was the last official test and the Air Force ordered the aircraft scrapped. The XB-46's nose section was shipped to the Air Force Museum[28] in Dayton, Ohio, and unfortunately the remaining sections of the XB-46 were destroyed in February 1952.

Glenn L. Martin Company XB-48: Rocky Arrival

The third medium-bomber competitor, and the first with a six-engine configuration, took to the air on 22 June 1947, from the Glenn L. Martin airport near Baltimore, Maryland. In the tandem-seat cockpit were Martin test pilots Pat Tibbs and copilot Dutch Gelvin. The XB-48 (Model 223) aircraft (t/n 59585) lifted off gracefully and, while maintaining a minimum angle of attack, retracted its landing gear. It continued a slow climb and flew for 37 minutes to the Naval Air Station (NAS) Patuxent River, Maryland, approximately 80 miles away. At an altitude of 10,000 feet, Tibbs reported that the right aileron snapped up too rapidly—a report noted in the Martin flight control room.

Upon landing, the XB-48 drifted off the centerline, and Tibbs's attempted corrections with rudder were ineffective. Subsequently, applying continuous brake pressure resulted in overheating and complete brake malfunction. Both sets of tires on the twin bogies were blown as the aircraft stopped just off the runway. The aircraft, however, was not damaged. Tibbs reported in the post-flight briefing that the braking system was unresponsive during landing rollout, and he had to apply heavy brake pressure.

The Convair XB-46 over the Mojave Desert. The Plexiglas bombardier blister is clearly visible. Although quite streamlined, the B-46's fuselage proved to be too narrow to accommodate the installation of operational radar and associated equipment. This aspect of the design received several negative ratings during the competition evaluation. (National Museum of the USAF)

A scene of what might have been: Two conceptual USAF/Convair B-46A medium bombers outfitted with jettisonable wing tanks. The banking medium bombers provide an excellent view of the white antiradiation paint that was introduced during the height of the Cold War. (Author Photo/Illustration)

The XB-48 featured a conventional monoplane configuration with a conservative straight wing. Martin officials also had access to the German World War II swept-wing wind-tunnel data, yet remained true to a more comfortable design configuration. The Martin team did incorporate several unique features, including tandem bicycle landing gear under the fuselage similar to the Boeing XB-47 design. Also similar to the XB-47 design were the thin wings required for speed. This dictated placing the main landing gear in the fuselage. Martin had previously successfully tested the configuration on a modified company B-26 Marauder, designated as XB-26H.

Closely embedded in two three-engine nacelles underneath the wings were six Allison J35-A-5 gas-turbine engines producing 3,820 pounds of thrust each. The nacelles were designed to create a lifting surface and appeared fused with the wing by an upper fairing.[29] Because of high engine temperatures, each cell of engines had a unique air cooling duct between them that exited out trailing ducts. The exhaust nozzles were also adjustable. Outrigger wheel assemblies were located underneath the nacelles and retracted with the main landing gear; the XB-47 also featured outrigger wheels under its engine nacelles. The bomb bay was designed to handle the oversized nuclear weapons of the time.

Second Prototype Approved

The original December 1945 AAF contract awarded to the Martin Company was modified to include funding for a second prototype. Martin met the required first-flight deadline of no later than 1 November 1947. Once again, it was the early days of jet engines, and all types of malfunctions were common. There were 14 J35 engine replacement episodes during the first 44 test flights.[30] The second XB-48 (t/n 59586) flew on 16 October 1948. In total, Martin test pilots accumulated 41 hours of flight time during 52 flights, with USAF test pilots notching-up an additional 64 hours in 50 flights.

After final speed tests were concluded, data showed the XB-48 had reached 454 mph, which was below the specified design criteria. The aircraft was also approximately 14,000 pounds overweight, nose-wheel steering was too sensitive, and turbulence occurred when the bomb bay doors were opened.[31] Air Force evaluators determined that Boeing's XB-47 entry was superior in several categories and would best meet their urgent requirement for a medium

This "what might have been" is a USAF/Martin B-48A medium bomber. (Author Photo/Illustration)

A detailed view of the XB-48's wingtip, engine nacelle, and forward section of the fuselage with the cockpit. (National Museum of the USAF)

An atypical color photograph taken at the Glenn L. Martin plant near Baltimore, Maryland, with its test facility runways in the background. (Martin)

The XB-48 number-one prototype (t/n 559585) over the Chesapeake Bay, not far from the Martin plant. Although larger in scale, the empennage is very similar to the World War II Martin B-26 Marauder medium bomber. (Martin)

Three-quarter aft-view of the Martin XB-48 at the Martin Plant. Although featuring clean lines, the overall Martin design did not offer any leading-edge innovation. (Martin)

bomber. In September 1948, the USAF canceled the XB-48 program. Martin offered to upgrade its prototype by installing the new XT40 turboprop engines recently developed by Pratt & Whitney, but the program office had gone though the turboprop data with Boeing and felt that jet-powered aircraft were the future for bombers.

Despite program cancellation, the second XB-48 prototype was authorized to fly as a testbed. Number-two XB-48 flew on 16 October 1948, after the medium-bomber production award to Boeing for the XB-47. The number-two XB-48 (t/n 45-59586) was completed very close to the original weight specifications but still needed required modifications. It was finally accepted by the Air Force on 23 February 1949. By the end of the summer of 1949, flight-testing was concluded.

For research purposes, Martin continued flying the number-two prototype while the first XB-48 was used for spares.[32] Martin officials considered critical data on engine cooling systems, F-1 autopilot technologies, deicing boots, and hydraulic systems of prime importance for future aircraft applications. However, the funding process did not work out as planned, and only the deicing tests were carried out. By mid-1951, prototype number two's last flight took it to the Aberdeen Proving Ground, Maryland, where static testing on the airframe until final destruction was done.[33] The number-one prototype, which had been cannibalized for spare parts, was also eventually scrapped.

Boeing XB-47 Stratojet: A Clean Sweep

Several days of rain preceded a very important day for Boeing. Gray skies, but improved conditions, at Boeing Field in Kent, Washington, welcomed 17 December 1947. Waiting for takeoff clearance was the technically secret six-engine swept-wing XB-47 (t/n 6065). Seated in tandem beneath the clear Plexiglas fighter-like canopy was Boeing project pilot Bob Robbins and copilot Scott Osler. Unlike Boeing's new commercial airplanes, this first flight was carried out with little fanfare and limited to only those people necessary. Boeing's entry into the medium-bomber competition was the last prototype to fly. Boeing had decided to gamble and insert innovative

The Martin XB-48 was the only other six-engine competitor in the medium-bomber contest. Overall the design was very conservative and shows off its pleasant lines. The XB-48's performance did not measure up during flight-testing. (National Museum of the USAF)

The XB-48 taxiing at the Martin facility. The massive three-engine nacelles feature unique cooling ducts located in between the engines. Also visible are the tandem fuselage landing-gear bogies and outrigger landing-gear struts under the nacelles. (National Museum of the USAF)

Although the Martin XB-48 never progressed beyond the prototype stage, this conceptual USAF/Martin B-48A medium bomber displays USAF Strategic Air Command markings. This hypothetical variant has a solid nose instead of the Plexiglas nose that appeared on the XB-48 prototype. This modification would have accommodated an MA-4 horizontal periscopic bombsight on the point of the nose. (Author Photo/Illustration)

Two conceptual USAF/Martin B-48A medium bombers leaving contrails at high altitude. (Author Photo/Illustration)

and potentially breakthrough technology into their candidate. The design team was about to learn if the wait had been worth it.

A P-80 chase plane had conducted an earlier 120-mile flight to Larson Air Force Base at Moses Lake, Washington, and back to check on weather conditions enroute and at the field. The site was the XB-47's destination for its first flight. Known for its remoteness and more stable flying weather conditions, Moses Lake hosted the initial XB-47 flight-test program.

Weather conditions improved, and the sleek bomber began its takeoff roll. At 100 mph a warning light indicated an engine fire. Robbins chopped the throttles and hit the brakes, aborting the takeoff. Osler checked the aircraft's systems and found the warning light had malfunctioned. After taxiing back to face the wind, Robbins noted that the brakes had not yet cooled down and would be less effective in the event of another abort. The XB-47 accelerated once again, and as the false warning light reappeared, Robbins pressed on; at V1, or 135 mph, the XB-47 lifted off. Seeming to leap into the air like a fighter, a spectacular and successful takeoff was executed. With the exception of Robbins having to activate a backup system to retract the flaps after takeoff, there were no other major anomalies with the new bomber.

The flight to Moses Lake was otherwise uneventful. During the landing approach, Robbins noticed an uninitiated 1.5-degree-per-second roll rate, which he corrected with yaw inputs. Being familiar with the long spool-up time of the J35s, Robbins kept the

A hypothetical USAF/Martin B-48A medium bomber in Strategic Air Command markings. It has a modified nose section, which was Plexiglas on the prototypes. In addition, the air-to-air refueling receptacle is visible aft of the cockpit area. (Author Photo/Illustration)

A USAF/Boeing B-47E (t/n 0-32271) with full antiradiation paint. (Aircraft, USAF; Background, Author)

In a low-profile manner, the still-secret XB-47 (t/n 6065) prototype was rolled out on 12 September 1947 at Boeing's Plant 2 in Kent, Washington. Only essential individuals were permitted to attend the event. Two months later on 17 December, the number-one prototype made its first fight, flying to Larsen AFB at Moses Lake, Washington, for the initial flight-test program. (USAF)

thrust high during the approach, resulting in an extended landing roll. The Boeing team celebrated their new bomber.

It All Began

Without the forward thinking of Boeing engineers and executive leadership, the XB-47 could have easily remained a standard straight-wing configuration based on the B-29. This would have dramatically altered the bomber competition by placing the XB-47 in a lower performance category. Two years prior in December 1945, when the AAF approved a contract for $9,357,800 to build the two prototypes, $1,500,000 in concurrent funding was provided for a backup to develop a straight-wing XB-47 powered by turbo-prop engines.[34] In reality, the program office persuaded Boeing to do more. The decision fell upon Boeing president William Allen, who had the courage to take the technical and scheduling risk and ordered the design of a better product with superior performance.

The leading-edge slats are clearly visible on the Boeing XB-47 prototypes parked in the hangar at the Moses Lake, Washington, facility. The layout of the hangar is eerily reminiscent of a scene in the classic 1955 movie Strategic Air Command. The scene takes place after Lt. Col. Robert "Dutch" Holland, played by Jimmy Stewart, became proficient flying the piston-powered SAC B-36 bomber. One day General Hawkes, played by Frank Lovejoy, brings Dutch to a hangar on base and opens the door to reveal the Air Force's new jet-powered B-47 Stratojet. Hawkes was attempting to persuade Dutch to remain in the Air Force Reserve. (Boeing Archives)

The number-one XB-47. While flying from Moses Lake, Washington, to the Congressional Air Show on 8 February 1949, the XB-47 prototype (t/n 6065) set a new cross-country speed record for a medium bomber, averaging 607.2 mph. (USAF)

On 15 February 1949, the latest USAF fighters and medium/heavy bombers were on display at Andrews AFB, Maryland, for the Congressional Air Show. President Harry Truman took a personal tour of the aircraft. Centered is the Convair B-36A Peacemaker heavy bomber, flown there by chief pilot Beryl Erickson. Just in front is the Northrop YB-49A flying wing. Maj. Bob Cardenas flew the YB-49A a total of 2,258 miles in record time for a heavy bomber from Muroc AFB, California, averaging 511 mph. (USAF) **Inset:** The XB-47 prototype is inspected at Andrews AFB on 8 February 1949, shortly after its record flight. Note the dissimilar appearance of the number-three engine cone; this engine lost power prior to arrival. (USAF)

After extensive wind-tunnel testing based on captured German wind-tunnel data, Boeing charted a different course for its medium bomber. Unlike its competitors, Boeing instituted major design changes, including a 35-degree sweep of the wing for the six-engine bomber. Four inboard engines were enclosed in nacelles slung below the wing on swept-back pylons. The two most outboard engines were attached directly to the underside of the wing. This kept the wing thin and aerodynamically clean, and in the event of an engine fire the disabled engine could drop free. The thin swept wing was key for increased airspeed, but there was no space for internal fuel. This forced the main fuel tanks to be located within the fuselage, negating the standard tricycle-landing-gear arrangement. Boeing engineers opted for tandem main landing gear bogies that retracted into the forward and aft sections of the fuselage, with smaller outrigger landing gear located under the inboard engine nacelles.

The new Boeing design was a major departure from the integral wing/engine arrangement being produced by competitors. The risky, yet critical, design innovation affected Boeing's schedule. By mid-1947 all of the straight-wing competitors—the NAA XB-45, Convair XB-46, and the Martin XB-48—had already conducted their first flights. As the first flight proved, the design changes had paid off handsomely in performance dividends, and the XB-47's destiny was set.

Record Setter

Through August 1948, test flying at the Moses Lake facility accumulated 83 hours, including 38 hours of Phase II flight tests. Flying for 3 hours and 46 minutes from Moses Lake on 8 February 1949 for the Congressional Air Show at Andrews AFB, the first XB-47 prototype set a new cross-country speed record of 607.2 mph. During mid-1949, the number-one prototype was fitted with uprated J35-GE-7/9 engines providing 5,200 pounds of thrust each.[35] The second prototype was equipped with the J35-GE-7/9 during assembly. Eventually, Boeing would accrue more than 330 test-flight hours on the number-one prototype over a period of six years.

A B-47B Stratojet (t/n 0014) on landing approach at Edwards AFB, California. Due to the slow spool-up of the early jet engines, during landing approach B-47s deployed a 16-foot-diameter drogue chute that increased aerodynamic drag. This enabled the pilot to keep higher thrust on the engines in the event of a go-around. (USAF)

The underside of an early B-47B (t/n 12363). After accepting 10 B-47As, the Air Force ordered 392 of the B variants. Compared to the competitor's very conservative designs, the clean lines and advanced appearance of the B-47 design are evident. (USAF)

Boeing B-47B (t/n 12212) of the 306th Bomb Wing (Medium) at MacDill AFB, Florida, deploys its 32-foot-diameter drag chute during landing. (USAF)

During June 1953, maintenance technicians at MacDill AFB examine the twin .50-cal. machine guns on a B-47B from the 306th Bomb Wing (Medium). Later B-47 variants were upgraded to twin 20mm cannons. (USAF)

A B-47B performs a dramatic takeoff at Edwards AFB using the RATO system. Until the B-47's engines were uprated, RATO was often used, combined with a light fuel load to be later topped off by aerial tankers. (USAF)

The USAF accepted the first prototype on 29 November 1949, and the second XB-47 (t/n 6066) was accepted in December 1949. Air Force Program Office officials were very pleased with the new bomber. Introduction of the XB-47 Stratojet would represent a dramatic shift in the performance of jet-powered aircraft. Even with new jet engines for propulsion, straight-wing configurations had reached their limit of performance. And although jets were in their embryonic stage, technical improvements would quickly increase their thrust capability and reliability. The revolutionary and futuristic-looking B-47 Stratojet would now begin a long, invaluable contribution to U.S. security and aviation history.

Ratcheting-Up Production

On 1 March 1950, the first B-47A (t/n 91900) was rolled out at the Wichita plant. It subsequently entered service with SAC at MacDill AFB, Florida, with the 306th Bombardment Wing, Medium, in May 1951. Aircrews were keenly aware that the B-47A in its current configuration was underpowered and required careful attention during all phases of flight. The 10 B-47As produced were used as trainers for SAC aircrews, preparing them for operational B-47Bs to follow. Production of the B-47B was carried out at Boeing's Wichita, Kansas, facility. The limited factory capacity coupled with demands of increased production soon required B-47s to be built by other contractors. In December 1950, Douglas Aircraft was awarded a contract under license, followed by Lockheed Aircraft. Eventually, Boeing produced 1,371 B-47s of all models, with Douglas and Lockheed bringing the total to 2,040, not including the original two prototypes—extraordinary numbers for a medium bomber produced after World War II.

A B-47B (t/n 92642) performs initial testing of the twin external wing tanks testing near the Boeing Wichita facility. For photo-tracking purposes, the tanks are painted in white and safety orange. The 1,760-gallon tanks were equipped with 8-foot-diameter parachutes; in the event of an emergency, they could be deployed from the tail cone to rip the tanks off their wing mounts. (Boeing Archives)

Inset: During late 1955, technicians at the Lockheed Aircraft Marietta, Georgia, facility install an external fuel pod on a B-47E (t/n 23346). Hundreds of SAC B-47s were modified to carry two of the jettisonable external fuel tanks. (USAF)

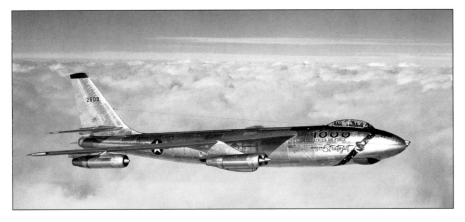

The 1000th B-47E (t/n 5609), which was delivered to SAC on 17 December 1954. The aircraft was stationed at Smoky Hill AFB, Kansas, with the 40th Bomb Wing (Medium). Eventually, a total of 1,341 B-47Es were built. (Boeing Archives)

A Boeing B-47E being refueled by a Boeing KC-97G tanker. By late 1964, SAC began modifying the KC-97G fleet with two added J47-25A turbojets mounted on wing struts. The KC-97L had an increase in speed by 25 percent and an operational altitude improvement of 60 percent. This allowed for a smoother refueling hookup, as the increased airspeed helped the B-47 remain stable. The KC-97L proved an effective interim aerial tanker until the all-jet Boeing KC-135 Stratotankers came online in 1955. (Author Photo/Illustration)

The YDB-47E was an E model modified to carry the Bell GAM-63 RASCAL air-to-ground missile. Once air launched, the 32-foot RASCAL carried a 3,000 to 5,000 pound nuclear payload at Mach 1.5 to 2.5. After launch from approximately 35,000 feet, the RASCAL would accelerate quickly and reach an altitude of about 60,000 feet. After its fuel was expended, the missile would dive on its target. Its range was a rather limited 100 miles. Operational carrier aircraft were designated DB-47E and were equipped with a drone director radome on the lower aft fuselage. (USAF)

To minimize the B-47's exposure to more sophisticated Soviet anti-aircraft defenses and blast effects, in 1955 a toss-bomb technique, or low-altitude bombing system (LABS) was developed. Target ingress with a nuclear weapon was executed at high speed and low altitude. At a predesignated point the aircraft would pull up and, just prior to going vertical, the bomb would be released toward the target. The B-47 would continue performing what is known as an Immelmann maneuver, a half-loop and roll upright heading at high speed away from the target. Several factors, including wing fatigue cracks caused by high-G loading, resulted in the discontinuation of the LABS program in 1959. (Author Photo/Illustration)

A B-47E (t/n 2311) in a hard bank displays its nimble handling during a Boeing factory test flight. The aircraft's new full anti-radiation paint is readily visible. This newer pattern is applied higher on the fuselage and up under the wing. (Boeing Archives)

SAC B-47Es on the flight line after a thunderstorm. During the late 1950s and the majority of the 1960s, B-47s were on 24/7 alert status during the Cold War. (USAF)

A SAC B-47E leaving contrails as it conducts a high-altitude training sortie. (Author Photo/Illustration)

Delivery of the improved B-47B began in 1952. A welcome factor for pilots was the more powerful General Electric J47-GE-23 engine, along with an increased number of solid-fuel rockets in the Rocket-Assisted TakeOff (RATO) system. The B-47 was easy to maintain compared to the piston-powered Convair B-36 Peacemaker, but it was demanding to fly and unforgiving of mistakes. Former SAC B-47 pilot and author Walter J. Boyne commented in late 2014, "It was a privilege to fly the B-47, although in truth we had no idea of how dangerous they were in certain circumstances. We knew that they had to be handled promptly and correctly in the event of losing an engine on takeoff, for example."[36]

In addition, the pilot deployed a small 16-foot-diameter drogue chute inflight at a designated point during the landing approach

to increase drag, but this necessitated higher engine thrust in the event of a go-around. Even the new, more powerful J47 engines were slow to spool-up, and higher thrust settings greatly improved safety. Because the aircraft was so streamlined it was also slow to decelerate, requiring both an anti-skid braking system and a 32-foot-diameter drag chute for the landing rollout.[37]

Other new equipment on the B model included a hydraulic boost on all control surfaces, an air-refueling receptacle, an AN/APS-54 warning radar, electronic countermeasures (ECM), and twin radar-guided 20mm cannons with a B-4 fire-control system.

Although the B-47's performance improved with the new engines, aircraft weight had increased from 120,000 to 202,000 pounds. This had a negative effect on both handling and the aircraft's performance in the thinner air at high altitude. Numerous deficiencies were subjected to a thorough SAC review, and improvement programs were headed by SAC vice commander Gen. Thomas Power. With the United States and Soviet Union in the midst of the ongoing and unpredictable Cold War, moving the impressive B-47 into the inventory was considered an excellent deterrent. Anomalies and specific deficiencies were gradually reduced under upgrade and retrofit programs code-named High Noon and Ebb Tide. The standardization greatly enhanced the fleet. In June 1953,

Various camera types (T-17C, T-11, and K-46) and ten flash bombs carried by the RB-47E reconnaissance variant on display. In addition to a 32.5-inch nose extension, the RB-47E variant had its offensive equipment removed and replaced with stations for 11 cameras and associated cooling systems. Its defensive tail-mounted 20mm cannons were retained. A total of 255 RB-47Es entered Air Force service. (USAF)

This particular WB-47E (t/n 7066) variant performed weather-reconnaissance missions with the Navy. In October 1969, the aircraft was flown to Boeing Field and turned over for display at the Museum of Flying. (Author Photo/Illustration)

the B-47 was ready for its first overseas power projection. Fifteen B-47Bs from the 306th Bomb Wing at MacDill AFB flew to RAF Fairford, England, via Limestone AFB, Maine. For the 90-day rotational training exercise, the aircraft were supported by the 306th Air Refueling Squadron's KC-97[38] aerial tankers.[39]

Perilous Surveillance: The Cost of the Cold War

The Air Force quickly recognized the potential of the B-47 as a fast high-altitude reconnaissance/surveillance platform. Develop-

ment of the RB-47 variant was initiated in March 1951, and specifications for the improved A-5 fire-control system for the defensive 20mm cannons, as well as uprated J47-GE-25 engines, were finalized in October 1952.[40]

The aircraft's standard bomb bay was modified to carry specially designed pods containing eight cameras. Basically, the operational RB-47s coming off the production line would closely resemble the E model, thus the RB-47E designation. Eventually 1,341 B-47Es[41] were built, and the first of 255 RB-47Es flew on 3 July 1953.

Surveillance of the Soviet Union to pinpoint offensive missile and long-range-bomber capabilities was a prime SAC mission goal. Flights even near denied airspace proved to be very hazardous, as previously experienced by RB-45Cs and other U.S. and Allied reconnaissance aircraft. Electronic listening intelligence (ELINT) missions were also conducted by EB-47Es. Col. Donald Hillman, deputy commander of the 306th Bomb Wing out of MacDill AFB, conducted the

The RB-47K variant is well known for its service record of flying dangerous Cold War reconnaissance missions. In addition to photographic gear, the K variant carried side-looking radar. Note the rectangular-shaped air refueling receptacle doors just below the stripes on the nose centerline. On earlier variants, the receptacle was circular in shape and located off-center and more forward on the nose. (USAF)

A Navy-operated EB-47E (t/n 24100) modified at the Douglas-Tulsa facility to perform missions as a missile-tracking aircraft. Two EB-47Es were flown by the Navy during missile tests and ECM testing. Various telemetry and electronic sensors could be carried on the drop tank pylons. (U.S. Navy)

first overflight. The 15 October 1952 sortie was approved by President Eisenhower. Originating from Eielson AFB, Alaska, the seven-hour 3,500-mile flight covered the Chukotski Peninsula in eastern Siberia and obtained vital radar and optical photographs of five Soviet air bases. During the 500-mile trek over Soviet territory, several MiG-15s attempted, but failed, to intercept the RB-47.[42]

In mid-1954, another RB-47 flying the same mission profile was attacked and nearly shot down. Additional missions flew just outside Soviet airspace, but were just as risky. On 1 July 1960, an RB-47H from the 55th Strategic Reconnaissance Wing flew over the Barents Sea on an ELINT mission probing Soviet radar systems. The RB-47H was attacked and hit by MiG-15 37-mm cannon fire and crashed. Unfortunately, the aircraft was carrying three additional electronic warfare officers. Out of the six aboard, only the copilot and navigator survived and were held by the Soviets for several months.[43] The term "Cold War" has always been a

A hypothetical camouflaged USAF B-47E. The B-47 did not perform any tactical bombing missions in Vietnam, but continued to serve in SAC until its retirement as a reconnaissance variant in 1969. The RB-47/EB-47 variants served during the Vietnam War performing surveillance and ELINT missions. The WB-47 variant also performed missions during the conflict. Neither type was painted in camouflage. (Author Photo/Illustration)

Two conceptual USAF B-47Es on a sortie in operational camouflage. The medium-bomber's retirement was expedited due to Sec. of Defense Robert McNamara's plan to retire the bomber as quickly as possible to preserve funding for ICBMs. (Author Photo/Illustration)

misnomer, for more than 40 different types of reconnaissance aircraft were shot down during the Cold War with the majority of the 200 crewmembers losing their lives while serving to protect U.S. security.

During the October 1962 Cuban Missile Crisis, RB-47Hs worked in conjunction with Ryan BQM-34[44] Firebee drones that had been air-launched by Lockheed DC-130 Hercules aircraft. These drones gathered SIGINT intelligence on Cuban air defense systems. During the escalating Vietnam War in 1964, the RB-47H was again called upon to collect intelligence on North Vietnam; this involved both SIGINT and ELINT missions. It's fascinating to reflect on the B-47's extensive history of projecting deterrence for SAC and the RB-47 variants carrying out dangerous reconnaissance missions during the Cold War. One thing is certain: The B-47's service life would have been much shorter if Boeing had not taken the risk to incorporate radical new technology that resulted in a truly exceptional aircraft.

Specifications

North American Aviation B-45A—Medium Bomber
Crew: 4—pilot, copilot, bombardier/navigator, and tail gunner
Wingspan: 89 ft. (27.1 m); with wingtip tanks 96 ft. (29.26 m)
Length: 75 ft. 4 in. (22.9 m)
Height: 25 ft. 2 in. (7.67 m)
Maximum weight: 81,419 lb (36,931 kg)
Empty weight: 45,694 lb (20,726 kg)
Range: 1,800 miles (2,896 km)
Maximum speed: 496 mph (798.23 km/h)
Cruising speed: 438 mph (704.89 km/h)
Service ceiling: 46,400 ft. (14,143 m)
Powerplant: 4 General Electric J47-GE-7/9 turbojet engines—5,200 lb (23.13 kN) thrust each
Payload: 22,000 lb (9979 kg) conventional/nuclear gravity bombs
Defensive Armament: Twin .50-cal. machine guns (Manned by tail gunner; Emerson Electric radar-directed twin .50-cal. machine guns planned for B-45B were not successful.)

North American Aviation RB-45C—Strategic-Reconnaissance Aircraft
Crew: 4 to 5—pilot, copilot, bombardier/navigator, and up to 2 reconnaissance systems operators
Wingspan: 89 ft. (27.1 m); with wingtip tanks 96 ft. (29.26 m)
Length: 75 ft. 9 in. (23.08 m)
Height: 25 ft. 2 in. (7.6 m)
Maximum weight: 110,700 lb (50,212 kg)
Weight empty: 49,600 lb (22,498 kg)
Range: 2,426 miles (3904 km)
Maximum speed: 573 mph (922 km/h)
Cruising speed: 466 mph (749.95 km/h)
Service ceiling: 41,500 ft. (12,649 m)
Powerplant: 4 General Electric J47-GE-15 turbojet engines—5,820 lb (25.88 kN) thrust each
Payload: 5 nose camera ports; modified bomb bay, 7 camera ports, 25 M-122 photoflash bombs: 188 lb (85 kg) each
Defensive Armament: None

Consolidated-Vultee (Convair) XB-46—Medium-Bomber Prototype
Crew: 3—pilot, copilot/radio operator, bombardier/navigator
Wingspan: 113 ft. (34.44 m)
Length: 105 ft. 9 in. (32.23 m)
Height: 27 ft. 11 in. (8.5 m)
Maximum weight: 94,400 lb (42,819 kg)
Empty weight: 48,000 lb (21,772 kg)

Range: 2,870 (4,618 km) approximate
Maximum speed: 425 mph (683.97 km/h)
Cruising speed: 381 mph (613 km/h)
Service ceiling: 40,000 ft. (12,192 m)
Powerplant: 4 Allison-built J35-C-3 axial-flow gas-turbine engines—4,000 lb (17.79 kN) thrust each
Payload: 22,000 lb (9,979 kg) gravity bombs

Defensive Armament: none (Proposed: Emerson Electric radar-directed twin .50-cal. machine guns.)
Boeing B-47E Stratojet—Medium Bomber
Crew: 3—pilot, copilot, navigator/bombardier
Wingspan: 116 ft. (35.3 m)
Length: 107 ft. (32.6 m)
Height: 28 ft. (8.5 m)
Maximum Weight: 230,000 lb (104,326 kg)
Empty weight: 79,047 lb (31,773 kg)
Ferry range: 4,100 mi. (6,598 km)
Maximum speed: 606 mph (975.26 km/h)
Cruising speed: 525 mph (844.91 km/h)
Service ceiling: 40,500 ft. (12,344 m)
Powerplant: 6 General Electric J47-GE-25 axial-flow turbojet engines—7,200 lb (32.02 kN) thrust each
Payload: 20,000 lb (9,071 kg) conventional/nuclear gravity bombs

Defensive Armament: GE A-5 fire-control system, twin radar-directed 20mm cannons in tail turret
Martin XB-48—Medium-Bomber Prototype
Crew: 3—pilot, copilot/radio operator, bombardier/navigator
Wingspan: 108 ft. 3 in. (33 m)
Length: 85 ft. 9 in. (26 m)
Height: 26 ft. 6 in. (8 m)
Maximum weight: 102,600 lb (46,535 kg)
Empty weight: 58,500 lb (26,535 kg)
Range: 2,500 miles (4,023 km)
Maximum speed: 495 mph (796.63 km/h)
Cruising speed: 360 mph (579.36 km/h)
Service ceiling: 39,400 ft. (12,009 m)
Powerplant: 6 Allison-built J35-B-1 axial-flow gas-turbine engines—3,820 lb (16.9 kN) thrust each
Payload: 22,000 pounds gravity bombs (est.)
Defensive Armament: none (Proposed: radar-directed twin .50-cal. machine guns.)

Chapter 2

CONTINUING THE JOURNEY TO JETS
NAA AJ-1 SAVAGE, NAA B-45, AVRO CF-100, MARTIN XB-51, ENGLISH ELECTRIC CANBERRA

In many aspects, the United States was shocked by the 25 June 1950 invasion of South Korea by North Korea. With no depth in the Air Force, the venerable Douglas A-26 Invader[1] was drawn into action. The piston-powered A-26s wound up attacking ground targets manned by North Korean and Chinese soldiers and equipped with the latest anti-aircraft systems provided by the Soviet Union. The United States and its allies were so ill-prepared that even World War II–era Boeing B-29[2] heavy bombers were deployed. The limitations of obsolete equipment once again highlighted the enormous misjudgments undertaken during the post–World War II drawdowns.

The USAF Board of Senior Officers initiated discussions concerning a new light bomber soon after the outbreak of hostilities on the Korean peninsula.[3] Overall experience from the conflict stressed the acute nature of the situation and the necessity of rapid procurement of a qualified aircraft for the light/tactical and night-intruder bomber role. The new competition would be carried out in a similar manner as the medium-bomber acquisition, with expediency being the guiding force. In the post–World War II world, the United States was in a numerical and technical catch-up phase with the formidable People's Republic of China (PRC) and its Cold War foe, the nuclear-capable Soviet Union.

Preliminary light-bomber requirements were issued in September 1950. They included a 40,000-foot service ceiling, a 1,150-mile range, and a maximum speed of 633 mph.[4] Additionally, all-weather day/night operations from austere airfields was added to the specifications. The new aircraft's payload would be both conventional and nuclear certified. Also included were forward-firing guns with the capability of seeking targets at low altitude. High-altitude reconnaissance was also a desired capability. The Air Force had gathered preliminary capabilities data on the English Electric Canberra and, to be fair to industry, the ensuing competition cast a wide net for potential candidates. Competing aircraft included the NAA B-45C Tornado medium bomber in service with TAC; the NAA AJ Savage, a U.S. Navy medium bomber that was carrier qualified; the Canadian Avro CF-100 Canuck; the Martin XB-51; and the English Electric

A conceptual USAF/Martin B-51G prepares to take on fuel from a USAF/Boeing KC-135A. (Author Photo/Illustration)

The B-45 Tornado served with SAC as a medium bomber and was eventually reclassified as a light bomber and transferred to TAC. For the new light-bomber evaluation, the B-45C was tested in the low-level mode, and Air Force evaluators rated the B-45C capable of night attack missions. Excessive aircraft weight proved to be a liability. (National Museum of the USAF)

A conceptual operational USAF B-45G Tornado Night Intruder in tactical camouflage. Note that the B-45G is equipped with the Tropic Moon III sensor suite in the nose section, and the Tornado's usual twin .50-cal. tail guns are removed for the low-altitude tactical-bomber role. (Author Photo/Illustration)

Canberra. As it turned out, the competition quickly narrowed to the XB-51 and Canberra.

North American Aviation AJ-1 Savage

As the NAA AJ-1 Savage emerged, it became a product of the deep rivalry involving the USAF and U.S. Navy nuclear attack capabilities. A memorandum issued by Rear Adm. Daniel Gallery on 17 December 1947 was critical of the USAF B-29 and B-36 in their role as nuclear bombers. He proposed that the U.S. Navy take on this task (the memorandum contained several far-out proposals that most likely diminished its relevance), yet it took on a life of its own.[5] A straight course for the United States was set in March 1948, when Sec. of Defense James V. Forrestal[6] and the Joint Chiefs of Staff established the Key West Agreement. Approved by President Harry S. Truman on 21 April 1948, the agreement ordered that the Air Force would be the primary service to develop nuclear weapon delivery systems. However, the Navy would also develop its own nuclear strike capability operating from a maritime perspective.

NAA was already ahead of the new Navy nuclear delivery strategy, having received a previous contract on 24 June 1946 for three XAJ-1 (NA-146) prototype medium bombers that would fit that potential mission. With NAA test pilot Bob Chilton in the cockpit, the first XAJ-1 Savage flew on 3 July 1948. Between October 1947 and May 1948 the Navy ordered 40 AJ-1 Savages.

During May 1949, NAA officials proposed the AJ-1 Savage for the USAF night-intruder tactical bomber/reconnaissance competition. Air Force evaluators looked seriously at the Savage. The AJ-1 and AJ-2P (reconnaissance variant) were powered by two R-2800 radial engines and a single J33 turbojet in the tail. The Savage could operate

A hypothetical scene of two B-45Gs operating as tactical bombers. The medium bomber was remotely qualified, but evaluated during the light/tactical bomber contest. (Author Photo/Illustration)

from austere airstrips, and its range/loiter capability was assessed as good. Bomb-load capacity exceeded requirements, the large aircraft had nimble maneuverability, and its stability for night attack missions was concluded as outstanding.[7] In addition, the basic internal layout and design favored future growth potential. However, in the final analysis, aircraft weight and lack of specified airspeed counted against the Savage.

An NAA AJ-1 Savage on a test flight over Southern California in 1950, prior to delivery to the U.S. Navy. The Savage was developed to fulfill the Navy's requirement for a nuclear-capable carrier-based aircraft. (U.S. Navy)

An interesting hypothetical view of a NAA Savage in USAF SEA tactical camouflage conducting a low-altitude bombing sortie. The Night Intruder versions have the Tropic Moon III sensor suite installed in a special nose fairing. Results from the Air Force light/tactical-bomber evaluation process determined that the piston-powered Savage lacked adequate airspeed. (Author Photo/Illustration)

Three U.S. Navy AJ Savages overfly the USS Forrestal during the late 1950s. A Vought F7U Cutlass making a catapult launch is leaving the deck. Although the North American Savage's positive qualities were recognized by USAF light-bomber evaluators, its lack of speed in the jet age was a negative factor. (U.S. Navy)

The XA2J-1 Super Savage was developed by NAA to greatly improve performance. It was powered by two Allison T40-A-6 turboprops with counter-rotating propellers that generated 5,035 horsepower plus 1,225 pounds of thrust each from the exhaust nozzles. The cockpit layout/canopy was greatly improved and the vertical tail was swept. Although the maximum speed increased to 451 mph, the prototype was consistently plagued with engine and propeller problems. (U.S. Navy)

The Canadian Avro CF-100 Canuck was originally developed during the Cold War and became the guardian of Canadian air defense. The two-seat twin-engine interceptor was evaluated during the U.S. light/tactical-bomber competition. (RCAF)

Avro CF-100 Canuck

A quirk of history cast a new spotlight on the Avro CF-100 Canuck interceptor. Originally developed during the Cold War, the stalwart of Canadian air defense found itself being considered as a U.S. light/tactical bomber. In operational coordination with U.S. interceptors, the CF-100 bolstered northern Canadian airspace and U.S. continental air defenses under the North American Air Defense Command (NORAD).[8] The indigenous two-seat twin-engine CF-100 Mk. 1 Canuck first took to the air on 19 January 1950. It entered ser-

vice with RCAF 445 Squadron in 1953. A total of 692 CF-100s were produced, including 53 exported for use by the Belgian Air Force, which actually selected the Canuck over the Northrop F-89 Scorpion for its air defense fighter. Variants Mk. 1 through the Mk. 5 gradually improved the aircraft. The CF-100 could be armed with eight .50-cal. machine guns in a belly-mounted pack that would lower into the slipstream to operate. Additionally, in a similar arrangement as the Northrop F-89 Scorpion, the CF-100 was equipped with wingtip pods armed with a total of 104 2.75-inch folding-fin Mighty Mouse air-to-air unguided rockets.[9]

More advanced air-to-air missiles, such as the Sparrow II and GAR-1A Falcon, were tested for use on the CF-100 Mk. 5 at Naval Air Station Point Mugu, California. But this slated capability improvement was inexplicably discontinued. The CF-100 had excellent range and sufficient speed, but as a potential light bomber the CF-100 design was out of its element. Although wing-mounted hardpoints capable of carrying bombs were tested with ordnance, they were never used operationally. As a potential light bomber, payload capacity would have been insufficient. Evaluators determined that too many extensive modifications would be needed. Although the top speed of the CF-100 was Mach 0.88 (669.8 mph), Avro chief developmental pilot Jan Zurakowski[10] believed the aircraft could exceed Mach 1. Piloting a CF-100 Mk. 4, he conducted a series of dives and exceeded Mach 1 (761 mph) on 18 December 1952. Notably, the CF-100 became the first straight-wing aircraft to exceed the speed of sound without

rocket assist. The RCAF Mk. 5 was the last variant produced and continued to serve in the defense of Canadian airspace until 1962, although several CF-100s remained in service as Electronic Warfare (EW) variants and target-tow aircraft. Canucks served for 29 years before being retired in October 1981.

During the 1950s, the Canadian aircraft industry was on firm footing, and ingenuity at the well-known Avro Warton facility was flourishing. A more advanced twin-engine swept-wing CF-103 variant was proposed, but this concept did not proceed. In May 1952, additional concept studies led to the superbly designed delta-wing CF-105 Arrow. With only initial flight-testing accomplished, the CF-105 Arrow program experienced a very controversial cancellation on 20 February 1959 by the Conservative Canadian government which had an immediate and long-term devastating effect on the Canadian aircraft industry.

In 1961, Canada began operating the two-seat McDonnell F-101B (RCAF CF-101B)[11] in the air defense role. The CF-101B was a

AN RCAF CF-105 Mk. 5 in formation with a conceptual operational camouflaged USAF Mk. 5 Canuck with two Mk. 82 500-pound smart bombs. The interceptor entry was a long shot, and no official designation was disclosed for a potential USAF CF-100 variant for a light-bomber variant. (Author Photo/Illustration)

less-capable aircraft compared to the CF-105 Arrow, and total acquisition cost would eventually amount to more than if the Arrow program had continued. Today, more than 60 years later, the end of the CF-105 still infuriates many Canadians who were familiar with the cancellation.

Martin XB-51: The Flying Cigar

Lt. Col. Fitzhugh "Fitz" Fulton[12] states in his book, *Father of the Mother Planes*,[13] "In my opinion and the opinion of several well respected test pilots, the airplane that should have been selected as the Air Force's newest light bomber in the early 1950s, was the three-engine Martin XB-51." Fulton continued, "It was a very advanced design. However, the Martin Company was apparently in political disfavor at the time." According to Fulton, there were unconfirmed rumors at the time that Air Force Chief of Staff Gen. Hoyt Vandenberg had been overheard mentioning that "the Air Force was not going to buy any originally designed airplane

from Martin."[14] The XB-51 concept originated in 1945 under an AAF requirement for a light bomber. Designated XA-45, the Martin Company won the competition for a high-altitude bomber with a six-member crew, top speed of 505 mph, and combat radius of 800 miles.[15] If a program could be labeled as a "back to the drawing board" airplane, the XA-45 would fit the title. In less than a year, during the spring of 1946, the AAF revised the light-bomber requirements. Under the direction of Gen. "Hap" Arnold, a new all-weather close-support bomber with increased performance was envisioned.[16] A designation of XB-51 (Model 234) was assigned to the prototype, and Martin engineers proceeded with a revised design. A contract for $9.5 million was issued on 23 May 1946 for the production of two prototypes.

In 1947, AAF Headquarters entered the fray with new revisions and expressed interest in seeking additional contractor proposals. AMC convinced AAF officials to stick with Martin to best utilize allocated funds and remain on schedule. Final specifications for the XB-51 included a crew of two, top speed of 599 mph, cruising speed 499.4 mph, and a bomb load of 4,000 pounds. Because the new requirements were for a low-altitude tactical bomber, eight forward-firing 20mm cannons were included, and combat radius was reduced to fit the existing Short-Range Navigation (SHORAN) system. SHORAN was limited to less than 230 miles. Another added feature was single-point ground refueling to enable quick sortie turnaround. Additionally, rearming had to be completed in less than 10 minutes.[17] Once approved by AAF Headquarters, Martin went to work again.

The XB-51 Unveiled

Roll out of the first XB-51 prototype (t/n 6685) at the Martin facility in Middle River, Maryland, took place on 16 September 1949. This was just over a year prior to the initiation of the light bomber competition. The Martin team was aiming high, and the outstanding

An XB-51 using water injection to increase engine thrust bolts off the runway with its three J47s smoking. In a combat environment, the XB-51's sleek profile may have presented less of a target for AAA than the larger broad-winged B-57. (USAF)

A rare color view of the number-one XB-51 prototype. In addition to the number-one and number-three engine-mounts, the bicycle landing-gear bogies are visible. (USAF)

design appeared well ahead of its time. Compared to their previous XB-48 medium-bomber design, this was a breath of new life. With its bare metal glistening in the sunlight was a stunning tri-jet aircraft with swept wings, an elongated 85-foot fuselage, and, topping it off, a T-tail[18] 17 feet 4 inches in height. (The XB-51 was the first bomber to incorporate a T-tail.)

As Boeing had done with its XB-47, Martin also incorporated a 35-degree wing sweep into their design and added a six-degree anhedral. In the lineup of contenders for the new light/tactical-bomber competition, the XB-51 was the only swept-wing candidate. The Martin engineering team had been privy to the shared government documents gathered from Operation LUSTY. They not only took advantage of the swept-wing technology data, they also mounted the two forward engines (engines number one and number three) on pylons on the lower part of the forward fuselage, a similar configuration to the Arado Ar 234B light bomber built for the Luftwaffe during World War II. Engine number two was mounted aft under the T-tail.

Although seemingly undersized compared to the fuselage, the XB-51's 53-foot 1-inch wings were considered cutting edge, with automatic leading-edge slats, slotted flaps, and spoilers. With no ailerons, the spoilers provided roll-control inputs. Another advanced

The XB-51 with a display of the types of weapons to be carried in its unique rotating bomb bay. Ordnance includes 5-inch HAVAR folding-fin rockets and 500/750/1,000-pound gravity bombs. The technicians are near a 4,000-pound gravity bomb. (Martin)

Toward the Unknown

XB-51 prototype number one (t/n 6685) was used in the filming of *Toward the Unknown*,[19] released by Warner Brothers in September 1956. The XB-51 represented the fictitious Gilbert XF-120, which had been approved for production by the Air Force. In reality, the XF-120 would have been an extremely large fighter. The story premise was centered on the XF-120's potential stability and control problems. A series of test flights were undertaken that would hopefully solve the airworthiness problem and save the program. First seeing the film as an impressionable youngster, the author recalls the remarkable flightline of aircraft on the Edwards AFB, California, ramp. These now-historic aircraft were viewed by test pilot Maj. Lincoln Bond (William Holden) as he walked across the tarmac to formally meet his new boss.

His commander was Brig. Gen. Bill Banner (Lloyd Nolan), who Major Bond had pulled from an F-102 fighter (actually the XF-92) that crash-landed the previous evening. In addition, James Garner made his screen debut as Maj. Joe Craven, who was later killed when a wing separated from the XF-120. A technical advisor on the film was test pilot Lt. Col. "Pete" Everest, known as the "Fastest Man Alive" for piloting the Bell X-2 to Mach 2.87 (1,900.34 mph). The movie featured numerous views of the sleek XB-51 in various phases of flight. For the filming, various XB-51 aerial scenes were flown by Everest, and the F-100 Super Sabre chase plane was flown by Bob Hoover. Unfortunately, XB-51 number one was lost in a takeoff accident on 26 March 1956 while enroute to Eglin AFB to film additional scenes. Typical for the era, the use of actual aircraft in flight scenes added greatly to the film's authenticity, which was far superior to the excessive use of nonrealistic CGI (computer-generated imagery) in today's aviation-themed movies.

Filming of a scene from Toward the Unknown *at Edwards AFB with actors Lloyd Nolan (left) and William Holden near the XB-51 painted with the fictitious Gilbert XF-120 markings. (AFFTC History Office)*

feature was the automatically adjustable wing incidence. The incidence is the angle between the wing chord and the aircraft's pitch axis, and the XB-51 could vary the pitch from three to seven degrees to increase drag for landings. A similar wing-incidence function was later used on the Vought F-8 Crusader to slow the approach speeds for carrier ops. This feature also helped slow the sleek XB-51 during landings. Opinions were mixed: Fitz Fulton commented on the high landing speed, while other pilots were satisfied with the landing approach speed. To retain a thin wing for increased speed, the aircraft's elongated fuselage featured tandem bicycle-type landing gear, with wheel bogies in the forward and aft fuselage and small outrigger wheels at the wingtips, similar to the XB-47 and XB-48. The wheel braking system utilized pneumatic pressure, which pilots reported was extremely noisy. Later a new Decelostat brake system was installed that greatly shortened landing rolls, and a drag chute was available as well.

An XB-51 prototype (t/n 6685) taking off at Martin's Middle River facility. Note the T-tail join point prior to the fairing that was added later to reduce vibrations in the higher-speed regime. (Martin)

A single pilot sat under a clear Plexiglas canopy with the SHORAN operator seated slightly lower and behind the pilot. The canopy was rather small and it is unfortunate that design engineers did not emulate Boeing's XB-47 cockpit featuring a two-seat tandem cockpit. This would have aided crew comfort and emergency egress. Bearing in mind the XB-51's unusual elongated shape, the aircraft was soon nicknamed "the Flying Cigar."

Slim Bird Takes to the Air

With Martin Chief Test Pilot Edwin "Pat" Tibbs at the controls, the first flight of the number-one XB-51 prototype (t/n 6685) took

XB-51 prototype number two (t/n 6686), with drag chute deployed, moves toward the ramp. Note the specially designed vibration-reducing fairing has been added to the aircraft at the T-tail join point. (National Museum of the USAF)

place on 28 October 1949. The aircraft used both water injection and RATO for takeoff. At an altitude of 10,000 feet a series of stalls was executed, and the dive brakes were tested.[20] After climbing to a maximum altitude of 20,000 feet, the aircraft gradually descended for a landing at NAS Patuxent River, Maryland. A drag chute was used for the first landing after the 34-minute flight. Testing for Phase I continued until the end of March 1951. During initial testing at Wright-Patterson AFB in Dayton, Ohio, the XB-51 experienced several landing-gear malfunctions due to mechanical and hard-landing pilot errors. It was concluded that the aircraft needed additional development testing, which was not unusual considering the new aerodynamic and propulsion technologies being evaluated. However, it was determined the aircraft did not require any extensive modifications. This positive conclusion was validated through Phase II testing, which ran from 4 April to 10 November 1950. With Martin test pilots at the controls, aircraft number one flew for 221 hours during 233 flights.[21] Additionally, Air Force pilots flew 221 hours in more than 200 flights.

The second XB-51 prototype (t/n 6686) flew on 17 April 1950, and was flown by company pilots for 125 hours in 168 sorties. Air Force testing was rather limited on the second prototype, recording only 26 hours during 25 flights. Although additional flight skills were required, Air Force test pilots rated the XB-51 highly and indicated that its unique design offered significant potential. In December 1950, a down-select decision favoring the English Electric Canberra as the new light bomber was concluded, but flight-testing of the XB-51 was permitted to continue.

The first XB-51 prototype's sleek elongated fuselage, 35-degree swept wings, and T-tail accentuated its jet age contours. (USAF)

Had the Martin XB-51 been selected as the new USAF light/tactical bomber, early B-51B variants may have appeared in an all-black scheme with bright-red USAF markings. The Martin B-57B Canberras appeared in this color scheme. (Author Photo/Illustration)

Flight Testing at Edwards AFB

XB-51 number-one prototype (t/n 6685) was transferred to Edwards AFB in 1952 where flight-testing continued. It was here the XB-51 gathered ballistic data during weapons drops that included bombs and land mines. New jet bombers dropped their ordnance at higher speeds with different aerodynamic effects, and the XB-51 featured a novel rotary bomb bay to deal with those factors. In lieu of bomb bay doors opening into the slipstream, which caused instability, the single curved door rotated 180 degrees, revealing the bomb racks. Additionally, Martin developed a pneumatic system to eject bombs through the high-speed slipstream and away from the aircraft. The inimitable rotary bomb system was later incorporated into the B-57 Canberra.

Then-Maj. Charles E. "Chuck" Yeager, first pilot to break the sound barrier on 14 October 1947 in the Bell X-1, also checked-out in the XB-51. A high-time XB-51 test pilot, Yeager flew the high-speed weapons delivery sorties. This included low-altitude high-speed dropping of 4,000-pound mines at Mach .92 into both designated water and land locations. Yeager commented, "Flying both ships one and two, I never had a hairy moment in the airplane." Yeager also added, "In a high speed dive the plane would max-out at .93/.94 Mach. The XB-51 was way ahead of its time."[22] Capt. Fitz Fulton began his test flights on the number-one prototype (t/n 6685) in 1953. He noted that other pilots had problems with the number-two aircraft, but Fulton reported no problems during his 40 flights that accumulated 33 hours of flight time. Fulton noted that the XB-51 was "a real pleasure to fly, although the landing and takeoff speeds were higher than contemporary airplanes."[23] From the onset of XB-51 flight testing, the two most-impressive features mentioned were its extremely smooth flight-control system and excellent speed on the deck, clocking in at 645 mph.

Additional Test Pilot Remarks

Col. Fred Ascani pointed out the importance of maintaining the proper landing speed/attitude and touching down on both landing-gear bogies simultaneously. He praised the XB-51's smooth flying qualities in the Mach .92/.93 regime. "On the deck at full speed, the XB-51 would have been difficult to intercept in a fighter," said Ascani.[24] In essence, the United States almost had its first supersonic bomber during the 1950s. Col. Robert Cardenas, noted for his accomplishments in the Northrop YB-49A flying wing, also flight-tested the XB-51. "As I remember it was extremely easy to fly." Cardenas also pointed out the proper landing procedure. He performed additional testing to confirm that the XB-51 was flying 50 knots (57.5 mph) faster than predicted. Testing proved that and related it to an early example of Richard Whitcomb's area rule. Cardenas continued, "I remember the B-57 short field landing tests. The Canberra landed short, rolling past his mark blowing tires trying to stop. I was amazed when they didn't buy the '51 and turned around and bought the Canberra."

Program Cancellation

The XB-51 program cancellation in November 1951 was unusual, but the Air Force was rushing to acquire a new light bomber. The Air Force actually canceled the program prior to delivery of the two prototypes to the service. One clarification provided stated that the XB-51 received a second-best rating compared to other aircraft designed to fulfill similar mission roles. No data was provided to identify the aircraft that were compared, yet that data established the XB-51's disappointing rating. According to the Air Research and Development Command (ARDC), the airplane in its current configuration did not meet the requirements, particularly in the range requirement of TAC.[25]

Regarding the rationale for canceling the XB-51, it was recalled that Gen. Boyd had zeroed-in on the cost of the Martin airplane. "The Air Force just could not afford to buy-in at that cost."[26, 27] In Boyd's opinion, the deal for the English Electric Canberra, which included all the engineering drawings and production rights, was the best course for the Air Force. It was only later in the acquisition

Based on the Martin Company's heritage World War II B-26 Marauder bomber, a name for the B-51 could have been the Marauder II. Two conceptual USAF/Martin B-51B Marauder IIs reveal their drop tanks and conventional 500-pound gravity bombs while enroute to a gunnery/bombing range. (Author Photo/Illustration)

With an active production and flight-test program, it is highly probable that additional YB-51A prototype aircraft would have been built. This is a conceptual view of a new YB-51A prototype (t/n 6688) as it peels off from a formation with a camouflaged operational B-51C Marauder II. (Author Photo/Illustration)

cycle that the Air Force would learn how many modifications would be needed to bring the Canberra in line with Air Force operational requirements.

New Specifications: Wingspan, Length, Height—and Politics

With the Martin Company also producing aircraft for the U.S. Navy, some individuals felt that Glenn Martin[28] had favored the Navy during the highly charged congressional budget battle that pitted aircraft carriers against the USAF/Convair B-36 heavy bomber. In the opinion of some, this may have hindered Martin as an Air Force customer during the critical selection process. Walter J. Boyne

A conceptual operational USAF/Martin B-51G Night Intruder variant prepares to take on fuel from a KC-135A Stratotanker. (Author Photo/Illustration)

Had the Martin XB-51 been selected, it is possible that the UK may have been interested in procuring the US-built B-51 aircraft for the RAF. This conceptual image of operational RAF PR.10 Marauder II reconnaissance variants conducting a power climb represents that potential quirk of history. (Author Photo/Illustration)

Prototype Accidents

The number-two prototype (t/n 6686) was transferred from Wright-Patterson to Edwards AFB in 1952. Martin and Air Force test pilots had successfully accumulated 151 hours in 193 sorties. On 9 May, test pilot Maj. Neil Lathrop was performing a series of low-level passes at Edwards. On the fourth pass a roll was initiated, but the aircraft remained too long in the inverted position. With one wing low, it flew into the ground, killing Maj. Lathrop; the SHORAN position was unoccupied for this flight.

Unfortunately, another accident occurred about four years later on 26 March 1956, when the first prototype was lost during takeoff at El Paso International Airport, Texas. After this refueling stop, the XB-51 was to continue to Eglin AFB for a firepower demonstration and to film additional flight scenes for the movie *Toward the Unknown*. The aircraft was painted with the "Gilbert XF-120" logo. With pilot Maj. James Rudolf and flight engineer Staff Sgt. Wilbur Savage aboard, the XB-51 started its takeoff roll at 10:30 a.m. CST. Eyewitnesses described the aircraft gaining about three feet of altitude and then settling back down. As it ripped through a barbed wire fence across an airport perimeter road, the XB-51 broke up and exploded. The flight engineer was killed instantly and Maj. Rudolf later died at the Air Force burn center in San Antonio.

Fitz Fulton, who had reported to Rudolf at Edwards AFB, was assigned as an accident investigating officer.[30] There was a single 8mm film of the crash taken by a private citizen, and it was thoroughly analyzed. According to Fulton, during takeoff the XB-51's front and rear bicycle landing gear normally rise off the ground simultaneously. At the halfway mark during the ill-fated El Paso takeoff, the front bogies lifted off first and the XB-51 remained at a slight nose-high angle-of-attack. At this point Major Rudolf was struggling to pull up, and the nose reached about 30-degrees angle-of-attack (stalled condition) with the rear wheels on the ground as the aircraft passed over the end of the runway.

Fulton noted that the El Paso airport runway was less than 8,000 feet in length and the elevation of the airfield was 4,000 feet, which will reduce engine thrust in conjunction with hot air temperature.[31] Today we are well aware of hot ambient temperature's effect on engine thrust, but at the time it was the early days of jet aircraft. The rationale for the XB-51 operating out of a limited commercial airport was that transient aircraft were not that welcome at SAC bases; they were usually parked far away from the operational flightline and had to wait for pilot ground transport, refueling, etc. Although Biggs AFB, Texas, was only five miles away with a runway capable of handling SAC bombers, it was not considered unusual that Maj. Rudolf elected to land at the civilian airport. With both XB-51 prototypes destroyed, there would be no additional testing of the unique jet bomber. Neither accident was attributed to any aircraft design flaw.

(aviation author and former director of the National Air & Space Museum) felt that there was an irrational USAF prejudice against Martin-designed aircraft, although not Martin-built products. Boyne also recounted that a significant amount of U.S. government records on the XB-51 program are missing.[29]

Two conceptual USAF B-51G Marauder II Night Intruders equipped with drop tanks to extend range/loiter time fly over the southwestern United States. (Author Photo/Illustration)

Another conceptual RAF/Martin PR.10 Marauder II on a training sortie in a later operational-camouflage scheme. (Author Photo/Illustration)

The number-one prototype B1 Canberra (VX165) first flew on 13 May 1949 at Warton Aerodrome, UK. USAF observers were on hand for the flight of the Canberra, which featured engine nacelles mounted in the low-aspect-ratio wings. (RAF)

The Canberra: English Import

From the start, the Air Force had already compiled a performance profile on the English Electric Canberra. Long before the light/tactical-bomber competition, the British jet had favorably impressed USAF staff officers as they witnessed its first flight at Wharton Aerodrome on 13 May 1949. At the time Great Britain was undeniably the leader in developing jet propulsion. By summer 1950, a selection committee reporting to Edwards AFB commander Gen. Albert Boyd had essentially expedited the evaluation of the Canberra. The initial report provided by the committee on 28 September indicated the Canberra was suitable as an all-weather fighter, for tactical reconnaissance, and as a medium-altitude bomber. The ground-attack category did not fair so well, however, as the report stated that the Canberra was unstable during low-altitude maneuvering. Some officials were perplexed that an airplane designed by the British as a high-altitude bomber would now be used at low altitudes. However, its tactical utility and ease of production[32] deemed it eligible for the Mutual Defense Assistance Program.[33] It was recommended that rigorous testing be carried out prior to any procurement, and a total of 25 recommended changes to the aircraft were identified.

Early Conclusions

With Gen. Boyd's report secured, during October 1950 the Board of Senior Officers formed a new committee under Brig. Gen. S. P. Wright, the deputy commander of the Air Proving Ground. The group, known as the Wright Committee, also included officers from AMC and TAC. The Wright Committee examined the data on the candidates and determined that the NAA B-45C Tornado[34] was too heavy to meet the criteria—plus its original design dated to the early 1940s, which would limit potential growth. The other NAA

A group of three RAF B2 Canberras on a training sortie over the English countryside. (RAF)

candidate, the AJ-1 Savage, lacked the necessary airspeed. The Avro CF-100 Canuck was an excellent interceptor but might prove difficult to adapt to the light-bomber role. In its concluding remarks the Committee noted that neither the Canberra nor the XB-51 fully met the night-intruder specifications. They unexpectedly endorsed both aircraft. Their recommendation was for the immediate procurement of the British Canberra to equip two light bombardment groups, with a future procurement of a similar amount of Martin B-51s.[35]

However, the Board of Senior Officers did not support the dual aircraft solution proposed by the Wright Committee. In their opinion, the Canberra was preferred, noting the XB-51's lesser combat radius. A Canberra from the UK joined the other candidate aircraft on 23 February 1951 at Andrews AFB for demonstration flights. Each aircraft performed a series of maneuvers for the evaluators. Although the XB-51 projected power with its sleek profile and speed, the aerial demonstration by test pilot Roland Beamont in the Canberra was impressive in this arena. Evaluators noted the Canberra's excellent routine, but concluded again that numerous modifications would be needed to perform the Air Force night-intruder role. In a final action on 26 February, the English Electric Canberra was down-selected, and Secretary of the Air Force Thomas K. Finletter, as well as early-on Martin Company critic Gen. Vandenberg, quickly agreed.

The Martin-built USAF B-57A featured a bubble canopy with the pilot slightly to port and the bombardier/navigator lower and to the starboard side. During flight operations, it was quickly recognized that this configuration was not adequate for the mission. As the B-57B came online, a noticeable improvement was the two-seater tandem-canopy arrangement. (USAF)

An early bare-metal USAFE RB-57A from the 30th Tactical Reconnaissance Squadron, 66th Tactical Reconnaissance Wing, based in Germany. (Author Photo/Illustration)

The Winner Takes All—Almost

The need for expediency in the procurement of a light/tactical bomber brought positive news to the Martin Company. Although Martin had lost the competition, the Air Force felt that their experience with developing an aircraft such as the unique XB-51 provided a sound base of proficiency for dealing with advanced jets. Hence, when it was concluded that the English Electric Company was overly burdened producing Canberras for the RAF, the Air Force began discussions on building the aircraft in the United States, and Martin was selected on 24 March 1951. Although they'd be building another contractor's design, the decision kept Martin in the advanced jet business. The selection was basically an off-the-shelf[36] order, yet the Board of Senior Officers wanted to keep modifications to a minimum. In addition to the known night-intruder modifications, there soon was a realization that numerous supplementary modifications of the British design for U.S. service would be necessary.

Details for the final contract order were worked out in discussions during late February 1951. In what would be considered a rather aggressive production schedule, the initial agreement would require Martin to deliver 250 B-57s between November 1952 and October 1953,[37] a peak production rate of 50 aircraft per month. On 24 March 1951,

a contract for 250 B-57 Canberras was issued to the Martin Company which received an advance payment of $6 million. This also included funding to acquire a licensing agreement[38] for the manufacture of the English Electric aircraft. This agreement was signed on 8 May 1951. Martin was also fully reimbursed for the $1 million cost of quickly acquiring two RAF Canberras during mid-1951 for detailed examination and flight-testing.

Nip and Tuck Modifications

The B-57A was equipped with a slightly modified oblong clear Plexiglas canopy, similar to the RAF B2 Canberra. The new canopy offered slightly better visibility and more room for the crew. In

An all-black RB-57A from the 363rd Tactical Reconnaissance Group; note its pronounced red/white-checkered tail. (USAF)

addition to the canopy changes, wingtip tanks were ordered to increase loiter time.[39] Since range/loiter time was one of the categories where the Martin XB-51 fell short, historians might wonder if there was ever any discussion regarding re-engining the XB-51 or adding drop tanks to extend its range. Also overlooked was the fact that, at the initiation of the competition, the range requirement was reduced to accommodate the SHORAN system's effective range. Additional modifications included replacing the British clamshell bomb bay doors with the lighter minimum drag/buffeting rotary door developed for the XB-51. Also, the Rolls-Royce Avon turbojets were replaced by U.S.-built Wright Aeronautical J65-W-1 turbojets that produced 7,200 pounds of thrust.

The factory-fresh number-one all-black B-57B, with wide wing chord, added tip tanks, and inert wing-mounted ordnance. Note the spacious tandem two-seat cockpit arrangement compared to the bubble canopy of the A models. (USAF)

Mockup Review

Martin completed a full-scale mockup of the B-57A, but the first inspection revealed several shortcomings. Recommendations included modifying the bomb bay for special weapons, adding weapon hardpoints to the wings, upgrading the landing gear and brake actuation system, adding wingtip tanks, strengthening the engine mounts, and improving the nose gear swivel. To top things off, the mockup board recommended the cockpit be redesigned. By January 1952, only 6 corrections for 35 design deficiencies had been approved and production delays loomed on the horizon. The Wright Air Development Center was concerned about Martin's ability to remain on schedule. First flight of a Martin-built B-57A finally took place on 20 July 1953. The 46-minute flight was considered successful and received wide media coverage. In reality, none of the B-57As ever went into operational service and were instead used as trainers by the Air Force. The A variant was considered too similar to the Canberra design, which contained inherent flaws. The B-57A was virtually canceled after only eight aircraft were produced.[40]

Super Canberra

During early 1951, the Martin Company offered a new blended design that incorporated the top characteristics of the Canberra and the XB-51. Martin designated the proposed design the B-51B Super Canberra. The configuration featured swept wings with embedded engine nacelles and the signature T-tail of the XB-51. A two-man crew would be located under an American-style bubble canopy. The primary feature for outstanding performance would be two afterburning engines that generated 21,700 pounds of thrust. According to Martin, a top speed of 724.9 mph (630 knots) at sea level would be achieved for both low-level attack and reconnaissance missions. Documents provided to the Air Force declared that the Super Canberra could be operational by 1954. However, wanting to avoid evaluating a new aircraft design, the Air Force rejected the Martin proposal in November 1951.

The best of both bombers: A conceptual Martin B-57B Super Canberra. Martin engineers thought they could greatly improve the selected English Electric Canberra by incorporating the best features of their XB-51 and the Canberra. The most notable proposed modifications were the swept wing with imbedded uprated engines and the removal of the tail-mounted number-two engine. (Author Photo/Illustration)

Asymmetric Thrust Hazard

After two accidents involving single-engine landings, the Air Force training syllabus added a new film for B-57 pilots. It featured an instructor in a classroom starting a 16mm projector and narrating two unsuccessful landing approaches and one successful one. Critical data was clearly stated: "For engine-out single-engine landing approaches in a B-57, you need full flaps, and never let the airspeed drop below 178 mph (155 knots). And remember, once your speed is below 178 mph (155 knots), you are committed to a landing; there is no go around." In other words, at 178 mph (155 knots) the B-57 will have adequate rudder and aileron control to complete a safe go around as single-engine full power is applied. The film documented

two examples of pilot error. As the approach speed dropped below 178 mph (155 knots), and a go around was attempted, both pilots lost control as their B-57s turned sideways and crashed. Fitz Fulton witnessed one of the B-57s crash at the Martin facility, which nearly hit the control tower as it exploded in a fireball.

The film was factually documented, except the author notes that the instructor never mentioned the term "asymmetric thrust," which was caused by applying full power to one engine only. Also not included is the fact that the pilot should be capable of applying approximately 200 pounds of force on the rudder pedal to compensate for the asymmetric thrust.

Pressing Ahead

Although the Canberra program was not dead, engineering was in process to produce an improved airplane, the B variant. The B-57B featured an entirely redesigned tandem cockpit with the pilot centered and the navigator slightly offset to the left. The requested hardpoints for ordnance under wings were installed, and the aft fuselage had dive brakes. Four 20mm canons replaced the original six .50-cal. machine guns in the wings. The B models were

A B-57B and a dual-control C model, at the Martin plant. Both featured a completely redesigned cockpit with the pilot and navigator seated in tandem. This arrangement offered greater visibility and aircrew comfort. (USAF)

An EB-57B Canberra (#519) from the Vermont ANG, aka the Green Mountain Boys. (USAF)

An RAF PR.9 Canberra reconnaissance variant from 39 Squadron. This English Electric–built Canberra adopted the U.S.-style canopy, although it was single-seat and positioned slightly to port. The navigator/RSO remained positioned behind and below the pilot. (Author Photo/Illustration)

To improve the night-interdiction mission in Vietnam, 16 B-57Bs were taken out of service and underwent extensive modifications during mid-1969. This resulted in the B-57G Night Intruder variant fitted with a Tropic Moon III sensor suite. The mods featured an APG-139 multifunction radar, with an additional lower nose fairing containing FLIR; low light level television; and laser/designator sensors. B-57Gs were the first combat aircraft to lase and drop PGMs independently. (Author Photo/Illustration)

A USAF B-57B with a modified radar nose cone accelerates during takeoff. Rockwell International's Autonetics group installed advanced radar and electronic gear in several types of aircraft and also test flew the aircraft. (USAF)

flight-tested extensively and initially considered slightly better than the Canberra. It made its first flight on 18 June 1954, and a total of 202 B-57Bs were built.

Meanwhile, 67 RB-57A reconnaissance variants were produced and delivered but continued to be plagued by engine, flight control, and structural problems. Despite these early bugs, RB-57As were first deployed in March 1954 to the 363rd Tactical Reconnaissance Wing (TRW) at Shaw AFB, South Carolina. Additional recently delivered RB-57As were quickly ferried across the Atlantic to Germany. The 10th TRW at Spangdahlem AB and the 30th Tactical Reconnaissance Squadron (TRS) of the 66th Tactical Reconnaissance Group (TRG) received the first aircraft.[41] The units provided vital Cold War reconnaissance data. RB-57As also transited the Pacific Ocean and operated with the 6021st and 6091st TRS at Yokota AB. A specially modified RB-57A with a large-aperture oblique camera was able to perform critical reconnaissance missions of North Korea and China.

Southeast Asia Combat Service

With systematic modifications and improvement programs, the B-57B and later models proved more successful. During early

A modified RB-57D in formation with a standard B-57B model clearly depicts the increased wing chord and wingspan of the D model. In June 1954, under the classified code name Bald Eagle, six B-57Bs were shifted from production and modified to the RB-57D configuration. This was the first radical modification designed for high-altitude reconnaissance. Achieving IOC in 1956, RB-57Ds performed critical reconnaissance missions during the Cold War at altitudes up to 70,000 feet. (USAF)

The greatly widened wing chord of NASA 926 WB-57F. The F variant also had an increased wingspan, from the RB-57D's 106 feet to 122.5 feet. After transfer from the Air Force, number 926 began operating with NASA supporting the Landsat program in 1972. NASA operated two WB-57F variants on various research programs. (NASA)

Beginning in the early 1970s, NASA operated a specially instrumented B-57B for various atmospheric research programs. The aircraft was retired in 1987. (NASA)

This is an excellent view of the changed nacelle contour of the new RB-57F variant, after installation of the uprated P&W TF33-P-11 turbofans. Each TF33 produced 16,000 pounds of thrust. Additionally, two removable P&W J60-P-9s (3,300 pounds of thrust each) were installed on wing pylons. The RB-57F had a service ceiling of 82,000 feet and flew classified missions during the Cold War. (National Museum of the USAF)

1965, B-57Bs were deployed to Bien Hoa Air Base, South Vietnam. After first performing reconnaissance missions on 19 February, the B-57B became the first USAF aircraft to drop live ordnance on enemy combatants.[42]

The EB-57B EW variant also flew surveillance missions in the combat zone. Additionally, Australia sent 16 Australian-built Canberras to assist the United States in the Vietnam War. Operating under the call sign "Magpie," RAAF No. 2 Squadron Canberras performed combat sorties from Phan Rang AB, South Vietnam. Meanwhile, Martin and Westinghouse modified existing B-57B airframes into the B-57G configuration to enhance capabilities for night-interdiction missions. The G model was equipped with the Tropic Moon III sensor suite that included Forward-Looking Infra-Red (FLIR), a low-light-level TV sensor, and a laser/ranger designator contained in a bulbous nose fairing. The modifications enabled the B-57G to carry four 500-pound Mk. 82 precision-guided munitions (PGMs) for greatly improved accuracy. Due to the aircraft's altered CG and the sensitive equipment, the standard four 20mm cannons were deleted.

During the early 1960s, extensive modifications performed by the General Dynamics[43] Ft. Worth Division on standard B-57B airframes created the RB-57D/F-WB-57F high-altitude variants. These modifications also focused on fixing the Canberra's inherent and ongoing single-spar wing structural problems. The large wings of the RB-57F were built with bonded honeycomb wing skins, which resulted in reduced drag and increased lift. The RB-57F's curved wingtips were made of plastic. From the original B-57B wingspan of 64 feet, the RB-57D increased to 106 feet, followed by the RB-57F at 122.5 feet. Built with the same process, the vertical tail area was increased to twice that of the B-57B to compensate for the higher-rated engines. Eventually 20 different versions of the Canberra were produced. In all, the Martin Company[44] built 422 B-57 variants for the USAF, and a total of 925 Canberras were produced in the UK for the RAF and foreign customers. The Air Force selection of a British-designed aircraft to fill the light/tactical-bomber role was certainly an eye-opening experience. Despite early problems, the B-57 Canberra's 29 years of USAF service was considered a success story.

Specifications

Avro CF-100 Mark 5 Canuck—Interceptor
Crew: 2—pilot, navigator/WSO
Wingspan: 58 ft. (17.75 m)
Length: 54 ft. 2 in. (16.7 m)
Height: 15 ft. 6 in. (4.76 m)
Maximum weight: 37,000 lb (16, 800 kg)
Empty weight: 23,100 lb (10,480 kg)
Range: 2,500 miles (4,000 km)
Maximum speed: 690 mph (1,110 km/h)
Cruising speed: 472 mph (759.6 km/h)
Service ceiling: 54,000 ft. (16,460 m)
Powerplant: 2 Orenda-14 turbojet engines—7,275 lb (32.4 kN) thrust each
Armament: 8 x .50-cal. machine guns mounted in a fuselage drop-down tray. During early testing, hardpoints carried 4 x 1,000 lb (450 kg) gravity bombs. The Mk. 4 variant tested wingtip rocket pods.

North American Aviation AJ-2 (A-2B) Savage—Carrier-Based Medium Bomber
Crew: 3—pilot, copilot, navigator
Wingspan: 71 ft. 5 in. (21.8 m)
Length: 63 ft. 1 in. (19.2 m)
Height: 20 ft. 5 in. (6.2 m)
Maximum weight: 50,954 lb (23,112 kg)
Empty weight: 27,558 lb (12,500 kg)
Range: 1,731 miles (2,787 km)
Maximum speed: 471 mph (758 km/h)
Cruising speed: 270 mph (434.5 km/h)
Service ceiling: 40,800 ft. (12,440 m)
Powerplant: 2 Pratt & Whitney R-2800-48 radial engines—2,500 hp (1,864 kW) each, plus 1 Allison J33-A-10 turbojet—4,600 lb (20 kN) thrust
Payload: 12,000 lb (5,400 kg) conventional gravity bombs; nuclear capable

Martin XB-51—Light/Tactical-Bomber Prototype
Crew: 2—pilot, SHORAN operator
Wingspan: 53 ft. 1 in. (16.2 m)
Length: 85 ft. 1 in. (25.9 m)
Height: 17 ft. 4 in. (5.3 m)
Maximum weight: 62,457 lb (28,330 kg)
Empty weight: 29,584 lb (13,419 kg)
Range: 1,075 miles (1,730 km)
Maximum speed: 645 mph (1,040 km/h)
Cruising speed: 269.6 mph (434 km/h)
Service ceiling: 40,500 ft. (12,300 m)
Powerplant: 3 General Electric J47-GE-13 turbojet engines—5,200 lb (25.88 kN) thrust each
Payload: Approximately 4,000 lb (1,814 kg) gravity bombs, or 8 x 6-in. high-velocity aerial rockets in internal bomb bay
Armament: 8 x 20mm cannon with a total of 1,280 rounds

Martin B-57B Canberra—Light/Tactical Bomber
Crew: 2—pilot, copilot
Wingspan: 64 ft. (19.5 m)
Length: 65 ft. 6 in. (19.9 m)
Height: 15 ft. 6 in. (4.7m)
Maximum weight: 58,800 lb (26,308 kg)
Empty weight: 49,600 lb (22,226 kg)
Range: 2,000 miles (3,218 km)
Maximum speed: 570 mph (495 km/h)
Cruising speed: 450 mph (391 km/h)
Service ceiling: 49,000 ft. (14,935 m)
Powerplant: 2 Wright J65-W-5 turbojets—7,200 lb (32 kN) static thrust each
Payload: 7,500 lb (3,401 kg) internal and external ordnance
Armament: 8 x .50-cal M3 machine guns or 4 x 20mm M39 cannon

Chapter 3

THE PENETRATION FIGHTER
McDONNELL XF-88, LOCKHEED XF-90, NAA YF-93A, McDONNELL F-101

An aircraft formation that never occurred. The three penetration-fighter competitors led by the McDonnell XF-88. The Lockheed XF-90 is at right echelon and the NAA YF-93A at top left. (Author Photo/Illustration)

As World War II in the European Theater came to a close in 1945, Allied attention was focused on finishing the war against Japan in the Pacific Theater. Looking ahead, the Army initiated discussions regarding a new jet fighter to escort heavy USAAF bombers. Experience from World War II concluded that bomber escorts greatly improved mission success. However, future projections of improved enemy air defenses and interceptors worried U.S. war planners. The operational B-29, and the massive six-engine Consolidated-Vultee (Convair) XB-36 Peacemaker under development, would need escort fighters.[1] This next area of activity would develop what would become known as a penetration fighter, an advanced long-range jet fighter with the necessary range and armament to clear a path for the heavy bombers.

The USAAF was competing several contractors with a goal to modernize its light and medium bombers. However, jet propulsion continued to present problems. Aircraft manufacturers were consistently coming up with interesting designs for new aircraft, yet were always forced to keep aircraft weight down. Similarly, as aircraft designs were refined, engine manufacturers battled to increase engine thrust and reduce fuel consumption. USAAF senior officers initiated the penetration-fighter competition hoping for the best. The first set of requirements was released on 28 August 1945 and updated the following 23 November. USAAF escort-fighter specifications included a top speed of 550 mph at an altitude of 35,000 feet, with a dash speed of 600 mph at sea level.[2] Climb rate should not exceed 10 minutes to reach an altitude of 35,000 feet, and the combat radius would be 900 miles. The proposed escort fighter would be armed with six .50-cal. machine guns or 20mm cannon.[3] It was recommended that only known operational engines be considered for propulsion, a somewhat limiting factor. Evaluators believed two 3,000-pound-thrust engines would suffice. Whereas most proposals allow for growth potential, this was a reversal on that process. Yet in a period when jet engine development had a nebulous future, one could agree with this. Only after an active and trouble-plagued teething period did jet engines manage to gradually mature.

Updated Requirements

On 15 October 1945, proposals were received by Consolidated-Vultee (later Convair), Curtiss-Wright, Goodyear, Lockheed, McDonnell, Northrop, and Republic.[4, 5] On 15 February 1946, only Convair and McDonnell survived the down-select. However, in an attempt to even the playing field, it was decided that Convair—with another fighter win under its belt, and the massive XB-36 program—would be directed to stand down. Yet the Army still wanted to keep two competitors in the game, so Lockheed was recontacted and instructed to upgrade the engine choice for its XP-90 proposal. With two Westinghouse 24C (XJ34) engines selected for propulsion, Lockheed's

The initial McDonnell XP-88 (Model 36C) full-scale mockup, which was inspected by the AAF customer during August 1946, featured a V-tail. Major changes were recommended, including changing to a more conventional empennage arrangement and sweeping the intakes back at a 40-degree angle. Later wind-tunnel testing confirmed possible stability problems with the V-tail. (National Archives)

amended XP-90 was awarded a prototype development contract on 20 June 1946.[6] The penetration-fighter competition now had two firm competitors, Lockheed Aircraft Company and McDonnell Aircraft Company. Subsequently, as predicted by the aircraft contractors, rapidly changing technology necessitated that the Army[7] adjust the specifications, which took place on 22 August 1947. The new aircraft's climb rate was increased to reaching an operating altitude of 50,000 feet within 10 minutes. Top speed was reestablished at 690 mph, with a combat radius of 1,500 miles. Although still in their infancy, air-to-air missiles with fire-control systems now entered the picture.

Believing in Voodoo

Two McDonnell XP-88 Voodoo[8] prototypes were ordered by the Army on 14 February 1947. The McDonnell team proceeded to construct a full-scale mockup at its St. Louis, Missouri, facility. To avoid the high-speed effects of compressibility, the prototype featured a V-tail configuration.[9] However, further wind-tunnel testing revealed an uncontrolled roll and instability while nearing a stall.[10] After several corrective redesigns, the McDonnell team shifted to a more conventional vertical and horizontal stabilizer. The final XP-88 configuration featured a tail empennage that was rather elongated and swept upright to a high vertical stabilizer. An official Army full-scale mockup inspection that took place on 21 to 23 August 1946 resulted in several design refinements. First, the customer agreed with the contractor's wind-tunnel calculations regarding the V-tail deficiencies and subsequent configuration changes. The customer recommended the XP-88's intakes be swept back 40 degrees and a boundary-layer ramp added to improve pressure recovery.[11] Additionally, in the review's concluding remarks the Army recommended adding afterburners to the number-two prototype's engines.

New USAF aircraft designations were ordered in June 1948,[12] and the XP-88 was redesignated to XF-88. The futuristic-looking XF-88

The number-one XF-88 Voodoo (t/n 6525) prototype in front of the main McDonnell Aircraft hangar adjacent to Lambert Field. The official rollout occurred on 11 August 1948. The prototype work was started as the XP-88 and changed in concert with the overall USAF aircraft designation conversion from P (Pursuit) to F (Fighter), announced in June 1948. (USAF)

twin-engine jet was rolled out at the St. Louis facility on 11 August 1948. Considering it was the late 1940s, the lustrous metallic jet was a spectacular sight. After conducting ground and taxi testing, all systems were deemed nominal. The aircraft was disassembled and shipped to Muroc AFB, California. With McDonnell Chief Test Pilot Robert Edholm in the cockpit, number-one XF-88 (t/n 6525) made its first flight on 20 October 1948. Although the aircraft handled well, initial performance was not impressive. This was mainly due to the additional weight accumulated during assembly, combined with a lack of engine thrust. Overall, McDonnell company pilots made 41 flights, racking up just more than 35.5 hours.

Phase II flight-testing commenced on 15 March 1949, and Air Force test pilots accumulated 17 hours and 57 minutes.[13] As predicted, the aircraft was severely underpowered. Similar to the early

light and medium jet bombers, low-engine thrust as well as reliability was a consistent problem; *underpowered* became a buzz word to describe new jet prototypes. Fortunately, the Air Force had previously requested that afterburners be added to the number-two XF-88 prototype (t/n 6526) and internal fuel capacity was also increased.[14] To reflect the uprated engines, the second prototype was redesignated XF-88A. With the McDonnell design proven flight worthy, the number-two prototype's maiden flight took place on 26 April 1949 at Lambert Field, located on the same property as the McDonnell facility.

McDonnell chief test pilot Robert Edholm made the first flight of the XF-88 on 20 October 1948 at Muroc. The XF-88 handled well, but as predicted the aircraft's engines lacked sufficient thrust. (National Museum of the USAF)

A rare view of both XF-88 prototypes at McDonnell Aircraft prior to shipping out to Muroc. The number-one XF-88 (t/n 6525) is in the foreground, and the number-two XF-88 (t/n 6526) has the six 20mm cannon installed in the nose section. McDonnell F2H-2 Banshees awaiting delivery to the U.S. Navy are in the background. (National Records Center, St. Louis, Missouri)

The number-one XF-88 shortly after arrival at Edwards North Base. (National Museum of the USAF)

The XF-88A number-two prototype (t/n 6526) was equipped with afterburners, which significantly improved performance during the evaluation process. Air Force evaluators also scored the XF-88 above the other competitors in capability to operate from standard tactical air base runways. (Photo of Aircraft, USAF; Photo of Background, Author)

Over the next two months the afterburners were carefully tested in flight. The XF-88A was also armed with the required six nose-mounted 20mm cannons. During the following August, the number-one XF-88 prototype was removed from flight status. This was not due to any defect or malfunction, but as a result of President Truman's previous order on 12 May 1948 declaring a ceiling on FY1950[15] military funding. The reality was that the penetration-fighter program lacked the funding to continue flying two prototypes. In fact, many programs were suffering under the new budget doctrine. In late 1949, the number-one prototype was removed from flyable storage at Muroc after the number-two aircraft was damaged during an emergency landing. The accident helped release some funding to repair and upgrade the aircraft. After shipment to St. Louis, it was brought up to flight status and had J34 engines with afterburners installed. The number-one prototype (retaining the XF-88 designation), returned to flight on 1 May 1950 at St. Louis and flew to Muroc in late May.

Critical Phase II testing took place during 5 May and 14 June 1950. Afterburners were definitely the key to emerging success for the McDonnell aircraft. The XF-88A in afterburner was able to increase its speed from 630 mph to 693 mph while flying at 15,000 feet. The XF-88A could exceed Mach 1 during a shallow dive, and Mach 1.18 was reached without any serious buffeting.[16]

Good News and Bad News

Just prior to the evaluation fly-off on 16 June 1950, the number-two XF-88A was damaged as a result of a belly landing. The jet had completed 105 flights that accumulated 82 hours and 45

Two conceptual operational USAF/McDonnell F-88As featuring "USAF" on their upper right wings. With more powerful engines, an increased DoD budget, and an assured mission, fate may have turned out differently for the XF-88. The XF-88 placed first in the competition, but McDonnell Aircraft had to wait to produce the F-101 Voodoo. (Author Photo/Illustration)

minutes of flight time. It was shipped to St. Louis but never flew again. McDonnell was now forced to use its number-one prototype for the final evaluation, and it was fortunate that this aircraft had been retrofitted with afterburners. On 29 June 1950, the fly-off evaluation of the three penetration fighters commenced—the McDonnell XF-88, Lockheed XF-90, and NAA YF-93A. Eight Air Force test pilots flew the XF-88 for 26 flights that accumulated 16 hours.

The fly-off ended on 10 July 1950, and on 3 August the number-one XF-88[17] was returned to St. Louis. McDonnell officials received the good news on 11 September 1950 when Air Force evaluators rated the McDonnell XF-88 number one over the other contenders. They also received the bad news that there was no budget to begin production of the F-88 penetration fighter. McDonnell did submit cost/analysis numbers for producing the F-88, which included additional fuel capacity to increase range. No production was ordered.

The Lockheed XF-90

Buoyed by the success of their P-80 Shooting Star straight-wing jet fighter, Lockheed was ready to tackle a new endeavor. The limited DoD budget that the USAAF was operating under forced continued merging of requirements that would hopefully produce an all-in-one fighter. To meet the penetration-fighter requirements with added ground-strike capability, almost 60 separate designs were considered. Kelly Johnson's Skunk Works design team first settled on a delta-wing configuration. A delta wing offered advantages in airframe strength and performance in the transonic regime, but cruising speed with stores on hardpoints would increase drag. This, plus limited engine thrust and a heavy fuel load for long range missions, added up to severe performance penalties. Johnson felt the only option was to move to a more conventional design. The XP-90 was conventional in a sense, but it still offered the customer advanced features.

Once unveiled, the media and public were presented with an exceptionally futuristic design.[18] As with several aircraft fighter/bomber contractors at the time, Lockheed took advantage of swept-wing technology acquired from captured German data. The XP-90 featured a 35-degree wing sweep. Wingtip-mounted auxiliary fuel tanks could be added for certain missions. The tip tank's attach points were at the end of the wing, unlike the P-80 with tip tanks slung under the wingtip. Wind-tunnel tests concluded there was significant decrease in drag with the XP-90 configuration.[19] The elongated fuselage reduced its diameter as it neared a sharply pointed nose section.[20] This limited available space, necessitating the location of the six 20mm cannons in a unique position underneath the fuselage, just aft of the wing's leading edge. Although requested by the customer to install afterburning engines, Westinghouse was encountering delays with the XJ34, so the first prototype did not have them. Additionally, in June 1948 in accordance with the USAF aircraft designation change, the XP-90 became the XF-90.

The XF-90 with wingtip tanks flying a test sortie over the Mojave test range. (Author Photo/Illustration)

A rare color photo of the first XF-90 at Lockheed's Burbank, California, facility during April 1949, just prior to shipment to Muroc AFB. (Lockheed Martin)

The number-one XF-90 prototype at Lockheed's Burbank Facility. (Lockheed Martin)

Lockheed ground personnel tow the number-one XF-90 prototype out of the hangar at Edwards North Base. (AFFTC History Office)

The XF-90 showing its classic lines during a test flight near Edwards AFB. Even with large tip tanks the aircraft appeared sleek. (Lockheed Martin)

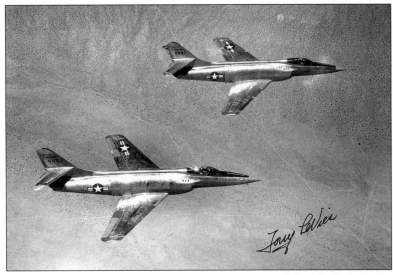

The dynamic shape of the Lockheed XF-90 in afterburner. (Author Photo/Illustration)

Both XF-90 prototypes without tip tanks in echelon formation over the Muroc test range. Lockheed test pilot Tony LeVier signed the photo. (AFFTC History Office)

Following the conclusion of the penetration-fighter competition, the Air Force tested the XF-90's capabilities as a ground-attack aircraft. Two 1,000-pound gravity bombs can be seen mounted on wing hardpoints. (AFFTC History Office)

A hypothetical view of a sleek operational USAF/Lockheed F-90A without tip tanks high above the Sierras. History may have turned out differently for the XF-90 program if uprated engines had been available. (Author Photo/Illustration)

After being transported by truck to Muroc AFB in late April 1949, the number-one XF-90 was reassembled and readied for its first flight. Legendary Lockheed test pilot Tony LeVier took the first XF-90 into the air on 3 June 1949. The first flight was quite an adventure according to LeVier. The XF-90 barely got off the ground after an extremely long takeoff roll, and LeVier noted that his altitude could not exceed more than 100 feet. He carefully made a wide circular track, with a radius of about 40 miles, flying over neighboring Palmdale, California, while nursing it back to Muroc.[21]

As flight-testing continued, RATO was consistently used for takeoff due to the lack of engine thrust from the non-afterburning engines. The following year, LeVier tested the XF-90 with afterburner-equipped engines that generated 3,950 pounds of thrust each. Even with the added thrust, with the aircraft's weight averaging 28,000 pounds, the XF-90 would have to enter a dive to exceed Mach 1. Testing in the transonic regime in prototype number one (t/n 6687) was slated for May 1950. On 17 May, at 40,000 feet, LeVier pushed the XF-90 into a steep dive and reached 800 mph at 27,000 feet, which exceeded Mach 1. LeVier had joined the Mach Busters club.[22] Both prototypes accrued a total of 15 supersonic flights in this mode. Although impressive for a heavy fighter, the XF-90 was not superior to the operational NAA F-86A[23] Sabre. Even NAA's F-86D Sabre Dog interceptor variant could climb to 40,000 feet in just over seven minutes. As with the XF-88, the XF-90 saga is an example of a sound airframe design being penalized by inadequate engines.

A conceptual view of two USAF/NAA F-93A single-seat variants. One aircraft is painted in interceptor flat gray, and the other in tactical fighter camouflage. In their original 1949 proposal, NAA developed computerized fire-control systems and an intercept autopilot to allow single-pilot operation during the demanding part of the mission. (Author Photo/Illustration)

The North American Aviation YF-93A

It was late 1947 and with confidence building in its XP-86 Sabre Jet, NAA proposed a modified Sabre Jet for the penetration fighter. The result was a modified NA-157 design that was designated P-86C. Originally, the commonality of the new modifications with the P-86A was favored by the Air Force. The prevailing procurement system was geared to funding known entities, and adding two P-86Cs onto an expected contract for the P-86A would attract less attention.

The number-one YF-93A prototype was towed onto Rogers Dry Lake for a photo session. Note the original flush intakes, in which NAA engineers utilized NACA-Ames data in their design. The increased aircraft weight over the standard F-86 necessitated twin tires on the main landing gear. (AFFTC History Office)

An active day at Edwards North Base for North American Aviation aircraft. The number-one YF-93A (right) is parked next to an F-86D Sabre Dog. Because of the NAA YF-93A entrant's commonality with the F-86, it was initially favored by the Air Force in the penetration-fighter contest. In addition, note the NAA B-45C Tornado in the background. (Bill Yenne Collection)

Note the leading-edge slats and open 20mm cannon access door of the number-one YF-93A. Rather than an XF designation, the YF (prototype fighter) designation was the assigned prefix for the NAA YF-93A entry. The rationale was that the two prototypes were added to a standard P-86C (F-93A) production order. Additionally, the YF-93A was the only competitor with USAF markings on the aircraft's wings. (Bill Yenne Collection)

ously approved order for 118 F-93A production fighters was canceled. What could have been worth up to $57.9 million (1949 dollars) was suddenly off NAA's books. The two YF-93A prototypes would continue on to the penetration-fighter competition.

After completing the first YF-93A prototype, the aircraft was transported by ground to Muroc in late 1949. NAA test pilot George "Wheaties" Welch took the YF-93A into the clear winter air above Edwards AFB on 25 January 1950. After the first flight Welch remarked, "A pilot could have been a one-man air force with the YF-93A in Southwest Pacific air battle."[25] NAA was keenly aware they were the last competitor to fly, and the competitors were hungry for work.

The number-one NAA YF-93A with the final intake modification allowing smooth airflow and minimizing drag. The original flush intakes that were developed with NACA wind-tunnel data successfully reduced drag, but hampered the airflow to the engine. The slight tucked-in area can be seen at the wing root. (AFFTC History Office)

The C variant would retain the basic Sabre wing and tail-assembly shape, although tail height was slightly increased. Fuselage length was increased by three feet to accommodate the more powerful J48 engine with afterburner. In lieu of an F-86-type single through-intake, the C variant's twin flush intakes were located on the sides of the fuselage, thus increasing fuselage width. The spacious nose section could now accommodate a 30-inch-diameter radar dish.

The increase in weight was thought to be well worth it, by having 8,000 pounds of thrust available when the pilot activated the afterburner. The P-86C would be armed with six 20mm cannons, an increase in firepower from the P-86A's six .50-cal. machine guns. The YF-93A fuselage featured a unique tucked-in segment adjacent to the wing root that was similar to the Coke-bottle shape later established by Richard Whitcomb's area-rule[24] research at NACA. The Coke-bottle shape in that fuselage area of high-performance aircraft reduced drag in the transonic regime which allowed a smooth transition to Mach 1 (761.2 mph at sea level). Whitcomb received the 1954 Collier Trophy for his research.

On 9 April 1948, NAA pushed confidently ahead with a proposal to manufacture 118 production versions of the new P-86C. The Air Force approved the proposal on 29 May and approved the initiation of fabrication of tooling. During September 1948, the Air Force determined there were enough major differences in the configuration and redesignated the two prototypes YF-93A and the production versions F-93A. Unfortunately, for the realm of the bean counters operating within stringent budget guidelines, these were turbulent times. Without warning on 25 February 1949, the previ-

Rating Positive and Negative

On the positive side, the aircraft handled well and was a stable gun platform. Further testing noted the outstanding climb rate in afterburner of 11,960 feet per minute. A setback occurred on 5 June 1950 as prototype number one (t/n 8317) was about to conduct a second sortie at the renamed Edwards AFB. An explosion occurred as the afterburner was engaged, and takeoff was aborted. The aft fuselage was damaged, and a broken afterburner fuel manifold drain line was found to be the culprit.[26] The second YF-93A prototype

The first prototype YF-93A after its transfer to NACA-Ames Research Center in Palo Alto, California, to undergo additional flight testing. The YF-93A's dive brake is extended under the fuselage, and a larger pitot tube has been added for in-flight data gathering. NACA test pilot Stew Rolls conducted flight tests with both prototypes to establish precise intake airflow data. (NASA)

Enormous operational pressure resulting from fiscal restraints governed the penetration-fighter competition from the outset. President Truman would not relent on his original FY1950 budget[27] request released during May 1948. Summarily, Sec. of Defense James Forrestal was forced to reduce the 1950 defense budget from $23.8 billion to $16.9 billion. To make things worse, President Truman then issued his new pay-as-you-go philosophy and set the defense budget at $14.4 billion. Shocked and perplexed, the DoD convened a special Senior Board of Officers, including SAC commander Gen. Curtis LeMay. The Board would decide what standing military assets would be cut and what new weapon systems, including aircraft, would be canceled.

(t/n 8318), which had arrived at Edwards during May 1950, was used to perform in the competition which commenced on 23 June 1950.

Air Force flight-test evaluations revealed several deficiencies with the YF-93A. This included insufficient range, an insufficient maximum airspeed of 715.5 mph (Mach 0.94), mild instability at 608.9 mph (Mach 0.80), continued afterburner use needed to maintain 25,000 feet altitude, and excessive airspeed bleed-off during maneuvering. Another test concluded that with landing gear and flaps extended, the aircraft could not maintain altitude at full power.

An Unglamorous Finish

As the Korean War came to a conclusion, the concept of a bomber escort, or penetration fighter, was becoming obsolete. Bombers were converting to jet propulsion and achieving higher airspeeds and longer range as a result. With bomber technology advancing in the Soviet Union, air defense of the U.S. and Canadian homeland was becoming a priority. This transformation in strategy combined with budgetary restrictions essentially ended the penetration-fighter competition in December 1950. The McDonnell XF-88 was rated first in evaluation points, followed by Lockheed's XF-90. Third was NAA's YF-93A.

Of the competing penetration fighters, only the McDonnell XF-88 design would reemerge in the form of the YF-101 Voodoo. Lessons learned by Lockheed would benefit the Skunk Works, which under Kelly Johnson would go on to develop some of the most advanced aircraft of the century. The two YF-93As were transferred to the National Advisory Committee on Aeronautics (NACA) for additional flight-testing. After additional flight-testing with NACA, the two YF-93A prototypes were scrapped in 1951. Despite the hasty Air Force evaluation process conducted under tremendous budget pressures, NAA also learned many lessons. Within a couple of years they would be producing the venerable F-100 Super Sabre, the first USAF operational supersonic fighter and trailblazer of the famed Century Series.

F-101 Voodoo: A Rebirth

After the Korean War, lessons presumably learned regarding military procurement were almost too numerous to list. One issue did stand out—the Air Force still needed a long-range fighter. As the Cold War continued to dominate military planning, it was realized that aging jet fighters such as the Republic F-84F Thunderjet would be

A conceptual F-93C variant in afterburner features vastly improved intakes and drop tanks as it flies a training sortie. With a more powerful engine, the YF-93A's evaluation prototype would have improved considerably. In reality, the YF-93A prototype placed third in the evaluation and was plagued with performance problems. An advanced two-seat USAF/NAA F-93C all-weather interceptor could have been developed had events turned out differently. (Author Photo/Illustration)

incapable of escorting B-36s on a mission into denied airspace over the Soviet Union. Continued design work and patience eventually paid off for McDonnell Aircraft, though. Per issuance of a General Operational Requirement for a long-range strategic fighter on 6 February 1951, all the original penetration-fighter competitors once again submitted proposals.

After a thorough review the following May, the Air Force selected the earlier winner: McDonnell. There would not be a fly-off for this aircraft, however. As a result of a good design effort, the new McDonnell jet would be a larger and more potent aircraft powered by twin Pratt & Whitney J57-P-13 turbojets. A development contract was awarded on 3 January 1952, and the aircraft was designated

F-101. The expedited schedule also ordered production variants to be produced without an experimental prototype (XF/YF-101) being built. Initially, McDonnell would build a single F-101A to complete Category II testing.

The production contract was awarded on 23 May 1953 for 39 aircraft. Within two months of the end of the Korean War on 27 July 1953, Air Force escort strategy shifted again. Concurrently, the new eight-engine Boeing YB-52 Stratofortress long-range jet bomber was now under development, resulting in a move away from the escort mission. Analysis concluded that the F-101A was compatible as an offensive platform, and a nuclear strike capability was added to the requirements.

Voodoo: The Need for Speed

Rollout of the first F-101A took place in August 1954, and the aircraft was then transported to Edwards AFB. First flight followed

The powerful McDonnell F-101A Voodoo climbs sharply during a test flight. The test article F-101A made its first flight on 29 September 1954, and featured an extended nose-mounted pitot tube. (Author Photo/Illustration)

Under the hot desert sun on Rogers Dry Lake, the number-one F-101A (t/n 32148) shows its distinct classic lines. After its rollout during August 1954, the F-101A was shipped to Edwards AFB for its first flight. (USAF)

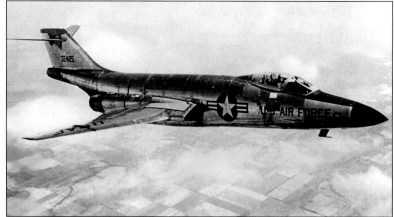

USAF F-101A Voodoo (t/n/ 32425); to extend range, later Voodoo variants were equipped with twin drop tanks mounted under the mid-fuselage. (USAF)

During late 1954, F-101A (t/n 32434) was transferred to NACA at Edwards AFB for additional flight-test research. The F-101A flew a series of flights from the NACA High-Speed Flight Station to conduct research on inlet-flow distortion. (NASA)

An early model of the two-seat USAF F-101B Voodoo interceptor variant over the test range at Edwards AFB. (USAF)

quickly on 29 September 1954, with McDonnell test pilot Robert C. "Bob" Little in the cockpit. The powerful jet climbed to 35,000 feet and reached Mach 0.9 (685 mph). It didn't take long to expand the envelope to Mach 1.4 (1,065.6 mph). On 12 December 1957, a new absolute world speed record was set by an F-101A over a specified course at the Edwards Test Range. Known as Operation Firewall, the early model Voodoo reached Mach 1.59 (1,207.6 mph) and became the fastest tactical fighter in the USAF. Although originally destined

for service with SAC, the F-101A went operational for only 59 days before being shifted to the Tactical Air Command.

Unit cost for the 77 F-101s as produced was listed at $2,906,373 each. Meanwhile, other Voodoo variants emerged, the 51st aircraft off the line being the C model which had been strengthened to perform in the low-level fighter/bomber role. With the Northrop F-89 Scorpion approaching obsolescence, the need for a new interceptor emerged. The idea of a two-seat version of the F-101 had been discussed in detail, and now a two-seat variant began to materialize. With an increase in fuselage length of five feet, the F-101B would be the most widely produced variant with 480 built.

After the sudden cancellation of the advanced Avro CF-105[28] Arrow interceptor on 20 February 1959, the Canadian government was in dire need of an interceptor to defend its enormous border. Other than a lack of understanding of the Arrow program, one of the reasons for the cancellation was that officials had been led to believe aircraft were becoming obsolete and

Recognized as the first jet aircraft to enter the Southeast Asia combat zone, RF-101C Voodoos first deployed to South Vietnam during October 1961. Under Operations Pipe Stem and Able Mable, the RF-101Cs operated out of Tan Son Nhut AB, South Vietnam, with the 15th TRS and at Don Muang Airport, Thailand, with the 45th TRS. (Author Photo/Illustration)

An RCAF CF-101B Voodoo climbs above the setting sun; 66 F-101Bs were converted to Canadian specifications (CF-101B). The United States helped finance the procurement and transfer of the CF-101s to the RCAF. This was arranged after Canada canceled its indigenous more-advanced Avro CF-105 Arrow interceptor. (Author Photo/Illustration)

that air defense could be entirely handled by missiles.[29] That rationale was totally misplaced and arrangements were made to acquire the F-101B. Beginning in 1961, 56 F-101B and ten F-101F variants with upgraded systems were transferred to the RCAF and received the CF-101B designation.

Sharp Eyes in the Nose

The most memorable Voodoo was the RF-101A reconnaissance variant. The A model first flew in June 1956, becoming a welcome replacement for the aging Republic RF-84 Thunderflash. The nose section of the RF-101A contained the Fairchild KA-1 framing camera and a CA1 KA-18 strip camera. The recce aircraft entered service during May 1957. As camera technology quickly advanced, RF-101As were retrofitted with the latest optical gear and redesignated RF-101G. The next reconnaissance variant was the RF-101C, of which 166 were built. On 27 November 1957, during Operation Sun Run, an RF-101A set a transcontinental speed record by flying from Los Angeles to New York nonstop and returning to Los Angeles in 6 hours and 46 minutes.

In Southeast Asia (SEA) RF-101Cs became the first jets to enter the combat zone in October 1961, performing dangerous reconnaissance missions over both South and North Vietnam. The Voodoo's cameras were updated with the KS-72A camera suite that was able to achieve clarity despite high speeds at low altitude. The RF-101C was also capable of high-altitude reconnaissance, providing critical data on the buildup of Soviet Intermediate-Range Ballistic Missile (IRBM) sites during the Cuban Missile Crisis in late 1962. During 82 sorties, the RF-101Cs would ingress very low and fast, providing an immediate tactical perspective of the situation. Concurrently, operating at altitudes of more than 75,000 feet, Lockheed U-2s were able to capture detailed overview coverage, as well as close-up imagery of contested areas of Soviet intrusion in Cuba. Aerial reconnaissance also provided critical imagery to confirm the dismantling of the Soviet missiles as the Cuban Missile Crisis was diffused.

An RCAF CF-101B during a visit to March AFB, California, in November 1982. (Author)

An RCAF CF-101B Voodoo crew prepares to close the canopy for takeoff. Four RCAF CF-101Bs performed aerobatics during the open house at March AFB, in November 1982. (Author)

RCAF CF-101B (t/n 101005) goes nearly vertical in afterburner. (Author Photo/Illustration)

Specifications

McDonnell XF-88 Voodoo—Penetration-Fighter Prototype
Crew: 1—pilot
Wingspan: 39 ft. 8 in. (16.5 m)
Length: 54 ft. 3 in. (16.53 m)
Height: 17 ft. 3 in. (5.2 m)
Maximum weight: 18,500 lb (9,616 kg)
Range: 1,737 miles (2,795.4km)
Maximum speed: 641 mph (1,031.5 km/h)
Service ceiling: 41,800 ft. (12,741 m)
Powerplant: 2 Westinghouse J34-WE-15 turbojet engines—3,000 lb (13.3 kN) thrust each with afterburner.
Armament: 6 x 20mm cannon; 2 x 1,000 lb (454 kg) gravity bombs or 8 x 5-in. (127mm) HVAR unguided rockets

Lockheed XF-90—Penetration-Fighter Prototype
Crew: 1—pilot
Wingspan: 40 ft. (12.9 m) without wingtip tanks
Length: 56 ft. 2 in. (17.12 m)
Height: 15 ft. 8 in. (4.8 m)
Maximum weight: 31,062 lb (14,089 kg)
Empty weight: 14,035 lb (6,366 kg)
Range: 1,967 miles (3,165.5 km)
Maximum speed: 708 mph (1,139 km/h)
Cruising speed: 633 mph (1,018km/h)
Service ceiling: 39,000 ft. (11,887 m)
Powerplant: 2 Westinghouse J34-WE-15 turbojet engines—4,100 lb (18.2 kN) thrust each with afterburner.
Armament: 6 x 20mm cannon; 2 x 1,000 lb (454 kg) gravity bombs or 8 x 5-in. (127mm) HVAR unguided rockets

North American Aviation YF-93A—Penetration-Fighter Prototype
Crew: 1—pilot
Wingspan: 38 ft. 9 in. (11.8 m)
Length: 44 ft. 1 in. (13.4 m)
Height: 15 ft. 8 in. (4.8 m)
Maximum weight: 26,516 lb (12,028 kg)
Gross weight: 21,610 lb (9.802 kg)
Range: 1,967 miles (3,165.5 km)
Maximum speed: 708 mph (1,139.4 km/h)
Cruising speed: 534 mph (859.3 km/h)
Service ceiling: 46,800 ft. (14,264.6 m)
Powerplant: 1 Pratt & Whitney J48-PW-6 turbojet engine—8,000 lb (35.6 kN) thrust with afterburner
Armament: 6 x 20mm cannon

McDonnell F-101A Voodoo—Penetration Fighter
Crew: 1—pilot
Wingspan: 39 ft. 8 in. (12.1 m)
Length: 67 ft. 5 in. (20.5 m)
Height: 18 ft. (5.4 m)
Maximum weight: 43,020 lb (19,504 kg)
Range: 1,380 miles (2,220.8 km)
Maximum speed: 1,070 mph (1,721.9 km/h)
Cruising speed: 550 mph (885 km/h)
Service ceiling: 50,300 ft. (15,331 m)
Powerplant: 2 Pratt & Whitney J57-PW-13 turbojet engines—15,000 lb (66.7 kN) thrust each with afterburner
Armament: 3 M-39 20mm cannon; low-altitude bombing system (LABS) capable

Chapter 4

THE HEAVY BOMBER COMES OF AGE
BOEING YB-52 VERSUS CONVAIR YB-60

A Convair RB-36F high-altitude reconnaissance variant. Under the Featherweight III program, reconnaissance-variant airframes were significantly lightened. Up to 14 cameras were mounted in the forward bomb bay, including long focal-length cameras that could resolve a golf ball from 50,000 feet. (Author Photo/Illustration)

One couldn't avoid searching the skies to track down the source of that unmistakable low rumble. It was the Convair B-36 Peacemaker, powered by six pusher-prop piston engines augmented by four GE J47 turbojets. As a youngster living in Miami, Florida, during the 1950s, this author recalls often tracking B-36s through borrowed binoculars. At the time, Homestead AFB, Florida, just 35 miles southwest of Miami, was a SAC base and transient B-36 flights over the area were routine. For several afternoons in 1958, the low resonance was greatly accentuated. Gazing upward, a group of us saw several impressive cells of low-flying B-36s heading toward the northwest. Unknown by us at the time, this procession must have been part of the B-36 fleet heading for retirement at Davis-Monthan AFB, Arizona. This was another personal encounter with the majestic six-piston/four-jet B-36 Peacemaker as it displayed proof of its then-popular descriptor: six turning and four burning.

The massive B-36 Peacemaker was the mainstay of America's long-range bomber force during the late 1940s and early 1950s. The prototype XB-36s first flew on 8 August 1946, and a total of 385 B-36s were delivered to the Air Force. This includes two B-36Fs converted into swept-wing versions, the YB-36G, later redesignated

YB-60 and B-60. However, the Peacemaker's days were numbered as U.S. adversaries introduced jet fighter interceptors and modernized their air-defense systems. By the XB-36's first flight, the Air Force already recognized the need to develop a fast intercontinental-range bomber. Initially, planners thought turboprops offered the best solution, sacrificing speed for range. As plans moved forward, turboprop concepts were held in reserve strictly as a backup.

On 12 February 1959, after nearly a decade of protecting the United States, the last B-36 flew into the twilight, having successfully carried out SAC's strong tradition of deterrence. The positive result of projecting strength was not having one bomb dropped in anger, thus confirming the concept of "peace through strength." The Peacemaker's mission had been accomplished, and now a jet-powered bomber fleet would proudly enforce that tradition.

Dueling Heavyweights

Moving forward with a long-range bomber replacement for the B-36 was not without numerous complications. A major gauntlet was politics. It is difficult to believe there were senior officials

An impressive B-36 production line at Convair's Fort Worth facility adjacent to Carswell AFB, Texas. A total of 385 B-36s, including the XB-36 and YB-36, were produced by Convair. (USAF)

Living up to its nicknames "Aluminum Overcast" and "Magnesium Monster," an RB-36D displays its underside. Ten RB-36Ds were later modified to carry a parasite fighter and flight-tested both a modified Republic RF-84F Thunderflash and the McDonnell XF-85 Goblin. (USAF)

Changing of the guard: Looking out from underneath the wing of the venerable B-36 Peacemaker on the tarmac at Edwards AFB as the Boeing XB-52 is readied for a test flight. (AFFTC History Office)

A stunning view of the Boeing XB-52 with its original tandem-seat fighter-like cockpit. SAC commander Gen. Curtis LeMay strongly suggested that Boeing modify the B-52 cockpit to a side-by-side seating arrangement. (Boeing Archives)

within the austere-minded Truman administration that favored continuing the XB-47[1] development and canceling the follow-on heavy long-range jet bomber program to replace the B-36. There was a general misunderstanding of the differences between a medium bomber (B-47) and a long-range heavy bomber with superior capabilities. Fortunately, more sophisticated minds prevailed and the AAF Board of Senior Officers was given the go-ahead for the development of a long-range heavy jet bomber, and on 13 February 1946, the AAF released a design directive to aircraft manufacturers.

There was maximum latitude of freedom in the design criteria.[2] Boeing, Consolidated-Vultee (Convair), and Martin all responded with preliminary proposals. It may have seemed unusual to be planning a new heavy bomber six months before the first XB-36 even flew, but with gradual improvement in turbojet engine reliability and performance, this reticence was diminishing. By June 1947, the criteria had been revised, with increased airspeed being the main driver. After about two years of revisions and design criteria variations, things began to calm.

Boeing Gets to Work

At Boeing, final work was already underway completing the six-engine XB-47 Stratojet which featured a 35-degree wing sweep. After its first flight on 17 December 1947, its success strongly influenced some of the B-52 designers, although not all were confident in jet engines, which up to this point were very thirsty when consuming fuel. The Boeing Model 452 was still destined for turboprop engines to achieve the range needed to meet required specifications. Meanwhile, chief aerodynamicist George Schairer, who had changed the XB-47 design with his recommendations on the advantages of a swept wing, conferred with engineer Ed Wells. The gradually evolving result was the Model 464-35 with a 20-degree swept wing, powered by six turboprop engines with contra-rotating propellers. This configuration appeared amazingly similar to the four-engine Soviet Tupolev Tu-95 Bear long-range bomber.

Schairer, Vaughn Blumenthal, and Art Carlsen presented their design to AMC at Wright-Patterson AFB on 21 October 1948. AMC officials consisted of Gen. Kenneth Wolf and Col. Henry Warden, both experienced World War II bomber and fighter pilots, respectively.[3] The meeting was rather brief, and the Boeing team was directed to eliminate the propellers and switch to jet engines. The team was somewhat surprised, as they had previously been directed by AMC to employ turboprops. Essentially, the new boss was in town and times had changed.

Flexibility Was Key

AMC agreed to meet with Boeing again, provided a new design could be presented. That was good to hear, but the meeting date was set for the following Monday, only four days away. Ed Wells immediately flew in from Seattle, and two additional Boeing engineers who were in Dayton joined the group that was now under severe pressure. George Schairer headed for a local hobby shop to pick up some balsa wood, a modeler's knife, and glue. The rationale was that a

The elegant Boeing YB-52 (t/n 9231) on a test flight off the coastline of Washington State. (National Museum of the USAF)

three-dimensional model always works better in a live presentation. What has become a legendary Boeing Company story is the redesign session that took place over a weekend in a Dayton hotel room.[4] The quickly assembled Boeing team of six worked out a configuration that would meet the performance parameters. This included increasing the wing-sweep angle from 20 degrees to 35 degrees and increasing wing area from less than 3,000 square feet to 4,000 square feet. At this stage there was a critical balance.

From lessons learned on the B-47, the new design incorporated a thicker wing than the Stratojet. Although not too thick for reduced drag, the wing would be easier to build, stronger, and less fatigue prone. Also in contrast to the medium-range B-47, the B-52's wings allowed for very large fuel tanks.[5] The bicycle landing gear that retracted into the fuselage followed the B-47's clean configuration, however. All these components were considered critical features to maximize range. In addition, eight Pratt & Whitney YJ-57-PW-3 engines would be mounted in pairs in four underwing pylons. Estimated top speed was more than 600 mph, and range was far greater than the B-47.

Let's Meet Again

During the critical Monday, 25 October, follow-up meeting, the team presented their 33-page design proposal along with the 14-inch-long balsawood model that was carved from scratch. The

In summer 1954, Air Force Capt. Fitz Fulton was copilot on the first delivery flight of a B-52B (52-005) from Boeing Field in Seattle to Edwards AFB. Upon touchdown on Edwards' new 15,000-ft. runway, warnings lights and horns activated when the landing gear handle moved to the "up" position and the gear began retracting right on the runway. Despite Fulton's best efforts to push the handle back down, the airplane slid to a stop with three of the four bogies retracted, and substantial damage to the gear doors. An investigation revealed a design flaw in the gear handle detent which Boeing took full responsibility for, and the problem was corrected on the production line. (USAF)

The XB-52 (t/n 9230) joined the flight-test program during Phase II. Note the F-86 Sabre Jet chase plane in the background of the massive bomber lining on the runway centerline at Boeing Field. (USAF)

B-52A (t/n 2001), featuring the new modified cockpit, landing at Boeing field after a test sortie. The number-one B-52A made its first flight on 5 August 1954. Out of the original B-52A order for 13 aircraft only 3 were completed, with the remaining 10 A models converted to B-52Bs. (USAF)

The graceful aerodynamic lines of the YB-52 Stratofortress. SAC was awaiting deliveries of the new jet bombers. (National Museum of the USAF)

Boeing configuration was a clean-sheet design; perhaps now a "clean balsawood" design. The Air Force was pleased and Col. Warden quickly headed to the Pentagon in Washington, DC. He carried with him Boeing's proposal and the balsawood scale model.[6] In short order, Warden's positive recommendation was accepted, and on 17 November 1948, the Air Force authorized Boeing to build a full-scale mockup plus two prototypes. Although the first two aircraft would be built identically, one would be designated XB-52 (t/n 9230) and the second YB-52 (t/n 9231). Formal inspection of the mockup took place in April 1949, and final design-tweaking recommendations were agreed to.[7] Continuing Boeing's "Strato" aircraft heritage, the name Stratofortress was accepted. Meanwhile the Air Force had approved a competing proposal from Convair to modify two B-36F airframes as jet-powered heavy bombers.

Because of a modified wing spar and late engine deliveries on the XB-52, the YB-52 was selected for the first flight. Both the YB-52

The active flight line at Edwards AFB with a Boeing XB-52 flanked by a Northrop X-4 Bantam in the foreground and two Convair B-36s in the background. (AFFTC History Office)

and XB-52 featured tandem cockpits similar to the B-47. Boeing Chief Test Pilot Alvin M. "Tex" Johnson was in the cockpit as the YB-52 made its first flight on 15 April 1952.[8] Following the flight path of the first XB-47 some five years earlier, the 235,000-pound bomber lifted off gracefully from Boeing Field and headed to Larsen AFB at Moses Lake, Washington. Initial flight-testing would be carried out at the Boeing facility there. In what might be a record for a first flight, the YB-52 remained aloft for 2 hours and 51 minutes. Johnson was impressed by the slow airspeed capability on landing approach resulting in very little braking on landing rollout. The drag chute was only deployed for testing.[9]

Initial reports on the YB-52 flight-testing were extremely promising, substantiating the design's jet-powered flight dynamics. The aircraft's spoilers, mounted on top of the wing, acted as ailerons that enabled quick reaction maneuvering for the large aircraft. By October 1952, 50 flight hours had been accumulated and speeds of Mach 0.84 and an altitude of 50,000 feet were achieved at less than full throttle. The prototype was accepted by the Air Force on 31 March 1953, and eventually the YB-52 accrued 738 hours during 345 test flights.

The XB-52 was rolled out on 29 November 1951, but it was almost a year before it flew. Its main participation was in Phase II flight testing.[10] The XB-52 encountered far more problems than the YB-52, requiring the airplane to be returned to the Boeing factory. After a flight with "Tex" Johnson, SAC Commander Gen. Curtis LeMay felt the B-52 was exactly what SAC needed to maintain peace during the Cold War. In a conversation with Boeing President Bill Allen, LeMay strongly recommended that the cockpit arrangement be changed to side-by-side seating for better crew interaction, as on all large bombers, and Boeing instituted that cockpit configuration change on production models.

Convair was Not Complacent

In the midst of restricted DoD budgets, and with its proficient B-36 production line already in place, Convair felt it had a lower-cost solution. On 25 August 1950, Convair proposed to the Air Force a swept-wing jet-powered version of the B-36. Two B-36Fs would be modified to an all-jet B-36G[11] configuration to be used as flight-test aircraft. In lieu of a formal agreement, on 15 March 1951 the Air Force modified the existing B-36 contract to authorize conversion of two B-36F airframes to the B-36G specifications outlined by Convair. The first prototype would be ready to fly by December 1951 and the second aircraft by February 1952.[12] Considering the obvious differences in the B-36F airframe, and potential increased performance, the Air Force redesignated the prototype YB-60.

The second airplane, which would closely resemble an operational version, was designated B-60. To avoid design redundancy and keep costs to a minimum, the Air Force authorized Convair to use Boeing-designed wing pylons and engine nacelles. In addition, the identical engine (P&W YJ57-P-3)[13] that would power the Boeing YB-52/XB-52 would be installed on the YB-60 and B-60. The YJ57 engine was a new breed designed for higher thrust and lower fuel burn. However, by early 1951 testing of the new prototype YJ57-P-3 turbojet had amounted to only 550 hours. With full production only initiated in early 1952, providing engines for both the XB-52/YB-52 and YB-60 at the start of test flights would be cutting it close.[14]

The basic YB-60 airframe remained intact, but propulsion was switched to all jet engines and swept wings were added through modifications. The six huge Pratt & Whitney R-4360 pusher piston engines and four General Electric J47 turbojets were removed. With the government furnishing the eight Pratt & Whitney YJ57-PW-3 turbojets, plus several additional ancillary items, Convair estimated the cost would be approximately $1 million per aircraft. Additionally, the YB-60 would have 72-percent parts commonality with the B-36. This shortened the assembly process, which eventually took only eight months.[15] Nevertheless, modifying a B-36 airframe and achieving the desired performance was a challenge, and Convair found itself in the midst of a paradox. The cost estimate would appear favorable in their proposal, yet would jet engines be enough to overcome obsolete B-36 airframe traits, specifically the thick wing? The B-36 wing's cross section was actually large enough for a crewmember to step inside the wing and inspect various engine systems while in flight.

The B-36 Going Swept

Each wing spar was cut just outboard of the main landing gear. Next a wedge shape was inserted that angled the main spar at 35 degrees. A new wing glove was installed along the leading edge of the center edge to provide a smooth line into the fuselage. A matching-angle wedge structure was installed in the wing box, or wing root location, to fill the gap of the now swept wings. This increased the wing area by approximately 500 square feet[16] and added room for ten fuel tanks capable of holding 42,106 gallons.

The number-one Convair YB-60 prototype (t/n 92676) on a medium altitude test flight. Its brilliant silver and red colors presenting a striking image in front of the clouds. (Author Photo/Illustration)

On 18 April 1952, with chief test pilot Beryl Erickson in command, the number-one YB-60 (t/n 92676) made its first flight from Carswell AFB, adjacent to the Convair plant. The tail landing gear had already been retracted prior to rotation. The dark smoke from the eight YJ57s has been airbrushed out by Air Force censors. Other released versions of this particular photo had the entire landing arrangement airbrushed out. (USAF)

This increased range, but with a penalty of increased drag. The original B-36 was not designed with an aerial-refueling receptacle and needed to carry huge amounts of fuel to perform its long-range missions. The advent of more advanced aerial-tanker platforms negated the necessity of having to carry excessive quantities of fuel at the expense of aircraft payload and range. Weight and drag have always been the enemy of aerodynamic performance, and while modifying the basic B-36 wing Convair engineers made the best of it.

As in the B-36 arrangement, the YB-60's main landing gear was retracted into the wing, leaving a slight bulge on both the upper and lower outer wing surfaces near the wing root. These drag-creating protuberances were considered an acceptable penalty when Convair engineers designed the wing modifications for the YB-60 configuration. Incorporating the Boeing XB-47's design of bicycle landing gear retracting into the fuselage, thus allowing for a thinner wing, was not an option. This would have involved a clean-sheet design negating Convair's low-cost approach. Subsequently, the YB-60's 35-degree swept wingspan was 206 feet, some 24 feet less than the B-36's 230-foot wingspan. To obtain more performance from the modified airframe, the horizontal stabilizers and vertical tail were also swept back. To increase rudder authority[17] the area and height

The Convair YB-60 on a test sortie over the Texas countryside, its large-area wing clearly evident. Chief test pilot Beryl Erickson conducted the Phase I test flights prior to the aircraft's ferry flight to Edwards AFB. (USAF)

of the vertical tail were increased, making the YB-60 13.7 feet higher than the B-36 and, unknown to Convair engineers at the time, 12.2 feet higher than the competing YB-52.

Also very different from the B-36 was a new aerodynamically shaped needle nose equipped with a large pitot tube. The widely recognized bulbous B-36 canopy over the flight deck remained essentially the same, as SAC Commander Gen. Curtiss LeMay favored this type of side-by-side seating for bomber crews. In the YB-60 prototype, all the B-36 remote-controlled guns were removed. In the pressurized forward compartment, the flight crew would consist of the command pilot, copilot, navigator, and bombardier/radio operator. The well-known B-36 fuselage tunnel used by crewmembers to move between the fore and aft compartments was eliminated from the YB-60 since required redundant operational systems were located in each compartment, negating the need for crewmembers to move.

The tail section was also modified to house a drag chute, and an aft landing gear was installed to prevent the aircraft from rocking back on its tail in an aft-CG condition on the ground. The fuselage would extend to 171.2 feet, approximately 9 feet longer than the B-36F.[18] Per contract, the YB-60 program was running late as preparations ensued for the first flight, a prime factor being delayed engine deliveries from Pratt & Whitney. In fact, the number eight YJ57-P-3 engine arrived only 12 days prior to the scheduled first flight.[19] Rollout took place on 6 April 1952, and Convair's new contribution to the jet-age was presented to the media.

The YB-60 prototype at the Convair plant. The thick wings were a constraint that Convair engineers had to work with in modifying a basic B-36 wing to the YB-60 jet-powered configuration. (USAF)

Punching Through the Clouds

It was 18 April 1952 and first flight day had arrived. Unfortunately, the Fort Worth area was hampered by poor weather conditions consisting of gusty winds up to 25 mph and a ceiling of 5,000 feet with scattered showers. Boeing's YB-52 had made its first flight three days prior, and Convair felt that getting off the ground as soon as possible was important for company morale. Late afternoon was looking better as the crew boarded the YB-60. In the command pilot seat was Chief Test Pilot Beryl Erickson, who had made the first flight of the XB-36 six years prior.[20] In the copilot's position was Arthur Witchell Jr., accompanied by flight test engineers J. D. McEachern and William Easley. At 4:55 p.m., during a break in the weather, the YB-60 lifted off the runway at Carswell AFB, adjacent to Convair's Fort Worth facility. The landing gear remained down during the 66-minute flight and all systems operated nominally. Fortunately for Convair, the inaugural flight was completed only seven days before Fort Worth experienced 15 hours of continuous rainfall. After two additional local flights, the YB-60 was flown to the Air Force Flight Test Center (AFFTC) at Edwards AFB. There, both Convair and Air Force test pilots would fly the new bomber.

An interesting variance that quickly attracted Convair engineers' attention was the aircraft's center of gravity (CG). Since the nose and main landing gear positioning were the same as the B-36, the new swept wings shifted the CG to aft. While on the ground and under certain load conditions, the tail could possibly settle. Convair engineers designed and installed a tail-mounted retractable landing gear that would keep the aft section off the ground. While parked, this addition greatly distracted from a sleek jet appearance, and as a result the aft landing gear was either airbrushed out or hidden by various objects in any publicly released Company photographs. The aft gear had to be retracted during the takeoff roll to allow the nose to rise for rotation. As one of two Air Force test pilots on the YB-60 program, Fitz Fulton[21] remarked, "The takeoff procedure was for the

The YB-60 at the Convair Fort Worth plant with the forward bomb bay doors open. (USAF)

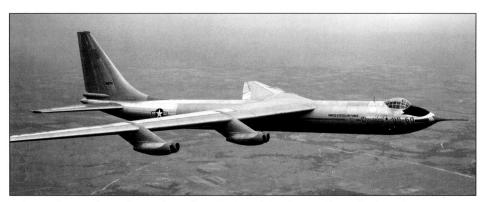

Prior to being ferried to Edwards AFB, Beryl Erickson pilots the YB-60 on a test flight on an overcast day over Texas. (USAF)

A rare color image captures the YB-60 (t/n 92676) on short final at Edwards AFB. The YB-60 was flown to Edwards during July 1954, and both Convair and Air Force pilots accumulated 66 hours of flight time on the number-one prototype. (AFFTC History Office)

The number-one YB-60 prototype and its unusual aft landing gear arrangement. The installation of swept wings on the B-36 airframe shifted the center of gravity, and the gear was installed to prevent the aircraft from settling on its tail. (USAF)

pilot to hold the control column forward until the speed reached about 70 knots. The copilot would then retract the rear-mounted landing gear and tail wheel. If it failed to retract he would hit a switch that would explosively blow off the gear and allow the takeoff to continue." Fulton continued, "Compared to the standard airplanes we were used to flying, this seemed like a fairly complicated and somewhat unorthodox procedure."[22]

Although the YB-60 was fitted with new ailerons, the overall configuration had been designed for slower airspeeds. With increased jet-powered airspeeds, the higher aerodynamic forces imposed on its flight-control system degraded performance considerably. This translated to speed limitations at low altitude and some instability traits. The Boeing YB-52 design, which utilized independent spoilers on top of the wings to act as ailerons, proved extremely beneficial. As flight records were tallied, it became clear to Air Force officials that Convair's entry was not going to achieve its desired performance parameters—the YB-60's top speed of 508 mph was approximately 100 mph below the YB-52. Other deficiencies included buffeting at high altitude, engine surge, vertical stabilizer flutter, and electrical system problems.[23]

A detail of the number-one YB-60 nose section. The second prototype (B-60) would have featured many of the attributes of an operational aircraft. This would have included a more aerodynamically shaped nose section without the large pitot tube. (USAF)

The Convair Cancellation

Convair and Air Force test pilots flew the YB-60 prototype for a total of 25 sorties, accumulating 66 hours of flight time, but overwhelming data pointed toward the competing YB-52's superior performance. On 4 August 1952, the B-60 program was canceled, and testing of the prototype ended in January 1953.[24] Unfortunately, the second aircraft (B-60), which was configured closer to a final operational bomber, never flew. This must have been very frustrating for Convair, because the B-60 was 93-percent complete and only needed its eight engines installed. Concurrently produced from another B-36F airframe, the B-60 would be equipped with retractable gun turrets (similar to the B-36), as well as tail-mounted twin 20mm cannons. The aircraft also featured a more aerodynamic nose that would have increased airspeed performance.

During this time Convair offered a back-up plan that would equip the prototypes with experimental turboprop engines and keep them flying. This type of propulsion was still considered by both the government and industry to be a suitable backup should jet propulsion hit a snag. However, budgets remained austere, and the turboprop concept was rejected. The total cost of both aircraft, including Convair's fee and termination costs, was estimated at $14,366,022 in 1954 dollars.[25] Once again, as if with a swift, thoughtless hammer, both the YB-60 and B-60 were regrettably scrapped by the end of June 1954, another sad commentary on the attitude of the times regarding the preservation of rare, unique, and historic aircraft.

The Stratofortress: Cold War Mainstay

The first formal agreement between Boeing and the Air Force was signed on 14 February 1951 for production of 13 B-52A[26] Stratofortresses.[27] An amendment later changed the order to RB-52A; through modifications, internal pods could be mounted in the bomb bay allowing the RB-52A to operate either as bombers or reconnaissance variants. Rollout of the first B-52A in Seattle on 30 June 1953 was a special occasion for the Air Force—it represented the new jet-age deterrence for SAC. Among the nearly 2,000 people in attendance was Air Force Chief of Staff Gen. Nathan Twining. During the ceremony Gen. Twining remarked, "The long rifle was the great weapon of its day. Today, this B-52 is the long rifle of the air age."[28] Twining continued to stress the B-52's symbol of deterrence. Less than two months later, on 4 August 1954, the number-one B-52A was airborne. The first B-52B[29] entered service with the 93rd Heavy Bomb Wing at Castle AFB, California. As with any new aircraft, the B-52 certainly had its share of problems, but none too severe to halt the program. There were two short incidents of aircraft groundings due to alternator, fuel system, and hydraulic pack anomalies.

During the summer of 1954, Air Force Capt. Fitz Fulton was copilot on the first delivery flight of a B-52B (52-005) from Boeing Field in Seattle to Edwards AFB. It was the seventh Stratofortress built.

The Convair YB-60 and its predecessor, the B-36 Peacemaker, parked on the ramp at Edwards North Base. (AFFTC History Office)

Upon touchdown on Edwards' new 15,000-foot runway, warning lights and horns activated when the landing gear handle moved to the "up" position and the gear began to retract right on the runway. Despite Fulton's best efforts to push the handle back down, the airplane slid to a stop with three of the four bogies retracted, and substantial damage to the gear doors. An investigation revealed a design flaw in the gear handle detent, for which Boeing took full responsibility, and the problem was corrected on the production line.

As B-52s progressed through the early models, the airframe appeared to be capable of a long service life. Past experience with the B-47 helped greatly in understanding maintenance support and, more importantly, airframe fatigue. Thus, the Air Force and Boeing were acutely aware and well prepared as problems emerged during the aircraft's service life. The versatility of the B-52 platform was unmatched, whether carrying conventional dumb bombs or smart bombs. Nuclear weapons were still in its pocket of offensive ordnance, as well as sophisticated standoff missiles. Additionally, upgrades to the bomber's defensive electronics suite have kept the B-52 up to date. However, even as the B-52 was proving itself as a vital flexible leg of the Strategic Triad, there were constant attempts to either retire the bombers in service or thwart further production. Astonishingly, there were concurrent efforts to consistently delay or cancel new, more-advanced replacement bombers.

Congressional Bomber Battles

During March 1961, quite a flap developed between the Air Force and Congress when President Kennedy reduced the Mach 3+ XB-70

As the YB-60 flies over the Edwards test range, Mojave Desert sand replaces the grass and trees of Texas. (USAF)

With two B-36s in the background, the Convair YB-60 takes off at Edwards AFB. In this Air Force–released photo, the water-injection dark exhaust has not been airbrushed out by the censors. (AFFTC History Office)

strategic bomber to only a development project. Additionally, Kennedy did not request any increase for the B-52 or B-58 bomber fleet. Were our adversaries watching? Note this was a year and a half before the Cuban Missile Crisis erupted. The President attempted to allay fears by promising that "the Skybolt missile would be good for the B-52 or successor bomber." During the following month, Congress questioned the flawed strategy recommended by President Kennedy and Secretary McNamara in their FY1962 DoD budget. In a wise move, the House Armed Services Committee (HASC) headed by Rep. Carl Vinson (D-GA), stepped forward and authorized an extra $337 million to continue production of the current strategic-bomber fleet.[30] The decision was left up to the Air Force to apply the funds to the B-52 and/or B-58. The dollar estimate was based on the cost of 15 B-52s and 16 B-58 Hustlers. At the time, B-52 production was scheduled to end in August 1962 and the B-58 in October 1962.

Testifying before the Senate Armed Services Committee (SASC), Secretary McNamara defended his recommended cuts to the U.S. strategic-bomber force. He was so fixated on costs that he compared the significant budget impact for procuring more manned bombers to the lower unit cost of single missile types. Secretary McNamara testified, "Minuteman in silo, $3.2 million; mobile Minuteman, $5 million; and Polaris, $9.7 million."[31] Yet not a single knowledgeable congressman stood up to question this unusual logic. Essentially, the

The massive B-36 Peacemaker was often referred to as the "Aluminum Overcast," and the YB-60 projects a similar impression. The chase plane moved under the massive YB-60 bomber to reveal a rather ominous profile; note the inboard flaps have been lowered slightly. (National Museum of the USAF)

fog of budget wars caused Secretary McNamara to completely misjudge the capabilities of a flexible, recallable manned bomber versus nuclear-armed ICBMs stored in silos. Any Commander-In-Chief knows that an ICBM launch is potentially the end of civilization.

Fortunately, during May 1961, the SASC increased the funding to $525 million. The committee overwhelmingly supported the continuation of the B-52 program eventually armed with the AGM-48A Skybolt Air-Launched Ballistic Missile (ALBM). In testimony, Secretary McNamara and Air Force Chief of Staff Gen. Thomas D. White both supported the B-52 and emphasized the importance of the combination of the bomber and the unique Skybolt[32] air-to-ground missile scheduled to enter the inventory in 1965. Gen. White estimated the Skybolt to have a service life of four to five years. Recall that was in 1961, and White also predicted the service life of the B-52G/H to be another eight years.[33, 34]

Both Secretary McNamara and General White emphasized that both the B-58 and the impending B-70 were not designed to carry the Skybolt. Although Convair had submitted a proposal to modify the B-58 to carry Skybolt, Gen. White commented that "the USAF is viewing this skeptically." What was not mentioned to the SASC was the fact that NAA was conducting XB-70/Skybolt compatibility studies. An operational B-70 heavy bomber would fly at subsonic speeds with two Skybolts mounted on wing pylons. After the Skybolt ALBMs launched 700 to 1,000 miles from their targets, the pylons would be jettisoned and the B-70 would accelerate to triple-sonic (Mach 3+) speeds. With approximately 28,000 pounds of internal payload, the B-70 would then head for a secondary target. This combination would have been difficult for an enemy to defeat.

ICBMs versus Manned Bombers

Secretary McNamara didn't give up. During November 1962, he proposed doubling the force of Minuteman ICBMs from 800 to 1,700. The Pentagon's FY1964 budget request would be issued at the expense of the B-52 fleet, which consisted of 700 aircraft. The FY1964 budget called for the phase-out of all 449 operational B-52A through B-52F[35] bombers over a three to five year period. Further examination of McNamara's plan revealed that the 193 B-52Gs and 102 B-52Hs might be facing the same fate. The G model was currently being modified to carry the subsonic NAA Hound Dog air-to-ground missile, and the H model was being modified to carry the Douglas Skybolt, a hypersonic air-launched ballistic missile. The Skybolt, with a ballistic trajectory and speed of Mach 12.4 (9,500 mph) would be a tremendous addition to the B-52's deterrence projection. Ironically, if deployed the Skybolt ALBM would actually have given the U.S. deterrent force another additional ballistic missile, only it would be air-launched.

While on a test flight over the Mojave Desert, the YB-60 presents an excellent view of the large modified wing. The wing area was increased by 500 square feet during the 35-degree-sweep modification process. (USAF)

Moving forward in a hypothetical history: A conceptual operational USAF/Convair B-60E in SAC markings, with white antiradiation paint applied to its underside. Had the YB-52 faltered in any way during the heavy bomber competition, perhaps the YB-60 would have been selected. (Author Photo/Illustration)

Attempting to analyze McNamara's thought process is challenging for historians. The secretary of defense had previously declared in 1963 that by 1965 Soviet air defenses would preclude any penetration by the B-52. SAC commanders were certainly aware of this prediction and were totally behind equipping the B-52 fleet with standoff weapons. The difference being the Air Force wanted to upgrade their recallable bomber fleet, and McNamara would do his best not to spend resources upgrading manned aircraft. After all, ICBMs were cheaper, and a trimmed budget could be presented to the president. Fortunately, the majority of the USAF B-52 bomber fleet was retained.

McNamara also seemed to be suffering from short-term memory loss regarding the value of the manned bomber. During the Cuban Missile Crisis, which occurred in October 1962, President John Kennedy had ordered SAC to maintain a large number of nuclear-armed B-52s to loiter just outside the denied airspace of the Soviet Union. As planned, the Kremlin knew they were there and, upon orders from the president, the bombers could immediately head to their assigned targets, remain on-station, or return to base. The loitering bombers provided crucial time for a peaceful diplomatic solution to be established. This cannot be done with nuclear-armed ICBMs. With missiles it's either all or nothing—a rather nightmarish thought.

Fuel Savings: Missed Opportunities

The history of the B-52 Stratofortress is pockmarked with missed opportunities to re-engine the venerable bomber. Whether the cause was budget constrictions or disagreement regarding the process, the

A hypothetical operational early-model USAF B-60B with fixed wing tanks. Although the YB-60's performance never met the Air Force requirements, or even approached that of the competing YB-52, in aviation history there is always the speculation of what might have been. (Author Photo/Illustration)

A conceptual view of a SAC B-60E on a training mission over the southwest United States. With its antiradiation flash paint and external wing tanks, the bomber almost appears similar to a SAC B-52E. (Author Photo/Illustration)

With the hypothetical service life of the B-60 continuing, it's fascinating to imagine the next variant: a G model in SEA camouflage with the distinctive shortened tail. (Author Photo/Illustration)

A Boeing B-52H Stratofortress flies over snowcapped mountains. (Author Photo/Illustration)

A publicity photo of the first Wichita-built B-52D (t/n 5049) Stratofortress destined for service with SAC. Note the white antiradiation flash paint applied to the aircraft's underside and the new large wing tanks. A total of 69 D models were built. (USAF)

A SAC aircrew scrambles aboard one of the first operational RB-52Bs from the 22nd Bombardment Wing at March AFB. With rapid bomb bay modifications, the RB-52B could operate as either a reconnaissance aircraft or a B-52B bomber. (USAF)

Two B-52s were converted to launch motherships for the NASA/NAA X-15 rocket-plane in 1959. "Balls Three," the third aircraft built (t/n 54-003), was modified and converted to the NB-52A while B-52 t/n 54-008, called "Balls Eight," was modified as an NB-52B. Throughout the decades, NB-52s launched numerous experimental aircraft, lifting bodies, and remotely piloted vehicles, up through the hypersonic X-51A WaveRider. (NASA)

A SAC B-52E takes on fuel from a KC-135A Stratotanker during early SAC refueling exercises. The photo was taken from another KC-135A. (USAF)

During the height of the Cold War, a sentry stands guard at the entrance to Offutt AFB, Nebraska, home of SAC Headquarters. The sign depicts SAC's mission: "Peace is our Profession." (USAF)

Gen. Curtis LeMay became Commander of SAC on 19 October 1948. SAC was quickly transformed into the best strategic deterrent force in the world. General LeMay later became the Air Force chief of staff during the Kennedy Administration. (Author Photo/Illustration)

The red telephone on the side of the senior controller at SAC HQ. Picking up this phone immediately links the controller to every SAC command post at bases throughout the world. (USAF)

job was never done. This is particularly disconcerting in light of the unqualified success of the KC-135R re-engining program. The only engine upgrades since the inception of the B-52 were to the G model with the installation of the GE J57-P-43WA turbojets and the H model with the P&W TF33-P3 turbofans. The TF33-P3 provided 17,000 pounds of thrust compared to the earlier J57 with 8,700 pounds of thrust.

In 1978, an opportunity occurred with a proposal from Rolls-Royce and Pratt & Whitney to mount four fuel-saving high-bypass turbofan engines on the B-52 fleet. Both the Rolls-Royce RB.211-535 and P&W PW2000 were flight tested on a B-52 testbed engine pylon. Both engines offered tremendous fuel savings, as well as less maintenance, noise, and air pollution, but nothing was done. In late 1996, an unsolicited proposal was submitted from Boeing and Allison Engine Group for a B-52 re-engining lease arrangement for the RB.211-535. This program would have also privatized engine maintenance, relieving the Air Force of this task. There would be a substantial increase in thrust, and range would increase by 30 percent. Cost savings for the Air Force ranged from $3 billion to $8 billion. A headline in the 17 November 1996 issue of *Defense News* read, "U.S.

Air Force Finds Merit in B-52 Engine Lease Plan." During the ensuing months there was disagreement on the number of bombers the Air Force would keep in service and the future cost of fuel. It's not rocket science to figure out that throughout modern history, with intermittent spikes, the cost of oil/fuel gradually escalates.

The Defense Science Board (DSB) carried out a review of a 1997 DoD study. It found that the DoD had failed to properly calculate the amount of fuel savings that would result from less in-flight refueling. It was estimated that if B-52s had been equipped with new engines during Operation Desert Storm, it would have required one less squadron of KC-135 tankers for support. And, again, it was

With water injection creating dark exhaust smoke, a B-52F takes off at Boeing Field carrying the new NAA GAM-77 (later AGM-28) Hound Dog air-to-ground missiles. The F models had two additional internal wing water tanks installed to provide longer injection for takeoff. The next G model became the primary carrier of the Hound Dog. (USAF)

The number-one B-52E (t/n 6631), built at Boeing Seattle, on a low-level test flight over the Pacific Northwest coastline. Both the E and F models were equipped with terrain-following radar (TFR). (USAF)

The good old days. It was mid-1957 when the USAF aircraft fleet posed at the Air Proving Ground Command at Eglin AFB. Observing clockwise around the outer circle, starting at six o'clock: Convair F-102A Delta Dagger, NAA F-100D Super Sabre, Martin B-57B Canberra, Douglas B-66A Destroyer, Boeing RB-47E Stratojet, Boeing KC-135A Stratotanker, Boeing B-52E Stratofortress, Douglas C-124A Globemaster II, Boeing KB-50 Superfortress, Lockheed C-130A Hercules, Grumman SA-16 Albatross, Northrop F-89D Scorpion, and McDonnell RF-101A Voodoo. On the inner circle, clockwise from lower left: NAA F-86D Sabre Dog, Lockheed F-94C Starfire, Lockheed EC-121 Warning Star, Convair B-36H Peacemaker, Boeing KC-97 Stratofreighter, Republic F-84F Thunderstreak, and NAA F-86E Sabre Jet. In the center: Sikorsky H-19 Chickasaw and Cessna T-37 Tweet. (USAF)

A B-52G carrying two AGM-28 Hound Dog air-to-ground missiles. If needed, the missile's air-breathing turbojet engines could be started in flight, providing the B-52G with a combined thrust of 10 engines for emergency dash capability. (USAF)

Ready to go B-52Fs on the flightline, each armed with two NAA AGM-28 Hound Dog air-to-ground missiles. An excellent standoff weapon with a 785-mile standoff range, the Hound Dog could be guided from the point of launch to the target. In addition, the missile's radar could be monitored, and it could receive course corrections. (USAF)

Under Operation Arc Light, on 18 June 1965 the first B-52s to deploy to Southeast Asia were the F models. Taking off from Anderson AFB, Guam, the B-52Fs supported U.S. ground troops in South Vietnam. With nonglare black paint on its underside, a B-52F from the 320th Bombardment Wing unloads a salvo of M117 750-pound conventional bombs from both its internal bomb bay and wing-mounted bomb racks. (USAF)

After landing during December 1976, a B-52G taxies in from the main runway at Homestead AFB. During the Cuban Missile Crisis in October 1962, Homestead AFB was a critical marshaling base for U.S. SAC bombers, TAC fighters, and tactical reconnaissance assets. (Author)

A well-worn SEA-camouflaged B-52G (t/n 60243) parked on the tarmac at Homestead AFB, Florida, on a late winter afternoon in December 1976. (Author)

The stinging section of a B-52G in the late 1980s. G models were armed with four .50-cal. M-3 machine guns on a three-dimensional moving turret. On the G model the tail gunner's position was moved to a forward crew station. (Author)

emphasized that a re-engined B-52 would have a 50-percent greater combat radius and twice the loiter time over the target area. In March 2003, the DSB recommended to re-engine the B-52H fleet at a cost estimate of $3.5 billion.

By mid-2003, the B-52 re-engining concept was revised yet again. Operating under a $3 million contract, Boeing requested engine manufacturers to submit bids for both four- and eight-engine configurations. Eight engines would eliminate the problem of an outboard engine failure during takeoff by having a remaining engine in the nacelle to counter the asymmetric thrust. Studies concluded that a B-52 with only four engines might not have enough rudder authority in a sudden outboard engine failure condition during take-off. For the four-engine configuration, Pratt & Whitney proposed an uprated variant of the C-17 engine, the F117X. For the eight-engine option, the PW6000 and JT8D-200 were considered candidates and Rolls-Royce offered its RB.211-535E4 with an alternate being the

BR.715 at 22,000 pounds of thrust. Also in the mix was General Electric with the CFM International CFM56-3. Again, nothing happened.

Better Late Than Never

Moving forward to October 2014 a familiar idea reemerged; imagine that. During an Air Force Association event, Lt. Gen. Stephen Wilson, commander of Air Force Global Strike Command (AFGSC), [37] commented, "A perennial B-52 upgrade idea of re-engining is being considered again. Plans call for the B-52 to remain in service until 2040, and possibly beyond—and an engine replacement might pay for itself by the mid-2030s." Gen. Wilson also remarked, "There's no money in the coming budget for new engines, but we're exploring whether Congress would be willing to allow the Air Force to use some money earmarked for energy-saving upgrades at installations for the project. Right now, the money can't be used for aircraft modifications."[38]

Some Explaining to Do

Clearer minds prevailed and the air-launched Hound Dog missile program went ahead, but Secretary McNamara[36] suddenly canceled the more advanced air-launched Skybolt ALBM on 7 November 1962. The B-52H lost a critical standoff weapon, and a side effect would occur as a diplomatic faux pas. The next month President John Kennedy attended a previously scheduled meeting with British Prime Minister Harold Macmillan in which the agenda was unexpectedly sidetracked by the Skybolt cancellation. Since March 1960, there had been an agreement in place to provide the RAF with 100 AGM-48A Skybolt missiles for their Vulcan bombers; without Skybolt the British bomber was virtually obsolete. The MoD had already spent 27 million pounds to modify the RAF Vulcans to carry the Skybolt. Kennedy seemed unaware of the importance of the missile program to the British strategic-deterrent posture. Additionally, McNamara had not provided an adequate heads-up to the British regarding the cancellation.

Interestingly enough, the Skybolt cancellation occurred during the same time period that the manned-bomber preservation argument was taking place. By eliminating a standoff capability, coupled with not being able to penetrate denied airspace, you have conveniently removed the need for the manned bomber. This McNamara strategy continued with the Mach 3+ XB-70 Valkyrie bomber, as step-by-step the program was emasculated and never tested with offensive/defensive systems.

A Cold War Mutually Assured Destruction (MAD) strategy began to evolve during the early 1960s. To McNamara MAD was simple, expedient, and cheaper than bombers, plus a trimmed DoD budget might be achieved. In theory, MAD worked as the United States and the Soviet Union achieved parity. No right-minded sta-

ble country would attack the other and suffer a retaliatory strike resulting in total annihilation of both nations. Living under that threat was a heavy price to pay during the Cold War. Under this precarious train of thought, the only flexible part of the nuclear arsenal was slowly being eliminated. Manned bombers were recallable and during a crisis situation they offer the president some wiggle room. Flexible response is even more pertinent today, with an irresponsible rogue nation or group possibly possessing a nuclear capability. At the time, SAC was able to present its case and the B-52 fleet survived. Ironically, on 15 April 2015, the B-52 celebrated 63 years since its first flight!

A B-52H conducts a fit-check flight with four Douglas AGM-48A Skybolt ALBMs on its underwing pylons. The Skybolt would fly a ballistic trajectory at Mach 12.4 (9,500 mph) and at a standoff range between 600 to 1,000 miles. Had it not been canceled, the Skybolt would have provided an additional potent deterrent for the B-52H fleet. (USAF)

A crewmember at Barksdale AFB, Louisiana, conducts a walk-around of a B-52H. The AGM-142 Have Nap Raptor air-to-ground missile on the left wing pylon was the first standoff weapon to be carried by the B-52H. The Israeli-designed Popeye missile was coproduced by Rafael Advanced Defense Systems and Lockheed Martin and introduced to the B-52H in 1986. As conventional CAL-CMs became available, the AGM-142 Raptor was retired in 1995. (Author)

A conceptual view of a Boeing B-52R re-engined with four high-by-pass turbofan engines and the standard drag-producing wing tanks removed. The first opportunity to re-engine the B-52H fleet occurred in 1978, but no action was taken then or on several other opportunities. After three decades of missing a potential savings of billions of dollars in fuel and reduced maintenance, during April 2015 there seemed to be new impetus from Air Force leadership to fund the program. (Author Photo/Illustration)

A Tanker Win-Win Decision

The Air Force KC-135 Stratotanker fleet was, and still is, critical in supporting the U.S. manned-bomber leg of the Strategic Triad. The first KC-135A entered service in June 1957, dating back to the time of the original B-52. Thirty-five years ago in January 1980, Boeing was awarded an Air Force contract to begin a study to replace the tanker's P&W J57 engines and retrofit 420 KC-135A/E Stratotankers with new and more-fuel-efficient engines. The CFM56 high-bypass engine produced by CFM International was selected, and the results were impressive. A single CFM56 produces 22,000 pounds of thrust, with the four engines providing a 60 percent increase in power. In addition to greatly reduced noise (an astounding 98 percent quieter than the KC-135A) and air pollution, the increased efficiency enables a single KC-135R to transfer 50 percent more fuel while reducing its own fuel consumption by 25 percent. In addition, two KC-135Rs can perform missions that would require three KC-135As.

The KC-135 re-engining program was the correct decision at the right time. It has been nothing short of outstanding. On 9 June 2005, the 420th KC-135R was delivered by Boeing to the Air Force, concluding the immensely successful modification program. In addition to the USAF KC-135 Stratotanker, 25 RC-135V/W Rivet Joint and RC-135U Combat Sent aircraft, plus 14 French Air Force KC-135Fs, were re-engined with the CFM56. One must wonder why the stars never lined up for the B-52. The majority of B-52 systems such as ECM, PGM capability, communications, etc., have been continually upgraded through the decades, but not engines.

A Boeing KC-135R Stratotanker (t/n 10280) from March Air Reserve Base, California. The KC-135A had been in service for 23 years when the decision was made in 1980 to re-engine the fleet of A and E models. The fuel-thirsty P&W J57-P-59Ws were replaced by CFM56 high-bypass turbofan engines. The re-engining decision resulted in higher thrust for safety, dramatic fuel savings, and far less maintenance, air pollution, and noise. (Author Photo/Illustration)

A B-52R with 12 AGM-86C CALCAMs mounted on its underwing pylons. The AGM-86C is the conventionally armed variant, and the AGM-86D bunker buster was designed for deep penetration of underground targets. Also mounted under its right wing is the Lockheed ATP-SE LITENING surveillance and targeting pod. (Author Photo/Illustration)

AGM-129A/B Advanced Cruise Missile (ACM) began development in 1988 and was approved for procurement in July 1991. Built by General Dynamics (later Raytheon Missile Systems), the nuclear-armed AGM-129B ACM was also known as the "stealth cruise missile." The B-52 could carry 12 AGM-129Bs[41] on underwing pylons, each one independently targeted.

Continuing the Lineage

Fortunately, the early B-52 D and F models were not scrapped per Secretary McNamara's budget-slashing plans in 1961. Congress had negated that order, and during the late 1960s and early 1970s, these bombers turned out to be the venerable workhorses of the Vietnam War. They carried out conventional bombing of enemy-held positions in South Vietnam. Later, during Operation Arc Light and Linebacker I/II, B-52s conducted bombing missions over North Vietnam.

When the first B-52G rolled off the assembly line, several visible and internal differences were evident. The G featured a vertical stabilizer eight feet shorter than previous models. Additionally, the

Again in April 2015, Gen. Wilson commented that he expected to have industry proposals in hand by summer for re-engining the B-52H bomber fleet. "They can give us a 35-percent more fuel-efficient engine. What that means is that I can get about 35-percent more range out of the B-52, which already boasts substantial reach. An even bigger payback could come from ripple effects in logistics and operations," said Wilson. "Initial analysis points to a one-for-one engine swap-out, thus keeping the B-52's eight-engine configuration instead of moving to four turbofans.[39] Substantial operational savings have been predicted by experts for decades, but were never realized. Many are hoping that finally, this time, the B-52H fleet will receive its new engines.

A Standoff Platform

A good portion of the success of the B-52's longevity has been the acquisition of sophisticated standoff weapons. After being modified to carry the AGM-28 Hound Dog during the Cold War, the B-52 went on to carry the Boeing Short-Range Attack Missile (SRAM). During mid-1979, competing contractors' Air-Launched Cruise Missiles (ALCMs) were test fired over the AFFTC Range at Edwards. A dual service selection resulted, and Boeing developed the AGM-86 while General Dynamics built the AGM-109. The AGM-86 was selected by the Air Force. The system was developed as both nuclear-armed and conventionally armed versions—the AGM-86B and AGM-86C,[40] respectively. Later, the AGM-86D conventional deep penetrator was developed.

The AGM-109 Tomahawk was developed as an extremely successful Navy shipboard and submarine Sea-Launched Cruise Missile (SLCM). The missile has a range of approximately 1,500 miles and can be launched toward multiple targets from a B-52, surface ship, or submarine. The subsonic low-flying missiles are equipped with GPS and terrain-following radar (TFR) and follow a preplanned track matched to a computerized flight-path/target map. The classified

During 2006, a B-52H from the 2nd Bomb Wing at Barksdale AFB exhibited the variety of ordnance that can be carried, from the M117 general-purpose bomb to precision guided munitions (JDAM). Additional weapons carried are the AGM-86B/C ALCM/CALCM, and AGM-129B ACM (retired-2012). After being in the inventory for more than 40 years, during June 2015 the last M117 conventional bomb was dropped by a B-52H from Barksdale AFB. (USAF Tech. Sgt. Robert J. Horstman)

A B-52H (No. 0050) conducts a drop test of the GPS-guided Massive Ordnance Penetrator (MOP). Developed by the Air Force and Boeing in 2007, the MOP weighs 30,000 pounds, including 5,000 pounds of high explosives. The MOP is the largest conventional weapon in the Air Force's arsenal, and when dropped at high altitudes its weight provides the kinetic energy to penetrate deep underground targets. The MOP is equipped with a hard-target void-sensing electronic fuse and internal observing features that provide "penetration situational awareness" to its command center. Over denied airspace, the Northrop B-2A stealth bomber is certified to operationally carry the MOP. (USAF)

A B-52G at Edwards AFB featuring the twin electro-optical pods that were installed on all B-52G and H bombers. (Author)

A B-52H with Raytheon ADM-160B Miniature Air Launched Decoy-Jammers (MALD-J) mounted on its underwing pylons. When launched the turbojet-powered MALD-J counters enemy radar, creates false radar signatures, and/or mimics a variety of radar cross section (RCS) signatures. (USAF)

A B-52H (No. 0050) BUFF (Big Ugly Fat Fellow) lines up on the Edwards AFB runway centerline using its unique bicycle landing gear arrangement to side-slip for a crosswind takeoff. The landing gear could be turned to an angle of up to 20 degrees. (Author)

bomber featured a wet wing with integral tanks for increased fuel capacity. Also, the large 3,000-gallon auxiliary wing tanks carried by preceding models were replaced with smaller and more aerodynamic 300-gallon fixed tanks. The G was also fitted with twin electro-optical pods to enhance low-light vision at low altitude. Aircraft weight was increased from 450,000 to 488,000 pounds.[42] B-52Gs entered service with SAC on 13 February 1959, and a total of 193 were produced at Boeing's Wichita, Kansas facility, with the last G model being retired during the early 1990s.

Model H for "Hell Raiser"

On 9 May 1961, the first B-52H began service with SAC. Although its vertical stabilizer was the same as the G model, the engine nacelles were shaped differently due to the installation of uprated 17,000-pound-thrust P&W TF-33-P-3 turbofan engines. Unfortunately, the B-52H was initially plagued with numerous engine problems. 102 B-52Hs were built at Wichita, and the H model is the only variant in service with the USAF today. As of mid-2015, the active fleet stood at 85 aircraft. During Operation Desert Storm in 1990, 40 percent of all ordnance was delivered by the B-52—a combination of gravity bombs in support of coalition troops and AGM-86C ALCMs for hard targets.

The B-52H can carry 20 AGM-86C CALCMs, and hundreds were used during Operation Desert Storm, Operation Allied Force, and Operation Desert Strike. During Desert Strike, the longest combat mission ever flown was recorded when a B-52H flew a distance of 16,000 miles during a grueling 34-hour round-trip mission from Barksdale AFB to Baghdad and back. Called into service again on 21 March 2003, B-52Hs launched 100 AGM-86C CALCMs during Operation Iraqi Freedom.

All B-52Hs were equipped with twin electro-optical viewing sensors and FLIR, and are now being upgraded to the latest Sniper Advanced Targeting Pod, mounted externally on the aircraft. The B-52H is being continually modernized with digital communications to improve situational awareness and mission effectiveness. In February 2015, Boeing was awarded a contract to install Combat Network Communications Technology (CONECT) on an additional ten B-52Hs, bringing the total to 30 aircraft so equipped. The update includes full-color LCD displays with real-time intelligence on map overlays. The B-52H will be connected to satellites to receive data for quick mission changes and new target identification, bringing this classic aircraft the agility and flexibility needed in the modern battlefield environment.

A total of 744 B-52s were built; the last H model was delivered to SAC in October 1962. Each subsequent model resulted in dra-

A majestic B-52 flies across the sunset. (Author Photo/Illustration)

matic improvements to the bomber's structure and internal flight and electronic systems. Prepared to operate in a network-enabled environment, the current B-52H fleet—which started in SAC and continues to serve today in Global Strike Command (and possibly to the year 2040)—soldiers on in the digital age. Despite decades of budget battles, and continued failure to re-engine the B-52, the Cold War–era Stratofortress has always managed to assert its resilience.

Specifications

Boeing XB-52/YB-52 Stratofortress—Heavy-Bomber Prototype
Crew: 4—pilot, copilot, navigator, bombardier
Wingspan: 185 ft. (56.3 m)
Length: 157.07 ft. (47.8 m)
Height: 48. 4 ft. (14.7 m)
Maximum takeoff weight : 390,000 lb (17,690 kg)
Range: 7,000 miles (11,265 km)
Maximum speed: 610 mph (981.7 km/h)
Cruising Speed: 525 mph (844.9 km/h)
Service Ceiling: 50,000 ft. (15,151 m)
Powerplant: 8 Pratt & Whitney YJ57-PW-3 turbojets—8,700 lb (38.6 kN) thrust each
Bomb capacity: 10,000 lb (4,535 kg)
Armament: None

Convair YB-60—Heavy-Bomber Prototype
Crew: 4—pilot, copilot, navigator, bombardier
Wingspan: 206.4 ft. (63 m)
Length: 171.2 ft. (52.1 m)
Height: 60.6 ft. (18.4 m)
Maximum takeoff weight: 410,000 lb (18,597 kg)
Range: 8,000 mi. (12,874 km)
Maximum speed: 451 mph (725.8 km/h)
Cruising speed: 440 mph (708 km/h)

Service Ceiling: 44,650 ft. (13,609 m)
Powerplant: 8 Pratt & Whitney YJ57-PW-3 turbojets—8,700 lb (38.6 kN) thrust each
Payload: 10,000 lb (4,535.9 kg)
Armament: None

Boeing B-52H Stratofortress—Heavy Bomber
Crew: 5—commander, pilot, radar navigator, navigator, EW officer
Wingspan: 185 ft. (56.4 m)
Length: 159 ft. 4 in. (48.5 m)
Height: 40 ft. 8 in. (12.4 m)
Maximum takeoff weight: 488,000 lb (219,600 kg)
Ferry range (unrefueled): 10,145 miles (16,232 km)
Combat range (unrefueled): 8,800 mi. (14,080 km)
Maximum speed: 650 mph (1,047 km/h)
Cruising speed: 525 mph (844 km/h)
Service ceiling: 50,000 ft. (15,151 m)
Powerplant: 8 Pratt & Whitney TF33-P-3/103 turbofans—17,000 lb (75.62 kN) thrust each
Payload: 70,000 lb (31,500 kg)—mixed gravity bombs, sea mines, JDAM, ALCM/CALCM, JASSAM
Armament: remote-controlled M61 rotary 20mm cannon, ASQ-21 fire-control system. Tail gun removed in 1991.

THE COLD WAR TACTICAL FIGHTER
REPUBLIC YF-105A VERSUS NAA F-107A

An incredible formation that never took place. During a training sortie over the United States, a Convair B-58 Hustler (Project Bullseye) operating as an armed pathfinder, leads a Republic F-105D and North American F-107D. Although testing took place, deployment of the fast and accurate B-58 to Vietnam was denied by Sec. of Defense Robert McNamara. Of the three aircraft, the F-105D was the only aircraft that served in Southeast Asia. (Author Photo/Illustration)

The legendary contest that supposedly pitted the Republic YF-105A against North American's F-107A never materialized into a formal competition. Republic was proceeding with a fighter-bomber contract, and concurrently NAA was proceeding with an interceptor concept that would be an improvement over their F-100 Super Sabre. As time passed, the concept evolved, and the NAA design moved closer to a fighter-bomber configuration, and basically the two programs converged into an indirect competition. Both contractors were continually checking their six, as the Air Force announced the F-107 program would be a backup for the F-105 program. Arriving at that point is an intriguing tale.

Evolution of the Thunderchief

Efforts to improve the weapons load of the Republic F-84F Thunderstreak gradually evolved into a new design. Chief Engineer Alexander Kartveli centered his efforts on the installation of an internal weapons bay. Numerous obstacles, such as a through-intake and potential increased aircraft weight, stood out. Engine-thrust capability at that time was limited, and any increase in weight was a non-starter. F-84 variants were already infamous for their long takeoff rolls, and Republic's efforts shifted to a new design based around an uprated General Electric YJ73 engine. Slightly resembling an RF-84F configuration, this new design moved away from a through-inlet and featured flush wing-root intakes. The nose section was now available for radar and a fire-control system. To strike a favorable chord with the Air Force customer, Republic included an internal weapons bay that could carry a 3,000-pound payload. Based on the availability of the YJ73, engineers predicted a speed of 920 mph at 35,000 feet—vastly superior to the F-84F.

In February 1952, the Republic proposal was submitted to the Air Force, which changed the engine to the Allison YJ71. On 25 September, the Air Force awarded Republic a letter contract for $13 million for production of 199 F-105A fighter-bombers (WS-306A).[1,2] The

The number-two Republic YF-105A looking pristine on the tarmac at Edwards AFB. The prototype was equipped with the original F-84-type inlets and smooth exhaust nozzle. (AFFTC History Office via Mike Machat)

Republic Aviation technicians pose in front of a hangar at Edwards AFB with the number-two YF-105A prototype. (Mike Machat Collection)

aircraft would reach Initial Operational Capability (IOC) in 1955. This contract fell under a modified version of the Cook-Craigie[3] concept of concurrency that did not require a YF or XF designation for the F-105. Oddly enough, initial F-105s carried Y designations for both prototype and preproduction development aircraft, while the NAA F-107A did not. Suddenly on 20 March 1953, the production was cut back to 37 aircraft; delivery would be three aircraft per month beginning in April 1955. In an amendment signed on 25 September 1953, nine RF-105[4] reconnaissance variants were added to the 37 F-105s.[5]

Due to technical problems with the YJ71 at Allison, Pratt & Whitney's YJ57 engine would be substituted as the powerplant. Without any further delays the full-scale mockup was completed and inspected by the customer. Noting approximately 152 minor changes, the program proceeded with the goal of an early 1955 IOC. Continuing the trail of instability, in December 1953 the F-105 contract was suspended. Reasons cited were program delays, increased aircraft weight, and non-delivery of the required YJ75 engine. Many of these delays and weight increases were due to customer requirements added to the aircraft. The F-105 started out as a basic fighter-bomber but was becoming increasingly complex. Thus, in the history of DoD procurement, the F-105 became an early example of requirements creep.[6]

Back on Track, Almost

The Air Force had been working with Pratt & Whitney to explore availability of the new YJ75 engine rated at 16,000 pounds of thrust. Pratt & Whitney assured the program office that this engine could be adapted to the F-105 airframe. As a result of that background effort, during 1954 the F-105 program was reinstated with $49.9 million allocated from FY54 funding. Fourteen YF-105As and a single YRF-105A would be funded, but all would be powered with the less-powerful YJ57 in order to get the aircraft into flight status more quickly.[7]

Continuing this seesaw of tendencies, on 2 September 1954 the Air Force cut the program again, this time to three aircraft with the

The improved YF-105B during assembly at Republic's Farmingdale, New York, facility. To boost high-speed performance, the modified forward-swept inlets were added to the B model. (Republic Aviation)

YJ57. An Air Force review stated, "There was a general lack of confidence in this contractor in fulfilling his commitments and meeting the performance guarantees on the F-105 weapon system." On 9 September, a stop-work order only authorized construction of two YF-105As powered by the YJ57, and one YF-105B powered by the new YJ75 engine. Three additional B models were added later. In early 1955, the numbers were juggled again, increasing the number of YJ75-powered F-105Bs to ten. Once again, the reconnaissance variant YRF-105B entered the picture with three aircraft authorized.[8]

Upon completion at Republic's Farmingdale, New York, facility, the first YF-105A (t/n 54-0098) was disassembled and airlifted in two C-124 Globemaster IIs to Edwards AFB on 28 to 29 September 1955. After reassembly the YF-105A was readied for its first flight. During this process everyone could sense the urgency to get the airplane

This low-angle view of the number-three YF-105B accentuates the sleek form of the fighter-bomber. (Republic Aviation)

into the air. On 22 October 1955, Republic Chief Test Pilot Russell "Rusty" Roth climbed into the cockpit and taxied out to Runway 04. The first flight resulted in zero anomalies, and Republic reported that the YF-105A had passed Mach 1. First flight was successful, but due to the limited powerplant and obsolete intakes, some within the industry were skeptical of the test margins.

Prototype Down

The number-one YF-105A was accepted by the Air Force after 12 flights. Unfortunately, on 16 December 1955 this aircraft experienced a problem. While flying 609.9 mph and conducting a 5.5-G turn, the right main landing gear extended and was torn off the aircraft. The aircraft made a belly landing on Rogers Dry Lake, suffering extensive damage, although, thankfully, Russell Roth was not injured. Aircraft number one had flown 22 test hours, but never returned to flight status, serving as a forward fuselage mockup for the still-born F-105C.

After C-124 cargo aircraft transported YF-105A prototype number two (t/n 54-0099) to Edwards, it was reassembled and made its first flight on 9 December 1955 with Roth again in the cockpit. He had tested the newly designed exhaust cone that also served as an adjustable four-pedal speed brake fitted to the first YF-105A, but number two had a smooth fixed-exhaust aperture.

By early 1956, the YF-105B was ready and featured forward-swept elliptical inlets with internal control ramps. Republic officials were excited as it was felt the B model would deliver the performance they were looking for. The first YF-105B (t/n 54-0100) took off from Edwards on 26 May 1956 flown by Republic test pilot Henry "Hank" Beaird Jr., who remained aloft for 64 minutes. A problem arose as Beaird began his landing approach—the nose gear would not extend, forcing yet another belly-landing on Rogers Dry Lake.[9] There was no serious damage until a crane operator dropped the aircraft while lifting it from the salt flat, causing the aircraft to remain out of service for several weeks.

Continuing Republic's tradition of prefacing their aircraft names with *Thunder*[10], company officials submitted *Thunderchief* for the F-105, and on 25 July 1956 the name was approved by the Air Force. Flight testing was accelerating, and the number-two YF-105B[11] (t/n 54-0101) flew at Edwards on 28 December 1956. The first YF-105B to fly from the factory runway at Farmingdale was number three (54-0102) on 29 April 1957.

Category II Testing

Flight testing under Category II occurred between 8 January and 7 March 1957. In this relatively short cycle, 18 flights were conducted totaling 13 hours and 45 minutes. The Air Force concluding report stated, "The YF-105B has the potential of becoming an excellent fighter-bomber. But it needed a large number of improvements before it could be considered acceptable for operational use." Additionally, the report disclosed, "The YF-105B is capable of Mach 1.95 in level flight at 35,000 feet, and 1.49 at 20,000 feet under standard temperature conditions." Details from the report indicated that flying above Mach 1.8 was not suitable because of poor acceleration qualities. The acceleration characteristics concern was backed up by a test in which the YF-105B took nearly nine minutes to accelerate from Mach 1 to Mach 1.95 at 35,000 feet.[12] After nine minutes in afterburner, however, fuel was nearly depleted. A sustained combat ceiling was established at 46,500 feet. Other areas of concern were the YF-105's range at 35,000 feet, which was 20 percent less than predicted by Republic, and problems with both the longitudinal and lateral control systems. A total of 50 recommended fixes were documented at the end of Category II testing.

A detailed view of the F-105 inflight refueling probe that utilized the hose-and-drogue system. Note the gun-bay gas purge vent just below the probe. Later D models were also equipped with a refueling receptacle in the nose to accept the USAF-type refueling boom. (National Museum of the USAF)

Number-three YF-105B (t/n 40102) begins refueling from the number-two YF-105A (t/n 40099) prototype that was equipped with a buddy-store refueling system under its starboard wing. Note the YF-105A has the early F-84-style intakes marked with International Orange paint and the original smooth single-piece exhaust nozzle. The YF-105B nozzle has been modified with the variable four-pedal speed brake. (USAF via Mike Machat)

The NAA F-107A: A Rocky Start

To put it simply, the emergence of the NAA F-107A configuration was analogous to the birth of a water buffalo—lengthy and arduous, but it felt great when the process ended. Prior to arriving at the final radical F-107A configuration, several iterations took place. The prelude to finding the correct path to a new fighter design consisted of a combination of budget restrictions and the vying of one

bureau of the Air Force against the other. The budget portion was best described by NAA's equipment supervisor for the F-100B Interceptor Project Group, Dave Wisted: "The F-107A was not derived from the F-100. The only reason for the F-100 designation was that the Air Force was having a much easier time finding money for modifications to fleet aircraft, rather than a new program."[13] Basically, applying the F-107A designation too early in the process would have killed it outright.

As proposed by NAA in August 1953, the F-100B was an improved F-100A in the interceptor role. In a two-pronged effort, NAA also added some features that could give the aircraft a fighter-bomber capability. The NAA proposal looked good to ARDC. On 2 October 1953, a recommendation was forwarded to Air Force leaders to proceed, with the provision that it be designated a fighter-bomber. The proposed aircraft had a 7.67-G limit. Later that month, Wright Air Development Center (WADC) conveyed their disapproval and declared that the complex design was moving forward too quickly. Although expressing confidence in the improvements over the current F-100A, the final opinion issued deferred a full production rate and focused on negating potential problems.

A critical configuration conference, which would have major implications for the program, was held at Wright Field on 24 June 1954. One conclusion was that the recommended load factor for the airframe should be 8.67 Gs, which diverged from the original F-100B requirements.[14] This would eventually lead to a fresh aircraft configuration, but would not solve the inter-agency quarreling. Meanwhile, in early August 1954 the Air Force conducted an engineering inspection that resulted in 135 recommended minor design changes. A full-scale mockup review took place in September and approximately 105 minor comments were noted. Air Force

A hypothetical view of a camouflaged operational USAF/NAA F-107D carrying an AGM-12B Bullpup and a F-107A prototype painted in original red accent markings. Had NAA won the competition, the Air Force may have ordered additional A models for pilot training. This F-107A is aircraft number five (t/n 55122). (Author Photo/Illustration)

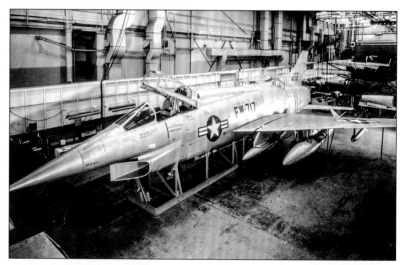

At NAA's Inglewood facility, the F-100B full-scale mockup displays its original lower lip–style intake. Several original F-100A Super Sabre traits are evident, including the rather short vertical stabilizer. (Boeing Archives)

Headquarters approval took place in December. Brig. Gen. Harold Estes Jr., the director of weapon systems operations at WADC, forwarded his recommendations to ARDC on the F-100B program. Very much aware of previous efforts to defer full production of the F-100B, Gen. Estes thought that other circumstances had entered the picture that called for accelerating the program:

- The concurrent F-100D fighter-bomber variant being developed would not meet all the mission requirements.
- The experiences obtained in the F-100A/C/D programs would prove beneficial to the F-107A program.
- A delayed schedule would place the F-100B (F-107A) in the inventory at the same time period as the more advanced F-105.[15]

A Tug of War Timetable

It was still uphill for NAA as a familiar bureaucratic segment of the customer. Despite Gen. Estes's suggestion, the WADC still rejected an accelerated program. In fact, WADC recommended canceling the F-107A and moving ahead with a new Fighter-Bomber, Experimental (FBX). Additionally, the concurrent Republic YF-105 would be tagged as high priority. Part two of the WADC recommendation was to reconfigure the F-107A to utilize the YJ75 or YJ76 engine. The F-107A could then serve as a backup for the F-105. Fortunately for NAA the FBX program was canceled six months later, and the F-107A remained alive while hoping for the uprated YJ67 engine to become available.

To NAA's consternation, on 25 August 1954, Air Force Headquarters constrained any further funding, and there was a six-month period in which no funding was available. The prior $6 million released in June had been intended to flow until October, but had been nearly expended, thus NAA remained cautious in ordering lead items. Fortunately, an additional $1.5 million was released in December of that year. The continuous hedging and indecisiveness did not make designing a new aircraft easy for NAA. It was also implied that NAA was to use some of its own funding if it wanted to develop the F-107A. The strategy was to proceed to keep the program on schedule and hope for later reimbursement.

In December 1954, Maj. Gen. Floyd Wood, Deputy Commander, Technical Operations, ARDC, put forward a 28-month development schedule requiring:

- A 1- to 2-month period from the completion of the first article to first flight
- A minimum 10 months of flight testing to gather sufficient data
- 18 months from the date of production release to a production go-ahead and subsequent rate determination

The variable-area inlet duct (VAID) is clearly visible on top of the intake of F-107A number two (t/n 55119). (Bill Simone Collection)

F-107A number one (t/n 55118) taking shape at NAA's Inglewood Facility. (Boeing Archives)

The NAA F-107A was impressive and it appeared ahead of its time. The aerodynamic shape of the variable inlet is clearly visible, and the leading-edge slats are fully deployed. (AFFTC History Office)

At this time, it became evident that the Pratt & Whitney YJ57-P-35 would not be available to meet the test-flight schedule, and the YJ57-P-11 would have to be installed in the first 14 aircraft. This engine was rated at approximately 15,500 pounds of thrust in military power and 23,500 pounds in full afterburner.[16] On 1 February 1955, a final plan for the program was laid out by Gen. Thomas Power, Commander, ARDC, and sent on to Air Force Headquarters. Essentially, he agreed with the go-slow approach to ensure an organized and systematic development. In a positive move, General Power stated that the F-107A met the General Operational Requirements (GOR) that placed the aircraft on a timetable to be a companion weapon system with the F-105. In conclusion, he recommended the Pentagon approve the development plan that called for IOC in February 1959 and combat readiness by the following July.

In a letter, agreed to by NAA on 20 April 1955, the Air Force "officially and openly" changed the designation from F-100B to F-107A. As previously mentioned, the F-107A never received a Y (prototype) or X (experimental) designation. The resulting openness of the F-107A designation was a psychological boost to NAA. This was thankfully followed by the release of $9 million for development, engineering design, and production planning. Another fact is that the F-107A is often referred to as the Super Sabre or Ultra Sabre. However, research and the author's personal interviews with former NAA employees confirmed that the F-107A was never given an official name.

Shaping the F-107A

As originally envisioned, the F-100B follow-on to the F-100 was designed as an interceptor, and fighter-bomber requirements were not involved. During the early 1950s, special weapons stores, or nuclear weapons, had not yet reached a sophisticated, miniaturized state of development. Because of their large size the centerline area of the fuselage was designated as essential to carry the special weapons. Fundamentally, the F-100B configuration would be suitable as an interceptor. However, even though NAA had added fighter-bomber aspects to their design, General Wood was not satisfied. He had informed AMC, where TAC was headquartered, that the F-100B (F-107)[17] with its original configuration of a lower air-inlet duct and asymmetrical stores, was completely unacceptable.[18] Gen. Wood felt that moving toward a centerline store[19] was the best course to pursue.

F-107A Emerges from its Cocoon

As Air Force contract negotiations were taking place, NAA engineers were already at work improving the F-107A configuration. They had arrived at a promising solution in February 1955. The new configuration featured a recessed midfuselage centerline area that held a semirecessed weapon store. As opposed to an internal bay, this design was far less complex, increased internal area, and helped reduce drag. To facilitate this weapons location, the lower-lip F-100B-style inlet duct was moved to the upper fuselage, just aft of the cockpit. The F-107A was equipped with a variable-area inlet duct (VAID) system. The complex inlet featured a bifurcated fixed vertical wedge, followed by stepped first and second movable ramp panels. Above the intake structure were exits for ramp boundary-layer-control bleed air. In addition to easing the transition to high-Mach flight, an added benefit of the ducts on top of the aircraft was the lessened potential for FOD ingestion on the ground.

The dynamics of the variable inlet[20] were sophisticated, leading to the technical expertise at which NAA was beginning to excel. Dave Wisted once quipped, "What was remarkable was the fact that the F-107A was not designed by the advanced design group, but on the floor by engineers not located in a secure area." This is noteworthy, because the F-107A represented many innovative features. Wisted[21] also remarked that he appreciated the valuable input he received from engineers in the area.[22]

F-107A number one (t/n 55118) on its takeoff roll. The first flight was completed at Edwards AFB on 10 September 1956 with NAA Chief Test Pilot Robert Baker in the cockpit. (AFFTC History Office)

A close-up of the F-107A retractable in-flight refueling probe. Had the F-107 gone into production, later models would have been equipped with a boom receptacle. (William Simone Collection)

F-107A rolls out after landing at Edwards AFB. On the second flight of aircraft number one, the drag chute deployed correctly. (USAF via William Simone)

An excellent view of the sleek aerodynamic shape of F-107A number one on a test flight. At this point in the flight, the leading-edge slats are slightly deployed and the flaps slightly lowered. (USAF)

As offensive armament, the F-107A would carry the T-171 cannon, later designated the M61 Vulcan 20mm rotary cannon.[23] At the time, the Air Force was uncertain which engine would meet the schedule. NAA allowed for three different engines to be accommodated by the airframe: the Pratt & Whitney YJ57, YJ67, or YJ75. Continuing the frustrating numbers game, on 17 March 1955, ARDC issued an order to AMC to reduce the number of development F-107As from 33 to 13. This detrimental DoD practice of reducing procurement numbers, resulting in increased unit prices, continues to this day. Emanating from the other end of the customer spectrum, TAC supported NAA by declaring that the F-107A configuration offered superior performance potential.

Deputy TAC commander Maj. Gen. Earl Barnes recommended that the F-107A's primary mission would be for nuclear weapons delivery. A secondary capability would be for conventional bomb payloads, along with rockets/cannon to be used against ground targets. If available, the NAA Autonetics–developed advanced XMA-12[24] fire-control system would be installed. The operational MA-8 fire-control system would be a backup. Initially, the powerplant lineup for the F-107As was as follows: two aircraft with the YJ75 engine, five aircraft with the YJ67, and two RF-107A reconnaissance variants with the YJ67. The sudden addition of a reconnaissance variant was certainly a real plus in the eyes of NAA. In mid-June 1955, Maj. Gen. Herbert Thatcher, assistant deputy chief of staff for development at Air Force Headquarters, issued his concluding remarks: "The F-107A program will be considered as a backup program for the F-105. It is desired that the F-107 development lag the F-105 as little as possible. Until further directed, these two developmental programs will be conducted with equal priority."[25]

A rare shot of the number-two F-107A (t/n 55119) with auxiliary drop tanks. (USAF)

Into the Light

Considering the continuous schedule, design, and budget pressures, morphing the original F-100B design to the final F-107A configuration was quite an accomplishment. NAA engineers' talents had culminated with a radically new design that was a pleasure to behold. At first glance, the F-107A was certainly impressive, beginning at its needle nose and sweeping back to the distinctive overhead advanced inlet. The aircraft looked fast even on the ground, an impression soon borne out in actual flight testing. The 45-degree swept wings featured automated leading-edge slats and unique spoiler-slot deflectors located on the upper surfaces. This ensured maximum roll-rate throughout the entire flight envelope.

F-107A Designated Flight-Test Assignments

- Serial number 55-5118: stability, control, and performance two-stage VAID system
- Serial number 55-5119: performance, integrated control system, weapons separation, two-stage VAID system, XMA-12 fire-control system (installed when available), M-39 gunnery testing (ground-air)
- Serial number 55-1120: fully automated VAID system, XMA-12 fire-control system (installed when available)

The empennage featured all-moving horizontal stabilizers and a 45-degree swept vertical stabilizer. The large vertical tail would ensure full rudder authority, avoiding problems associated with early-model F-100 Super Sabres. The F-107A ejection seat was based on the F-100 seat design. Pilot ejection would be upward, with the seat riding on extending guide rails to clear the inlet. The ejection system was thoroughly tested up to 1,075.2 mph (947.34 knots) using a full-scale cockpit/nose section mounted on a rocket sled at the Edwards AFB high-speed track. Successful testing determined the overhead intake would not present any problems whatsoever for emergency escape.[26]

Take It to the Limit

F-107A number one (t/n 55-5118) was trucked from NAA's Inglewood, California, facility to Edwards AFB on 16 August 1956. After taxi tests and high-speed ground runs, the F-107A was ready to fly. With NAA test pilot Robert Baker Jr. in the cockpit, the F-107A headed east and lifted off Edwards Runway 04 on 10 September 1956. Phase I testing had begun. The F-107A was accompanied by a two-seat YTF-100C Super Sabre flown by J. O. Roberts, and in the backseat was Air Force project pilot Capt. James Carson. Roberts would later become NAA's chief F-107A pilot. Anomalies may occur in any first flight, and this flight was no exception. After climbing to 5,000 feet the landing gear was retracted, but a landing-gear-door warning light illuminated. Baker climbed to 10,000 feet and reduced airspeed to 287.7 mph (250 knots). Another recycling of the gear was successful—no warning lights. At 35,000 feet altitude and Mach .91, an oil-sump master warning light illuminated. Baker dropped the nose slightly, and the aircraft easily passed Mach 1.[27] Thrust was set to idle, and Baker prepared to land immediately, per recommendation of Pratt & Whitney's procedure. Most significant, however, the

The number-two F-107A presents a clear view of the semirecessed aerodynamically shaped centerline 500-gallon fuel tank. The original requirement was to carry a 1,680-pound Mk. 7 tactical nuclear weapon. Different tanks could carry a combination of special stores, cameras, or fuel. Modified to a reduced 250-gallon tank, the Sandia Shape could carry 27 sensors. (USAF)

The rate of climb of the F-107A was impressive. In afterburner the F-107A was able to reach 30,000 feet from sea level in 1.4 minutes. This is approximately 30,000 feet per minute, but at 45,000 feet altitude this rate dropped to 2,200 feet per minute. During zoom climb testing the number-two F-107A with Al White on board reached 69,780 feet. (USAF)

F-107A had achieved Mach 1 on its first flight. Upon lowering the flaps for landing, Baker encountered roll control problems. Remarkably, although unable to extend full flaps, he was able to slow the approach speed in an attempt to save the tires. Unfortunately, the drag chute failed to deploy and the F-107A overran the end of the 15,000-foot runway, safely rolling onto the dry lakebed. All seemed okay until the nose gear encountered an unmarked shallow wash and snapped off. However, the aircraft was quickly repaired.

Program Reductions Continue

NAA had just reported that the development of the prototype Autonetics XMA-12 fire-control system was nearly completed. Then, out of nowhere in August 1956, Air Force Headquarters further curtailed the program. It reduced the number of F-107A aircraft to be acquired to three. Additionally, it recommended to continue testing the XMA-12 in an F-86K; the system was never installed in the F-107A. The versatile XMA-12 could compute control of several air-to-ground and air-to-air modes. This included radar ranging for bombing, gunnery, and rockets.

"Go!" for Mach 2

With J. O. Roberts at the controls of aircraft number one, Mach 2+ was reached on 3 November 1956. This achievement capped off a primary goal of Phase I, demonstrating the competence of the design. Upon landing, it was found that the red paint on the nose had blistered from the generated heat, even though the paint had been pretested for the high-Mach environment.[28] USAF project pilot Capt. James Carson, who had flown in the first flight YTF-100C chase plane, took the F-107A to Mach 1.4 and Mach 2+ a few days later. The aircraft was now considered flightworthy enough that Gen. Albert Boyd, commander, AFFTC, and his director, Col. Horace Hanes, both

The third F-107A (t/n 55120) lifts off at Edwards AFB. This aircraft was the most advanced and was equipped with a fully automated VAID system. Aircraft number three conducted a total of 118 test flights. A black-and-white version of this photo graced the cover of Aviation Week magazine on 9 December 1957. (USAF)

The number-two F-107A with its canopy in the ingress/egress position. Visibility from the cockpit was excellent, however the intake position did prevent aft viewing if the angles were less than 50-degrees. According to Air Force evaluators, this would have to be corrected should the F-107 ever go into production. (Boeing Archives)

A rare view of all three NAA F-107As on the tarmac at Edwards AFB. (USAF)

F-107A (t/n 55120) was loaned to NACA (which became NASA in 1958) in late 1957, where it was equipped with a side-stick controller on the pilot's right. The standard F-107 control stick remained, and a switch could activate either system. This side stick was used to test the X-15-type control stick. NACA also evaluated the F-107A's all-moving vertical tail, VAID inlet system, and spoilers for lateral control. (NASA)

The F-107A in a steep bank reveals the aerodynamic 500-gallon auxiliary fuel tank in the semirecessed centerline area. The competing F-105 internal bomb bay, which played a key role in helping the F-105 during the competition, was never used to carry bombs. (USAF)

flew sorties during November 1956. Interestingly, Air Force F-105 project pilot Maj. Stuart Childs flew two sorties in the F-107A. Childs commented favorably that the new airplane "felt solid in 2-G turns at 1.6 Mach number at 35,000 feet. Stick force per G is good, [it] can hold G easier in a turn than with the F-100."[29] Although several aircraft anomalies occurred throughout the flight tests, it quickly became apparent that the basic design was sound and could easily be brought to operational status. Phase I flight-testing achieved 35 flights accumulating 21 hours on aircraft 55-5118.

The Phase II Flight Evaluation Program took place from 3 December 1956 to 15 February 1957. Capt. James Carson was the primary pilot. As in Phase I, several anomalies occurred throughout the flight tests, although it quickly became apparent that the climb rate was most impressive. The F-107A was able to achieve Mach 1 in a vertical climb, with an impressive rate of climb of 1.4 minutes to reach 30,000 feet. After passing 40,000 feet there was a drop-off in the rate of climb to approximately 2,200 feet per minute. During zoom climb testing, F-107A number two, piloted by Al White, reached 69,780 feet, although the YJ75 suffered compressor stalls. This was comparable to other Century Series jets at the time and was attributed to the limits of the YJ75-P-11 engine. Additional successful speed runs were performed at 45,000 feet at Mach 1.95[30] and above. Sorties also included testing the aerodynamics of the 500-gallon semirecessed fuel tank.[31] Also on the positive side, the flight-control problem associated with the flaps was solved and landing speeds became manageable both with and without the drag chute.

Test pilot Al White[32] was selected for the weapons-drop testing series. During these tests, F-107A (t/n 55119) successfully completed seven separation drops: five with the TX-28 nuclear shape and two with the Sandia-developed nuclear weapons shape. Weapons separation was ensured with 10,000 pounds of ejection force. Additionally, speeds were impressive, ranging from Mach 1+ up to Mach 2. These high-speed weapons-separation tests were a first for any aircraft. In fact, SAC's new B-58 bomber would not accomplish high-Mach weapons separation until 10 February 1961, some three years later. Even at that time, the B-58 required extra testing before it was cleared to drop its centerline weapon pod at Mach 2. Phase II accumulated just more than 19 hours during 32 flights.

Program Conclusions

Although the decision had been made two months earlier, negative news arrived at NAA on 22 March 1957 in the form of an official F-107A termination. Terms included the continued testing of the first two aircraft until the funding expired. However, on 29 April, a limited 47-hour test program to expand the VAID system was approved, with the goal of testing the system to its full capability. J. O. Roberts was project pilot for this phase, which commenced on 7 June 1957. Aircraft number three (t/n 55120) was employed with a step-input variable-area inlet duct. Additionally, instrumentation was installed in the centerline tank. The second and third prototypes (t/n 55118-55120)[33] were both loaned to NACA (which became NASA on 1 October 1958). In total, all three F-107A prototypes flew a combined 272 times and accrued 176.3 hours of flight time.[34] There would be no production of NAA's F-107A. Witnessing a design with such potential never flying again and being placed in storage was extremely disappointing to those who designed, built, and flew the unique F-107A.

A sad ending: Exposed to the elements, the number-one and number-two F-107A aircraft in outdoor storage at Edwards South Base, circa 1960–1961. Both aircraft had participated in Phase II flight evaluation between 28 November 1956 and 18 February 1957. During this time the third aircraft (t/n 55120) was stored at Norton AFB, California. (AFFTC History Office)

For the 1964 air show season, the USAF Thunderbirds Aerial Demonstration Team transitioned from the North American F-100C Super Sabre to the Republic F-105B. Had the North American F-107 gone into service, the Thunderbirds would have transitioned to the F-107B and NAA company field support would have continued. (Author Photo/Illustration)

Competition Analysis

By piecing together the web of the existing bureaucracy at the time, it is possible to examine the selection of the F-105 over the F-107A. As previously mentioned, internal bureaucratic tensions were evidence that the Air Force was still forming itself into a fighting force. With the overwhelming threat of nuclear war and the buildup of U.S. deterrence, certainly SAC had the budget advantage. In a strategy similar to what the U.S. Navy employed to promote and establish their own nuclear role, TAC needed an aircraft that could perform that mission. The solution was a bomb bay. TAC and ARDC had formulated the F-105 concept around the ability to carry nuclear weapons. On the other hand, the F-107A concept was encouraged by AMC believing that NAA could produce an advanced tactical fighter. Hence, the seeds of a harmful competition between Air Force bureaus were planted. On 24 October 1956, Under Secretary of the Air Force,[35] James H. Douglas Jr., conducted a fact-finding mission to Edwards AFB. He did not seem to be interested or informed about the F-107A.[36] Other influences included the fact that Republic was in desperate need of acquiring a new aircraft contract to keep its capabilities intact while NAA was currently producing the F-86 Sabre

With the F-107 in production, it would have been feasible that a reconnaissance variant would have been produced to compete against the McDonnell RF-101C Voodoo. In a three-ship formation, a conceptual camouflage RF-107C variant flies with two early model F-107Bs, each carrying a centerline tank and wing drop tanks. RF-107C underside reveals an attached reconnaissance pod containing several types of cameras. North American Rockwell would later develop a larger pod known as "the canoe" for U.S. Navy RA-5C Vigilante carrier-based recce aircraft. (Author Photo/Illustration)

A "what might have been" variation of a well-known photo from the Vietnam War. The black-and-white version depicts a Douglas EB-66B Destroyer pathfinder leading a flight of four F-105Ds on a radar-bombing mission during 1966. (DOD) A hypothetical view at left depicts an EB-66B leading a flight of four F-107Ds as they each release two M117 bombs over North Vietnam. EB-66B provided advanced bomb/navigation system for bomb release cueing, improved accuracy, and ECM protection. (Author Photo/Illustration)

A conceptual operational F-107D carrying 500-pound general-purpose bombs in echelon with an updated Douglas EB-66E pathfinder. Designated for Electronic CounterMeasure (ECM) missions, 34 RB-66 Destroyers were converted to this configuration. (Author Photo/Illustration)

On a low-level reconnaissance mission and just prior to jettisoning its drop tanks, a conceptual USAF RF-107C goes into afterburner. The RF-107C was equipped with cameras only, and its four M-39E 20mm cannons were removed. (Author Photo/Illustration)

Jet and F-100 Super Sabre. NAA officials did have an ace in the hole: They were initiating a design for a much-needed Mach 3+ interceptor, the F-108 Rapier.[37]

Shortchanged

An excerpt from the Operational Programming Document, Headquarters AFFTC, dated 1 January 1957, indicates the forthcoming misfortunes of the F-107A. At that time the Phase II Flight Evaluation was not complete, and the number of F-107As to be built had been reduced to only three. Surprisingly, the AFFTC informed all Center entities that after Phase II there would not be any continuation of flight testing. Phase VI and V had been canceled even before Phase II had been completed. Essentially, the Air Force had selected the F-105 for production and the F-107A would only undergo limited testing.

During Phase II Flight Evaluation, the F-107A had accumulated only 9 hours and 5 minutes of flight time. What is unusual is that Phase II evaluation of the improved YF-105B had not yet commenced at this point. That occurred on 8 January 1957, seven days after the 1 January unofficial termination of the F-107A (the official termination letter was dated 22 March 1957). Interestingly, additional flight testing of the F-107A was approved by the Air Force the following

Performing the SEAD (Suppression of Enemy Air Defenses) mission, a speculative two-seat USAF F-107G Wild Weasel, armed with an AGM-45A Shrike antiradiation missile, speeds through the danger zone over North Vietnam. The Soviet-built SA-2 Guideline SAM was a two-stage missile, with the solid-fuel first stage burning for six seconds and the liquid-fuel second stage guiding to the target. The SA-2 had a top speed of Mach 3.5 and a maximum range of 27 miles up to 60,000 feet altitude. SA-2 SAM sites were a constant threat to U.S. aircraft. (Author Photo/Illustration)

Many decades after the Republic YF-105A selection decision, aviation author Robert F. Dorr recalled a telephone interview with former Republic F-105 test pilot Henry "Hank" Crescibene. Crescibene remembered being told to prepare for the F-107A. "Our perception was that the Air Force liked North American, and liked North American's design better than ours."[39] Furthermore, while examining the history of the NAA F-107A, author and historian William J. Simone also uncovered an interesting account that had been published in *Flight Testing at Edwards, Flight Test Engineers Stories 1946–1975.* Flight-test engineer Jack Wesesky commented on an event that took place several weeks after the YF-105A selection. "As we were reviewing the F-105 phase II report, the Project Engineer came into my office and dropped a large package on my desk. It was still wrapped and sealed from the printing office. The bundle contained the Republic's report on our tests (USAF Phase II testing). I noticed numerous discrepancies, redlining each to show Mr. Bikle (AAFTC Technical Director). Two of the most glaring that I recall were that only half of the takeoff performance data were presented. Data scatter was eliminated by only presenting the most favorable points. A maximum speed data point of a 2.07 Mach number was shown from Republic (Phase I Testing); however, the maximum we found was about 1.85 Mach. The Republic data point was made on an unusually cold day, after a diving descent into the jet stream, hardly a stabilized standard test condition. I was instructed to destroy the package," said Wesesky.[40]

April. The extremely short Phase II Flight Evaluation of the YF-105B consisted of nine flights (6 hours, 50 minutes) which ended on 7 March 1957.[38] In addition to the comment that there were major problems, during this period there were two major accidents that destroyed two aircraft. In the end, the Air Force was betting on the F-105 greatly improving with time.

The Thunderchief Enters Service

Production go-ahead was given, although the 50 recommended improvements and fixes had not been remedied at the time. During 1955, the initial nine F-105Bs were on the assembly line at Farmingdale, New York. The production B model was two feet longer than the YF-105B, and the vertical stabilizer was increased in height by two feet, two inches. This would increase rudder authority for the expected increase in speed.[41] Also on the assembly line were the three RF-105B[42] reconnaissance variants. With Republic still awaiting delivery of the more powerful 24,500-pound-thrust J75-P-19, the first batch of F-105Bs would be powered by the lower 23,000-pound-thrust YJ75-P-9 engine.

Production of the F-105B was delayed by several months as the intakes were modified to a forward sweep, and the fuselage was modified into an area-rule shape. The internal mechanism for the F-105B inlet was originally developed by Dr. Antonio Ferri, who at the time

A spectacular lookdown view of an F-105D with its unique three-tone tan and reddish brown "Desert Fox" camouflage from the 466th TFS at Hill AFB, Utah. (Author Photo/ Illustration)

F-105B Thunderchiefs lined up on the tarmac. The B model became operational in the USAF in 1958. (National Museum of the USAF)

Historic Significance

Fortunately for aeronautical history, the NAA F-107A has received a somewhat kinder fate than other aircraft. Escaping the previous poor judgment exhibited at the conclusion of several past fighter/bomber competitions, none of the three prototypes were used as gunnery targets, and they were instead temporarily stored. Unfortunately, someone authorized the transfer of the most-advanced number-three F-107A (t/n 55120) to Oxnard AFB, California—for use as a firefighting training aid. This decision resulted in the complete destruction of the airframe. When you think of the numerous retired airframes of all aircraft types available at the time, it's inexplicable why the rare F-107A was chosen for this fate. Thankfully, the two remaining F-107A prototypes were eventually restored. They are now on permanent display for future generations to learn from. Aircraft number one is on display at the Pima Air and Space Museum, and the number-two prototype is located at the National Museum of the USAF. Author and historian William Simone was personally responsible for saving aircraft number one (t/n 55118).

With the hose-and-drogue system, a Boeing KB-50D aerial tanker simultaneously refuels a (clockwise) Republic F-105D, NAA F-100F, and McDonnell RF-101C. Both the F-105 and RF-101C were later modified to also accept the USAF-style refueling boom. The Thud retained a dual capability. (USAF)

The first F-105B assigned to the USAF Thunderbirds Aerial Demonstration Team was t/n 75782. The aircraft was modified at Republic and delivered to Nellis AFB on 25 January 1964 to prepare for the air show season. (USAF)

The Thunderbirds' Thunderchiefs go vertical: The Republic F-105B began its brief career with the Thunderbirds in the 1964 season. Aesthetically, the futuristic shape of the F-105B was a dramatic shift from the NAA F-100C Super Sabre. Basic modifications to the aircraft included the fuel system for inverted flight and added ballast to improve maneuverability. In addition, the F-105Bs were equipped with dual smoke probes providing a choice of red, blue, or mixing the colors. Not as agile as the previous F-100C, the F-105B was noted for its wide turns during air show routines. Unfortunately, after only six performances an accident occurred, and during an operations shutdown the team was ordered to switch to the updated F-100D. (Author Photo/Illustration)

This camouflaged F-105B (t/n 823) at Hill AFB during August 1980 was from the last batch of B models. (Warren Munkasy)

The first F-105D (t/n 81146) Thunderchief at Republic's Farmingdale facility. (National Museum of the USAF)

headed the Brooklyn Polytechnic Institute's Department of Aeronautical Engineering and Applied Mechanics. Ferri's previous work at NACA's Langley Aeronautical Laboratory had developed an inlet with the advantage of combining the efficiency of an internal compression shock system with the more reliable handling qualities of an external type.[43] Republic had considered this inlet design for its Mach 3–capable dual-cycle XF-103, which only reached the mockup stage and was canceled on 21 August 1957.

The F-105B inlets utilized moving plugs inside the lip. The engine airflow is cut back to make it easier for excess air, which builds up behind the shockwave as it moves into the inlet, to spill over the top and bottom of the inlet. The movable plugs hold the normal shock wave, once it is inside, at its most efficient position. A Republic engineer related that the oblique shock produced achieves only 5 percent of the compression work of the inlet system,[44] while the normal shock does the rest.[45] The F-105's unique forward-swept elliptical inlets provided maximum recovery at supersonic speeds and reduced whetted-area turbulence flowing over the tail. To ensure afterburner cooling, a single thin air duct was located at the base of the vertical stabilizer.

On 26 May 1958, the first F-105B (t/n 54-0111) was delivered to the 335th Tactical Fighter Squadron (TFS). Although based at Seymour-Johnson AFB, North Carolina, at the time the squadron was deployed to Eglin AFB for weapons testing. Republic built a total of 75 F-105Bs prior to initial deliveries of the all-weather-capable F-105D. The uprated D model "Thud" soon followed, deploying to the 335th TFS on 28 September 1960. During May 1961, F-105Ds began to arrive at Bitburg AB in West Germany to bolster USAFE forces. With their all-weather capability, they gradually replaced the F-100 Super Sabres based there and fit well in the European environment.

F-105D pilots had recently undergone extensive tactical training at Nellis AFB, Nevada.[46] The F-105D was equipped with the AN/ASQ-19 Thunderstick bombing and navigation system for both air-to-ground and air-to-air engagements. The D was also equipped with the North American R-14A Autonetics search and ranging radar

An early F-105D-10-RE (t/n 00459) on the flight line; the D model was powered by the J75-P-19W delivering 26,500 pounds of thrust. (National Museum of the USAF)

(NASARR); both systems were developed by NAA's Autonetics Division. With the J75-P-19W installed, the 26,500 pounds of thrust provided 2,000 pounds of additional thrust over the B model. The D was the most widely produced F-105 variant[47], of which 610 were delivered. Fifty-five two-seat F-105G Wild Weasels were originally F models modified as a more advanced SAM killer. Republic produced a total of 833 Thunderchiefs in all variants.

The Thud in Combat

Under orders from President Lyndon Johnson, the F-105D Thunderchief found itself in Southeast Asia shortly after two incidents in the Gulf of Tokin on 2 to 4 August 1964. America was officially entering combat in Southeast Asia. Affectionately known as the "Thud" or "Lead Sled," the F-105D flew 20,000 tactical sorties during the Vietnam War, carrying 75 percent of all ordnance delivered in North Vietnam. These missions, flown under tight targeting restrictions, were quite different than what the Thud was designed for originally: flying supersonically and carrying nuclear weapons to

F-105D (s/n 59-1719) peels off, again displaying its underside aerodynamic shape. (National Museum of the USAF)

An F-105B displaying the variety of ordnance it could carry. (USAF)

targets in the Soviet Union or its Warsaw Pact allies in the Cold War. During the Vietnam War, both the F-105 tactical fighter-bomber and the Boeing B-52 strategic nuclear bomber were flying missions neither were ever designed for.

Republic designed their F-105 around a standard internal weapons bay. TAC favored this approach to counter SAC's bomber fleet. Aerodynamic drag was greatly reduced, but when the bomb bay doors were opened at supersonic speeds, the severe airstream entering the bomb bay caused separation problems. The internal bomb bay proved unsuccessful and was never used in combat. Instead, that space was used for an internal conformal auxiliary fuel tank. It remained closed for all F-105 missions. Ironically, the internal weapons bay was a major plus in the Air force evaluation process against the F-107A.

The F-105 was also never designed to ingress in waves into a heavy-threat zone while banking and jinking at medium to low

Three F-105Ds in formation. The clean aircraft displayed their new TAC patch on their tails. (USAF)

The Lead-Sled: A freshly camouflaged F-105D carrying an AGM-45 Shrike antiradiation missile during a sortie on the test range. (USAF)

An F-105D with M117 750-pound conventional bombs on underwing racks. Under the Thunderstick II program, the installation of the long-range navigation (LORAN) radar system enabled a CEP (Circular Error Probable) of approximately 50 feet from an altitude of 15,000 feet. (USAF)

speed. Many combat losses were due to North Vietnamese Firecan radar-directed Anti-Aircraft Artillery (AAA) that surrounded designated targets along with SA-2 SAM sites. The F-105's hydraulic systems were vulnerable on the underside of the aircraft. Modifications were eventually made, but losses eventually amounted to 321 aircraft plus another 60 due to accidents. In contrast, based on its experience with the F-86 Sabre Jet in the Korean War, NAA designed a triple-redundant system[48] for the F-107. Mounted far apart in the upper fuselage, it consisted of three separate 3,000-psi constant-pressure units—one utility and two flight-control systems.

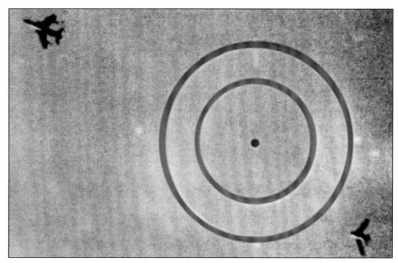

Aerial engagement over North Vietnam: Captured through the gun camera reticle, a F-105D leads a VPAF MiG-17F (lower right) as the Thud pilot attempts to protect another F-105 from the closing MiG-17F. Thud pilots had to avoid a turning fight with the MiGs, as the F-105 was sluggish when airspeed bled off. As an adversary initiated a turn in the horizontal plane, the F-105 would climb at approximately 60 degrees and roll over (F-105 roll rate: 385 degrees/second) while pulling the stick back to keep a visual on the bogey. The F-105 in afterburner and nose down had an advantage for quickly gaining speed. The goal was to fall in behind the adversary. During combat over the North, F-105s were able to shoot down 27.5 VPAF MiG fighters. (USAF)

Four fully armed F-105Ds prepare to take on fuel from a SAC KC-135 during the 1965–1966 transition period, when the F-105s were being painted in SEA camouflage. In assigned routes, the tankers would orbit in cells, approximately 200 miles from fighter bases. (USAF)

The initial hits of 20mm cannon shells on the left wing and drop tank of a VPAF MiG-17 are captured by an F-105D gun camera. This kill was shared between two pilots on 3 June 1967. (USAF)

An F-105F begins its takeoff roll from Korat RTAB. Just prior to afterburner engagement, the pedal speed brake opens to a nine-degree angle. The Wild Weasel was capable of homing in on the SAM site's Fan Song guidance radar dish. The early AGM-45A Shrike could not lock on if the radar system was switched off. The later AGM-78A Standard ARM, with a larger warhead, would continue to home-in on the coordinates of the last transmissions. (USAF)

Thuds on the move over South Vietnam during May 1970. The F-105D (foreground) and F-105F are both carrying 500-pound general-purpose bombs. (USAF)

During 1966, three F-105Ds begin a simultaneous takeoff roll. The Thud conducted a total of 20,000 combat sorties during the Vietnam War. (USAF)

A Flawed Strategy

The United States committed its military to South Vietnam with very honorable intentions—to prevent South Vietnam, a free and independent country, from being overrun by Communist-led North Vietnam. However, prior to entering a conflict you must have a strategy in place that supports clear objectives. You must acquire an all-aspect situational awareness that includes both the military and political situation. Knowing that your adversary is very determined and will not back down in the face of idle threats, is critical, and you can't ever forget that fact. You must apply the military pressure necessary to ensure your goal will be achieved in the shortest time span possible to reduce casualties on both sides. A protracted war of attrition only favors your enemy. Paramount in the process is that politicians listen to advice from military experts. Unfortunately, during weekly White House target-planning meetings, no military professionals were present, not even the chairman of the Joint Chiefs of Staff, until late 1967.[50] President Johnson, [51] far from qualifying as a military planner, was determined to micromanage the Southeast Asia combat arena under his terms. Johnson once pompously boasted, "I won't let the Air Force generals bomb the smallest outhouse without checking with me."

By not hitting the entry port of Haiphong and storage centers near Hanoi, the president's team chose to do it the hard way. U.S. pilots had to search for hard targets after they were already dispersed and loaded on thousands of trucks, bicycles, small boats, and rafts—and then sent down rivers and hidden trails. Searching for and destroying these numerous small targets exacted a high price for the United States.[52] To compound the situation, within the office of the Secretary of Defense lurked more arrogance. An intransient wall that prevented cross-communications had been initiated by Sec. of Defense Robert S. McNamara[53] under the previous Kennedy administration.

The National Security Action Memorandum (NSAM) 228[54] issued by Secretary McNamara ordered the Joint Chiefs of Staff to develop plans of graduated overt pressure on North Vietnam. This unfortunately included a 30-day notice for scheduled raids and a 72-hour warning to Hanoi for any retaliatory raids.[55] There must have been severe cringing within the walls of the Pentagon. This could be a Hollywood comedy, but unfortunately it was real, and the valuable lives of our soldiers and airmen were at stake. This was a bad situation waiting to get worse.

Within the broad scope, President Johnson feared that any serious attack on Hanoi or Haiphong would initiate a response from the Soviet Union or Communist China. In reality, based on its bloody experience during the Korean War, Chairman Mao Tse-tung of China had nullified a mutual defense pact with North Vietnam in 1964. If President Johnson didn't know this, he should have.[56] In addition, it is very doubtful the Soviet Union would have responded militarily in that geographical area, for the October 1962 Cuban Missile Crisis with the United States was still fresh in their memory. In Vietnam they were acquiring what they wanted, testing their air-defense equipment, and their advisors were obtaining combat experience. They could cut and run at any time, and push North Vietnam for a negotiated settlement. The basic strategy of North Vietnam and its allies was to continue a long, costly, drawn-out war that slowly drained U.S. resources, as well as the patience of the American public, while occasionally enticing the U.S. president that they might be willing to negotiate to bring about bombing halts. These temporary cessation of hostilities worked perfectly for the repair, rebuilding, and shipment of more arms into South Vietnam. In essence, the Johnson administration was adhering to North Vietnam's plan perfectly.

These two independent systems were provided for the horizontal/ vertical stabilizer, spoiler and deflector, and flaps. A completely independent utility system provided hydraulic pressure for the landing gear, wheel brakes, inlet ramps, gun drive, and air-refueling probe.

Thud pilots learned to not engage in a turning fight with Vietnam People's Air Force (VPAF) MiGs, as the F-105 was sluggish at slower speeds. Flat-out high speed on the deck was the F-105's advantage. During the test-flight phase, the F-107A exhibited a much better turning radius than the F-105. However, at the time the Air Force was not looking for a dogfighter, but rather a straight-on supersonic nuclear-capable fighter/bomber. In air-to-air combat F-105s shot down 27.5[49] MiG-17s during their deployment. On 4 June 1983, an impressive F-105 24-ship diamonds-on-diamonds formation flew over the active service retirement ceremony at Hill Air Force Base, Utah. The Thud continued to serve in the Air Force Reserve until 25 February 1984. Combined with the indisputable courage and skill of USAF airmen, the rugged F-105 stood the test of time during service in the Vietnam War. The Thud endured the punishment inflicted by the enemy while performing a mission it was never intended to fly. Numerous F-105s returned to base with severe battle damage. Now, like its predecessor, the famed P-47 Thunderbolt of World War II fame, the F-105 is forever imbedded in the history books.

F-105G Wild Weasel with an AGM-45A Shrike on its left wing hard point. The F-105G was capable of homing in on the SAM site's Fan Song guidance radar dish. The early Shrike could not lock on if the radar system was switched off. The later AGM-78A Standard ARM, with a larger warhead, would continue to home in on the coordinates of the last transmissions. (USAF)

Specifications

Republic Aviation YF-105A Thunderchief—Tactical Fighter/Bomber Prototype
Crew: 1—pilot
Wingspan: 34 ft. 11 in. (10.6 m)
Length: 63 ft. 1 in. (19.6 m)
Height: 19 ft. 8 in. (6 m)
Maximum takeoff weight: 46,998 lb (21,317.9 kg)
Range: 2,200 miles (3,540.5 km)
Maximum speed: 1,375 mph (km/h)
Cruising speed: 581 mph (935 km/h)
Service ceiling: 48,100 ft. (14,660.8 m)
Powerplant: 1 Pratt & Whitney YJ57-PW-25 turbojet—16,000 lb (71 kN) thrust with afterburner
Bomb Capacity: 8,000 lb (3,628 kg)
Armament: 1 General Electric M61A1 Vulcan 20mm cannon (1,028 rounds)

North American Aviation F-107A—Tactical Fighter/Bomber Prototype
Crew: 1—pilot
Wingspan: 36 ft. 6 in. (11 m)
Length: 60 ft. 10 in. (18.5 m)
Height: 19 ft. 6 in. (5.9 m)
Maximum takeoff weight: 41,537 lb (18,840.8 kg)
Range: 1,570 miles (2,526.6 km)

Maximum speed: 1,520+ mph (2,446 km/h) Mach 2+
Cruising speed: 600 mph (965.6 km/h)
Service ceiling: 48,000 ft. (14,630 m)
Powerplant: Pratt & Whitney YJ75-P-11 turbojet—24,500 lb (109 kN) thrust with afterburner
Bomb capacity: 8,000 lb (3,628 kg)
Armament: 4 Pontiac M-39E 20mm cannons, 108 x 2.57 in. rockets

Republic Aviation F-105D Thunderchief—Tactical Fighter/Bomber
Crew: 1—pilot
Wingspan: 34 ft. 11 in. (10.6 m)
Length: 64 ft. 5 in. (19.6 m)
Height: 19 ft. 8 in. (6 m)
Maximum weight: 52,838 lb (12,181 kg)
Empty weight: 26,855 lb (12,181 kg)
Range: 2,390 miles (3,846 km)
Maximum speed: 1,390 mph (2,236.9 km/h)
Cruising speed: 778 mph (1,252 km/h)
Service ceiling: 51,000 ft. (15,544.8 m)
Powerplant: 1 Pratt & Whitney J75-P-19W turbojet—26,500 lb (117.8 kN) thrust
Bomb Capacity: 16,500 lb (7,484 kg)
Armament: 1 General Electric M61A1 Vulcan 20mm cannon (1,028 rounds)

PHANTOMS AND CRUSADERS
McDONNELL F4H-1 PHANTOM II
VERSUS CHANCE-VOUGHT F8U-3 CRUSADER III

A USAF F-4E Phantom II in afterburner screaming at low altitude across a valley. (Author)

The U.S. Navy competition that pitted McDonnell Aircraft against Chance-Vought emerged from earlier roots. A rivalry began in mid-1953 with a competition for a single-seat Navy fighter/bomber (McDonnell designation F3H-G[1]) designed for carrier operations. McDonnell was confident of winning because they had previously produced the carrier-based FH-1 Phantom, F2H Banshee, and F3H Demon fighter jets for the Navy. This competition, however, was lost to Chance-Vought's F8U-1 Crusader. The Crusader, the Navy's first operational supersonic aircraft, emerged as a rugged and venerable aircraft that established an impressive combat record. In the rapidly changing aviation world during the 1950s and 1960s, McDonnell knew the Navy would be looking again.

Rise of the Phantom II

As closely predicted by McDonnell officials, by 1955 another Navy RFP emerged for an uprated carrier-based all-weather fighter/

bomber. Naval requirements were for the aircraft to remain on station 250 miles from the carrier, with a complete deck cycle time of three hours. After process and design reviews, McDonnell felt it was ready this time and submitted its AH-1 configuration. After subsequent Navy reviews, and a mission change to interceptor/fighter, the design was revised and it received a new designation of F4H-1.

The McDonnell team, which was headed by project manager David S. Lewis and senior project engineer Herman D. Barkey, conducted extensive design work[2] and wind-tunnel tests to arrive at a high-performance configuration.

Originally sporting a simple and clean 45-degree swept wing with a slight anhedral, the F4H-1 wound up with a 3-degree dihedral. Additionally, to increase high-speed directional stability, the dihedral of the outer-wing sections was increased to 12 degrees. The outer panels also began with a sawtooth leading edge, which later became a Phantom II trademark look. These unusual wing-design steps were taken to avoid redesigning the complex titanium wing

The original single-seat F3H-G/H fighter full-scale mockup in 1954. The proposed F3H-G/H would be powered by two Wright J65s or, if available, two GE J79 turbojets. Following the configuration requirements, note the nose ports for the four 20mm cannons. The next competition would require the removal of all guns and would be armed with missiles only. (National Museum of Naval Aviation)

The full-scale mockup of the F4H clearly depicts the morphing of the new design to a fleet defense fighter. Traits of the impending Phantom II's classic lines, with its two-seat cockpit, wing configuration, and semirecessed Sparrow missiles, are clear. (National Museum of Naval Aviation)

box section, which engineers wanted to retain. Adding to the Phantom's unique appearance were all-moving horizontal stabilizers, which had a 23.5-degree anhedral. The new twin-engine two-seat all-weather interceptor would carry four semirecessed Sparrow III[3] air-to-air missiles under the fuselage and two additional missiles on wing hardpoints. The F4H-1 would not have a cannon.[4] The spacious nose radome fairing would house a Westinghouse AN/APQ-72 radar/fire-control system with a 32-inch dish. The infrared search and track (IRST) system would be housed just below the radome fairing.

Phantom II Takes Flight

Streaking off the Lambert Field runway adjacent to McDonnell Aircraft, the first F4H-1 prototype (BuNo.142259) made its initial flight on 27 May 1958. McDonnell chief test pilot Bob Little was at the controls. The flight was conducted at low speed and termi-

nated early due to several minor anomalies. Little was precluded from going Mach 1 on the first flight. This included having to leave the landing gear in the down position. However, with a new right engine and the inlet ramp doors repositioned four degrees, a second flight occurred on 29 May. Prior to being ferried to Edwards AFB for Phase I testing,

A planform view of the U.S. Navy F4H-1 (BuNo.142259) and its prominent wing configuration. Also visible is the extended sensor-laden pitot tube. (U.S. Navy)

The number-one F4H-1 (BuNo.142259) on a test flight at approximately 18,000 feet with its landing gear extended. The aircraft's high-approach speeds were later mitigated with factory mods on the leading and trailing edges of the wings. The aircraft is also carrying inert Sparrow missiles for fit checks. (U.S. Navy)

aircraft number one completed 11 test flights. Little also took the F4H-1 to 50,000 feet at a speed of Mach 1.68.

Flight testing at Edwards AFB was basically free of major anomalies,[6] except for one aborted takeoff on 21 August 1958 that blew the tires, causing the landing-gear doors to suffer fire damage.[7] Initially designed for lower weight, the F4H-1's wing size caused increased approach speeds. The Navy was aware of weight increases to the airframe and agreed to a wing fix beginning with the sixth preproduction aircraft. Factory mods on the wing leading and trailing edges mitigated these potential carrier-landing approach problems. A definite positive noted for McDonnell was the excellent acceleration achieved by the F4H-1 in the transonic regime (Mach 0.9–1.4). Initial comments from evaluating test pilots included experiencing a heavy stick, but superb power with the twin engines. Regarding the later F-4C model, USAF F-4 combat veteran Ralph Wetterhahn commented, "Control sensitivity varies widely. It takes full aft stick to raise the nose for takeoff, yet at certain fuel loadings and at speeds just above Mach 0.9 at low altitude, moving the stick only one inch can produce 6 Gs on the airframe. At above Mach 2, on the other hand, the shock wave that is created moves the center of lift so far aft that pulling the stick all the way back produces only about 2 Gs."[8]

The Three Missileers

At the time another type of fleet defense aircraft was under consideration. Fitting into the realm of a missile truck, three primary contractors responded to a 1957 Navy RFP for a carrier-based fleet defense fighter that became known as the F6D-1 Missileer. The three missileers were Douglas, McDonnell, and North American Aviation. Grumman also responded to the RFP, but as a secondary contractor through the Bendix Corporation, which was developing the advanced AAM-N-10 Eagle air-to-air missile.

Unlike the powerful F4H-1 or F8U-3, the F6D-1 was not intended as a fast attack jet, but was essentially a high-altitude subsonic missile platform. Requirements included extended loiter time (up to six hours) and a capability to patrol long distances from the carrier attack group. An advanced Westinghouse AN/APO-81 Doppler radar with a range of approximately 138 miles would be capable of tracking six bogeys simultaneously. The newly developed Mach 4.5–capable AAM-N-10 missile would engage and destroy nuclear-armed Soviet bombers well away from naval fleet assets.

Douglas had an excellent head start with its existing F3D Skynight, which featured a side-by-side cockpit, high-aspect-ratio wings, and imbedded nonafterburning engines in the lower fuselage. To secure the extra loiter time, the proposed F6D-1's wingspan was lengthened from 50 to 70 feet. This not only would provide excellent range, but also adequate space for the large underwing-mounted AAM-N-10 Eagle missiles. For better carrier-deck stowage, the wing folding points were nearly at the halfway mark. New Pratt & Whitney TF30-P2 non-afterburning turbofans would deliver plenty of power with low fuel consumption. The F6D-1 had an excellent chance to fly its mission profile successfully; the downside was the fact that the avionics/weapon systems the crew depended on were entirely new, raising the risk factor significantly.

The F6D-1 Missileer program fell victim to the Eisenhower administration's fixation on leaving office with a balanced budget. The very promising NAA Mach 3–capable F-108 Rapier interceptor program was also caught up in this DoD budget-cutting effort. Secretary of Defense Neil McElroy canceled the F-108 on 23 September 1959 and deleted funding for the impending F6D-1 for Fiscal Year 1962. McElroy hoped the Missileer would be restarted, but the outgoing Eisenhower administration was unaware that the new secretary of defense, Robert McNamara, would have even less enthusiasm for new military programs that weren't his original idea. Although probably not one of the best-conceived Cold War projects, the F6D-1 Missileer was canceled by Secretary McNamara in December 1961.[5] However, many of the technological advances from that program emerged in follow-on programs such as the F-111 (TFX) and F-14.

A conceptual U.S. Navy/Douglas F6D-1 Missileer unleashes two long-range Mach 4.5 Bendix AAM-N-10 Eagle air-to-air missiles. As a Navy fleet defender, the F6D would patrol well away from the carrier attack group and defend against enemy bombers. Unfortunately, the F6D-1 Missileer was caught up between the outgoing Eisenhower administration, and the incoming Kennedy administration. The Missileer program was canceled in December 1961. (Author Photo/Illustration)

The Chance-Vought Crusader III

During 1958, veteran Navy aviator and test pilot Cdr. Robert M. Elder was director of the Naval Flight Test Center (NATC) at NAS Patuxent River. Elder had eight NATC evaluation test pilots under his command. During this time a spectacular new generation of advanced naval aircraft were flying: the McDonnell F4H-1, Chance-Vought[9] F8U-3, and North American Rockwell A3J-1 Vigilante. During Elder's tenure, one of the controversies was whether the Navy should buy the F4H-1 Phantom II or the F8U-3 Crusader III. Based on its performance, Elder favored the F8U-3. Decades later he commented, "The F8U-3 outperformed the F4H-1 in almost every category. It was like a freight train going downhill; the faster it went the faster it wanted to go." However, the Navy made the right choice since mission-systems complexity was a serious consideration, and the F4H-1 was a two-seater.[10] Thus, the never-ending saga continued, pitting the two-seat twin-engine aircraft against the single-seat single-engine fighter.

Well aware of McDonnell's design efforts to please the Navy and go for a two-seater, Vought conducted extensive research on a two-seat version. Both tandem and side-by-side seating were studied, and there was a substantial weight penalty that could hurt performance, especially in lieu of new Navy-requested changes to the original configuration. With a wider fuselage, the side-by-side arrangement degraded performance, similar to the Convair TF-102, and this configuration was rejected. One F8U-1 (TF-8-1) was built as a tandem two-seater and performed well. (It was nicknamed the "Two-sader.") However, to accommodate a second crewman, Vought would have to stretch the F8U-3 fuselage by 50 inches and absorb an estimated weight penalty of more than 1,000 pounds. Some Pentagon officials indirectly informed Vought there was interest in an all-weather Mach 2–capable single-engine fleet-defense fighter, and Vought proceeded with a single-seat design for its advanced Crusader. The powerplant would be the powerful Pratt & Whitney J75. Even though avionics were becoming vastly more complex for a single pilot, Vought felt that automated systems developed for their Regulus II surface-to-surface missile would mitigate the need for a second crewman.

As Vought produced the F8U-2 Crusader II, which upgraded various systems on the F8U-1, their advanced Model V-401 was given the designation of F8U-3. There were radical differences in the new

The number-one F8U-3 in afterburner pulls up and approaches a vertical climb. (Author Photo/Illustration)

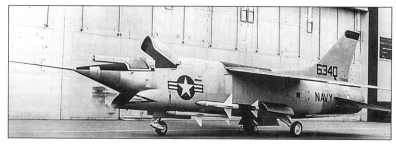

The rollout of the futuristic-looking number-one F8U-3 Crusader III (t/n 6340) took place in April 1958 at the Chance-Vought Grand Prairie, Texas, facility. Although having many differences from the previous F8U-1/2 Crusader, the Crusader III retained the F8U designation due to U.S. Navy budgetary procedures. (Vought)

The magnificent design of the F8U-3 had a dramatic aerodynamic shape. The test flights proceeded with dummy Sparrow missiles in their semirecessed positions. The retracted ventral fin can be seen just behind the ground technician. (Vought)

Clear differences can be discerned between Vought's second prototype F8U-3 (t/n 6341) Super Crusader and the two F8U-1 Crusaders also parked on the flightline. In 1958, the second prototype was flown nonstop from Vought to Edwards AFB for preliminary evaluation tests. (Vought)

air inlet was designed for the Dash 3. To accommodate the semirecessed mounting for the forward-mounted Sparrow missiles, the nose-wheel assembly was located slightly offset to the right.[11]

Crusader Rabbit III Goes Airborne

The flight-test programs of the F4H-1 Phantom II and Chance-Vought F8U-3 Crusader III signaled that the aircraft industry was experiencing a new era. After years of frustration, suitable jet engines were finally available for the advanced airframes being developed. This included dramatically increased thrust and greatly improved reliability. Shipped to Edwards AFB in two sections[12] via a C-124 Globemaster cargo aircraft, the F8U-3 was reassembled and prepared for flight. After

F8U-3, but the Navy opted not to use an available F9U-1 designation. This was similar to the situation that existed with NAA's Air Force F-100B proposal. As it evolved into a vastly different configuration, the F-107A designation was kept in the dark for quite a while. This was due to the DoD budget situation. At the time, new program starts had a very good chance of winding up dead in the water, while variants of an existing program had a much better chance of proceeding. Thus, the new Super Crusader designation only added a "Dash 3." If the F8U-3 had gone into service, would the new F9U-1 designation have been assigned post-competition? For those fully aware, the Navy's designation strategy of not assigning F9U-1 at this point made sense for funding reasons. On the other hand, when it came down to picking one of the competitors, were there some uninformed individuals who may have wondered if they were actually funding a new airplane or just an improved Crusader? This was important because the competition was extremely close.

Initial engineering studies also confirmed that for Mach-2 flight the F8U-3's vertical tail area needed to be increased and its ventral fins needed to be larger to increase lateral stability. Finally, a more radical area-rule design would be incorporated into the fuselage. To maximize the J75's capability at high Mach, a modified extended-lip

Vought Chief Test Pilot John Konrad took the number-one F8U-3 Super Crusader (t/n 6340) on its first flight on 2 June 1958. The extended ventral fins provided the F8U-3 with a futuristic look. (AFFTC Office of History)

Close Performance Parameters

Interestingly, the expected performance parameters of the single-engine F8U-3 and twin-engine F4H-1 were very close:

	F8U-3	F4H-1
Maximum speed at 35,000 ft.	Mach 2.02	Mach 2.02
Supersonic combat ceiling	52,100 ft.	51,900 ft.
Subsonic combat ceiling	45,700 ft.	42,600 ft.
Stall speed at landing weight	124 mph	115 mph
Combat Air Patrol (CAP)	2.98 hours	3.00 hours
Engine thrust at sea level	24,500 lb	2 x 17,600 lb each
Engine thrust at 35,000 ft.	23,400 lb	2 x 15,600 lb each

The number-one F8U-3 prototype takes another test flight at Edwards AFB. The next aircraft to feature a large ventral fin was the Lockheed YF-12A. (AFFTC Office of History)

Test pilots reported that the F8U-3 wanted to continue to accelerate as it approached the structural limits of the aircraft. Later in the flight test program, an area-rule shape was added along with the ventral fins being extended. (AFFTC Office of History)

A clean-looking number-three F8U-3 prototype taxis with its canopy open. The wings are in the raised position which provides greater lift during takeoff and reduced landing speed for carrier landings. Twin actuators were employed to raise and lower the wing incidence, as opposed to a single actuator for the earlier F8U-1/2. Mockup Sparrow missiles are clearly seen in their semirecessed positions. (U.S. Navy)

high-speed taxi tests[13] were completed and data from the static-test airframe was brought to 120 percent without structural failure, everything was considered ready. Vought chief test pilot John Konrad lifted the Super Crusader off the runway on 2 June 1958. Despite McDonnell Aircraft having a one-year head start on F4H-1 development, the Vought F8U-3 made its first flight within six days of the F4H-1 Phantom II's first flight.[14]

Although the Crusader III was ready to accelerate on that flight, a problem with the throttle limited the speed to 402.7 mph, with altitude held at no higher than 20,000 feet. In addition, with landing gear extended, low-speed buffeting of the ventral fins was also noted—the tip of one of the ventrals actually departed the aircraft. Konrad landed after 38 minutes in the air and commented enthusiastically during the debriefing, "This airplane is going to be a real

weapon. It's got an ease of control and a sense of power that fighter pilots will like. Another thing is it's engineered so you can forget the little things and concentrate on clobbering your target. This airplane gives the pilot a whole new dimension."

Testing continued during June, and the flight envelope was expanded to Mach 1.7 and 47,500 feet. On 12 June, modifications commenced with the installation of a larger vertical stabilizer as well as larger ventral fins to control lateral stability for the impending high-Mach flights. After resumption of flying, the F8U-3 reached Mach 2.92 by its 13th flight at the end of June.[15] Despite the advanced inlet design, the aircraft suffered a series of compressor stalls reminiscent of the YF-105A/F-107A testing, but a series of improvements to the inlet and fuel control seemed to bring things back to normal. It was noted in the flight-test record that despite early compressor stalls in the transonic regime, the F8U-3 had better high-altitude maneuverability and, more importantly, high-speed acceleration to reach the potential intercept target.

Vought test pilot Joe Angelone recalled flying the F8U-3: "It had superb handling qualities. It was a 40,000-pound airplane with around 25,000 pounds of thrust. It was amazing at high Mach numbers, as we would typically throttle back at Mach 2 on our early test flights. We were limited by windshield and lower wing-skin temperatures as higher Mach numbers were explored." Angelone continued, "A typical flight would involve taking off from Edwards and climbing to 40,000 feet to the eastern boundary of California. Here we would turn west and enter the supersonic corridor with a USAF F-104 chase plane. We would accelerate out to Mach 2, throttle back at this speed, and run through our test plan. As we passed over Edwards, we would drop subsonic and say goodbye to the 104, as he was about out of fuel. We would then pick up an F-100 chase for the remaining tests. As a former Air Force fighter pilot, I got a perverse chuckle out of running their Starfighter out of fuel halfway through our test plan."[16]

Although a formation flight of two F8U-3 prototypes never occurred, this hypothetical view provides an impression of two of the powerful fighters together. (Author Photo/Illustration)

Showing its graceful lines, the number-one F8U-3 prototype flies over the Gulf of Mexico coastline. (Author Photo/Illustration)

As more flight hours were accumulated, the F8U-3 was portrayed as having superior qualities to the previous F8U-1 Crusader. This included power control and approach/touchdown characteristics during landing. Meanwhile, on the opposite side of the spectrum, high speed was coming naturally to the Dash 3. By August 1958, the flight envelope had increased to Mach 2.2 at 43,000 feet.

Anticipating higher Mach numbers, the second prototype featured the larger tail and increased ventral fin size. Konrad flew it on a checkout sortie from the Vought facility on 27 September 1958. Within a few days Angelone ferried it nonstop to Edwards to join the number-one prototype.

Test pilots reported the F8U-3 wanting to continue accelerating, but they were approaching the structural limits of the aircraft. During a particular flight the F8U-3 entered a turn at Mach 1.05 and held 3.8 Gs while maintaining Mach 0.95. High-speed capability was critical to the Navy for defending the carrier attack group during the Cold War. Reaching the incoming bogeys (Soviet bombers) as quickly as possible to prevent an atom bomb detonation too close to the fleet was a high priority. The Air Force followed this same strategy to develop interceptors that could reach speeds of up to Mach 3. Unfortunately, two very promising USAF interceptor programs, the NAA F-108 Rapier and Lockheed F-12B Blackbird, were canceled prior to production.

Retracting its landing gear, F8U-3 (BuNo.147085) aircraft number three lifts off the runway at Edwards AFB. This aircraft was actually a production aircraft configuration. (AFFTC Office of History)

Single-Seat Strategy

The Navy had been through the single-seat versus two-seat drill previously in the 1950s when the McDonnell F2H-2N Banshee and the Douglas F3D Skyknight were flown against each other. The F3D featured side-by-side seating with a pilot and radar operator. The faster F2H-2N was a single-seater. The F3D with less performance possessed a superior search radar system with the operator's focused attention. Performance won out, however, and the F2H-2N Banshee beat the F3D, becoming the primary carrier-based fleet-defense fighter. The Skyknight operated mostly from land bases and performed well as a night interceptor during the Korean War, making the first radar-directed night kill in history. However, it was determined that at critical times the pilot could handle the radar with autopilot engaged, and so the follow-up McDonnell F3H Demon and F4D Skyray were also single-engine single-seat fighters.

This view of F8U-3 (t/n 7085) accentuates the unique forward-swept inlet lip as compared to the F8U-1/2. (Vought)

When Vought was not down-selected, company officials contacted both the USAF and the Canadian government about the capabilities of the F8U-3 Super Crusader. Although the potential sales outreach was unsuccessful, this hypothetical view shows a conceptual USAF F-8U-3 escorted by a Navy F8U-3 prototype. (Author Photo/Illustration)

Another conceptual view of two single-seat USAF F8U-3s in formation. With extensive automated system background experience with its unmanned U.S. Navy Regulus II missile program, Vought had confidence that F8U-3 intercept missions could be handled by a single crewmember. (Author Photo/Illustration)

A conceptual two-seater F8U-3 (F-9D) Crusader III from VF-111 Sundowners. The earlier F-8E Crusaders of VF-111 served during the Vietnam War. Had the Vought F8U-3 Crusader III won the competition, it possibly could have replaced the F8Us in Vietnam. The early F8Us had four 20mm cannons, which proved very effective in aerial combat. However, the F8U-3 most likely would have followed the same procurement strategy and would have entered service without an internal gun. In the Phantom II program this wasn't corrected until the E model. (Author Photo/Illustration)

As predicted at the onset of the competition, a second seat degraded performance such as endurance on station. An additional study conducted by the Naval Research Laboratory (NRL), concluded that the maximum potential gain in detection range with a dedicated radar operator on board was only 5 percent.[17] Vought did submit a detailed backup plan for an F8U-3 two-seat design to the Navy. Subsequent analysis of all the research data plus several other factors helped convince the Vought team that all along they were pursuing the correct course with its single-seat design.[18] Vought even built a mission simulator to validate the single-crewmember interception mission.

Decision Time Viewed from the Vought Side

As contractor D-day approached, both McDonnell and Vought knew the competition would be very close. Behind the scenes each held out hope there would be room for two naval aircraft types should they lose this competition. It was a time of rapid development for multiple new advanced aircraft, which both the Navy and Air Force were simultaneously flying and testing. It seemed a good bet that funding could be approved for aircraft that had both performed so well and were so close to each other in overall capability.

George Spangenberg, director of aircraft design at Naval Air Systems Command (NAVAIR), later commented, "The F8U-3 was faster, more maneuverable, had better flying qualities, cost 20 percent less, and had more range on internal fuel than the F4H-1 with an added external drop tank." He continued, "In the normal sense the F8U-3 won the fly-off. It had the best flying qualities with better legs and higher speed—the climb rate and ceilings were about the same." Depending on whom you asked at the time, the competition was very close behind the scenes, but in publicly released statements the F4H-1 Phantom II was the clear winner.

Another "what might have been" view of two F8U-3 (F-9D) Super Crusaders from VF-111. (Author Photo/Illustration)

Essentially, the contest narrowed down to the two-seat twin-engine advantage of the F4H-1. Unfortunately, this time Congress was going to fund only one aircraft. It was a tough decision for the Navy. Each contractor first received a heads-up phone call from the Pentagon. On Wednesday, 17 December 1958, after the stock market closed on the East Coast, McDonnell Aircraft was publicly announced as the winner for the Navy's all-weather fighter. The Navy felt it had thoroughly examined two of the most heavily armed and technologically advanced fighters ever flown. A news release reiterated that the McDonnell F4H-1 best met all of the requirements for the Navy's fleet defense.[19] It also pointed out that having the second crewman (radar operator) and twin engines were decisive factors in the selection. Vought was well positioned with field support for the F8U-1 and was also producing the uprated F8U-2 Crusader. However, a week

USAF F-4G Wild Weasel. (Author Photo/Illustration)

It was 6:04 a.m. PDT on 16 July 1957 when USMC Maj. John H. Glenn took off in an F8U-1P (BuNo.144608, later RF-8G) Crusader from NAS Los Alamitos, California. The flight established a transcontinental speed record averaging 725.25 mph. Glenn landed at Floyd Bennett Field, New York, 3 hours, 23 minutes and 8.4 seconds after takeoff. The F8U-1P only departed supersonic speed four times to slow to approximately 300 mph to refuel from AJ-2 Savage tankers. This was five years prior to John Glenn achieving household-name status when he became the first U.S. astronaut to orbit the earth in Mercury Friendship 7 on 20 February 1962. After the record flight, the Navy wanted to show off their new Crusader, and Glenn performed at several air shows in the summer of 1957. At the age of 10, the author was fortunate to have seen Glenn perform at NAS Masters Field, Florida. The lasting impression and overwhelming sound during the aerial display of the powerful F8U-1P certainly helped direct me toward an aviation career. Some 40 years later, the author was again lucky to have met Sen. John Glenn while working communications for the B-1B Lancer at Rockwell International. (U.S. Navy)

A conceptual view of a USN/LTV F8U-3P (later RF-9G) reconnaissance version of the Super Crusader. The various camera ports are visible that contain both forward-looking, downward wide angle, and oblique view cameras. It's interesting to postulate what would have happened if the F8U-3P had been in service and available for Major Glenn's record speed run. (Author Photo/Illustration)

after the F8U-3 Crusader III loss, the Navy also canceled their Regulus II submarine-launched surface-to-surface missile program. Vought initiated a marketing program to offer the F8U-3 to the USAF and RCAF[20] but to no avail. To put it mildly, 1958 ended badly for Vought. The next step for the F8U-3 (BuNo.147085) was an assignment to NASA Ames Research Center to flight-test its advanced features. After NASA flight testing, both F8U-3 prototypes were declared surplus and eventually scrapped.

Phantom II: The Winner

As bad as December 1958 was for Vought, it was a good month for McDonnell's St. Louis facility. Company founder and president James S. McDonnell[22], known as "Mr. Mac," announced on the public-address system that the company's F4H-1 had won the Navy competition for a new all-weather fighter.[23] On 17 December, the official contract was issued for 24 production aircraft. Following McDonnell's tradition of occult-derived aircraft names, on 3 July 1959 (the 20th anniversary of McDonnell Aircraft), the F4H-1 was christened Phantom II. This extended the short-lived FH-1 Phantom I legacy.[24]

Navy Phantoms: Testing and Breaking Records

1960 was a fast-paced year for the Phantom II. F4H-1 number 5 (BuNo.143390) was ferried to MCAS El Centro, California, for ground-attack testing. Beginning on 15 February, the 6th F4H-1 (BuNo.143391) participated in carrier-suitability tests aboard the USS Independence (CVA-62). The 11th F4H-1 (BuNo.145310) tested the Phantom II's bomb-load capability by carrying and releasing 22,500 pounds of Mk.83 conventional gravity bombs. Another F4H-1 (BuNo.146817) evaluated the maximum air-to-air missile-carrying capacity by test flying with six AIM-7 Sparrow missiles. On 29 December 1960, NAS

Miramar in Southern California received aircraft number 28 for testing. The Navy was very enthusiastic about their new fighter. This was vividly expressed by Vice Adm. Clarence Ekstrom, who commented after the F4H-1 established one of its world speed records of 1,217 mph in 1960. "This speed means more than a record; it means that we now have a weapon system capable of operating from aircraft carriers that can go higher, faster and farther, and be able to intercept any attacker aircraft." Ekstrom further emphasized that "the Phantom's capabilities give adversaries reason to reassess possible acts of aggression."[25]

During early carrier ops aboard the USS Forrestal, an F4H-1 Phantom II from VF-102 prepares for a catapult launch. (U.S. Navy)

F4H-1 prototype number six undergoing land-based carrier catapult launches at NAS Patuxent River, Maryland. (U.S. Navy) **Inset:** *Close-up of the nose landing-gear extension to increase lift during catapult launches. (U.S. Navy)*

Déjà Vu All Over Again

At the time of the McDonnell F4H-1 selection over the Chance-Vought F8U-3, Lyndon Johnson was a senator from Texas and actually from the Fort Worth area where Chance-Vought was located. Johnson was also on the Preparedness Investigating Subcommittee of the SASC. Rear Adm. Robert E. Dixon, chief of the Bureau of Aeronautics (BuAer), sent Senator Johnson a letter on 17 December providing details of the selection of McDonnell over Vought. He emphasized the closeness of the competition, but noted that the deciding factor was the McDonnell F4H-1 had two crewmen, including a radar operator and twin engines. Its interception performance would be superior to the single-crewman Vought F8U-3.[21] One can certainly imagine that Senator Johnson was thinking he wasn't going to let that happen again without a fight. It was only four years later, in November 1962, when President Johnson presided over the controversial TFX-competition decision. General Dynamics, located in Fort Worth, Texas, and Boeing, located in Seattle, Washington, were in a tight competition to build the Navy's newest carrier-based fighter/bomber. Disregarding recommendations of top Navy officials and experts, the Johnson administration, through Sec. of Defense Robert McNamara, picked General Dynamics over Boeing to build the TFX (F-111) in Texas.

Under Project Top Flight, the number-one F4H-1 prototype takes off from Edwards AFB on 6 December 1959. The Phantom II set a world altitude record of 98,557 feet. (AFFTC Office of History)

The Air Force flight-tested and evaluated the reconnaissance variant Phantom II under the designation RF-110A Spectre. The distinctive nose section has been modified to house photographic systems. When the DoD standardized USAF and USN aircraft designations on 18 September 1962, this version became the RF-4C. (USAF)

The number-one F-110A Spectre (BuNo.149405) was delivered to the Air Force for evaluation at Langley AFB. It was one of two F4H-1s bailed from the Navy in January 1961. Although marked with the USAF F-110A designation, this aircraft was actually an F4H-1. (USAF)

An excellent ground-level portrait taken in 1965 of an early USAF F-4C Phantom II with underwing stores. (USAF)

Air Force Phantoms

The F4H-1's impressive performance had already caught the attention of Air Force officials when, under direction from Secretary McNamara in January 1961, the Air Force acquired two Navy F4H-1s for evaluation. McNamara was determined to achieve more commonality between the services to save development costs. The Air Force was developing the Convair F-106A Delta Dart air-defense fighter and competed the F4H-1s, flown with the F-110A Spectre designation, against it. Under Operation Highspeed—conducted at Langley AFB, Virginia, in early 1962—the F-110A outperformed the F-106A in all criteria categories. In fact, the Phantom II appeared to be more capable than the USAF F-101 Voodoo and F-105 Thunder-

chief. The Air Force was impressed with both the interceptor and potential ground-attack capabilities of the F-110A.[26]

There was more good news for McDonnell Aircraft when the Pentagon announced on 30 March 1962 that the McDonnell F-110A[27] Spectre would become the Air Force's primary tactical fighter. McDonnell received an Air Force contract for a single F-110A and two reconnaissance variants, designated RF-110A.[28] Although the Air Force version would retain the folding outer wings and tail hook, there were some changes in the airframe to incorporate certain Air Force requirements. This included specified avionics systems and cockpit configuration. USAF aircraft would also feature dual cockpit flight control-systems. In addition, Air Force versions would eliminate the Navy probe-and-drogue aerial-refueling

A U.S. Navy McDonnell F-4B Phantom II of Fighter Squadron VF-111 Sundowners drops 500-pound Mk. 82 bombs over Vietnam during 1971. The Navy quickly adapted its all-weather fleet-defense fighter Phantom II to a ground-attack aircraft. (U.S. Navy)

The new F-110A Spectre designation didn't last too long. In an effort to standardize Navy and Air Force aircraft designations, on 18 September 1962 the DoD instituted numerous changes. Retaining F for fighter with an added dash, Navy aircraft would start at number one: F-1, F-2, etc. The existing Banshee was now F-2 and the Demon F-3. The new Navy F4H-1 and Air Force F-110A were now designated F-4 Phantom II for both services. The Navy variant was F-4B while the Air Force had the F-4C. The number-one USAF F-4C Phantom II made its first flight on 27 May 1963.

Prudent Advice Went Unheeded

Despite being consistently ignored, Gen. Curtis LeMay kept trying to convince Secretary McNamara to utilize airpower more effectively. However, on 1 February 1965, Gen. J. P. McConnell, who was handpicked by McNamara, succeeded General LeMay as Air Force chief of staff. Any balancing influence was now quashed, and the door for suggesting any fresh ideas was now closed. McNamara had the people in the Pentagon that he wanted. The rules of engagement stipulated that U.S. pilots could only attack enemy SAM sites if they fired at their aircraft first. Navy pilots actually spotted 111 SA-2s SAMs loaded on railcars near Hanoi, but permission to destroy them was denied. Our pilots had to wait until the SAM sites were set up and missiles were fired at them, resulting in the loss of millions of dollars worth of aircraft and many valuable American airmen.[29]

Once the North Vietnamese knew the exact location and parameters of the restricted and prohibited zones, they set up SAM sites within those zones. Essentially, SAM launch sites could be immune from attack, but the SA-2's range still allowed it to engage U.S. warplanes outside the zone.[30] This was just one of the many examples of

system with the boom-type receptacle mounted on the fuselage spine aft of the cockpit. Another exterior difference was the wider main gear tires. A full-scale Air Force variant mockup inspection took place at McDonnell's St. Louis facility during April 1962. Prior to the delivery of the USAF production aircraft, 29 Navy F-4Bs were borrowed and delivered to MacDill AFB during November 1963 for testing and training.

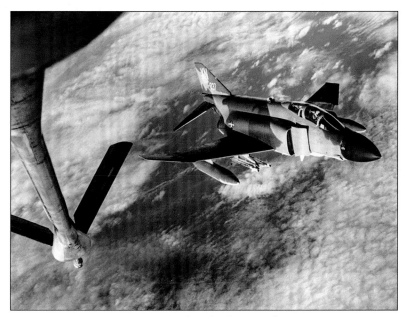

An F-4D prepares to move under the boom of a KC-135. (USAF)

This low-altitude look at a typical North Vietnamese SA-2A Guideline SAM site was captured by an unmanned Ryan BQM-34L Buffalo Hunter UAV. (USAF)

Side-view of the reconnaissance USAF RF-4C shows the distinct nose shape carrying the side-oblique and forward-looking cameras. (Author Photo/Illustration)

the United States fighting with one hand behind its back. This was not rocket science, but evidently beyond the Johnson administration's[31] realm of comprehension.

Early on, the Pentagon had drawn up a list of priority targets. Much could have been done to slow North Vietnamese aggression in the beginning. The North had no MiGs, no SAMs, and limited AAA. But the U.S. administration decided to wait until it became a fiery trap for our pilots.[32] As Thud Driver Col. Jack Broughton described, "It was utterly frustrating to see the MiGs, like sitting ducks in take-off position on the end of the runway, and not be allowed to splash them. As we passed them heading south, they would take off to the north and turn onto our tails.[33] VPAF airfields were off limits to air-strikes, but it was OK for the Viet Cong to attack our air bases in South Vietnam that killed people and destroyed aircraft."

The F-4 in Combat

At the start of Southeast Asia hostilities, there was the opportunity to quickly accomplish the goal of hitting North Vietnam's strategic targets in the Hanoi and Haiphong areas. This would have dramatically changed the course of the war or, most likely, short-ened it considerably. Instead, the Johnson administration waited until North Vietnam received massive Soviet and Chinese military equipment shipments through Haiphong, which was off limits to U.S. air strikes.[34]

Beginning in early 1965, USAF F-4 Phantom IIs began support-ing the F-105s during bombing missions in Vietnam and gradually replaced them in the fighter/bomber role. Entering aerial combat in Vietnam, the F-4 Phantom soon encountered new difficulties. On 3 April 1965, rather obsolete VPAF MiG-17Fs took a few chunks out of a Navy F-8E Crusader in an air-to-air encounter and later downed two USAF F-105Ds. Early dogfights with MiG-17Fs demonstrated that the F-4's tactical advantage was coming in high with power and acceleration. As experienced with the F-105s, getting into a tight-turning aerial fight was a no-go. The F-4's speed would bleed

An F-4D Phantom II mixes it up with two VPAF MiG-17Fs over North Vietnam. Although not always operating with the proper equipment, the skill of USAF and U.S. Navy airmen proved worthy, as they shot down a total of 137 MiGs, of which 61 were MiG-17Fs. (Author Photo/Illustration)

A Soviet-built VPAF Mikoyan-Gurevich MiG-17F Fresco in after-burner. The subsonic MiG-17F dated from the mid-1950s, but proved effective during low-altitude tight-turning aerial engage-ments. The MiG-17F was armed with internal nose-mounted 23/37mm cannons and could also carry AA-2 Atoll air-to-air missiles. VPAF pilots preferred sticking with cannons only. (Author Photo/Illustration)

With the USAF Thunderbirds F-4Es in the background, a General Electric (later General Dynamics) M61A-1 Vulcan 20mm rotary cannon is displayed at a Homestead AFB open house during November 1972. The Vulcan weighed 248 pounds, and its fire rate was 6,000 rounds per minute with a muzzle velocity of 3,450 feet per second. (Author)

The F-4E models were first delivered in 1967 with the internally mounted Vulcan M61A-1 20mm cannon. This is an F-4E from the 31st TFW at Homestead AFB in May 1975. The E model also carried the updated solid-state AN/APQ-120 radar. At the time the author inquired about the unusual lime green that was added to the standard TAC camouflage, but no one had an explanation. (Author)

off quickly, and the aircraft would lose energy, with handling becoming sluggish. In addition, air-to-air missiles didn't function well in a high-G environment, having a low percentage of successful hits.

The original decision to completely depend on air-to-air missiles, which were still maturing, was questionable at best. Air Force and Navy airmen soon found that missile malfunctions and a lack of guns was costing both U.S. aircraft and potential kills. Despite this, there were some successes using air-to-air missiles. Navy F-4B Phantoms from VF-21 scored the first aerial victories on 17 June 1965 with the downing of two MiG-17Fs. The following July, USAF F-4Cs from the 45th TFS also shot down two MiG-17Fs. Air Force Phantoms had dual controls, with qualified pilots occupying the rear seat. The position was later occupied by weapon-systems operators (WSOs), affectionately known as "Wizzos."

A Navy F-4J (BuNo. 154785af) on a test flight in late 1967. Although in Navy markings, this J variant Phantom II would go into service with the U.S. Marines. (U.S. Navy)

Have Gun, Will Travel

According to Ralph Wetterhahn, "The C variant had a number of design problems, and one of the biggest was lack of a gun.[35] The rules of engagement over Vietnam required that an adversary be identified visually before a missile could be fired at it. Both the MiG-17F and MiG-21 had small visual profiles, and to make the positive ID, shooters had to get close. Unfortunately, many times it was too close for the AIM-7 radar-guided and AIM-9B heat-seeking missiles to lock-on."[36] Initially, a temporary solution was the installation of the SUU-16/A gun pod containing the M61A1 20mm cannon on a centerline hardpoint; up to three gun pods could be carried for

CAS. This proved effective in the ground-attack role, but degraded the high performance needed for air-to-air combat. A second problem was that the C variant did not have a lead-computing gun sight and the pod-mounted M61A1 did not have tracer shells[37] for correcting aim during aerial engagements. Then, in May 1967, the McDonnell Douglas[38] F-4D was delivered. The D model introduced a lead-computing optical sight for use with the gun pod. In addition, the normal ammunition load now included tracers.[39]

In 1962 there had been another opportunity to correct the gun situation, when the Air Force tested the F-4B and then procured the Phantom (F-110A, later F-4C). It didn't happen, even though the Air Force mission did not encompass fleet defense and would involve a much larger scope. Even with Secretary McNamara's so-called defense experts, known as "the Whiz Kids," hard at work monitoring

During 1972, a Royal Navy FG.1 (F-4K) of No. 892 Squadron aboard HMS Ark Royal hits the afterburners prior to a catapult launch. The F-4Ks delivered to the UK were F-4Js modified to accommodate the British Rolls-Royce Spey turbojets and associated avionics. (National Museum of Naval Aviation)

After an early morning engine start, a USMC F-4J of VMFA-312 at NAS Key West, Florida, prepares to taxi during January 1976. (Author)

The USMC F-4J's two-seat arrangement for the pilot and radar-intercept officer (RIO) at NAS Key West. (Author)

the Pentagon, no one brought up the internal gun issue. It wasn't until 1968, some eight years after entering service, that the F-4E model was introduced with an internal nose-mounted Vulcan M61A1 20mm rotary cannon, which solved that problem. The E[40] model's 20mm rotary cannon operated in conjunction with the new AN/APQ-120 fire-control system. In conclusion, it was the skill of USAF and U.S. Navy airmen that proved worthy, as they eventually shot down a total of 137 MiGs, of which 61 were MiG-17Fs.

The Wolfpack

Col. Robin Olds, commander of the 8th TFW Wolfpack, and Capt. John Stone planned and organized the unique and most-successful MiG hunting expedition of the Vietnam War, Operation Bolo. The mission goal was to lure MiG-21s up to engage in what the enemy perceived as a large contingent of bomb-laden F-105Ds. Only this time the more agile F-4Cs, armed with air-to-air missiles, would be waiting. The Wolfpack F-4Cs would also be equipped with QRC-160 pods that emanated signals that the F-105Ds would normally emit. In addition, the cloaking F-4Cs would fly the exact same ingress profile as the F-105s.

The Soviet-built Mikoyan-Gurevich MiG-21PF Fishbed was capable of Mach 2. Introduced in early 1966, the VPAF flew MiG-21s in bare metal, and some were later camouflaged to mask their planform profile against the ground terrain. The MiG-21PF was equipped with both AA-2 Atoll missiles and a twin-barrel 23mm GSh-23 cannon. (Author Photo/Illustration)

During engine shutdown, a ground crewman checks an F-4E from the 31st TFW at Homestead AFB. Note that the tail hook is extended. (Author)

U.S. Navy F-4N Phantom IIs of VF-101KW greet a winter morning during January 1976 at NAS Key West. (Author)

On the morning of 2 January 1967, a contingent of more than 100 aircraft—also including F-105F/G Wild Weasels, F-104 Starfighters, an EC-121 Warning Star, EB-66 Destroyer ECM aircraft, and special eavesdropping Silver Dawn C-130B-IIs—accompanied the F-4C attack group. The VPAF MiG-21s fell for the ploy and headed into the trap. During the mission Col. Olds and his Wolfpack managed to shoot down seven MiG-21s with zero U.S. losses. As a result, the VPAF disappeared for a month or so to regroup and strategize.

Turning a New Strategy Leaf—Too Late

President Richard M. Nixon developed and initiated a strategy to bring North Vietnam to the bargaining table through the proper use of military force. This included bomb-for-effect missions and the mining of Haiphong Harbor. Positive results ensued and the Paris Peace Talks commenced. President Nixon's policy would have deterred any takeover of South Vietnam. However, as the peace process continued, the Watergate scandal materialized, forcing Nixon to resign in August 1974. Unfortunately for the United States, the war was now overshadowed as a top priority. Many members of Congress were so enthralled with a chance to politically attack President Nixon, they ignored the fact that the United States had to continue supporting South Vietnam in order to enforce the Paris Accords peace agreement.

Congress cut funding for the war and President Gerald R. Ford was powerless to support our military. The United States had to quickly evacuate friendlies from South Vietnam as North Vietnam's leaders took advantage and fully invaded the South. It was a sad moment in history considering all the sacrifices in cost and human lives the United States, its allies, and South Vietnamese soldiers had

An F-4G Wild Weasel 5 from the 37th TFW goes vertical in early 1982. The Air Force publicity photo represents the full complement of armament, including the AGM-45C Shrike and Standard ARM AGM-78 on the right wing and the AGM-65A Maverick and AGM-88A HARM on the left wing. (USAF)

During the Proud Phantom exercise in 1980, an Egyptian Air Force F-4E (t/n 60366) flies with a USAF F-4E from the 347th TFW. The author was on assignment at Homestead AFB in 1978, and the escort asked me not to photograph a particular flightline of F-4Es from the 31st TFW, which were marked in standard camouflage. Following orders, I continued photographing other aircraft. Later, I learned that a first batch of 18 F-4Es were delivered to Egypt under the Peace Pharaoh program in October 1979. Those F-4Es were originally from the 31st TFW and repainted in Egyptian Air Force markings. (USAF)

Two F-4Es sport new two-tone wraparound gray camouflage. (USAF)

Two JASDF Mitsubishi-built F-4EJ Phantom IIs take off from Hyakuri Air Base, No. 302 Squadron. Mitsubishi Heavy Industries built the first 14 Phantom IIs from McDonnell-supplied kits, and assembled an additional 125 F-4EJs in Japan under license. (JASDF)

An F-4E taxiing during November 1983. This E model was stationed at the AFFTC at Edwards AFB. (Author)

made. The Communist takeover cost thousands of additional lives and severely affected millions of others. In the end, it was the U.S. Congress that was responsible.

Outstanding Career

The Phantom II was a remarkable aircraft with a remarkable sustained production run of nearly 5,200 aircraft and a proven combat record that included more than 280 air-combat victories.

It was the first U.S. jet fighter to reach 5,000 units built and was flown by the U.S. Navy, USAF, and USMC. Variants were operated by allies around the world, including Australia, Egypt, Germany, Greece, Iran, Israel, Japan, South Korea, Spain, Turkey, and the United Kingdom's Royal Air Force and Royal Navy. USAF F-4G Wild Weasels also served during various operations in Iraq and flew their last SEAD mission in 1996. The McDonnell Douglas F-4 Phantom emerged as a true military classic that has withstood the test of time.

Two Luftwaffe F-4Fs of Jagdgeschwader 74 (74th Fighter Wing) move away from a USAF KC-135R after receiving fuel. The Luftwaffe operated a total of 113 F-4E that were approximately 3,300 pounds lighter than the standard F-4E. The German fleet was equipped with an updated F/A-18 AN/APQ-65 radar and carried both the Sidewinder and BVR AIM-120 AMRAAM. The F-4E entered service in 1973 and was retired as the Luftwaffe switched over to the Eurofighter on 1 July 2009. (USAF Tech. Sgt. Brad Fallin)

Specifications

Chance-Vought F8U-3 Crusader III—Tactical Fighter/Bomber Prototype
Crew: 1—pilot
Wingspan: 39 ft. 11 in. (11.9 m)
Length: 58 ft. 8 in. (17.9 m)
Height: 16 ft. 4 in. (4.9 m)
Maximum weight: 40,086 lb (18,143 kg)
Combat weight: 30,578 lb (13,607 kg)
Range: 1,755 miles (1,609 km)
Maximum speed: 1,819 mph (1,609km/h)
Cruising speed: 575.3 mph (925.8 km/h)
Service ceiling: 41,800 ft. (12,468 m)
Combat ceiling: 55,000 ft. (16,764 m)
Powerplant: 1 Pratt & Whitney J75-P-6—23,500 lb (104.5 kN) thrust with afterburner
Bomb capacity: Test equipment carried in prototype
Armament: None

McDonnell F4H-1 (F-4B) Phantom II—Tactical Fighter/Bomber Prototype
Crew: 2—pilot, radar-intercept officer (RIO)
Wingspan: 38 ft. 5 in. (11.7 m)
Length: 58 ft. 3 in. (17.7 m)
Height: 16 ft. 3 in. (4.9 m)
Maximum weight: 54,600 lb (24,493 kg)

Maximum range: 2,300 miles (3,218,6 km)
Combat range: 400 miles (643 km)
Maximum speed: 1,485 mph (1,609 km/h)
Service ceiling: 62,000 ft. (18,897 m)
Powerplant: 2 General Electric J79-GE-8A/B/C turbojets—17,000 lb (75.6 kN) thrust each with afterburner
Bomb capacity: 16,000 lb (7,257 kg)
Armament: 4 AIM-7D or AIM-7E Sparrows, 2 AIM-9 Sidewinders

McDonnell Douglas F-4E Phantom II—Tactical Fighter/Bomber
Crew: 2—pilot, RIO
Wingspan: 38 ft. 4 in. (11.7 m)
Length: 62 ft. 9 in. (19 m)
Height: 16 ft. 4 in. (4.9 m)
Maximum weight: 61,651 lb (27,669 kg)
Range: 1,885 miles (1,609 km)
Combat radius: 533 miles (857.7 km)
Maximum speed: 1,485 mph (2,389.8 km/h)
Cruising speed: 595 mph (957.5 km/h)
Service ceiling: 62,250 ft. (18,974 m)
Powerplant: 2 General Electric J79-17—17,900 lb (79.6 kN) thrust with afterburner
Bomb/missile capacity: 16,000 lb (7,257 kg) mix of missiles/bombs/rockets
Armament: 1 General Electric M61 20mm Vulcan rotary cannon

Chapter 7

PURSUIT OF CLOSE AIR SUPPORT
NORTHROP YA-9A VERSUS FAIRCHILD YA-10A

USAF A-10A taxiing in the sunset. (Author Photo/Illustration)

In an era of fast jets the DoD saw the need for a dedicated aircraft that could support troops in the battle arena. Experience garnered from the Vietnam War proved that although the tactical fighters at the time could provide CAS, their high speed and decreased loiter time greatly hindered their effectiveness. The venerable piston-powered Douglas A-1 Skyraider (affectionately referred to as "Spad" or "Sandy"[1]) was the stalwart performer most called upon to support the ground troops. The A-1's slow speed and extended loiter time was key for the pilot to get eyes on the target. These attributes were also ideal for keeping enemy combatants at bay during rescue missions, while rescue helicopters recovered downed pilots in hostile territory. However, all Sandy pilots wished the A-1 had a larger gun.

The concept for a dedicated CAS aircraft began in 1963 when the U.S. Army Close Air Support Board concluded that there was a need for a specialized aircraft[2] that was simple, rugged, tough, reliable, easily maintained, and capable of immediate response and continuous operation in a forward battle area. In congressional testimony before the Pike Committee two years later, the conclusion was that the Air Force had several multipurpose aircraft but no true CAS aircraft. By March 1966, the philosophy of the Air Force began to shift from developing multipurpose aircraft to aircraft designed for a specific mission. Examples were the air superiority F-15, interdiction F-111, and the impending B-1 for strategic bombing.[3]

A-X Start-Up

In September 1966, Air Force Chief of Staff Gen. John McConnell got the ball rolling. He directed that the attack-experimental program move forward with an aircraft possessing better performance than the Douglas A-1 and that would be simpler and less costly than the Vought A-7. The momentum for the program began to spin up, and by January 1969 Sec. of the Army Stanley Resor indicated he

The number-two YA-10A (t/n 11370) prototype. Fairchild was very confident that their unusual design would be an effective CAS aircraft. (Fairchild Republic)

The YA-10A on the tarmac at Edwards with the flight-test evaluation M61 20mm Vulcan cannon mounted in the nose. The GAU-8/A 30mm Avenger was not yet available for the competition, but later would appear much more menacing. (Fairchild Republic)

was lockstep with the Air Force on formulating CAS. The Army, of course, would be the ultimate customer. With this consensus, the CAS program would yield more weight before the U.S. Congress, which held the purse strings.

The following year, Secretary Resor voiced strong support for the USAF CAS program, saying, "The aircraft will provide increased capabilities to the firepower options of the ground commander, and thus the Army supports the development, procurement and deployment of the CAS aircraft."[4] A late 1966 DoD news release described the basic criteria for the CAS aircraft: "Contractors are expected to explore various design concepts for the A-X which would be relatively inexpensive, rugged and highly survivable." Although the concept of a competitive fly-off was not new, a new descriptor for the fly-off concept of doing DoD business was now termed "fly before buy." The general philosophy was to drive down development costs

With Fairchild test pilot Howard "Sam" Nelson at the controls, the YA-10A (t/n 11369) made its first flight at the Edwards Flight Test Center on 10 May 1972. The YA-10A handled very well and all systems were nominal during the first flight. (USAF)

through a step process of actually proving performance and flying qualities with competing prototypes.

On 6 April 1970, Sec. of Defense Melvin Laird approved the A-X program and officially authorized a competition between contractors. After an initial down-selection, two remaining contractors would be chosen to compete their prototypes. In May, the Air Force issued 12 RFPs, and seven contractors responded with their concepts for a specialized low-cost and survivable CAS aircraft. According to plan, seven months later in December 1970, Fairchild Industries and the Northrop Corporation were selected as the final two competitors—both companies would construct two prototypes.

The DoD pricing target for the CAS program was $1.2 million per aircraft, with a price ceiling of $1.4 million in 1970 dollars. This included aircraft avionics and was based on a buy of 600 aircraft.[5, 6] Upon completion of their respective prototypes, Northrop and Fairchild would fly a rigorous flight-test regime. After this phase of extensive contractor testing, the aircraft would be transferred to Air Force Systems Command (AFSC) and TAC. AFSC was responsible for development and delivery of aircraft assets, and TAC pilots would evaluate the A-X competitors.

Birth of the Thunderbolt II

As it entered the A-X competition, the design team of the Fairchild Republic Division of Fairchild Industries reflected on its great history of building combat fighter aircraft. The legacy ranged from the legendary World War II P-47 Thunderbolt to its most recent Mach-2 F-105 Thunderchief. Both aircraft were renowned for their ability to take extensive punishment from enemy fire and return to base. For the team, however, the A-X creation would have to be unique since the CAS mission was quite different. Its new airplane

The YA-10A had a low-mounted wing with hardpoints carrying practice stores. The nose landing gear was built off center to the starboard to provide room for the GAU-8/A 30mm cannon on the longitudinal centerline of the aircraft. For the flight-test program, the YA-10A was equipped with the 20mm Vulcan cannon. (Fairchild Republic)

must be able to take hits, but now fly low and slow. Additionally, a very long loiter time plus rapid turnaround under austere conditions were mandatory. While working with the Air Force requirements, the Fairchild team always kept in mind the additional goal of low cost. A new and distinctive aircraft shape would soon appear from within Republic's Farmingdale, New York, facility.

A Functional Design

The Fairchild A-X, which received the YA-10A designation on 1 March 1970, featured a low-mounted wing with a highly cambered airfoil section. Two high-bypass turbofans were uniquely mounted[7] high on the aft fuselage. The wing configuration would allow for optimum lift at low speed and had distinctive drooped wingtips. Wind-tunnel testing conducted by Fairchild confirmed that this feature further enhanced lift at low speed and virtually eliminated wingtip drag. The YA-10A's wing section also featured unique podded wheel wells, leaving the main gear tires partially exposed when retracted. This low-cost approach avoided having to cut into the wings or fuselage for the main gear positions. Fairchild engineers determined that the engines provided ample thrust to overcome any aerodynamic drag produced by this arrangement.

Outboard of the aft-mounted engines were twin vertical stabilizers on each end of the horizontal stabilizer. The high-mounted engines would avoid possible FOD while operating from unpaved runways, and, during quick forward-airfield turnaround, maintenance and weapons loading could be carried out while the engines were running with minimum hazard. In addition, the location of the vertical tails would aid in blocking the engine's infrared (IR) signature. A third strategy of the engine positioning would also keep the inlets as far away as possible from potentially ingesting the gases emitted from the nose-mounted GAU-8/A 30mm cannon. Fairchild engineers also aimed the exhaust nozzles a few degrees upward to negate the possibility of dust and dirt being kicked up

during taxiing at unprepared forward airstrips. The CAS requirements basically narrowed down the choice of engines to the General Electric TF34 and the AVCO Lycoming YF1-2-LD-100. Fairchild selected the 9,000-pound-thrust TF34, a version of which was already in service on the Navy's Lockheed S-3A Viking.

The YA-10A cockpit position allowed for a 360-degree view for air-to-air defensive and possible offensive maneuvering, 40-degrees from side-to-side and 20-degrees over the nose. Ten ordnance hardpoints were located under the wings, plus an additional single centerline fuselage hardpoint. Two wing inboard hardpoints were also available for optional drop tanks. For protection in the close-in combat environment, the pilot would be surrounded by a 1,200-pound bathtub of titanium armor designed to withstand hits from 23mm projectiles. However, for the prototype flight-test program, the armored structure would be made of aluminum. For quick turnarounds from forward operating bases (FOBs), a refueling access point was located on the left wing sponson. This access point ensured that hot refueling or defueling could be accomplished without interfering with other ordnance loading/unloading activities. For additional safety, the location of the running engines would place them well out of the way.

Thinking in the Box

YA-10A number one (t/n 11369) was rolled out of Final Assembly Building 17 at Fairchild Republic's Farmingdale facility on 22 April 1972. However, it was not the usual rollout with associated fanfare, as there was no ceremony and no viewing crowd on that rainy day. Instead, the YA-10A prototype was in boxes. It had been disassembled, packed and prepared to be transported to Edwards AFB. Fuselage, wings, empennage, and engines were all moved out

The YA-10A prototype number one with conventional iron bombs mounted on wing hardpoints. Flight evaluations included bomb drop accuracy tests, as well as firing the Vulcan 20mm rotary cannon on the Edwards range. (USAF)

The number-one YA-10A (t/n 11369) prototype fitted with dummy AGM-65 Maverick air-to-ground missiles. (USAF)

A preproduction A-10A with dummy AGM-65 Maverick air-to-ground missiles landing on Rogers Dry Lake at Edwards AFB. The aircraft's split aileron/speed brakes are open to slow airspeed during final approach, landing, and rollout. (USAF)

to the tarmac and loaded aboard a C-124 Globemaster II. A large banner was strung above Building 17's main door reading "NEW THUNDER A-X FOR USAF."

Concurrently, Fairchild had fully staffed its operations at the A-10 Flight Test Site at Edwards AFB. Some 70 employees would support YA-10A flight operations during the A-X fly-off competition. Former USAF test pilot Bob Scott was the test-site manager who directed day-to-day efforts of the site's personnel. Integration of the flight-test requirements into the overall A-10 program was the responsibility of Deputy Program Director John Williamson. Other Fairchild team members were Project Engineer Joe Otto, Safety Engineer Carl Bellinger (former Republic test pilot for the P-47, F-84, and XF-91), Crew Chief Dorman Steele, and Flight Data Engineer Mitch Lopatoff.[8]

The team was on hand to accept, reassemble, and prepare the YA-10A for flight. Ground system checks went satisfactorily, as well as slow- and high-speed taxi tests. The Fairchild team was very excited on 10 May 1972 as the YA-10A (t/n 11369) lifted off Runway 22 on its maiden flight. Northrop test pilot Howard "Sam" Nelson took it aloft. The aircraft handled well and it looked as though Fairchild was headed for a great flight-test program. After delivery to Edwards, also via C-124, the second YA-10A (t/n 11370) prototype was reassembled and successfully flown. Over the next two months, Nelson and Jim Martinez accumulated approximately 330 hours on both YA-10A prototypes.

The A-X competition, which featured two distinctive, dissimilar aircraft designs vying for the CAS mission, was perhaps one of the smoothest fly-off programs ever recorded at Edwards AFB. Only one incident occurred when the main landing brakes locked-up on the number-two YA-10A prototype during a landing. The tires blew out, resulting in the aircraft skidding off the runway. Although the main gear collapsed, the YA-10A was repaired within 33 days.

Northrop YA-9A

In previous decades Northrop had been known as the designer of such exotic aircraft as the flying wing, and tailless aircraft became its signature. Most recently, Northrop had designed and built the

The number-one YA-9A prototype on a test sortie over the Edwards AFB range. (Author Photo/Illustration)

successful F-5 Freedom Fighter series. Not only was the F-5 design perfect for the export fighter market, the mass-production experience was very important. However, the CAS mission was quite different, and this time Northrop engineers designed an aircraft to fit an entirely new role, and its shape would fit the mission. Interestingly, with the same requirements as the Fairchild team, Northrop engineers came up with a completely dissimilar design.

Unusual Looking, But Stable

Northrop's CAS prototype received the YA-9A designation on 1 March 1971. The preliminary design and proposal effort was headed by Walt Fellers, manager of Advanced Systems. Dave Deering directed the prototype development. Appearing very unlike Northrop's previous designs, the YA-9A featured a straight shoulder-mounted wing with twin engines mounted on the lower sides of the fuselage. Like the Fairchild aircraft, Northrop's was a single-pilot configuration. The two YA-9A prototypes were constructed of all-metal riveted aluminum alloy, semimonocoque with stressed skin. A honeycomb structure, along with chemically-milled skins, was also incorporated in the airframe.[9]

The forward nose section of the Northrop YA-9A during assembly at the Hawthorn, California, facility. In the operational version, the pilot would be surrounded by a titanium bathtub for protection against ground fire. For the flight-test evaluation, the YA-9A prototype used aluminum. (Northrop Grumman Corporation)

Northrop flight test director Lew Nelson enters the cockpit of the YA-9A. The ground crewman provides excellent scale for the large size of the intake. The YA-9A's wingspan was 5.3 feet wider than the Fairchild YA-10A. (Northrop Grumman Corporation)

Along more than half the wingspan of YA-9A prototype number one (t/n 11367) are large Fowler-type flaps, with associated guide tracks positioned off the wing trailing edge. (Northrop Grumman Corporation)

Under contract with Northrop, AVCO Lycoming would provide the YF1-2-LD-100 turbofan engines, which developed 7,500 pounds of thrust. The YA-9A's engines were mounted low on the fuselage separated by the width of the fuselage for increased survivability. Handling the integration was George Gluyas, Northrop's engine program manager. The main landing gear retracted into the engine nacelles. The wing contained self-sealing fuel tanks that would release foam to prevent fires in the event of projectile hits. In addition, the wings held separated redundant flight-control systems. A Northrop-designed triple-redundant hydraulic system was also incorporated in the YA-9A.

The YA-9A's wingspan was 58 feet, and the wings were equipped with ten hardpoints[10] for mixed ordnance and/or drop tanks. Along more than half the wingspan were trailing-edge Fowler flaps. Additionally, a Northrop-designed[11] feature of large ailerons on the outboard third of the wing were split into upper and lower sections. This dual capability provided both the aileron function and a speed brake. Extremely large lift spoilers on the upper wing trailing edge were designed to quickly kill lift upon landing touchdown, which would be especially effective for short-field operations. The spoilers would automatically deploy at runway touchdown with the thrust below 85 percent.[12]

In the context of the entire airframe, the vertical stabilizer and rudder design were rather large. This arrangement would provide effective directional authority. Mounted on the sizable tail was the horizontal stabilizer with 10-degree dihedral. Aircraft stability would also be further enhanced by a pitch-and-yaw-axis stability augmentor. The oversized rudder worked in conjunction with the Northrop-designed side-force control (SFC) system. Northrop's engineers were well aware of the requirements that low-to-medium speed maneuverability was critical. The SFC would utilize the rudder and asymmetric use of the split aileron speed brakes to activate yawing forces during flight. With this system the pilot does not have to bank the aircraft.[13] Although the pilot had the option of engaging the SFC, this capability during the attack mode eliminates jinking S-turns and yawing the aircraft. Northrop studies concluded that an operational A-9A in a 45-degree pop-up target approach dive could achieve up to twice the tracking accuracy (bombs and/or cannon) with the SFC[14] system.

The large bubble canopy was well placed for greater all-aspect visibility during tight turns and jinking maneuvers. The forward windscreen and canopy would be projectile-resistant up to 20mm. In addition to armor plating for protection of vital aircraft systems, as with the YA-10A design, the YA-9A would also have a titanium armor bathtub surrounding the cockpit to protect the pilot from ground fire up to 23mm. Also like the YA-10A, this area would be constructed of aluminum for the flight-test program.

Northrop's entry for the A-X competition made its first flight on 30 May 1972. Lew Nelson successfully flew the YA-9A for 58 minutes and described the flight as "routine and as planned." A camouflaged USAF A-37 is in the background flying chase. (National Museum of the USAF)

The YA-9A's extremely large lift dumpers on the upper wing trailing edge were designed to quickly kill lift upon landing. For austere short-field operations, the lift dumpers automatically deployed as the landing gear compressed at touchdown with thrust below 85 percent. Just outboard of the lift dumpers was another Northrop-designed feature: large ailerons split into upper and lower sections. This dual capability served both the aileron function and speed brake. (Northrop Grumman Corporation)

Quick Turnaround

In the realm of the CAS mission, minimizing rearming and refueling time was critical. The YA-9A was designed so that all in-field services could be performed at an easy-to-reach ground level. The twin engines were at chest-level, and removal and installation of a new engine was timed-out at less than 60 minutes.[15] The high wing location on the fuselage would allow for smooth access to ten underwing hardpoints for ground and ordnance crews, enabling a quick turnaround.

The Air Force pressed A-X competitors on the importance of cost. There was a feeling that even after this competition, the program would be challenged by those who would offer other alternatives to perform the CAS mission. The advice boiled down to "save money and don't strive for exceeding the performance requirements." Based on this direction from the customer regarding cost control, Northrop proceeded to incorporate as much parts-redundancy as possible, sometimes at the sacrifice of performance. In addition to off-the-shelf hardware, in-house studies concluded that interchangeable left- and right-side components could be used, including the main landing gear, flaps, speed brakes, ailerons, spoilers, and the engines.

YA-9A: Ready for the Competition

Rollout of the YA-9A took place in March 1972 at Northrop's historic Hawthorne, California, facility. Northrop employees were finally able to view the unusual-looking aircraft that had been assembled behind secure walls. Northrop's Hawthorne site was a factory with a formidable history. The classic Northrop flying wings first took to the air from Hawthorne's runway during the late 1940s and were followed by other unique designs. However, the YA-9A would not make its first takeoff from Hawthorne. The aircraft was immediately partially disassembled and prepared for ground transport to Edwards AFB.

With its landing gear in the extended position, the number one YA-9A tests handling characteristics. The large rudder is evident, as well as a Plexiglas window near the tail assembly which housed cameras that recorded stores coming off the hardpoints during weapons drop tests. During the testing each wing hardpoint held double ejection racks for multiple ordnance. This allowed for 18 Mk.82 500-pound bombs to be carried. (National Museum of the USAF)

Onsite at the Edwards test center, Northrop technicians reassembled the YA-9A. After ground-system testing and low/high-speed taxi tests, the YA-9A was ready. Northrop Flight Test Director Lew Nelson took the number-one prototype (t/n 11367) into the air on 30 May 1972. The maiden flight lasted a total of 58 minutes and, as reported by Nelson, all was nominal. During the post-flight debrief, Nelson described the flight as "routine and followed as planned."[16] Northrop test pilots flew both prototypes extensively to prove various handling characteristics and aircraft systems.

On 23 June 1972, Maj. Larry D. Fortner became the first USAF pilot to fly Northrop's YA-9A. By fall 1972, a joint Air Force Test Team of AFSC and TAC pilots took the prototypes through a rigorous

Beware the Avenger

The General Electric (now Martin Marietta Armament Systems) GAU-8/A Avenger[17] 30mm seven-barrel rotary cannon was the designated gun for the A-X program. Both competitors designed their aircraft for this weapon system. This was not a minor task—the GAU-8/A was a massive 20.9-foot-long 679-pound cannon. To prevent recoil problems that could produce yaw, the rotating barrel of the 30mm cannon would occupy the aircraft's longitudinal centerline. In their respective designs, the Northrop YA-9A had its nose wheel gear offcenter to the left, and the Fairchild YA-10A nose landing gear was positioned offcenter to the right. However, the GAU-8/A was still under development and was not available for the fly-off competition. Thus, both prototypes would be equipped with the smaller but well-proven M61A1 20mm Vulcan cannon.

Initially, the GAU-8/A offered an option of firing rates of 2,100 or 4,200 rounds per minute. Later, during the 1980s, it was determined that this dual-rate selection offered no real advantage, and it was eliminated. The gun was set at 3,900 rounds per minute, and the engines' ignition timing was synchronized with the gun trigger to prevent flameouts. The 30mm shell capacity would be 1,174 rounds contained in a linkless ammunition feed system. Spent cartridge cases are not ejected from the aircraft after firing, but are dispatched to a storage drum. The hefty 30mm shells would consist of armor-piercing high-explosive incendiary (HEI) shells (1.6 pounds) and depleted-uranium (DU) shells (.94 pounds).

During July 1974, Fairchild released this photo to show the scale of what the A-10A would be carrying into battle. A full-scale mockup of the General Electric GAU-8/A Avenger 30mm rotary cannon was placed next to a Volkswagen. The bulletproof drum holds the 30mm ammunition and retains the expended shells. General Electric's GAU-8/A won the Air Force contract to arm the A-10 after a three-month shoot-off at Eglin AFB. (Fairchild Republic)

The depleted-uranium shells rely totally on their weight plus kinetic energy to neutralize the target. The average firing range was approximately 4,000 feet, and a one-second burst averaged 50 rounds; the second one-second burst would fire 70 rounds. Eighty percent of the rounds fired from 4,000 feet would hit within a 20-foot radius.[18] Pilots have commented that the gunsight pipper can be right on the target, with no drop in the round's trajectory. With a muzzle velocity of 3,240 feet per second, the 30mm rounds would impact before the second one-second burst is fired. These short trigger presses would eliminate a main battle tank or cut through a concrete building. Tanks could be destroyed at a range of up to 6,000 feet, and thin-skinned targets would be at risk at a range of up to 11,000 feet.

With access doors open, the positioning of the GAU-8/A Avenger 30mm cannon is clearly visible. Additionally, the YA-10A nose-wheel assembly is seen in its off-center starboard position. (Fairchild Republic)

The 30mm round for the GAU-8/A Avenger rotary cannon was 11.5 inches long. The high-explosive incendiary (HEI) round weighed 1.6 pounds, and the depleted uranium (DU) round weighed .92 pounds. (Author)

two-month plan to meet flight-test goals. This included gunnery and bombing scoring on the Edwards Range. Since the GAU-8/A 30mm cannon was not available for the competition, both the YA-9A and YA-10A were equipped with the temporary Vulcan 20mm rotary cannon. It was disappointing that the Northrop YA-9A with its SFC system and the Fairchild YA-10A were not able to perform with the GAU-8/A 30mm cannon.

Fairchild A-X Down-Select

On 18 January 1973, Secretary of the Air Force Verne Orr announced that the Fairchild YA-10A prototype had been selected for full-scale development of the A-X CAS aircraft. The Air Force AFSC/TAC evaluators had compiled 328 hours flying the YA-10A. Fairchild was ecstatic and anxious to show that their unique design would prove its merit as the new USAF CAS aircraft. During a press briefing in Washington, DC, Fairchild Republic vice president Charles Collis remarked, "Experience has proved that there is only one way to perform the CAS mission effectively. And that is to operate under the weather, close-in, and using the human eye to distinguish targets, coupled with a weapon that is [as] accurate and lethal as has ever been installed on any operating aircraft: the 30mm cannon. This is the only way to do the Close Air Support job!"[19]

There was no respite in activity at the A-10 Flight Test Site. The two YA-10A prototypes were prepared for additional testing; new flight tests included stores certification, air-to-air refueling, stall and post-stall spin prevention. Following that, ground tests included escape systems, bird impact, anti-icing, and defogging tests.[20] On 1 August 1974, Deputy Sec. of Defense William P. Clements Jr. approved the overall design and manufacturing planning for the A-10. By late 1974, manufacture of outer wing panels, nose, and cen-

A good side view of the number-one YA-9A prototype depicting a fairly sleek profile. (Author Photo/Illustration)

ter and aft fuselage sections for five RDT&E A-10s were completed at Farmingdale. A company milestone was achieved with the delivery of the first General Electric FT34-GE-100 engine, which had accumulated 2,181 test hours.

No Hawg Heaven for Northrop's YA-9A

After the Air Force announcement, there was disappointment at Northrop. Their unique YA-9A design would not proceed into production. In general, Air Force test pilot reports were favorable regarding the YA-9A during a total of 307 flight hours. Many references were made to slightly better handling than the competing Fairchild YA-10A. Additionally, the overall conclusion was that the YA-9A was an excellent aircraft and quite capable of performing the CAS mission. Northrop was aware of Fairchild ending production of the F-105, and this factor had entered into the competition decision process. Northrop's prediction of being able to produce its CAS aircraft for a unit flyaway price of $1.4 million (1970 dollars) was confirmed. Although it did not receive the production contract,

A YA-9A on a test flight; note the large tail assembly and horizontal stabilizer with 10-degree dihedral. This arrangement provided effective directional authority, and aircraft stability would be further enhanced by a pitch-and-yaw-axis stability augmentor. The oversized rudder worked in conjunction with the Northrop-designed side-force control (SFC) system. (National Museum of the USAF)

Functionally designed for the CAS mission, the Northrop YA-9A cruises above the clouds. The Plexiglas camera-housing window on the forward part of the tail is clearly visible. (Photo of Aircraft, USAF; Photo of Background, Author)

During July 1976, the two Northrop YA-9A prototypes (t/n 11367 and 11368) are seen resting in the desert sun in outdoor storage at NASA Dryden FRC. (Author)

Northrop officials were confident that they had verified their strategy of building an aircraft that met the specifications and was delivered on budget.[21]

YA-9A Survivors

In mid-1973, the two prototypes were turned over to NASA Dryden Flight Research Center (DFRC). The four AVCO Lycoming YF1-2-LD-100 engines were removed from both YA-9As and installed on a C-8 Buffalo that was used on the NASA/Boeing Quiet Short-Haul Research Aircraft program. The YA-9A airframes were placed in outdoor storage at NASA DFRC. During the ensuing five or six years, it

A conceptual operational USAF/Northrop A-9A carrying four 500-pound GBU-12 laser-guided bombs. Note the A-9A with the GAU-8/A Avenger 30mm cannon and the Warthog mouth and eye painted on the nose. Unfortunately, during the fly-off the GAU-8/A was not available. (Author Photo/Illustration)

was fortunate that both YA-9As were not destroyed. The number-one prototype YA-9A (t/n 11367) is awaiting restoration at the AFFTC Museum at Edwards AFB, and the second YA-9A (t/n 11368) is on display at the March Field Air Museum at March ARB in Riverside, California.[22]

Congressional Meddling: Not Out of the Woods Yet

Despite being chosen to develop the YA-10A into the new CAS aircraft, Fairchild learned that the SASC and HASC were going to mandate another competition. This would be against the LTV (Ling-Temco-Vought) A-7D Corsair II already in the inventory. Stung by the Vietnam War experience, Congress was suddenly awakened and anxious to become more involved with DoD procurement. With a magnifying glass on the DoD budget, the focus was primarily on the cost of new weapon systems. The Congress-directed evaluation would determine which most cost-effective aircraft could better perform the CAS mission. This was especially frustrating for the Air Force, since a concerted effort had already been instituted to keep costs under control within every aspect of the CAS program.

Until the new competition was completed, Congress withheld $30 million of A-10A long-lead items and added money for the procurement of an additional 24 A-7Ds to keep LTV's line open. This basically delayed introduction of the A-10A in the Air Force inventory. Even though a prototype YA-10A would be flying against a proven operational ground-attack A-7D, the fly-off commenced

A conceptual USAF/Northrop A-9A pulls up sharply after hitting targets on the test range. The Northrop SFC system would have increased strafing and conventional bomb drop accuracy. (Author Photo/Illustration)

Two conceptual USAF A-9A CAS aircraft with PGMs and drop tanks to increase ferry range. The GAU-8/A 30mm cannon and AN/AAS-35V Pave Penny laser-spot tracker pod look like a good fit on the A-9A. (Author Photo/Illustration)

A-10A Enters Service

During the height of the Cold War, TAC's first priority was to get the A-10 in a position to counter any possible Soviet/Warsaw Pact aggression in Europe because the A-10 was capable of defeating Soviet T-62 main battle tanks. Events began to accelerate quickly to meet that deployment goal. As the two YA-10As continued testing at Edwards AFB, concurrently on 31 July 1974, $39 million for the first 52 A-10s was authorized. The first production A-10 (s/n 75-00258) flew on 21 October 1975, and deliveries to the 333rd Tactical Fighter Training Squadron at Davis-Monthan AFB were scheduled

in April 1974. Data obtained demonstrated once again that the A-10 was the ideal platform to perform the CAS mission. The A-7D needed to operate from paved runways and did not have the long loiter time of the YA-10A. LTV even later offered a lengthened A-7D fuselage to carry the GAU-8/A cannon, but it still would not be able to carry as much ammunition as the A-10. Basically, an expensive fly-off was held that resulted in data that Air Force CAS program planners already knew. During July 1974, Clements stated in congressional testimony, "Based upon my review of the flight evaluation, I can certify that the A-10 was the winner of this comparative flight evaluation."[23]

for April 1976. By February 1976, Fairchild had increased production to 15 aircraft per month.

On 1 July 1977,[24] the first operational squadron (356th TFS) was established at Myrtle Beach AFB and spooling up to combat readiness took place in a remarkably short three months.[25] For weapons

Two conceptual USAF A-9A CAS aircraft with drop tanks bank toward the mountains of Southern California. Note the false canopy paint on the underside of the cockpit area that was designed to confuse enemy aircraft. (Author Photo/Illustration)

A USAF A-10A exhibiting its original aesthetic beauty high above the clouds. (Author Photo/Illustration)

A-X Program Milestones

- 7 May 1970: RFPs issued to 12 companies for competitive prototype development phase of the CAS aircraft.
- 10 August 1970: Proposals submitted by Boeing, Cessna, Fairchild, General Dynamics, Lockheed, and Northrop for development of A-X dedicated CAS aircraft.
- 18 December 1970: Fairchild and Northrop selected to participate in a competitive prototype development phase for CAS.
- 1 March 1970: Designations assigned to prototypes—Northrop YA-9A and Fairchild YA-10A.
- 10 May 1972: Fairchild YA-10A prototype first flight at Edwards AFB.
- 30 May 1972: Northrop YA-9A prototype first flight at Edwards AFB.
- 10 October 1972: USAF flight evaluation fly-off begins at Edwards AFB.
- 9 December 1972: Flight evaluation of both competing A-X prototypes completed at Edwards AFB. Combined aircraft flight time 328.1 hours.
- 18 January 1973: Fairchild selected by the Air Force to proceed with full-scale development of the A-10A.
- 1 March 1973: Air Force awards Fairchild $159.2 million cost-plus-incentive-fee contract to continue prototype testing and develop and build 10 preproduction aircraft. General Electric awarded $27.6 million contract to develop and deliver 32 TF34 engines.
- 22 August 1973: General Electric selected to produce the GAU-8/A 30mm gun system. A three-year contract for $26.6 million is awarded for development.
- 26 February 1974: Number-one YA-10A prototype first in-flight firing tests of GAU-8/A.
- 31 July 1974: DoD releases $39 million to proceed with initial production of 52 A-10As.
- 18 September 1974: First launch tests of carriage/compatibility of unguided AGM-65A Maverick air-to-ground missiles completed at Edwards AFB.
- 14 February 1975: YA-10A prototypes log 1,000th flight hour since first flight on 10 May 1972.
- 13 November 1975: A-10A successfully demonstrates GAU-8/A 30mm lethality against tank targets at Nellis AFB.
- 10 February 1976: Deputy Secretary of Defense authorizes Air Force to proceed from initial production rate to A-10A rate production of 15 aircraft per month.
- April 1976: 333rd Tactical Fighter Training Squadron at Davis-Monthan AFB receives A-10As.
- September 1976: YA-10A (s/n 73-1669), the last preproduction aircraft, deployed to Homestead AFB for tropical high-humidity testing of the GAU-8/A.

A Soviet Sukhoi Su-25K, NATO code name Frogfoot-A. Developed after, but somewhat parallel, to the U.S. A-X program, the Su-25 made its first flight on 22 February 1975. Numerous reports have noted that the configuration is similar to the Northrop YA-9A. Although the engines are located on the fuselage, the Su-25 had a wing swept 10 degrees as opposed to the YA-9A straight wing. The YA-9A was a much larger aircraft, at almost twice the weight and payload. The Su-25's twin-barrel 30mm cannon has a capacity of only 220 rounds. (Author Photo/Illustration)

A Sukhoi Su-25UB Frogfoot-B two-seat training version taxis after a flight demonstration at the June 1989 Paris Air Show. The two-seat variant can be used in combat. Approximately 1,024 Su-25s were produced for the Soviet Air Force, and Russian Air Force. Hundreds were exported to more than a dozen countries, and the type remains in service today. (Author)

- 9 March 1977: First A-10A arrives at Myrtle Beach AFB, South Carolina, for maintenance training.
- 14 June thru 8 July 1977: PACAF tour of three A-10As from Davis-Monthan AFB.
- 1 July 1977: First operational squadron of A-10As activated at Davis-Monthan AFB.
- 15 October 1977: IOC achieved; the 356th TFS at Myrtle Beach AFB becomes first combat ready A-10A squadron three months ahead of program plan.
- December 1977: First GAU-8/A 30mm ammunition loading system (ALS) delivered to Myrtle Beach AFB.

- 3 January thru 23 February 1978: Four A-10As deploy from Nellis AFB to Ramstein AB, West Germany, for Maverick infrared-seeker testing under operation Coronet Jay.
- January 1978: YA-10A (s/n 73-1669) deployed to Eielson AFB for cold-weather testing.
- 29 March 1978: A-10A (s/n 77-0177) is first production aircraft to fly with the ACES II high-technology ejection seat.
- 3 April 1978: 100th A-10A delivered to TAC at Fairchild's Hagerstown, Maryland, facility. A-10A officially named the Thunderbolt II.

On a gloomy late afternoon in September 1976, the last preproduction YA-10A (s/n 73-1669) rests on the tarmac at Homestead AFB. The aircraft was deployed there for tropical high-humidity testing of the GAU-8/A. (Author)

A-10A (t/n 31665) at Edwards AFB in April 1980. (Author)

A dramatic wide-angle view of the GAU-8/A Avenger on A-10A (t//n 31665) shows the gas residue on the aircraft paint and one of the gas shields that was tested to divert the gases away from the engine intakes. All shields, including the Battelle Laboratory version, suffered from vibration problems. (Author)

training, the 66th Fighter Weapons Squadron was established at Nellis AFB. After a series of training operations it became apparent that an inertial navigation system and radar altimeter would be needed for A-10 operations in Europe. The European climate of persistent clouds, rain, and haze would present problems during high-speed low-altitude sorties. Although not without a fight, funding was eventually allocated to add the systems to the A-10 fleet.

Operating with the USAFE over Germany, two Phantom II variants accompany an A-10A Thunderbolt II in vintage European One camouflage. An F-4G Wild Weasel from the 81st TFS, 52nd TFW, is in the foreground, and an RF-4C from the 1st TRW flies above. (USAF)

Expelled gases from the GAU-8/A Avenger cannon envelop an A-10A during a strafing run. The average firing range was approximately 4,000 feet, and 80 percent of the rounds fired from 4,000 feet hit within a 20-foot radius. (USAF)

Even though the official name "Thunderbolt II" was established by the Air Force in April 1978, this proper-sounding name was receiving a second look as the aircraft was seen at more bases during demonstrations. Based on the ungainly appearance of the A-10, pilots and aircrews soon came up with "Warthog"—with affection, of course. It stuck and soon evolved into the "Hog" or "Hawg." Interestingly, many of the Republic employees who designed and built the A-10 Thunderbolt II began their careers designing and building the original P-47 Thunderbolt.

In total, 715 airplanes were produced, the last being delivered in 1984. Constant upgrades—including a wing replacement program and avionics and software upgrades—have kept the A-10 up to date. In fact, the upgrades were extensive enough to have the jet's designation change from A-10A to A-10C. On 20 January 2005, the first upgraded A-10C was flown by the 40th Flight Test Squadron at Eglin AFB. As of mid-2015, there were about 340 Warthogs in the inventory.

Who Let the Hawgs Out

After its initial tank-busting assignment to counter Soviet and Warsaw Pact armor across Europe during the Cold War, every time the international scenario changed the A-10 was there and ready. In January 1991, the A-10 was called to duty during Operation Desert Storm. The objective of the U.S.-led coalition forces of ground and air power was to boot Saddam Hussein's Iraqi army out of Kuwait. Operating with many aircraft types, A-10s flew 8,100 sorties with a mission-capability rate of 95.7 percent. Using both the GAU-8/A cannon, AGM-65 Mavericks, and PGMs, the Warthogs took out 987 Iraqi tanks, 926 artillery pieces, 501 armored personnel carriers, and approximately 1,106 trucks.

A standard A-10A was modified to create the only two-seat YA-10B. The purpose was to determine pilot workload for Single-Seat Night Attack (SSNA) missions. Aircraft (t/n 31664) was equipped with TFR, a wide field-of-view HUD, and FLIR and IR imaging for the AGM-65 Maverick missile laser designator. This was in addition to the standard GAU-8/A 30mm cannon. (USAF)

An A-10 Warthog pulling up hard after a strafing run. (Author)

One for the Log Book

During the Cold War, the A-10 would be critical in providing close air support to protect the East-West border from the Baltic to the Alps. Initial A-10A deployment took place in January 1979 to RAF Brentwaters for training to eventually support British and West German forces. Combat crews from the Air Force 81st Tactical Fighter Wing were gathering experience and assimilating the A-10A. Training missions were also carried out in support of the U.S. 7th Army in Southern Germany. This involved A-10As coordinating with Army AH-1S Cobra gunship helicopters to support ground troops. All aspects of the training were going smoothly except on the gunnery range. The standard RAF targets were supported by telephone-pole-sized logs. Through the years they sustained hits with standard 20mm practice round hits from aircraft. However, the targets and supporting logs were no match for the GAU-8/A; the 30mm practice shells had so much kinetic energy that a single shell was snapping the logs in half or uprooting them, along with destroying the target. The rapid fire rate placed so many rounds on the target area that it was impossible for the A-10 pilots to avoid the supports. At the time the Air Force was working with the RAF to find stronger target supports that could withstand the 30mm projectiles.[26]

In 1994, A-10s participated in the U.S./NATO operation in Bosnia-Herzegovina to counter Bosnian Serb aggression. In the skies over and near Kosovo, the A-10 was an effective CAS aircraft as well as an Airborne Forward Air Controller (AFAC), leading in strike packages of U.S. and NATO aircraft. The A-10 not only guided the ground attacks, it delivered its own heavy weapons. Then in 2002, the CAS attributes of the A-10 were once again called upon in Iraq and Afghanistan to battle the Taliban terrorist organization.

The A-10's Legacy Continues

It is certainly true that we have other assets performing the CAS role, including the F-16, F-15E, and B-1B. The F-16 and F-15E can deliver PGMs from a standoff position, as well as strafe. In many combat scenarios, the JTACs release the F-16s and F-15Es and request that the B-1B remain on station because of its massive payload and extended loiter time. Aircraft performing CAS usually coordinate with the A-10s, which are able to get eyes-on-the-target close to avoid hitting friendlies or innocent civilians. This is of primary concern because of terrorist groups' use of civilians as shields.

Today, the A-10 should be embraced for its systems modernization and its execution of the CAS mission in a variety of scenarios from the Cold War, countering the Soviet Union and the Warsaw Pact, to Iraq, Bosnia, and Afghanistan. In its latest task against asymmetric terrorist warfare, the A-10 has adapted and served. In fact, the A-10 was the perfect solution to counter the ISIS (Islamic State of Iraq and Syria) terrorist group, which emerged in 2014.[27] After initial battlefield successes, ISIS abandoned their dispersal methods and traveled during daylight on open roads in a long line of captured vehicles, ideal targets. Yet, U.S. air assets were held back from conducting airstrikes. This conformed to the Obama

A close-up of the only YA-10B in outdoor storage at Edwards AFB North Base in October 1988. During trials, a qualified A-10 pilot rode in the backseat to monitor pilot workload during night missions, which at times dropped down to an altitude of 200 feet. The Single-Seat Night Attack (SSNA) program ended in December 1983. (Author)

A USAF A-10C Warthog painted in standard tactical gray camouflage in a 90-degree bank demonstrating its narrow turning radius and maneuverability. Several hardpoints are visible, which can be added or removed; the full complement is 11 hardpoints. (Author)

An A-10 from the 188th TFW Arkansas ANG unleashes an AGM-65D Maverick air-to-ground missile. The A-10 had to fly straight for several seconds to get a lock on the target, then turn or begin jinking, as the Maverick was a fire and forget weapon. (USAF)

Two A-10As from the 355th Fighter Wing at Davis-Monthan AFB, Arizona, during a routine training mission. (Author Photo/Illustration)

A visiting A-10A from the 355th Fighter Wing David-Monthan AFB takes off from Nellis AFB, Nevada. (Author)

An A-10C taxiing at Edwards AFB. The first upgraded A-10C variant was test flown on 20 January 2005 by the 40th Flight Test Squadron at Eglin AFB. A-10Cs could be armed with JDAM. (Author)

administration's[28] foreign policy of remaining behind the power curve in the Middle East. By the time airpower was deployed, the majority of ISIS members had melded back into the innocent civilian population. Once approval for U.S. and coalition airstrikes was granted in late 2014, the A-10s were performing 11 percent of the missions. Now the task of defeating ISIS is much more difficult.

Hawgs and Predators

It seems that old Hawgs can learn new tricks. The unmanned General Atomics MQ-1 Predator UAV is primarily known for conducting prolonged surveillance and locating enemy combatants. Upon receiving clearance, the Predator can launch AGM-114 Hellfire missiles at the target. Often going unreported was the coordination of manned aircraft with the UAVs: the manned aircraft being the A-10 Warthog. These unique missions took place during Operation Enduring Freedom (OEF) in Afghanistan in combat actions against the Taliban. During a 2006 mission, A-10s operating in the arena were able to successfully integrate their updated systems with the UAVs. This brought interoperability of the best attributes of both aerial systems.

Former A-10 pilot Gary Wetzel pointed this out in his 2013 book, *A-10 Thunderbolt II Units of Operation Enduring Freedom*. With a superior sensor to the A-10's targeting pod (TGP), the Predator's ability to find and track targets permitted a successful engagement on numerous occasions. One mission flown by Lt. Col. Brian Borgen illustrated the growing ability of the two platforms to collaborate in OEF. A single sniper had been harassing U.S. ground troops in

An A-10 from 355th EFS takes on fuel from a KC-135R tanker as the wingman waits in the foreground. (USAF)

Afghanistan for several days. His firing position was within a civilian building and very difficult to isolate. The MQ-1 Predator assisted friendlies in locating the sniper's position. The sniper was forced into the open, and the A-10s received targeting data from the Predator on a single individual hiding in a field. In this particular case the A-10 pilot could not see the sniper and asked the Predator to lase the target with a laser designator. The A-10's An/AAQ-28 Litening II TGP was then engaged to follow the laser. Borgen received Joint Tactical Air Controllers (JTAC) clearance to fire and strafed the area with the 30mm cannon—without physically seeing the target. Borgen later remarked, "Taking out a solitary figure running across an open field in an A-10 was something we could never have done without the targeting pod, and its laser capability and integrating with the Predator. Although eradication of a single sniper was somewhat anti-climactic when compared to taking out a whole group of bad guys, it clearly illustrated the pinpoint accuracy of the technology that had been added to what was a 30-year-old airplane."[29]

Retiring the A-10: A Rocky Start

Rumors had persisted for many years regarding the retirement of the A-10 fleet, but the requirement for the A-10's CAS capabilities kept reappearing. However, with severe self-imposed budget cuts, known as sequestration, in force something had to give. During a 24 February 2014 Pentagon press conference, Secretary of Defense Chuck Hagel dropped a PGM on the A-10. Hagel began with the upside rationale. "For the Air Force, an emphasis on capability over capacity

A precision lineup of A-10Cs from Air Force Reserve Command 442nd Fighter Wing on the tarmac at Tallil AB, Iraq. (USAF)

Former Warthog Driver and Lawmaker Strafes A-10 Retirement Discussion

Rep. Martha McSally (R-AZ) is a retired Air Force colonel with 325 combat hours in the A-10 in Iraq and Afghanistan. Col. McSally also commanded an A-10 squadron. On 29 January 2015, she sent a letter to President Obama and Secretary of Defense Chuck Hagel urging them not to retire the A-10 in their fiscal 2016 budget request. The Air Force had attempted to retire the jet last year, but Congress blocked the move.

McSally wrote, "From my experience as an A-10 pilot and squadron commander, I know firsthand the unique capabilities of the A-10 in close air support, forward air control-airborne, and combat search and rescue missions. The Warthog is anything but a 'single mission aircraft' and there is simply no other asset that can match its lethality, loiter time, and survivability. The decision to retire it is reckless and will put American lives at risk."

The Air Force said it would save $3.5 billion over five years by phasing out the A-10. The move would free up money and personnel to help bed down the F-35 over that time span. The A-10 was originally expected to stay in the Air Force until at least 2028 following new wings and other lifespan-extension projects, and was recently deployed to the Middle East to fight the Islamic State terrorist group.

McSally continued, "Other Air Force assets have been engaged in operations against ISIS since August, but the Air Force did not start deploying the A-10 until November. That the A-10 was used in 11 percent of all operations in just three months signals the Air Force is frequently using the aircraft against the group. In fact, recent reports stated that an A-10 mission carried out airstrikes that killed and wounded dozens of ISIS components near Mosul. Iraqi News went so far as to note that 'the aircraft sparked panic in the ranks of ISIS.'[32]

An A-10A from the 81st Fighter Squadron based at Spangdahlem AB flies the skies above Germany. The A-10A has an ordnance load of AGM-56D Mavericks, Snakeye bombs, LAU-131/A WP rocket pod, AIM-9 Sidewinders, and an ALQ-131 ECM jamming pod. (USAF)

Approaching at a depressed angle of 20 degrees, an A-10C begins a strafing run with its GAU-8/A Avenger. The new, larger antenna just aft of the cockpit indicates installation of one of the recent upgrade programs, the beyond-line-of-sight Airborne Radio Communications-210 system for satellite communication. (Author)

Continuous Upgrades

Since 2004, the A-10 has undergone continuous improvements to its airframe and systems, including the ongoing re-wing program. At the time of Secretary Hagel's 24 February 2014 press conference, the Boeing Company was in the middle of executing a $2 billion replacement wing set contract awarded in 2007. Boeing is scheduled to re-wing 242 A-10s by 2018. It was during July 2006 as the re-wing program was getting underway that Air Force Chief of Staff Gen. T. Michael Moseley stated the service will completely re-wing those A-10s needing the fix, which ACC reported as 210 aircraft. The modification will involve structural refurbishing; USAF will not just re-skin them. As a result of the "Hog Up" program, the A-10 "now will be a significantly different airplane than it was before," Moseley asserted.[33]

Additional A-10 Upgrade Programs
- February 2004 Lockheed Martin Systems Integration (LMSI) contract for the integration of the Sniper XR targeting pod. Included FLIR and CCD-TV laser spot tracker.
- A-10C precision Engagement Upgrade Program—JDAM and WCMD extend service life to 2028. Includes LMSI multifunction cockpit displays ("glass cockpit") contract. Helmet-mounted sighting system integrated with Sniper XR or the An/AAQ-28 Litening II TGP. A-10C pilots also equipped with night-vision goggles.
- Boeing awarded two $4.2 million contracts for A-10 modernization of 283 aircraft under Thunderbolt Life-Cycle Program Support (TLPS). Includes Aircraft Structural Integrity Program (ASIP) and avionics architecture to increase data capacity. Includes the Situational Awareness Data Link (SADL).
- First A-10C flew in January 2005, and the C variant achieved IOC in August 2007.
- The A-10C was operating in the Iraqi theater of operations by September 2007. 100 A-10As had been completed to the A-10C upgraded configuration by January 2008. The upgraded A-10C can perform the CAS mission, Forward Air Control (FAC), and Combat Search and Rescue (CSR) missions.
- 2014: Northrop Grumman awarded a $24 million Life-Cycle Program Support contract with a goal to keep A-10s flying until 2028.
- 2014: DoD determined that the previous $1.3 billion allocated to re-wing the A-10 fleet would avoid costly future repair work.

Coming in low over the gunnery range, an A-10A fires an AGM-65D Maverick. The AGM-65D weighs about 500 pounds and has an effective range of 13 miles. (USAF)

In a 90-degree bank, an A-10C demonstrates its excellent low-altitude maneuverability. (Author)

An A-10C backs away from a KC-135 tanker after refueling. The A-10's refueling receptacle door is still open. (USAF)

An A-10A Warthog from the 355th Fighter Wing at Davis-Monthan AFB flies over the rugged terrain of New Mexico. (Author Photo/Illustration)

meant that we protected its key modernization programs, including the new bomber, the Joint Strike Fighter, and the new refueling tanker. We also recommended investing $1 billion in a promising next-generation jet-engine technology, which we expect to produce sizable cost savings through reduced fuel consumption and lower maintenance needs. This new funding will also help ensure a robust industrial base, a very strong and important industrial base, itself a national strategic asset."

Next, it was the bad news for the Warthog. Hagel continued, "To fund these investments, the Air Force will reduce the number of tactical air squadrons including the entire A-10 fleet. Retiring the A-10 fleet saves $3.5 billion over five years and accelerates the Air Force's long-standing modernization plan, which called for replacing A-10s with the more capable F-35 in the early 2020s.

"The Warthog is a venerable platform, and this was a tough decision. But the A-10 is a 40-year-old[30] single-purpose airplane originally designed to kill enemy tanks on a Cold War battlefield. It cannot survive or operate effectively where there are more advanced aircraft or air defenses. And as we saw in Iraq and Afghanistan, the advent of precision munitions means that many more types of aircraft can now provide effective close air support, from B-1 bombers to remotely piloted aircraft. And these aircraft can execute more than one mission.

"The A-10's age is also making it much more difficult and costly to maintain. Significant savings are only possible through eliminating the entire fleet, because of the fixed cost of maintaining the support apparatus associated with that aircraft. Keeping a smaller number of A-10s would only delay the inevitable while forcing worse trade-offs elsewhere."[31]

A-10 Replacement

During early 2015, Air Combat Command (ACC) conducted a sweeping review of CAS needs. "A follow on may be something we need to think about," said the commander of ACC, Gen. Herbert "Hawk" Carlisle, during a 12 February 2015 roundtable with reporters at the annual Air Force Association Air Warfare Symposium in Orlando, Florida. "Nothing is off the table." The CAS review was a week-long session that included officials from the Army, Marine Corps, and Navy. At issue was how to conduct CAS in a contested environment. Carlisle remarked, "This means that aircraft are threatened, but not necessarily operating in the highly defended

An A-10C from the 184th Fighter Squadron, Arkansas ANG, 188th Fighter Wing, ejects defensive flares designed to confuse enemy heat-seeking missiles. (USAF)

heed Martin in October 2001, and only the USMC F-35B variant achieved IOC on 31 July 2015, some 14 years later. Because the Block 3F software was not available, the F-35B's externally mounted GAU-12/U 25mm cannon pod will not be in service until 2019. In other words, no gun for another four years for the F-35B CAS mission. The USAF F-35A is scheduled for IOC in 2019—18 years after the JSF contract award.

An Inconvenient Sleuth

It seemed so clean and simple: retire the A-10 fleet and $3.5 billion would be available. Recent DoD budget reductions have produced heated and opinionated debates regarding the retirement of the A-10 fleet. Strong arguments have been presented from both sides, yet the A-10 retirement remains elusive.

However, after Secretary Hagel's press conference, reaction from all corners was swift, as numerous flaws in the A-10 retirement logic were pointed out. Regarding the A-10 description as a 40-year-old single-purpose airplane, Hagel was correct that the CAS aircraft began service in 1975. However, no mention was made of the huge DoD investment in the A-10 program that resulted in the upgraded A-10C. As far as being a single-purpose airplane, the A-10 performs the CAS, AFAC, and CSAR missions.

One point that substantially damaged the credibility of Hagel's argument was the DoD statement that without the retirement of the A-10 fleet, there would not be enough F-35A maintenance personnel available. The personnel are needed for the F-35As that will be entering the fleet. Essentially, operation of the A-10 fleet was delaying F-35 IOC. Most Congressional members were shocked and well aware of all the funding that had gone toward getting the F-35 variants ready for IOC—and suddenly the A-10 fleet would have to pay the price.

The Air Force is working very hard to operate within sequestration, and it is extremely difficult. During a Pentagon press briefing on 30 July 2014, Secretary of the Air Force Deborah Lee James stated, "The USAF will once again build a two-tiered budget for the coming year. One that spells out what 'we really need' and one which, under sequester, USAF will have to live with." In essence, the aircraft retirement controversy reaches way beyond the A-10 saga; it boils down to a partially dysfunctional Congress that must quickly realize the damage that sequestration is doing to U.S. military readiness. This factor, combined with a nondirectional and reactive U.S. foreign policy, has a huge impact internationally. General Welsh, a

air space of a near peer." Mission area working groups consisting of officers from each of the services will look at the state of CAS now and into the future once the A-10 retires and the F-35 is brought into service.[34]

This type of future planning is prudent and necessary. However, operational timetables are critical regarding the retirement of assets[35] and bringing new aircraft types online. The primary pitfall would be a premature retirement[36] of the A-10 before a new CAS aircraft is ready. It can take up to ten years or more to field a new aircraft. For example, the JSF contract was awarded to Lock-

An A-10C from the 184th Fighter Squadron, Arkansas ANG, 188th Fighter Wing on a training flight over the southwestern United States. (USAF)

Three upgraded A-10Cs carrying PGMs, AGM-65Ds, and AIM-9 Sidewinders. (USAF)

An A-10C Warthog from the 355th FW at Davis-Monthan AFB taxiing at Edwards AFB. (Author)

ness of the A-10 in action against ISIS, both Saudi Arabia and the United Arab Emirates have expressed interest in the A-10.

Boeing has almost completed the re-wing contract that involves 173 A-10Cs; 173 wing sets have been installed. The A-10s have already received updated communications systems and instruments (glass cockpit). Boeing would like to complete the contract, which would be more economical. If the Air Force retires the A-10 fleet, there would be costs involved in terminating the Boeing contract, and recently upgraded and re-winged A-10Cs would be placed in the boneyard. In an era of tight budgets this simply doesn't make sense. However, on 23 July 2015 the Air Force released a statement: "There are no anticipated sales of A-10 aircraft to anyone." Essentially, the A-10's capabilities are too good to export, and the Air Force will continue to push for retirement of the recently upgraded A-10 fleet. The Air Force plans to save approximately $4 billion over five years, and direct that to the F-35. Meanwhile, several billion dollars already invested in A-10 upgrades will be resting in the desert sun.

During summer 2015, Rep. Randy Forbes (R-VA), member of HASC and chairman of the Seapower and Projection Forces Subcommittee, remarked to an American Enterprise Institute forum that opposition to sequestration by the public and lawmakers has grown. "Today, the Air Force has not only aged and high-flight-time aircraft, but the numbers are critically low.[37] The Navy is also lacking the number of ships needed for the rebalance to Asia-Pacific, and the Army's troop strength is dropping to dangerous levels." Rep. Forbes continued, "I see the pendulum moving back to support for repealing sequestration, at least

former A-10 pilot, added, "The decision was not about the A-10. It's about balancing an Air Force to provide the spectrum of missions we provide to a combatant commander. I now have a list of 15 things they'd prefer us to spend the money on, and that $20 billion in cuts to the Air Force under sequestration was to blame."

Boeing announced at the June 2015 Paris Air Show that it was interested in handling the export of the A-10, should the Air Force retire the aircraft. The company is working with the Air Force on this proposal. Boeing would complete the upgrades and sustain the fleet for any potential foreign customer. After witnessing the effective-

for defense. But, we have to have the leadership from the White House[38] to help convince the public." It does appear that for FY 2015 the A-10 will keep flying. If sequestration continues, the retirement issue will return for each DoD budget Fiscal Year.

Author Note: As this book goes to press, the Pentagon announced on 2 February 2016 that the retirement of the A-10 fleet will be delayed until 2022. During a Pentagon press briefing, Sec. of Defense Ashton "Ash" Carter acknowledged that the A-10 has been performing extremely well in the fight against ISIS under Operation Inherent Resolve.

As two A-10s fly into the sunset, hopefully the program will continue until a capable CAS aircraft replacement is operational. (USAF)

Specifications

Northrop YA-9A—Close Air Support Prototype
Crew: 1—pilot
Wingspan: 58 ft. 1 in. (17.7 m)
Length: 54 ft. 6 in. (16.3 m)
Height: 17 ft. 1 in. (5.2 m)
Maximum weight: 42,000 lb (19,050 kg)
Ferry range: 3,622 miles (5,829 km)
Maximum speed: 449 mph (722.5 km/h)
Cruising speed: 322 mph (518 km/h)
Service ceiling: 40,000 ft. (12,192 m)
Powerplant: 2 Lycoming YF102-LD-100s—7,500 lb (33.3 kN) thrust each
Bomb capacity: 16,000 lb (7,200 kg) mixed ordnance on 10 wing hardpoints
Armament: 1 General Electric Vulcan M61A1 20mm rotary cannon

Fairchild Republic YA-10A—Close Air Support Prototype
Crew: 1—pilot
Wingspan: 57 ft. 6 in. (18 m)
Length: 53 ft. 4 in. (16 m)
Height: 14 ft. 8 in. (4.4 m)
Maximum weight: 50,000 lb (23,000 kg)
Maximum range: 2,580 miles (4,152 km)
Combat radius: 300 miles (482.8 km)
Maximum speed: 450 mph (724 km/h)
Cruising speed: 335 mph (539 km/h)
Service ceiling: 44,200 ft. (13,472 m)
Powerplant: 2 General Electric YTF34/F5 turbofans—9,000 lb (40 kN) thrust each
Bomb capacity: 16,000 lb (7,200 kg) mixed ordnance
Armament: 1 General Electric Vulcan M61A1 20mm rotary cannon

Fairchild Republic A-10A/C Thunderbolt II (Warthog)—
Sustained Close Air Support/Forward Air Control/Combat Search & Rescue Aircraft
Crew: 1—pilot
Wingspan: 57 ft. 6 in. (18 m)
Length: 53 ft. 3 in. (16.2 m)
Height: 14 ft. 6 in. (4.4 m)
Maximum weight: 51,998 lb (23,586 kg)
Range: 474 miles (763 km)
Maximum speed: 439 mph (707 km/h)
Cruising speed: 335 mph (539 km/h)
Service ceiling: 34,695 ft. (10,575 m)
Powerplant: 2 General Electric TF34-GE-100 non-afterburning turbofans—9,000 lb (40 kN) thrust each
Bomb capacity: 16,000 lb (7,200 kg) mixed ordnance and AIM-9 air-to-air missiles on 11 hardpoints
Armament: 1 Martin Marietta Armament Systems GAU-8/A Avenger 30mm seven-barrel rotary cannon—1,350 rounds

Sukhoi Su-25K Frogfoot-A (two-seat Su-25UB Frogfoot-B)—Ground Attack Aircraft
Crew: 1—pilot
Wingspan: 47 ft. 1 in. (14.36 m)
Length: 50 ft. 11.5 in. (15.53 m)
Height: 15 ft. 9 in. (4.8 m)
Maximum weight: 38,800 lb (17,600 kg)
Range: 317 miles (510 km)
Ferry range: 1,450 miles (2,333.5 km)
Maximum speed: 606 mph (975 km/h)
Service ceiling: 22,965 ft. (7,000 m)
Combat ceiling: 16,000 ft. (5,000 m) max load
Powerplant: 2 Soyuz/Gavrilov R-195 turbojets—9,921 lb (44.18 kN) thrust each
Bomb capacity: 9,700 lb (4,399.8 kg) mix of rockets, bombs, and R-60 air-to-air missiles

Chapter 8

BATTLE OF THE LIGHTWEIGHT FIGHTERS
GENERAL DYNAMICS YF-16 VERSUS NORTHROP YF-17

The competing General Dynamics YF-16 and Northrop YF-17 fly in formation. (USAF)

It all began in the 1970s as the concept of prototyping and fly before buy was renewed within the DoD and Air Force. The initial starter was the Lightweight Fighter (LWF) program, and on 6 January 1972 the Air Force's Prototype Programs Office at Wright-Patterson AFB issued an RFP. The refined LWF concept was originated by what became known as the "Fighter Mafia." This renowned group of aeronautical experts and test pilots included John Boyd, Tom Christie, John Chuprun, Harry Hillaker, Chuck Meyers, Pierre Sprey, and Everest Riccioni. Their combined input and expertise would literally change the direction of fighter procurement.

LWF specifications called for the development of a highly maneuverable fighter, with emphasis on light weight and low cost. Unlike several previously held competitions, there would be no hiding the development of a new-start airplane because of budget restraints or giving and taking of funding in a disorderly manner. The LWF budget was established and a plan of action was approved: reduce the competitors to two contractors and fly their prototypes against one another. Five major aircraft manufacturers responded: General Dynamics, Boeing, Lockheed, LTV, and Northrop. On 13 April 1972, the Air Force announced the field had been narrowed to General Dynamics and Northrop who would each build two prototype fighter airframes.

In view of continued cost increases for large and complex multimission fighters, in April 1974 Secretary of Defense James R. Schlesinger issued instructions to examine a low-cost Air Combat Fighter (ACF) which could emerge from the successful development of an LWF prototype. The results of this LWF/ACF program would fit into the DoD's new strategy of a high-low fighter mix for the Air Force and Navy.

YF-16: A Classic Design Emerges

Although the F-16 has evolved in many ways, its original design still stands as an iconic aircraft. The LWF program was a concept of a smaller, less-costly, and less-expensive aircraft to be produced in large quantities. These attributes were transformed by General Dynamics into the unique YF-16. The basic design combined a host of advanced technologies never before used in previous operational fighters. The

Amid quite a fanfare, the sleek red, white, and blue YF-16 LWF competitor was rolled out at the General Dynamics Fort Worth factory on 13 December 1973. (General Dynamics)

Early program publicity photograph of the number-one YF-16 (t/n 01567) prototype at the General Dynamics Fort Worth facility. (General Dynamics)

The number-one YF-16 prototype on a test flight near Edwards AFB. The first official flight was made on 4 February 1974 with Phil Oestricher in the cockpit. (USAF)

YF-16 design team had a secret weapon in the talent of Harry J. Hillaker, deputy chief engineer; he was later referred to as "father of the F-16." Hillaker's career began in 1942 at Consolidated Aircraft with the conceptual design of the B-36 Peacemaker. He also worked on the jet-powered follow-on YB-60, the supersonic B-58 Hustler, and the variable-geometry-wing F-111 Aardvark. Hillaker was on the ground floor for the initial launch of the LWF program in 1965.

The main wing and fuselage were blended variable-camber wings with forebody strakes that provided additional lift. The aircraft utilized a digital fly-by-wire system providing excellent response that also simplified the electronic systems as well as eliminated heavier hydraulic structures.[1] The advantage of fly-by-wire controls is that it allows for relaxed stability—basically an aircraft that is inherently unstable, with increased agility. The YF-16 also featured a side-mounted control stick and throttle, Head-Up Display (HUD), 30-degree reclined seat, and large single-piece bubble canopy. These design features would offer combat pilots both improved G-tolerance and situational awareness. These technologies, although explored in other aircraft types, were featured together for the first time in the YF-16.[2] The small jet fit the bill for a lightweight fighter, weighing-in at 14,023 pounds with two AIM-9 Sidewinders.

Off-the-shelf equipment utilized in the YF-16 prototypes:

- B-58 Hustler: main landing gear tires
- Concorde SST: emergency power unit
- A-4 Skyhawk: ejection seat
- SR-71 Blackbird: forked air-data probe
- F-111 Aardvark: leading edge slats servo rotary actuators from F-111 bomb bay doors
- Martin X-24 lifting body: canopy design and latching system

Rollout and Going Airborne

Amid celebrations on 13 December 1973, the first YF-16 (t/n 01567) was rolled out at the General Dynamics facility in Fort Worth, Texas. Its unique futuristic shape was accentuated by a handsome and colorful red, white, and blue color scheme. General Dynamics received additional kudos for producing the first prototype less than two years after go-ahead. Media coverage was extensive and promoted great interest in the new lightweight generation of fighters. Aviation writers noted that the United States had learned hard lessons from the Vietnam War and would no longer limit fighter aircraft to a single mission with a narrowly focused capability. Both the F-105 Thunderchief and F-4 Phantom II were built with the Cold War tactical (nuclear option) mission in mind and not designed for close-in dogfighting; adding to the miscalculation, the F-4 was fielded without an internal gun.

Within two weeks of the rollout, the YF-16 was partially dismantled and loaded onto a Lockheed C-5 Galaxy cargo aircraft for a flight to Edwards AFB. The company support team was already in place at the Flight Test Center. After ground tests and slow-speed

The number-two YF-16 (t/n 568) has two inert AIM-9 Sidewinder air-to-air missiles for fit checks. (USAF)

The experimental blue-and-white "broken sky" camouflage of the number-two YF-16 (t/n 568) did not provide any advantage during the evaluation and was eventually replaced with overall flat gray. (General Dynamics)

taxis, the YF-16 was almost ready for its first flight. On 20 January 1974, with General Dynamics test pilot Phil F. Oestricher in the cockpit, the number-one prototype conducted a high-speed taxi. To Oestricher's surprise, the YF-16 lifted off and the right horizontal stabilizer scraped the runway surface. Quickly reacting, Oestricher increased thrust and continued to take off rather than try to stop the aircraft. The unplanned flight lasted for about six minutes, and thankfully Oestricher landed without incident. The planned first flight took place on 4 February. This time Oestricher flew a flawless 90-minute sortie. Events included cycling the landing gear at 15,000 feet, and with the gear retracted, he proceeded to 30,000 feet maintaining an airspeed of 345 mph.[3] The side control stick performed well through three-axis maneuvers and turns limited to 3 Gs at 15,000 feet. Low-speed handling characteristics were tested at the same altitude with the landing gear down.

Oestricher commented after landing, "It was a completely successful flight and a most enjoyable experience. The airplane was responsive to the controls at all times. Acceleration to maximum planned speed was accomplished very quickly." Oestrich added, "Another feature of the airplane that will impress all fighter pilots is the outstanding visibility through the single-piece canopy."[4] The rapid pace was maintained with the delivery of the number-two

prototype (t/n 568) to Edwards on 22 February 1974. The second airplane was painted in a new experimental blue-and-white camouflage scheme, designed to simulate the sky with broken clouds. This aircraft was equipped with the M61 Vulcan 20mm cannon.

After General Dynamics test pilots completed confirmation of specifications flight tests, ASD and TAC pilots began their evaluation. Test pilot groups were rotated between the competing YF-16 and YF-17. Detailed reports on technical and performance merit compiled by the test pilots would be used to formulate the Air Force's final decision on the winning contractor. About one month prior to the competition's conclusion in November 1974, the two YF-16s had accrued 376 flight hours, 12 of which were supersonic including flights at Mach 2.

Top ceiling reached was just above 60,000 feet. Aerial gunnery with towed targets and strafing on the Edwards range resulted in the firing of more than 12,500 20mm rounds from the M61 Vulcan. Live testing of the AIM-9 Sidewinder and live Mk.84 bomb drops were also conducted. Air-to-air tactics and ACM were flown against adversarial fighters such as the F-4E Phantom II. The test pilots grew familiar with the side control stick, although it was force-sensing with no movement. This prevented the pilots from obtaining any

A publicity photo of the number-one YF-16 prototype (left) and the first FSD F-16 (t/n 50745). (General Dynamics)

true tactile feel for the flight controls. Eventually, the side stick was modified with a slight movement to resolve the problem.

Basically, both YF-16s performed flawlessly, the exceptions being an engine and landing gear malfunction. During September 1974, an engine malfunctioned during takeoff when a large plume was expelled from the exhaust nozzle, and the pilot aborted the take-off. No serious damage to the engine or aircraft occurred. During a company test flight in the number-two YF-16 near the Fort Worth facility with General Dynamics chief test pilot Neil Anderson at the controls, one of the main gear struts failed to lower into position. All attempts to free the gear failed, and Anderson was force to make a belly landing. The aircraft was quickly repaired.

This particular view of the first full-scale development F-16 (t/n 50745) accentuates its sleek, futuristic lines. The various international customer flags are painted on both sides of the nose. (USAF)

YF-16 Flight Test Program Highlights

No. 1 prototype first flight—2 Feb. 1974
No. 2 prototype first flight—9 May 1974
Total flight hours—376 (as of Nov. 1974)
YF-16 attains supersonic speed—Feb. 1974
Total supersonic flight hours—12 (as of Nov. 1974)
Total flights in single day (prototype No.1)—6
Single month flight number record—47
Maximum speed—Mach 2 plus
Maximum altitude—60,000 feet plus
Maximum airframe G—9.0
Number of air-to-air refuelings—86 (as of Nov. 1974)

Northrop's Preliminary Work for the LWF

The Northrop Corporation was already ahead in the late 1950s as it began to reshape their design team. A precursor to the F-5 light-weight low-cost export fighter series was a futuristic looking design designated N-102 Fang. A full-scale mockup was built for customer

An excellent depiction of the Northrop YF-17 Cobra's leading-edge extensions (LEX) along the fuse-lage and canted vertical stabilizers. (Northrop Grum-man Corporation)

A conceptual camouflaged Northrop N-102 Fang lightweight day fighter. Former North American Aircraft designer Edgar Schmued (P-51, F-86, F-100) was recruited by Northrop and was key in the N-102 development as an export fighter in 1956. The single-seat Fang featured an inlet located below the fuselage optimum for handling relatively uniform airflow and effective during high angle-of-attack maneuvers. Powered by the General Electric J79 with afterburner, the Fang would have been capable of Mach 2. How-ever, the N-102 concept only reached the mockup stage, but with this design experience Northrop moved ahead with the successful F-5, T-38, and P-530/600/YF-17 Cobra. (Author Photo/Illustration)

review. The new aircraft was an initial project for former NAA engineer Edgar Schmued, a pioneer in the design of the P-51 Mustang, F-86 Sabre, and F-100 Super Sabre. Schmued had resigned from NAA on 1 August 1952 and was working as an independent consultant when he was recruited by Northrop in 1954. As a new Northrop vice president, his first tasks were to turn around two problematic programs, the F-89 Scorpion interceptor and SM-62 Snark cruise missile. Working with Welko Gasich, Northrop's chief of preliminary design, Schmued's insight for producing unique design elements while reducing the trend of increasing cost and size was evident in the N-102 Fang.

Introduced in 1956, the Fang weighed less than half of the F-89 Scorpion and would be powered by the General Electric J79 turbojet with afterburner. The Fang would be capable of Mach 2, a service ceiling of 59,300 feet, and a ferry range of 2,030 miles.[5] Way ahead of its time, the single-seat N-102 Fang featured an inlet[6] located below the fuselage that would be optimum for receiving relatively uniform airflow, especially during high angles-of-attack (AOA). A full-scale mockup was displayed at Hawthorne for marketing, but unfortunately the N-102 Fang did not garner any orders and further development was suspended. However, with this advanced design experience, Northrop was now poised to plan the N-156 and N-156T. They evolved into the enormously successful supersonic F-5 Tiger II export fighter and two-seat T-38A Talon supersonic trainer.

Hooded Cobra

From these innovative design successes the P530 Cobra would proceed. Senior executives at Northrop were still eyeing the export market and wanted to produce a front-line fighter with twice the

A full-scale wooden mockup of the Northrop P530 Cobra was completed in December 1972 and displayed at Northrop's Hawthorne plant. The particular hood-like appearance of the Leading-Edge Extensions (LEX) along the forward fuselage provided the impetus for the name Cobra. Note the mockup is marked with a Dutch military serial number, as they were a potential customer. (Northrop Grumman Corporation)

range and maneuverability of current fighters. Of particular importance was a unit cost–competitive price. The manager of Advanced Systems, Walt Fellers, guided the P530 from its embryonic stage to a final design in 1967; Lee Begin headed-up the project office.[7] By March 1968, the proposed powerplant for the twin-engine P530 was the 10,000-pound-thrust General Electric J1A2. The aircraft would also feature an aerodynamically curved wing and leading-edge extensions (LEX) for increased lift and airflow control, especially useful during tight turns, and at high AOA. The LEX sections essentially double the main wing lift and also serve as turning vanes to channel air more directly into the intakes during high-AOA maneuvering. The P530 also featured twin vertical tails that were slightly canted outward. By mid-1968, Northrop submitted a detailed report on the P530 to the Aeronautical Systems Division (ASD) of the Air Force. Essentially, the Air Force agreed with the performance and cost predictions based on a production run of 1,000 aircraft.[8]

With its focus on air superiority and achieving a balance for maximum multirole capability, the P530 concept continued to evolve and improve. By 1970, it was in its fourth design iteration. A two-dimensional fixed-ramp inlet replaced the fixed cone inlet, the LEX shape was refined, the cockpit was improved for increased visibility, and engine thrust was increased to 13,000 pounds with the uprated J1A5. To support the air-superiority mission and ground attack, the operational aircraft would feature advanced avionics, search radar, and nine wing store hardpoints. To meet the goal of reduced weight and cost, Northrop also incorporated its experience on the F-5 program with graphite-epoxy composites.

A full-scale P530 mockup was built and placed on display for review by international customers.

Good Timing

As Northrop executives examined the LWF requirements, they quickly realized how fortunate it was that they had been developing the P530 Cobra. Based on their research and design work, they had an excellent head start for the LWF competition. As it pursued the LWF contract, Northrop would still attempt to market their P530 Cobra in the international arena. The next steps were to refine the P530 design to conform with LWF requirements. The powerplant was uprated to the 14,800-pound-thrust General Electric YJ101-GE-100. In addition, wing area was reduced to 350 square feet to improve supersonic performance. To keep within specifications, approximately 900 pounds of lightweight graphite composites were used in the airframe. For increased performance in the transonic regime area-rule design was added to the upper fuselage along the LEX and the shape of the intakes on the fuselage underside.

The aircraft was in the 20,000-pound weight class and received a new company designation of P600.[9]

The Northrop LWF proposal was submitted to the Air Force in 1972. In April 1972, Northrop received word of selection by the Air

An excellent wide-angle publicity photo taken shortly before the rollout of the Northrop number-one YF-17 prototype showed its advanced planform. (Northrop Grumman Corporation)

The 4 April 1974 rollout of the YF-17 Cobra was a festive occasion at Northrop's Hawthorne, California, facility. A large silk tarp was raised to reveal the sleek new jet fighter to the attendees. (Northrop Grumman Corporation)

Force to build two prototypes and that General Dynamics would also build two prototypes. The General Dynamics aircraft was designated YF-16, and the Northrop aircraft received the designation YF-17. Northrop's marketing of the Cobra continued for a brief period, but no foreign sales materialized, and eventually in 1974 the best of the P600 and YF-17 were merged.

Rollout

On 4 April 1974, the Northrop Corporation's Hawthorne facility hosted another unique aircraft rollout—this time it was the high-tech-appearing number-one YF-17 Cobra prototype (t/n 01569). Although described as a rollout, the YF-17 was located just outside the hangar, and with live music in the background a giant silk tarp was lifted to reveal the sleek fighter. The audience, consisting of Northrop employees, the media, and the keynote speaker, Secretary of the Air Force John L. McLucas, were impressed. The overall mood was celebratory. This aircraft seemed to be the one that would place the Northrop Company back on top once again. In describing the company's accomplishments in producing the low-cost T-38 Talon, F-5A/B, and the F-5E Tiger II, Northrop president Thomas V. Jones remarked, "These aircraft demonstrate the successful 20-year evolution of Northrop's application of technology to design advanced fighters at a cost which has permitted procurement of the aircraft in necessary quantities." Jones also mentioned that Northrop had produced more than 2,000 F-5/T-38 aircraft that were in service, or on order, with 23 nations around the world.[10]

The overall LWF program did not commit to production, but an Air Force goal was set at a flyaway cost of $3 million per air-craft (1972 dollars), based on a production run of 300 aircraft at a rate of 100 per year. Northrop vice president and YF-17 program manager Roy P. Jackson noted, "The combination of advanced aerodynamics and engines is an excellent example of the way in which creative technology can be applied to increase performance and reduce costs." There was little time to take a breather, for there was a competition to win. The YF-17 was partially disassembled and prepared for land-transport to Edwards AFB. Similar to the previous YA-9A test team, Northrop YF-17 technicians and ground crew at Edwards reassembled the YF-17 and prepared for the first flight. Aircraft weight was 23,000 pounds, and the twin General Electric YJ101-GE-100 turbojets were now rated at 15,000 pounds of thrust each with afterburner.

Accelerating Change

With no plan for production, the Air Force allowed for considerable latitude in the contractors' aircraft designs and flight-test programs. Unlike previous concurrent fly-offs, each contractor would conduct an independent one-year flight-test program, beginning with their first flight. General Dynamics began their YF-16 flight testing in February 1974, and Northrop later commenced with the YF-17 in June. However, with gradual evolvement of the USAF LWF program into the USAF/USN ACF program, Northrop compressed its YF-17 flight schedule to six months to meet a new source-selection deadline of March 1975. After additional input from four NATO countries who wanted to replace their F-100D, F-104G, F-4, and F-5 fighters, the ACF selection deadline was moved forward to January 1975.[11]

Flying the Twin-Engine Twin-Tailed Fighter

The big day was 9 June 1974 as the sleek twin-tailed YF-17 Cobra fighter lifted off the Edwards runway for the first time. Northrop

With Northrop's Chief Test Pilot, Hank Chouteau, at the controls, the first flight of the YF-17 (t/n 01569) took place on 9 June 1974. The flight lasted for 61 minutes and reached 610 mph over the Edwards range. (USAF)

Chief Test Pilot Hank Chouteau was at the controls and flew the YF-17 for 61 minutes. During the flight the YF-17 reached 610 mph at an altitude of 18,000 feet. During the first flight debrief an enthusiastic Chouteau remarked, "When our designers said that in the YF-17 they were going to give the airplane back to the pilot, they meant it. It's a fighter pilot's fighter."[12]

Two days later, on 11 June, Chouteau flew the YF-17 to Mach 1 in level flight at 30,000 feet without afterburner. This was a first for a U.S.-built fighter airplane, and the technique would later become known in the ATF as "supercruise." Chouteau flew the first three flights, with the YF-17's second flight lasting 45 minutes. The YF-17 was taken beyond Mach 1 with afterburners and on one engine to simulate single-engine approaches. The third flight was just short of an hour at 56 minutes. For the fourth flight the YF-17 was piloted by Col. James G. Rider, USAF, commander of the LWF Joint Test Force at Edwards.[13] The Air Force was able to gain its first preview of the YF-17's capabilities for one hour and six minutes, an aircraft designed to be 50 percent more maneuverable than contemporary fighters.

Normally air-to-air refueling is part of the flight-test program, but Northrop actually used this to accelerate its test goals. "We used aerial refueling to give us more data for a given flight than we have had ordinarily had conducted the tests on a flight-by-flight basis,"

A YF-17 Cobra prototype lifts off the runway at Edwards AFB. During testing, a military power takeoff from brake release to leaving the runway at 138 mph spanned 13 seconds and covered about 1,600 feet. With afterburner, takeoff took only 9 seconds and covered approximately 1,200 feet. (USAF)

As the number-one YF-17 Cobra prototype begins a 360-degree roll, the aircraft's underside reveals the leading-edge extensions that increase lift and airflow control. This is especially useful during tight turns and at high angle of attack. (USAF)

Early in the evaluation, the Northrop team announced that the YF-17 was the first aircraft to go Mach 1 vertically. The YF-17's area-rule "pinched fuselage" improved performance in the transonic regime. The LEX sections essentially doubled the main wing lift and also served as turning vanes to channel the air more directly into the intakes during high angle-of-attack maneuvering. (USAF)

The number-two YF-16 in its new flat gray camouflage takes on fuel from an ANG KC-97L as the number-one YF-17 and YF-16 look on. The faster jet-powered KC-135 Stratotankers were used during the LWF evaluation, but the piston-powered ANG KC-97 tankers were heavily relied upon to keep the test program on schedule. (AFFTC History Office)

Pilots pointed out that the YF-17's small frontal area, forward of the LEX, was a visibility and situational-awareness advantage during aerial combat. (USAF)

Rider said. "On certain occasions, aerial refueling has given us a 4:1 or 5:1 flight ratio because we could go up and plug into the flying gas station and then go back and do some more tests." In-flight refueling services, which were provided on a rotating basis by several Air National Guard (ANG) units still flying piston-powered Boeing KC-97s, significantly extended airborne endurance of the YF-17s, especially during high-speed tests that involved high fuel-consumption rates.

Chouteau was grateful to the ANG, noting, "If it had not been for the ANG we would have had a problem accomplishing as much as we did without them. Depending only on Edwards support they would have needed three or four additional tankers and crew." Basically, the increased frequency of air refueling cut the cost of some

flight operations by reducing the number of takeoffs and landings needed to complete certain test segments. Each time an aircraft was refueled in flight, savings were accrued in fuel, engine cycles, and brake and tire wear that would have been required for ground servicing.[14] Joseph B. Jordan, the second Northrop test pilot assigned to the YF-17 program, along with Hank Chouteau, was a Northrop representative on the LWF/ACF Joint Test Force. Jordan commented on the flight schedule, "The increased airborne endurance gave the flight-test program a great deal of flexibility, and made it possible to complete performance testing in about ten days instead of the usual six weeks."[15]

By December 1974, the number-one prototype had logged more than 185 hours during 159 flights, and the number-two prototype (t/n 01570) approximately 91 hours during 71 test flights. Nine hours of flight time were flown at supersonic speed including above Mach 2. Number-one aircraft was used for control system evaluation, stability and control investigations, and 20mm cannon firing. The second aircraft flew the majority of the structural demonstration and flight performance tests, and was used in the stall/post-stall program after the air combat maneuvering series. In all, the second prototype was flown to 100 percent of design air loads. Performance of the General Electric YJ101-GE-100 was exceptional through all flight parameters. "Essentially, it's the unrestricted flight envelope which allows us to fly 'head out' all the time. We don't have to worry about the engine envelope because we know that if we push the throttles we're going to get power," said Joseph Jordan.[16]

Chouteau was particularly complimentary about the cockpit visibility. With no bow supports in the canopy and no support post behind the seat, pilots had unrestricted aft visibility. Visibility runs in an arc from the nose to 190 degrees to the rear, enabling the pilot to see over the right shoulder and see the left vertical stabilizer. Fold-out handgrips[17] are mounted on each side of the forward cockpit so the pilot can twist the upper body to look aft. In the prototype, the ejection seat is tilted back 18 degrees; a production aircraft's seat will have a 25-degree aft pitch. This tilt angle, combined with raised heel cups on the rudder pedals, greatly improves G tolerances. The only anomalies experienced by the Northrop YF-17 were an in-flight FOD ingestion that caused an engine shut down and a fuel-valve failure causing another engine shutdown. In another incident the canopy shattered during a flight, but Hank Chouteau was able to land safely.

A New Kid in Town

Air Force pilots were quickly learning that the new YF-17 had impressive capabilities. A TAC pilot conducted a military power takeoff and accelerated to Mach 0.9 during a climb through 50,000 feet. At that altitude and speed, the rate of climb was more than 2,800 feet per minute. During another test, the YF-17 made a maximum

The number-two YF-17 (t/n 01570) joined the fly-off evaluation with a new experimental two-tone camouflage. Test pilots noted that the YF-17's landing gear retraction cycle was exceptional, taking about six seconds. This was fortunate, since the YF-17 accelerated so quickly during takeoff in afterburner. For landing, the landing gear was designed to be extended safely at 276 mph but could be extended in an emergency at 345 mph. (USAF)

YF-17 Program Milestones: 1974

- 9 June: First flight of prototype No. 1 (t/n 01569)
- 28 June: Multinational Fighter Program Committee viewed YF-17 at Edwards AFB
- 21 August: First flight of prototype No. 2 (t/n 01570)
- 12 September: NATO defense ministers from Belgium, Denmark, Netherlands, and Norway viewed the YF-17 at Edwards AFB
- 23 September: 100th-flight milestone reached
- 7 October: Northrop-McDonnell Douglas agreement to develop U.S. Navy version of YF-17 ACF prototype announced
- 1 November: F-17 ACF production proposal submitted to U.S. Air Force
- 15 November: Second hundred flights completed in 29 scheduled flying days
- 2 December: McDonnell Douglas-Northrop U.S. Navy ACF proposal submitted

YF-17 Flight-Test Program Highlights: December 1974

- No. 1 YF-17 fast-turnaround capability demonstrated on 20 December with 7 flights within 6 hours and 30 minutes. Average turnaround, chock to chock: 15 minutes. In addition, 25 sorties in 5 days (9–13 December) by both prototypes and with 6 sorties per day on 12 and 13 December.
- Maximum speed to date: Mach 2+ and demonstrated design acceleration performance. Maximum altitude to date: 50,000 feet.
- Longest flight with aerial refueling: 4 hours and 15 minutes. Shortest turnaround time with ground refueling: 10 minutes; aircraft airborne in 15 minutes.
- Longest flying day: 20 November; 9 hours and 26 minutes during four YF-17 flights.
- Supersonic flight without afterburners. Failure-free afterburner light-off during high-altitude maneuvers. No afterburner blowouts during flight test program.
- Throttle bursts from idle to full afterburner at high angles-of-attack and from idle to maximum power during full stick back maneuvers.
- Single-engine landing demonstrated twin-engine YF-17 recoverability.
- No departure tendencies at angles-of-attack of 63 degrees at 57.5 mph, and sideslip of 36 degrees and 58-degrees angle-of-attack.
- Achieved 9 Gs in one part of flight envelope. Sustained 6- and 7-G turns without buffet at transonic and supersonic speeds.
- 40 to 50 percent superior maneuverability than other operational fighters in its class demonstrated in competitive flight maneuvers.
- Landing and flight capability with two 600-gallon external wing-mounted fuel tanks, confirmed combat radius in excess of 500 miles.
- Aerial firing of 11,427 rounds from the M61 20mm Vulcan cannon, including firing at subsonic and supersonic speeds, air-to-air ground strafing, and firing at towed targets. Gunsight and tracking testing to 5 and 6 Gs.
- Ten Mk.84 2,000-pound bombs dropped in level flight and in 30-degree dives. Strafing at varying angles-of-attack both day and night. Symmetrical (with two bombs) and asymmetrical (one bomb) landings conducted.
- Seven AIM-9E Sidewinder air-to-air missiles launched at subsonic and supersonic speeds.

performance formation takeoff with a McDonnell Douglas F-4E Phantom II and was climbing through 45,000 feet 2 minutes and 45 seconds after brake release. When the YF-17 reached 46,000 feet, the F-4E was just passing 26,000 feet. Northrop Chief Test Pilot Chouteau also stated that at 35,000 feet the YF-17 routinely passed through Mach 1 in military power—contemporary fighters would need to go into afterburner to achieve this. On the other end of the spectrum, at altitudes up to 45,000 feet, the YF-17 can perform 30-degree banked turns at 172.6 mph. In addition, the ability to remain at high altitudes is considered an advantage of air dominance. The YF-17 was comfortable at 40,000 to 45,000 feet even at a 5- to 10-degree negative angle to remain there and observe bogies—then dependably accelerated when needed.

After the LWF/ACF fly-off, the Northrop number-one YF-17 (t/n 21569) was transferred to NASA Dryden Flight Research Center for additional flight-test research. After a series of flight tests, the YF-17 was turned over to the Navy for testing on the new F-18 program. (NASA)

Selection Day

By the end of 1974, the Air Force had concluded the flight evaluation of both the General Dynamics YF-16 and Northrop YF-17. On 13 January 1975, Secretary of the Air Force John L. McLucas announced that the General Dynamics YF-16 was the winner. During the Pentagon press conference McLucas remarked, "The flight-test program that was conducted on the two lightweight fighters went extremely well. Both of the aircraft performed very well. Both of the contractors did an excellent job of supporting the prototype test program. Both of the engine companies did a good job of supporting the aircraft companies." He continued, "On the other hand, there were significant differences in the performance of these prototypes. The YF-16 had many advantages in performance over the YF-17. It had advantages in agility, in acceleration, in turn rate, and endurance over the YF-17. These factors applied principally in the transonic and supersonic regimes. There were other advantages to the YF-16 over the YF-17. These factors included better tolerance of high-G because of the tilt-back seat, better visibility, and better acceleration. In any case, the YF-16 met all performance goals that we had established for it. The YF-17, while performing very well, did fall short of some of these goals. In the subsonic mission areas, the YF-16 and YF-17 were not as far apart as they were in supersonic. This is indicative of the fact that the YF-16 had lower drag and was a cleaner design."[18]

The second Northrop YF-17 (t/n 01570) shown in-flight during post LWF/ACF competition testing for the U.S. Navy F-18 program. For promotion of the new program, the aircraft was marked as an F-18 prototype and received a Cobra insignia painted on the nose. (Author Photo/Illustration)

New Design Emerges

The Air Force statement was intended to confirm a clear winner, and certainly the Northrop YF-17 team was disappointed. However, the team was aware of the Navy's preference for twin-engine aircraft for carrier-ops. The Navy was already considering a lightweight fighter to complement the larger and more complex Grumman F-14 Tomcat in their own high-low mix. The program was dubbed

The first McDonnell Douglas F/A-18A Hornet (t/n160775) on a test flight. During its rollout on 13 September 1978 at St. Louis, Missouri, the aircraft was painted with Marines on the starboard side and Navy on the port side. (U.S. Navy)

The number-four FSD F/A-18A (t/n 160778) Hornet flares during a landing after a test sortie. (U.S. Navy)

The F/A-18A Hornet FSD number six (t/n 160780) was the first test aircraft painted in red-and-white markings. At NAS Patuxent River, this Hornet underwent high angle-of-attack and spin-recovery testing. (U.S. Navy)

VFAX and the new jet would replace Navy/Marines F-4 Phantoms, F-8 Crusaders, and A-7 Corsair IIs. Although six contractors were working on proposals that fit aircraft-carrier requirements, Congress unexpectedly opted to reduce costs and redundancy and cancel VFAX. In Congress's view, the YF-16/YF-17 ACF competition would produce a suitable aircraft. However, when the single-engine YF-16 was selected, the Navy was not convinced that this aircraft fit their requirements.

Northrop discussions were already underway with a partner with extensive experience producing carrier aircraft: McDonnell Douglas. Under a joint agreement between Northrop and McDonnell Douglas, the YF-17 evolved into the Navy Air Combat Fighter (NACF) for the U.S. Navy. Northrop issued an internal employee announcement regarding the joint agreement: "Northrop Corporation and McDonnell Douglas today announced that the two aerospace firms have entered into an agreement under which they will jointly develop and propose an air combat fighter for the U.S. Navy which is based on the YF-17 design. Under the teaming agreement, McDonnell Douglas will have the prime contract responsibility for a carrier-suitable version of the YF-17 to meet the requirements of the proposed NACF. Northrop will have prime contract and design responsibilities for YF-17 variants for use by NATO nations and other allies."[19]

General Dynamics also teamed with a Navy aircraft production expert, LTV, to "navalize"[20] the F-16. However, finding commonality in Air Force and Navy aircraft is difficult, even though the services and contractors are continually ordered to try. Carrier operations

are quite different from land-based operations. The YF-16's single engine did not enhance its case, and other factors such as reduced landing-approach speed and strengthened fuselage and landing gear all require modifications and add weight. Both General Dynamics and Northrop presented their NACF proposals to the Navy, including three separate variations for a navalized F-16. On 2 May 1975, the Navy announced the selection of the F-17 variant. This evolved into the F-18A and the land-based version, F-18L.[21]

Onward to Full-Scale Development

With the LWF/ACF contract in hand, the General Dynamics team immediately began the transition from prototype aircraft to a production version, or full-scale development (FSD) aircraft. YF-16 testing validated the aerodynamics, propulsion, and handling qualities of the basic design—factors considered a major hurdle and now out of the way as General Dynamics looked ahead to FSD. The Fort Worth production line was set up to produce the first eight FSD F-16As. To preserve the superior flying qualities, there would be limited external differences, with the majority of FSD changes being internal. To enable the new multirole-fighter requirement that included enhanced air-to-ground capabilities, fuselage length was increased by 13 inches. The nose would now house a Westinghouse APG-66 radar. Additionally, the vertical stabilizer and wing were expanded by 15 percent to enable external loads, and the wing area was expanded from 280 to 300 square feet—the maximum allowable without further lengthening the fuselage. The FSD F-16A now had nine wing hardpoints. Early FSD F-16As were recognizable with their all-black radomes. This was later eliminated as a result of recommendations made by mock U.S. adversary pilots who noted that the black radomes made the F-16s visible from quite a distance

The number-one FSD F-16A (t/n 80001) with its new flat gray camouflage. The early FSD aircraft had distinct black radomes that were later eliminated because they were easily spotted by Aggressor jets during Air Combat Maneuvering. (USAF)

The General Dynamics F-16/101 testbed at Edwards AFB during February 1981. General Electric modified the F101 B-1A bomber engine as an alternative engine to the P&W F100 for the F-16. The F-16/101 Derivative Fighter Engine (DFE) program evaluated the engine. (Author)

during Air Combat Maneuvering (ACM) training. In the cockpit, a lighter weight Stencil SIIIS ejection seat was substituted for the prototype's ESCAPAC seat. The canopy was also strengthened to withstand a four-pound-bird strike at 402.7 mph. For simplification, twin nose-gear doors were replaced by a single door, and a self-contained jet fuel engine starter was installed.[22] General Dynamics was making serious strides to keep low cost in the equation.

Use of off-the-shelf equipment on F-16 FSD aircraft:

- LTV A-7 Corsair II: Modified HUD
- F-4 Phantom II: nose-gear wheel and tire
- A-10 Thunderbolt II: signal data recorder
- F-5E Tiger II: oxygen-quantity indicator
- T-39 Sabreliner: nose-wheel steering system
- F-15 Eagle: modified P&W F100 engine

The General Dynamics–proposed Swept Forward Wing (SFW) F-16 concept. The program was later designated Forward Swept Wing (FSW). Advances in aeroelastic tailoring that allowed aircraft wings to twist and change shape prompted the Defense Advanced Research Projects Agency (DARPA) to initiate the FSW program during the late 1970s. General Dynamics submitted FSW proposals along with Rockwell International and Grumman. The F-16 SFW concept was eliminated, and DARPA/NASA continued studying the Rockwell Sabrebat FSW concept, which reached the full-scale mockup stage. In December 1981, Grumman was chosen to build two FSW prototypes that were designated X-29. The first X-29 first flew on 14 December 1984 at Edwards AFB. (Author Photo/Illustration)

Under a $5.6 million (1978 dollars) Air Force contract awarded on 27 December 1978, General Dynamics would modify F-16 FSD (75-750) into an advanced fighter technology demonstrator. The Advanced Fighter Technology Integration (AFTI)/F-16 program was managed by the Air Force Flight Dynamics Laboratory and focused on development and evaluation of promising technologies for future tactical fighter operations. Distinctive modifications on the aircraft were the forward twin ventral canards used for direct side-force and yaw-pointing control. The decoupling of lateral and yaw control allowed for independent aircraft nose pointing and lateral motion. (NASA)

In-flight view of the USAF/NASA F-16D automatic collision-avoidance technology (ACAT) testbed. Led by NASA's Dryden Flight Research Center, the program concluded with the completion of flight-testing development of the Automatic Ground-Collision-Avoidance System (Auto GCAS) in August 2010. The project then transitioned to the Air Force Flight Test Center's 416th Flight Test Squadron for additional testing. (Author Photo/Illustration)

F-16 Milestones

- August 1972: USAF selects General Dynamics and Northrop to build LWF prototypes
- December 1973: Rollout of No. 1 YF-16
- January 1974: Inadvertent first flight of No.1 YF-16 during high-speed taxi test
- February 1974: First official flight of No. 1 YF-16
- May 1974: First flight of No. 2 YF-16
- January 1975: USAF selects F-16 as its Air Combat Fighter, plans for procurement of 650 aircraft
- June 1975: Belgium, Denmark, Norway, and the Netherlands announce plans to acquire 348 F-16s
- June 1975: YF-16 performs at Paris Air Show
- July 1975: YF-16 longest flight with refueling (nine hours)
- August 1975: F-16 manufacturing begins
- October 1976: Rollout of No. 1 F-16
- November 1976: No. 1 FSD F-16 viewed by NATO customers at Fort Worth
- December 1976: First flight of No. 1 F-16
- January 1977: USAF announces plans to acquire an additional 738 F-16s
- June 1977: F-16 makes second appearance at Paris Air Show
- August 1977: Maiden flight of first two-seat F-16B
- October 1977: DoD endorses full production of F-16
- August 1978: First production F-16 completes maiden flight

A two-seat F-16B assigned to the AFFTC at Edwards AFB. (Author)

An F-16C Viper taxis at Chino Airport after performing an aerial display. (Author)

A Lockheed Martin F-16 from the Demo Team Royal Netherlands Air Force (RNLAF) performs a knife-edge pass during the RIAT (Royal International Air Tattoo) at RAF Fairford in July 2007. At the time the F-16 was based at Volkel AB, Netherlands, and the team rotated every other year to Leeuwarden AB, Netherlands. The F-16 Demo Team members are composed of 322 and 323 Squadrons. The first RNLAF F-16 was delivered on 6 June 1979. (Author)

Two Royal Danish Air Force (RDAF) F-16MLUs fly in formation. Denmark took delivery of the first Block 10 F-16 for Squadron 727 on 28 January 1980 at Skrydstrup Air Base in Jutland, Denmark. (Author Photo/Illustration)

F-16 Milestones CONTINUED

Swiss Air Force F/A-18As over snowcapped mountains. Switzerland accepted 34 F/A-18A/B Hornets. The initial two Hornets were built at McDonnell Douglas in St. Louis, and the remaining were delivered in kit form and completed at Swiss Aircraft and Systems in Emmen, Switzerland, by 1997. (Author Photo/Illustration)

- June 1979: Royal Netherlands Air Force accepts its first F-16
- January 1979: Delivery of first operational F-16 to USAF's 388th TFW at Hill AFB, Utah
- January 1979: Belgium Air Force receives its first F-16
- January 1980: Royal Danish Air Force accepts its first F-16
- January 1980: Royal Norwegian Air Force accepts its first F-16
- January 1980: Israeli Air Force accepts its first F-16
- June 1980: Egypt signs Letter Of Agreement (LOA) to purchase 40 F-16s
- July 1980: F-16 officially named "Fighting Falcon" by USAF
- October 1980: F-16 achieves IOC
- October 1980: First flight of F-16/79 intermediate variant
- December 1980: First flight of F-16/101 DFE development aircraft
- March 1980: USAF announces that Thunderbirds will fly F-16s
- July 1982: Rollout and first flight of first F-16XL (single-seat variant)
- July 1982: AFTI/F-16 makes first flight
- October 1982: Two-seat F-16XL variant with GE F101 engine makes first flight
- April 1983: First public air show featuring F-16 Thunderbirds
- July 1983: Delivery of 1,000th F-16 to Hill AFB
- June 1984: F-16C variant first flight
- January 1985: USN selects F-16N as it adversary flight training aircraft (14 aircraft)
- August 1986: USAF F-16 fleet exceeds 90 percent mission capable rate, exceeding TAC standard
- February 1989: First USAF F-16 Aggressor delivered in MiG-29 Fulcrum paint scheme
- April 1992: First flight of VISTA/F-16 Variable In-Flight Simulator Testbed Aircraft
- March 1993: Lockheed completes purchase of General Dynamics military aircraft business, creating the Lockheed Fort Worth Company
- May 1993: Delivery of the first USAF F-16 Block 50D
- July 1993: Modified F-16 with GE AVEN engine in Multi-Axis Thrust Vectoring (MATV) program begins test flights
- February 1994: First demonstration of high off-boresight missile launch using helmet-mounted sight
- March 1995: Lockheed Corporation merges with Martin

A USAF F-16C Aggressor from the 64th AGRS in lizard camouflage at Nellis AFB takes off during a May 2004 Red Flag exercise. Nellis is the home of the USAF Warfare Center and Aggressor pilots use call signs such as Flanker, Ivan, and MiG. An electronic detection and countermeasures device is mounted on the port wing missile rack. (Author)

A two-seat Israel Defense Force Air Force (IDFAF) F-16I Sufa (Storm) and F-16C Barak (Lightning) fly in formation. The first F-16A Block 10 aircraft were delivered in July 1980, and the latest F-16 variant delivered to the IDFAF is the F-16I. Similar to Royal Norwegian Air Force F-16s, the IDFAF F-16Cs have a brake-parachute compartment in the lower vertical stabilizer. Since the IDFAF F-16s do not use parachute braking, the area is thought to contain ECM equipment. (Author Photo/Illustration)

Marietta, forming Lockheed Martin

- April 1995: 3,500th F-16 delivered to USAF
- September 1995: NASA begins flight testing F-16XL for future supersonic transport (SST) research
- September 1995: USAF F-16s set new safety record with less than 2.4 mishaps per 100,000 flight hours
- August 1996: F-16 is first USAF aircraft to perform guided launch of AGM-145 Joint Standoff Weapon
- September 1996: Ground testing completed on F-16 with P&W low observable axisymmetric nozzle, potential application on JSF prototype
- September 1996: USAF F-16s set new safety record for Class A rate of 2.1 mishaps per 100,000 flight hours
- November 1996: USAF Thunderbirds fly 1,000 performances in the F-16 since 1983
- April 1988: Flight testing of X-35 JSF flight-control software begun using the VISTA/F-16 testbed
- September 1998: 3,000th F-16 delivered: Block 52 for Singapore

The first FSD aircraft was delivered in December 1976 and was used for flutter, propulsion, performance, and flying-qualities testing. This aircraft was the first one powered by the General Electric F101 Derivative Fighter Engine (DFE),[23] which later evolved into the F110 that equipped the Block 30 F-16s. The second FSD F-16 was used for structure and performance testing. The number-three FSD aircraft was the first F-16 with a full avionics suite, and testing commenced on the avionics, fire-control-system vibration, and acoustics. Electromagnetic tests were also conducted. After being damaged in a landing accident on Rogers Dry Lake, this particular F-16 was later modified with a two-seat cockpit and a crank-arrow delta wing, becoming the experimental F-16XL. Number-four FSD F-16 concentrated on flying qualities, performance, avionics, and weapons-separation tests.

The fifth FSD F-16 continued this phase of testing and was later converted into a single-seat F-16XL while the sixth FSD aircraft headed to the climatic chamber at Eglin AFB and was later converted into the Advanced Fighter Technology Integration (AFTI) F-16 testbed. AFTI modifications researched several advanced technologies, including electric-actuator technologies for the future JSF. The seventh FSD aircraft was the first two-seat F-16B. This aircraft was primarily involved in maintenance and reliability testing. Number seven also had larger tail surfaces, which would signal the transition to Block 15 aircraft. Number-eight FSD F-16, also a two-seater, was focused on maintenance training and reliability. Later during 1980, this aircraft tested the General Electric J79-GE-119 engine, a derivative of the powerplant on the F-4 Phantom II.[24] The worldwide F-16 fleet now operates with both the Pratt & Whitney F100 and

F-16 taxiing in the sunset at Edwards AFB. (Author)

A USAF/Lockheed Martin F-16C Viper displays its superb acceleration capability as it goes vertical in afterburner. (Author)

A U.S. Navy/Boeing F/A-18F Super Hornet pulling up to go vertical. (Author Photo/Illustration)

A Boeing F/A-18C Hornet from the USS Carl Vinson preparing to move forward on the deck for a catapult launch during November 2000. This was shortly before the F/A-18E/F Super Hornets arrived aboard to start their squadron carrier sea trials. (Author)

General Electric F110-GE-100[25] engine. Operating with two basic engine types is an overall prudent strategy for single-engine operation safety. This will also prevent the grounding of the entire fleet in the event of an engine anomaly.

Vipers: Going Operational

The first F-16A Block 1 (78-0001)[26] was first flown at Fort Worth during August 1978 and was delivered to the USAF during the same

In the twilight over the Pacific Ocean off the California coast, a U.S. Navy F/A-18C Hornet conducts a catapult launch from the USS Carl Vinson during November 2000. (Author)

month. Number one was received at Hill AFB by the 388th TFW. IOC was achieved on 1 October 1980.

The pace of the F-16 program was rapid, with 94 Block 1 and Block 5 aircraft being manufactured through 1981. The majority of Block 1 and Block 5 F-16s were upgraded in 1982 to a Block 10 standard under the Pacer Loft program. In all, 321 new Block 10 F-16s rolled off the Fort Worth production line through 1980.[27] On 21 July 1980, the F-16 was officially named the "Fighting Falcon," although the more appropriate "Viper" was eventually preferred by pilots and it stuck.

The Block 30 variant at 983 units was the most widely produced. Two hardpoints were added to the inlet chin to accommodate sensors, and the vertical stabilizer size was increased by 30 percent. As production was ramped up in Europe for NATO F-16s, production of the F-16 amassed astounding numbers. Block 15 aircraft were upgraded with improved radar systems and fire-control systems for the AGM-65 Maverick and AIM-120 Advanced Medium-Range Air-to-Air Missile (AMRAAM). Subsequent Block 25–30/32–40/42–50/52 and Block 60 aircraft have continued to vastly update and improve the F-16 fleet for all customers. The remarkable success of the F-16 program is marked by the 4,565 F-16s of all variants that have been produced as of August 2015.

Sting of the Hornet

Initially, the U.S. Navy would procure the F-18 fighter version. The U.S. Marines, who provide CAS and ground attack, had the

A U.S. Navy F/A-18C (VFC-12) Aggressor prepares for takeoff and an Air Combat Maneuvering (ACM) sortie at NAS Oceana, Virginia, during May 2012. (Author)

The fourth FSD F/A-18E Super Hornet painted in Day-Glo orange and white. The Super Hornet was a quantum improvement over the F/A-18C/D. Its wing area was 25-percent larger and other features included larger trapezoidal intakes with low-RCS technology, improved GE F414-GE-400 engines rated at 22,000 pounds of thrust each, a Multifunctional Information-Distribution System (MIDS), APG-73 Advanced Targeting Forward-Looking Infrared (ATFLIR), and a joint helmet-mounted cueing system (JHMCS). Additionally, the Super Hornet had a 40-percent increase in range and loiter time over the F/A-18C/D Hornet. (U.S. NAVY)

A-18. As the aircraft could easily be mission switched, eventually the designation was merged for all customers as the F/A-18. For the ground-attack role the F/A-18 could carry more than 17,000 pounds of ordnance on its nine underwing hardpoints. Secretary of the Navy W. Graham Claytor announced on 1 March 1977 that the aircraft was named the "Hornet." With McDonnell Douglas test pilot Jack Krings in the cockpit, the number-one F/A-18 made its maiden flight at St. Louis on 18 November 1978. After testing at NAS Patuxent River, the F/A-18A completed carrier trials aboard the USS *America* (CVA-66) in November 1979.

In 1983, Hornets entered service with the U.S. Navy, USMC, and Royal Canadian Air Force. The first export was to Canada with 24 CF-18As (RCAF designation CF-18). Additional export orders followed quickly with 75 Hornets going to the Royal Australian Air Force and, in May 1983, 72 EF-18As to Spain. Improved F/A-18C (single-seat) and F/A-18D (two-seat) variants were introduced. On 13 November 1981, F/A-18A Hornets arrived at NAS Lemoore, California, to a mixed USN/USMC squadron, the Rough Raiders of VFA-125. By the end of 1981, a total of eight Hornets were based there.

The Super Hornet

The next Hornet iteration, the Super Hornet, took to the skies at the McDonnell Douglas St. Louis facility at Lambert Field on 29 November 1995. The F/A-18E was the single-seat version, and the F/A-18F was the two-seater with a WSO. The Super Hornet offered a dramatic improvement in capability over the Standard Hornet. Wing area was 25-percent larger, with a Multifunctional Information-Distribution System (MIDS), an APG-73 advanced radar, and Advanced Targeting Forward-Looking Infrared (ATFLIR). The pilot was equipped with a Joint Helmet-Mounted Cueing System (JHMCS). Larger trapezoidal-configured intakes with low-RCS technology fed two improved GE F414-GE-400 engines that generated 22,000 pounds of thrust each. The Super Hornet has a 40-percent increase in range and loiter time over the F/A-18C/D Hornet. The Navy took possession of the first Super Hornet in December 1998; IOC occurred in November 1999. Boeing modified the two-seat F/A-18F into a new airborne electronic attack aircraft to replace the Navy's Northrop Grumman EA-6B Prowler. Named the Growler, the EA-18G entered service in 2009 and has proved to be an outstanding aircraft.

With its tailhook extended, a U.S. Navy F/A-18C Hornet (VFA-113) prepares to move into the downwind leg and a trap landing. (U.S. Navy)

The Hornet 2000 Study

The F/A-18E/F Super Hornet is an impressive aircraft, but its design history could have turned out very differently. During the early 1980s, the Navy was considering several upgrades to the F/A-18C/D Hornet that would complement new advanced aircraft slated to enter the inventory. At the time, the classified stealthy A-12 Avenger II attack aircraft was being designed, and a Navy Advanced Tactical Fighter (NATF) could possibly emerge to replace the F-14 Tomcat.

To keep the Hornet viable into the next century, in 1987 McDonnell Douglas established the Hornet 2000 Study. Two F/A-18C/D upgrade configurations were considered: Option IIIC and IV. Outwardly, Option IIIC was basically the Super Hornet of today: F/A-18E (single-seat) and F/A-18F (two-seat). Option IV was a far more radical design and was dubbed the "Super Hornet Plus." The Plus featured a cranked-arrow wing, forward-swept canards, and large-area canted twin vertical stabilizers. Powered by two uprated General Electric F404-GE-400 engines, the intakes would be modified to handle increased airflow. This new configuration would improve maneuverability and supersonic flight performance. Included would be upgraded weapon-systems architecture, and the configuration variations would be handled by incorporating new flight-control software. With these dramatic changes to the Hornet's configuration, it was hoped that foreign participation in the program would drive down production costs, thus reducing the unit cost for the U.S. Navy.

The Super Hornet Plus (Option IV) was first offered to France in 1987 as a codevelopment project to replace the French Navy's aging Vought F-8E (FN) Crusaders. However, France opted to proceed with their indigenous Rafale fighter. At about the same time, France dropped out of the joint European Fighter Aircraft (EFA) consortium. Concurrently, the Japanese government was offered the Plus for the JASDF. Mitsubishi Heavy Industries (MHI)[28] had previously built the McDonnell Douglas F-4EJ Phantom II and was successfully producing the McDonnell Douglas F-15CJ/DJ Eagle under license. The Super Hornet Plus would have been an excellent follow-on. However, this sales effort did not produce an agreement either.

During January 1988, McDonnell Douglas presented the Super Hornet Plus (Option IV) to the EFA consortium and European military officials as an alternative to the EFA (later Eurofighter-Typhoon). The offer was based on a 250-aircraft buy, and would be only 30 percent of the cost of the EFA, approximately $27.5 million per copy (1988 dollars). EFA consortium members[29] Great Britain, West Germany, Italy, and Spain were all offered a coproduction stake in the Super Hornet Plus program. The United States had estimated that the EFA program would cost $8 to 10 billion.

In March 1988, the EFA consortium announced its rejection of the Super Hornet Plus coproduction offer. Despite being saddled with the high cost of developing the Eurofighter, there were many other considerations, including politics, technological pride, and retention of high-tech jobs.

Although taking 20 years to enter service, the Eurofighter eventually became the successful Typhoon fighter aircraft. With

A conceptual U.S. Navy F/A-18 Super Hornet Plus from VFA-125. This was the Option IV of an upgrade plan for the Navy/USMC F/A-18C/D Hornet. The Plus featured canards, a cranked-arrow wing, canted twin vertical stabilizers, and two uprated General Electric F404-GE-400 engines. This new configuration would improve maneuverability and supersonic performance. (Author Photo/Illustration)

A conceptual JASDF F/A-18 Super Hornet Plus. During the late 1980s, McDonnell Douglas offered Japan a coproduction plan to build the advanced Super Hornet Plus fighter, but the deal was not accepted. (Author Photo/Illustration)

The Hornet 2000 Study *CONTINUED*

no Japanese or European participation in producing the Super Hornet Plus, McDonnell Douglas and the Navy pressed ahead with developing the very capable Option IIIC, which became the F/A-18E/F Super Hornet. The timing was fortunate, since the Navy A-12 Avenger II was canceled on 7 January 1991, and the NATF did not materialize. Although we will never see the radical looking Super Hornet Plus take to the skies, the F/A-18E/F Super Hornet progressed into a tremendously successful program serving as the backbone of modern U.S. carrier operations around the globe. The aircraft is still in production in 2016.

Two U.S. Navy F/A-18E Super Hornets stationed at NAS Oceana flying over snow-capped mountains. (Author Photo/Illustration)

A U.S. Navy/Boeing F/A-18F Super Hornet from VFA-213 Black Lions has changed the back-seater and prepares for another sortie May 2012 at NAS Oceana. (Author)

The latest variation to the Super Hornet is the Navy EA-18G Growler, a supersonic replacement for the Northrop Grumman EA-6B Prowler. The carrier-based two-seat airborne electronic-attack aircraft has AESA upgrades, conformal fuel tank, advanced cockpit, Advanced Tactical Data Link (ATDL), and ALQ-218 radar warning upgrades. Although currently equipped with the standard ALQ-99 jammer, a new-generation jammer is under development. (U.S. Navy)

The General Dynamics F-16XL

Perhaps the most unusual and graceful F-16 variant was the F-16XL developed in 1981. Famed F-16 designer Harry Hillaker was now a vice president and the F-16XL deputy program manager. Under the guiding hand of Hillaker, supersonic/maneuverability research conducted during the 1970s led to the Supersonic Cruise and Maneuver Prototype (SCAMP) program. After approximately 3,600 hours of wind-tunnel tests, the cranked-arrow delta

The F-16A (left) on the tarmac with the F-16XL. The cranked-arrow delta wing had over twice the wing area of a standard F-16, yet the skin friction drag was only 22 percent more, partially due to the elimination of the F-16XL's horizontal stabilizer. The new wing combined with a 56-inch fuselage extension, increased the internal fuel capacity by 82 percent, increasing the combat radius by 45 percent. The weapons load was 120 percent better than the standard F-16. (General Dynamics)

The two-seat NASA F-16XL (t/n 848) with an active Supersonic Laminar Flow Control (SLFC) glove installed on its port wing and a passive glove on the starboard wing. The port wing titanium glove had 12 million microscopic perforations designed to pull in airflow. The NASA laminar-flow study was dedicated to supersonic-transport research. The two-seat F-16XL was powered by the General Electric F110 turbofan, and first flew on 29 October 1982. (NASA)

wing was selected. This new wing's leading edge sweeps backs sharply 70 degrees to a 50-degree outboard section. The configuration is designed to obtain the low wave drag associated with highly swept or thin wings, without the aerodynamic penalties of sweep or structural problems of the thin sections.[30] The secret was controlling vortices over the wing surfaces to obtain maximum performance at both high and low speeds and high AOA. The number-three FSD F-16 (75-0749) was modified and designated F-16XL. The crank-arrow delta wing had over twice the wing area of a standard F-16, yet skin friction drag was only 22 percent more, partially due to the elimination of the F-16XL's horizontal stabilizer. The new wing, combined with a 56-inch fuselage extension, also increased internal fuel capacity by 82 percent, resulting in a dramatic increase in performance and payload capacity. Combat

While assigned to NASA, the single-seat F-16XL (t/n 849) flew research missions for both laminar flow and the Digital Flight Control System (DFCS). The single-seat F-16XL was powered by the Pratt & Whitney F100 turbofan, and its maiden flight took place on 3 July 1982. (Author Photo/Illustration)

A single-seat F-16XL (t/n 849) with clearly marked visual reference points on the cranked-arrow delta wing in order to follow airflow. Smoke and cloth attachments were also used for increased visual reference that was videotaped by chase planes. (NASA)

radius was increased by 45 percent, with the weapons load 120 percent better than the standard F-16.

The single-seat F-16XL, powered by the Pratt & Whitney F100-PW-200, engine first flew on 3 July 1982. After the 1 hour, 5 minute flight, General Dynamics test pilot Jim McKinney remarked, "The XL performed as predicted, but it is a very different aircraft from the standard F-16, with a solid ride." During the

flight the F-16XL reached 30,000 feet and a speed of Mach 0.9. Also noted was the takeoff angle of attack of only eight degrees and on landing approach ten degrees, as compared to much higher angles on conventional delta-wing aircraft.

A second standard F-16 (75-0747) was modified with a two-seat cockpit and crank-arrow delta wing. This second F-16XL

A NASA F-16XL (t/n 849) in a sleek black-and-white paint scheme escorts a NASA SR-71A Blackbird (t/n 844) trisonic research aircraft. Both aircraft were used in the sonic-boom flight research of the Cranked-Arrow Wing Aerodynamics Project (CAWAP). Although conceived with very different designs and missions, they were indeed spectacular aircraft. (NASA)

A USAF/Boeing F-15E Strike Eagle engages its afterburners. The two-seat General Dynamics F-16XL and a two-seat McDonnell Douglas F-15 competed for the Air Force Enhanced Tactical Fighter (ETF) aircraft. The F-16XL performed extremely well but, once again, the variant's single engine counted against it. The winner became the very successful ground-attack USAF F-15E Strike Eagle. (Author Photo/Illustration)

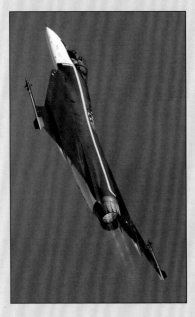

During the mid-1980s, Lockheed Martin proposed a tailless version of its F-16XL cranked-arrow variant as a research program for NASA. To fly a tailless aircraft successfully requires an active computerized flight-control system, but the advantages would offer a lower Radar Cross Section (RCS), save weight, and increase maneuverability. These advantages could be applied to future fighters. During the early 1990s, the Rockwell/MBB X-31A EFM program also considered a tailless variant. Neither program was funded. (Author Photo/Illustration)

A conceptual USAF F-16XX highly maneuverable fighter design that capitalized on the unmanned Rockwell HiMAT (Highly Maneuverable Aircraft Technology) design that first flew in 1979. This type of design would allow a fighter to sustain high-G turns without bleeding off airspeed. The basic XL configuration has been modified to allow the interactive canards/fins to be control configured with the cranked-arrow delta wing. Additional IR masking features have also been added. (Author Photo/Illustration)

was powered by the General Electric F110-GE-100 turbofan with 29,000 pounds of thrust with afterburner. After taking flight on 28 October 1982, it joined the number-one F-16XL in a 240-flight test program. The crank-arrow delta wing was developed to provide a balance of excellent supersonic and low-speed characteristics, shorter runway requirements, and high penetration speeds with significant increases in combat performance and range. The XL variant proved impressive with a maximum speed of Mach 2 (1,400 mph), cruise speed of 600 mph, and a range of 2,850 miles, twice that of the standard F-16.

The Air Force initiated the Enhanced Tactical Fighter (ETF) competition in March 1981. The requirements fit the low-level supersonic capable attack strike aircraft that would eventually replace the General Dynamics F-111 Aardvark. McDonnell Douglas offered a two-seat derivative of the F-15 Eagle fighter, and General Dynamics would propose its two-seat F-16XL. Both contractors felt the rear-seat WSO position was critical for the mission. With its increased wing area, the F-16XL was now equipped with a total of 17 weapon stations on 29 hardpoints—double the payload of the F-16. Both aircraft types performed extremely well during the competition. However, in February 1984 the Air Force selected the F-15, which became the F-15E Strike Eagle. Although the F-16XL[31] was an excellent-performing aircraft, once again its single-engine counted against the General Dynamics entrant. For deep strikes within denied airspace, the Air Force selection board felt that the twin-engine design had an improved survivability rate. Although the F-16XL did not succeed in achieving supercruise—supersonic flight without the use of afterburner—the design performed superbly. The two F-16XLs were temporarily placed in flight-worthy storage, and later used by NASA for numerous aeronautical research programs. Both F-16XL aircraft were permanently retired in 2009.

On a Multiyear Purchase (MYP) basis, the Navy has continued to acquire additional F/A-18E/F Super Hornets as a hedge against the F-35C Lightning II that has fallen behind schedule and increased dramatically in cost. Boeing's marketing strategy is to emphasize the upgrades and cost advantage of the proven Super Hornet, compared to the unit cost of the new F-35C. Boeing has also flown a modified Super Hornet that is being offered to the Navy. The Advanced Super Hornet emphasizes the F/A-18E/F's growth potential and is equipped with conformal fuel tanks, enclosed weapons pod, enhanced avionics, and additional developments to increase range and reduce the aircraft's RCS.

During the late 1980s, Lockheed proposed a big-wing UCAV (Unmanned Combat Air Vehicle) variant of the F-16. It would have been a demonstrator for future autonomous UCAVs, and would feature a high-aspect-ratio wing spanning 60 feet with hardpoints for ground attack and air-to-air missiles. Internal fuel capacity would be 22,000 pounds, enough to have an eight-hour loiter time for air combat patrol or ground attack with PGMs. (Author Photo/Illustration)

After a flight training sortie, a U.S. Navy/Boeing F/A-18F Super Hornet from VFA-213 Black Lions taxis toward the flightline at NAS Oceana during May 2012. (Author)

F/A-18E Super Hornet going vertical in the sunset. (Author Photo/Illustration)

On 5 February 1999, in commemoration of the 25th anniversary of the F-16's first official flight (4 February 1974), approximately 100 F-16s and several thousand F-16 personnel gathered at Edwards AFB. The number-one F-16B was painted in original colors to recreate the first YF-16 rollout ceremony. Guests included YF-16 first-flight pilot Phil Oestricher; F-16 chief designer Harry Hillaker; USAF historian Dick Hallion; Col. Jeffrey Riemer, director, F-16 System Program Office; and Bob Elrod, executive vice president of Lockheed Martin Tactical Aircraft Systems. (Author)

Utilizing a standard F/A-18C, the HARV (High Angle-of-Attack Research Vehicle) program was begun in 1987. Under the auspices of NASA Ames, Langley, and Lewis research centers, the HARV program's primary purpose is validating wind tunnel and computer data on high-angle-of-attack flight to eventually provide improved maneuverability in future high-performance aircraft. The F/A-18 with its LEX feature was a very capable AOA fighter, but the HARV was able reach 55 degrees AOA of controlled flight. (Author)

A predelivery Lockheed Martin F-16C Block 60 Desert Falcon destined for the United Arab Emirates (UAE). The Block 60 order will also include the two-seat F-16D. Powered by the increased-thrust General Electric F110-132, the Block 60 has a dorsal spine fairing, conformal fuel tanks, and the Northrop Grumman APG-80 agile beam AESA radar. (Author)

With additional modifications, phase two of the HARV program commenced in mid-1991. Three spoon-shaped paddles were added near the engine's exhaust nozzles. This was a similar arrangement as the Rockwell X-31A Enhanced Fighter Maneuverability (EFM) aircraft. The redirecting of engine exhaust added control during high-angle-of-attack modes when normal flight controls were ineffective. (NASA)

The LWF Competition Was Unique

The manner in which the LWF evolved into the ACF for the Air Force and, from the same competition, the NACF, was truly unique. It was a plus for all the customers, including future international customers. In an article written for the Society of Experimental Test Pilots (SETP), Northrop test pilot Paul Metz stated, "Both Northrop and General Dynamics were asked to build a new fighter unconstrained by conventional design criteria while using existing technology. The YF-16's tilt-back seat, side controller and fly-by-wire control system were truly unique, but they were based on existing technologies with significant laboratory and flight test equipment behind them. The LWF program was successful and produced two fine fighter aircraft, the F-16 and F-18."[32] The unique designs of both the F-16 and F/A-18 have allowed for extensive upgrades that have resulted in dramatic performance

RCAF F/A-18 (CF-188) Hornet. (RCAF)

Lifting off the Nellis AFB runway in afterburner, an EF-18A Hornet from the Spanish Air Force participates at Red Flag during May 2004. The Spanish Air Force took delivery of 72 Hornets by the late 1980s and received an additional 24 former USN Hornets in 1996. (Author)

A USAF F-16C at the June 2005 Paris Air Show displays the Identify Friend or Foe (IFF) antennas just ahead of the canopy. This configuration allows the antennas to also act as vortex generators. (Author)

A USAF/Lockheed Martin F-16C Viper in afterburner with vortices coming off the leading-edge strakes. (Author)

improvements and decades of reliable service. Today, they serve in the inventories of the U.S. Air Force, U.S. Navy, U.S. Marine Corps, and 25 foreign air forces. As manufacturing companies' names have changed through acquisitions and mergers, the aircraft types have for decades survived the test of time. These iconic fighters are the Lockheed Martin[33] F-16 (formerly General Dynamics) and the Boeing[34] F/A-18, formerly (McDonnell Douglas).

The unique LWF/ACF competition set the standard for future aircraft-procurement programs and, with two winners, had an unprecedented impact on the aerospace industry. As of August 2015, 4,565 F-16 Fighting Falcons (Viper) in all variants/block numbers have been produced by Lockheed Martin. Evolving from the YF-17, more than 700 F/A-18 Hornets and more than 500 F/A-18E/F Super Hornets have been delivered by the Boeing Company. Additionally, more than 100 EA-18G Growler electronic attack variants have been delivered to the U.S. Navy.

Specifications

General Dynamics YF-16—Air Superiority Fighter Prototype
Crew: 1—pilot
Wingspan: 32 ft. 10 in. (9.7 m)
Length: 49 ft. 6 in. (14 m)
Height: 16 ft. 5 in. (5 m)
Maximum weight: 29,896 lb (13,560 kg)
Maximum range: 1,407 miles (2,264 km)
Combat radius: 500+ miles (804+ km)
Maximum speed: 1,345 mph (2,164.5 km/h)
Cruising speed: 577 mph (928.5 km/h)
Service ceiling: 55,000 ft. (16,764 m)
Powerplant: 1 Pratt & Whitney F100-PW-100—23,830 lb (106 kN) thrust with afterburner
Bomb capacity: 16,000 lb (7,200 kg) mixed ordnance of air-to-air/air-to-ground
Armament: 1 General Electric Vulcan M-61A1 20mm rotary cannon

Lockheed Martin F-16C Block 50 Fighting Falcon (Viper)—Multirole Fighter
Crew: 1—pilot
Wingspan: 32 ft. 8 in. (9.9 m)
Length: 49 ft. 5 in. (15 m)
Height: 16 ft. (4.8 m)
Maximum weight: 42,300 lb (19,200 kg)
Ferry range: 2,280 miles (4,220 km)
Combat radius: 340 miles (550 km)
Maximum speed: 1,320 mph (2,120 km/h) Mach 2
Cruising speed: 335 mph (539 km/h)
Service ceiling: 50,000 ft. (13,472 m)
Powerplant: 1 General Electric F110-GE-100—28,600 lb (127 kN) thrust each
Bomb capacity: 17,000 lb (7,711 kg) mixed ordnance of air-to-air/air-to-ground
Armament: 1 General Electric Vulcan M-61A1 20mm rotary cannon

Northrop YF-17—Air Superiority Fighter Prototype
Crew: 1—pilot
Wingspan: 35 ft. (10.6 m)
Length: 56 ft. (17 m)
Height: 14 ft. 6 in. (4.4 m)
Maximum weight: 24,900 lb (11,294 kg)
Maximum range: 2,600+ miles (4,184 km)
Combat radius: 500 miles (804 km)
Maximum speed: 1,522,mph (2,449 km/h) Mach 2 class
Cruise speed: 647 mph (1,041 km/h) Mach 0.85
Service ceiling: 60,000 ft. (18,288 m)
Powerplant: 2 General Electric YJ101 turbojets with afterburner—15,000 lb (66.7 kN) thrust each
Bomb capacity: 16,000 lb (7,257 kg) mixed ordnance of air-to-air/air-to-ground
Armament: 1 General Electric Vulcan M-61A1 20mm rotary cannon

Boeing F/A-18E/F Super Hornet—Air Superiority/Ground Attack Aircraft
Crew: E model, 1—pilot; F model, 2—pilot, WSO
Wingspan: 44 ft. 11 in. (13.4 m)
Length: 60 ft. 4 in. (18.4 m)
Height: 16 ft. (4.8 m)
Maximum weight: 66,000 lb (29,937 kg)
Maximum range: 2,580 miles (4,152 km)
Combat radius: 1,467 miles (2,360 km)
Maximum speed: 1,475 mph (2,373.7 km/h) Mach 1.8+
Service ceiling: 50,000 ft. (15,240 m)
Powerplant: 2 General Electric F414-GE-400 turbofans—22,000 lb (97.8 kN) thrust each with afterburner
Bomb capacity: 17,000 lb (7,711 kg) mixed ordnance of air-to-air/air-to-ground
Armament: 1 General Electric Vulcan M-61A1 20mm rotary cannon

WINGS OVER THE MOJAVE DESERT: THE ADVANCED TACTICAL FIGHTER
LOCKHEED MARTIN YF-22 VERSUS NORTHROP YF-23

Up through the late 1980s, the desert skies over historic Edwards AFB had witnessed unprecedented progress in aviation. Test aircraft that once symbolized the embryonic jet age gradually evolved into the era of stealth and supercruise. No other program represents this dramatic advancement in technology more than the ATF program. The skies over Mojave would soon witness two advanced shapes that would usher in the future of aviation.

The ATF program's roots date back to the late 1960s, before the classic F-15 Eagle Air Superiority Fighter and F-16 Lightweight Fighter took to the air. TAC planners officially formulated the ATF program in 1971, which was sometimes referred to as the Advanced Offensive Strike Fighter (AOSF).[1] The effort was a peek at what future TAC requirements would look like. In addition to no DoD funding being available for a new-start aircraft, the superior performance of the F-15 and F-16 instilled confidence within Air Force leadership not to rush. However, the Soviet Union had started fielding more advanced fighters, and information gathered by intelligence seemed to signal that the Soviet aircraft bureaus were hard at work on the next generation. The ATF could no longer wait. Although the ATF was promoted as an air-dominance fighter, an air-to-ground capability would be included in the requirements.

In June 1981, a request for information (RFI) was initiated by the Air Force. Responses were received from seven major contractors: Boeing, General Dynamics, Grumman, Lockheed, McDonnell Douglas, Northrop, and Rockwell International.[2] The formal ATF System Program Office was created in early 1983 and headed by Col. Albert C. Piccirillo at Wright-Patterson AFB. In early 1998, Col. Piccirillo remarked, "Originally, the ATF program did not contain stealth. People on the program were aware of what was going on with the F-117 and the B-2 programs. We would have been really stupid to develop an advanced fighter without using this new technology. Without stealth, I am not sure the Air Force could have justified ATF."[3] The ATF program was declared a top-secret black program that required special access. It was code named "Senior Sky."

In May 1983, a concept-definition investigation (CDI) for the ATF was issued, quickly followed by a $1 million contract to the seven contractors that would extend the investigation for nine more months. The ATF concept was so advanced that a separate new-generation engine competition would be concurrently held. The two primary engine manufacturers, General Electric and Pratt & Whitney, pursued their own technical efforts

The Northrop YF-23A and Lockheed YF-22A fly together over the Edwards AFB test range. The signatures of chief test pilots Paul Metz and Dave Ferguson are visible with the aircraft types they flew. After the ATF competition, Metz left Northrop and joined Lockheed to fly the F-22A. (USAF)

The proposed Rockwell International ATF design was in the 50,000-pound class and featured a large blended delta wing, twin-canted vertical stabilizers, and twin engines embedded on the underside. Within the flat aft exhaust area were thrust-vectoring nozzles. Advanced technologies included blended fuselage/wing areas and lightweight composite airframe structure materials. (Author Photo/Illustration)

An early version of the McDonnell Douglas ATF proposal. This concept featured an elongated blended delta wing and a single vertical stabilizer. The twin-engine design featured embedded inlets widely separated below the fuselage and close-positioned thrust-vectoring nozzles. The inlet's location was similar to the YF-23A. Final proposal featured twin vertical stabilizers. (Author Photo/Illustration)

to come up with the type of engine required to fit this radically new fifth-generation fighter.

To Fly-off or Not to Fly-off?

The fly-off evaluation between two of the most advanced fighter prototypes in decades almost didn't happen. Despite the success of the YF-16/YF-17 competition, the Air Force was pursuing a Demonstration/Validation (Dem/Val) option. Under Dem/Val, after designing the aircraft based on a computer database, only wind-tunnel testing and radar-cross-section model tests would take place prior to declaring a single winner. Then a prototype demonstrator would be built for flight testing. After analysis of ATF requirements and complexity, plus pressure by the Packard Commission,[4] the direction of the ATF program was changed in May 1986. Instead of proceeding with a single contractor after the Dem/Val phase, two contractors would be selected to build demonstrators. Based on recent experience, the Air Force realized that a fly-off competition appeared to be the most efficient way to proceed after all.

Additionally, General Electric and Pratt & Whitney had to change gears. They were preparing to build competing engine prototypes for ground testing, and now they were going to physically power the prototypes for a fly-off. Engine weight and thrust generation became much more critical. Meanwhile, the Pentagon encouraged the responding airframe contractors to team.[5] Despite two airplanes flying concurrently at the same AFFTC, with an eventual winner being chosen, the Pentagon refused to call the Dem/Val phase a fly-off competition.

Gen. James A. Fain, USAF ATF program director, noted, "The acquisition strategy has always been for the contractor to conduct the test program he thought appropriate to his design. He has total freedom in this program to optimize his design in the way he thought would best

suit our very general stated requirements. Therefore, the flight tests had to be different, because the designs were different." Both General Fain and Gen. Ronald W. Yates, commander of Air Force Systems Command, repeatedly stressed that the ATF Dem/Val prototype phase was not a classic fly-off competition, but a data acquisition exercise in preparation for full-scale development. Yates commented, "It is part of a risk-reduction program, along with other major components." Fain added, "The purpose of this program was to establish a technology base, so when we stated FSD we'd have a good well-defined set of requirements and known technologies. Therefore, we would have a known price for the program. Flying the aircraft is just part of that."[6]

Lockheed was teamed with Boeing and General Dynamics,[7] and Northrop teamed with McDonnell Douglas. On 31 October 1986, the field was narrowed down as the Air Force awarded contracts to Lockheed and Northrop. The Dem/Val phase would be the last step prior to a final FSD award—the Air Force used this as a demonstration of the technical and management capability able to meet the objectives plus mitigate technical risk as well as cost. The plan was to produce at least 750 ATFs to eventually replace the aging F-15C Eagle fleet, which had begun service during the mid-1970s. In a paper for SETP, Northrop test pilot Paul Metz commented, "The YF-16 and YF-17 were Technology Demonstrators, while the next ATF competitors in the 1990s, the YF-22 and YF-23, would be Risk Reducers. The difference is much more than semantics."[8]

Northrop YF-23A: Rolling Out the Future

The Northrop/McDonnell Douglas F-23 Team promoted their capabilities and proven strengths based on 16 years of team experience producing and supporting F/A-18 Hornets and producing and fielding more than 10,000 jet fighters. They also had experience in innovative design, low observables, weapon systems integration, and USAF/USN supportability. Although Northrop was concurrently developing the B-2A stealth bomber, lessons learned were transferred to the YF-23A program. No clear picture on this process has ever been revealed, as the B-2A program was highly classified and extensively compartmentalized.[9] The YF-23A later proved so competent in the low RCS area that Air Force officials with access to the Lockheed F-117A program did not believe some of the Northrop test data. They attended an RCS test in person and were surprised but quite satisfied with Northrop's figures.

During May 1990, YF-23A PAV-1 (Prototype Air Vehicle-1) had been partially disassembled and shipped by truck from Hawthorne to Edwards AFB. The aircraft was carefully reassembled and prepared by the Northrop ATF F-23 Team for rollout and first flight. On 22 June, there was tremendous excitement just outside the Advanced Tactical Fighter Combined Test Force hangar at Edwards AFB. The results of all the hard work, long hours, and intense secrecy would now be revealed to the world. General Yates opened the ceremony, stating, "In a few moments we'll see an airplane that's no longer a paper list of specifications, or artist concept, but a modern miracle representing the world's most advanced technology in engines, avionics and materials." The commander of TAC, Gen. Robert D. Russ also commented, "By the time the ATF enters the operational inventory, most of our F-15s will be more than 20 years of age, so the time is upon us to produce a new air superiority fighter."[10]

As the YF-23A PAV-1 (s/n 87-800) emerged from the hangar there was excited applause and tremendous pride was evident throughout the audience. This was a first look at a new-generation ATF, since Lockheed's YF-22A had not been rolled out yet. Anyone not privy to the design procedure had no idea of what to expect, and the first impression was quite dramatic. As the aircraft was towed out of the hangar, the YF-23A's long and slender forward fuselage with a nose chine first appeared similar to a gray SR-71. Its length was 67 feet 5 inches, but it looked longer. Aerospace media accustomed to standard canted twin vertical tails were drawn to the large all-movable ruddervators canted outward 45 degrees. The large canted fins were actually one-fourth the size of the wing and had a 40-degree range of motion controlled by very-high-speed actuators. The feature was designed to reduce the RCS yet provide rapid-response agility; this would hopefully compete favorably with the vectored-thrust system of the YF-22A.

The Northrop Tacit Blue single-seat Battlefield Surveillance Aircraft Experimental (BSAX), also known as "the Whale," was first flown in total secrecy in February 1982. It was developed to flight-test low-observable (LO) techniques for a future battlefield-surveillance aircraft. Tacit Blue's elongated fuselage was 55 feet 10 inches long and had twin vertical fins with curved tips. The airframe tested the curvilinear form of LO assembly. This LO design technique, combined with radar-absorbent materials (RAM), later emerged on the B-2A and YF-23A. In particular, the similar nose chine is quite evident on the YF-23A. The single Tacit Blue aircraft flew 135 test flights and retired in 1985. It was eventually sanitized and declassified in April 1996. It is now on permanent display at the National Museum of the U.S. Air Force. (Author Photo/Illustration)

A high-angle view of the Northrop YF-23A reveals its dynamic futuristic shape. The aircraft is parked just outside the ATF Combined Test Force hangar. (USAF)

The YF-23A PAV-1 in April 1991. The trapezoidal inlets were separated by one engine diameter below and one diameter to the side, and blended into the underside. Additionally, the interior of the inlets curve up and inward to shield the fan blades from incoming frontal-emitted radar waves. The engines were mounted above the wing plane, similar to the B-2. (Author)

Even the YF-23A's canopy was designed with stealth in mind, and it was produced with a combination of glass and polycarbonate to provide nonreflectivity and excellent visibility. Chief Test Pilot Paul Metz once commented, "It felt like I was sitting on top of the airplane instead of in it." (Author)

This close-up of the YF-23A PAV-1 at Edwards AFB during April 1991 shows standard elbow-type pitot tubes on each side of the nose. On the underside of the nose chine are four flush-mounted air-pressure sensors in a diamond shape. These are similar to the B-2's sensors and do not reflect radar. They were used during the flight-testing, and the pitot tubes verified the data. During RCS testing the elbow pitot tubes were removed. (Author)

The Northrop YF-23A PAV-1 parked next to a General Electric YF120-100 engine in April 1991. Neither the YF-23A, or the GE YF120-100 engine was selected at the end of the Dem/Val. The YF-23A excelled in the stealth and speed categories, and the GE dual-cycle YF120-100 engine was reported as the higher-performing engine by test pilots. (Author)

The YF-23's 43 foot 3 inch wingspan had a 40-degree sweep on both the leading and trailing edges. Large flaps working interactively with the canted ruddervators would provide quick and positive flight control plus excellent aerodynamic braking during landing rollouts. Northrop President and Chief Executive Officer Kent Kresa commented, "We are witness to the emergence of a new generation of aircraft that represents a turning point in tactical military air-power."[11] To achieve the absolute minimum radar return, the YF-23A featured an overall edge-aligned planform and a coated skin featuring seamless unbroken lines. Northrop engineers employed a curvilinear[12] shape as with the B-2 stealth bomber.

Each YF-23A prototype would fly with the competing Pratt & Whitney YF119-100 turbofan and General Electric YF119-100 dual-cycle engines. The trapezoidal inlets were separated by one engine diameter below and one diameter to the side, and they were blended into the underside. Engines were mounted above the wing plane.[13] Additionally, the interior of the inlets curved up and inward to shield the fan blades from incoming frontal-emitted radar waves. Twin exhaust nozzles were located on top of the fuselage, well forward of the aft-end serrated edge of the fuselage. This provided space for long exhaust troughs covered with specialized heat-resistant tiles to reduce the IR signature. Also within this area was another feature: cooling tiles with thousands of tiny holes to run cooled air from an air compressor through the troughs. This was critical to keep the afterburners from damaging the aft section.

Ahead of the nozzles on the exhaust deck were what the F-23 ATF Team referred to as the "bread loafs." They were designed to accommodate the thrust reversers, but late in the process the Air Force deleted that requirement, and there was simply no time anywhere in the schedule for a redesign of that area.

On the F-23A production version these bread-loaf zones would have been much slimmer and produced less drag. Throughout the design phase, low RCS was a high priority. Even the canopy was designed with stealth in mind and was produced with a combination of glass and polycarbonate to provide nonreflectivity and excellent visibility. Chief Test Pilot Paul Metz once commented, "It felt like I was sitting on top of the airplane instead of in it."

Flying the Black Widow II

Northrop Chief Test Pilot Paul Metz would take PAV-1 on its first flight. During the initial slow-speed taxi run the flight-control computer started making corrections to smooth out the bumps in the runway. The ruddervators and ailerons could be seen in motion. The flight-control software was doing its job, but was too sensitive and was corrected. 27 August 1990 was the magical day for Northrop employees as they waited to watch the YF-23A take to the air. Metz applied full military power and the YF-23A accelerated nicely, lifting off Runway 04 at 120 knots (138 mph). Throughout the observation area there were cheers and tremendous applause as employees watched four years of work become airborne. Metz raised the landing gear and took PAV-1 to 25,000 feet. First flight was successful and PAV-1 quickly flew its assigned tasks in the compressed Dem/Val schedule. The YF-23 is the first fighter in history to achieve and sustain supercruise at above Mach 1.5. On what was termed "surge day," the YF-23 PAV-1 completed its Dem/Val flight tests on 30 November 1990 with 6 flights completed within 10 hours. This demonstrated a surge capability, with average turnarounds of 61 minutes. Northrop test pilot Jim Sandberg was chosen to pilot PAV-2 on its first flight. Powered by the YF-120 engines, PAV-2 took off on 26 October 1990. During the flight, Sandberg cycled the landing gear. Then he lowered them again. Metz, the chase pilot, notified Sandberg that only the nose gear came down. Sandberg retracted the gear again and lowered it for a test. All three bogies lowered. Metz recommended leaving the gear down for the remainder of the sortie which brought a few laughs in the headsets. PAV-2 landed without incident.

The YF-23A's twin exhaust nozzles were located on top of the fuselage, well forward of the serrated aft section. Within this area there were cooling tiles with thousands of tiny holes to run cooled air from the air compressor through the troughs. This was critical to keep the afterburners from damaging the aft section. (National Museum of the USAF)

Northrop Chief Test Pilot Paul Metz began the initial slow-speed taxi tests. During the initial run, the flight-control computer started making corrections to smooth out the bumps in the runway. The ruddervators and ailerons could be seen in various motions. The flight-control software was doing its job, but was too sensitive and was subsequently corrected. (USAF)

Sandberg commented on the YF-23A's performance in the transonic region: "I just put the plane into military power and watched the Mach meter move from 0.98, 0.99, 1.00, 1.01, 1.02. It was a very smooth transition, with no discernible effects, such as buffeting, etc." Sandberg recalled putting the YF-23A through sustained high-G turns at Mach 1.4. "It was smooth with no speed bleed off, and while conducting a proficiency flight in an F-16, I replicated this maneuver but at only Mach 0.8. The G-forces I experienced in the F-16 at Mach 0.8 were very similar to the YF-23A at Mach 1.4—it was impressive." Additionally, because of their large size, during maneuvering the ruddervators barely moved, keeping the aircraft's RCS extremely low. During flights at slightly above Mach 1, both aircraft experienced cracks in the polycarbonate-composite canopy, but returned safely to base; the canopies were replaced with no interruption in the schedule. In all, the YF-22A and YF-23A experienced one-third less fuel burn in supercruise than contemporary fighter aircraft in afterburner. The maximum speed released to the public was Mach 1.8, and a maximum altitude of 50,050 feet was reached. YF-23 PAV-2 continued its test program into December 1990.

The Black Widow Hourglass: During the YF-23A PAV-1's first flight on 27 August 1990, a vent access door that had been painted red by a Northrop ground crew member for safety reasons is visible. However, when this photo appeared on the cover of the 17 September 1990 issue of Aviation Week, senior Northrop officials ordered the painted hourglass immediately removed. (USAF)

The YF-23A's lower-mounted inlets internally curve inward and upward to the engines mounted above the wing-line. Referring to the outward-canted ruddervators, pilot Jim Sandberg called the YF-23 "the world's fastest Beechcraft Bonanza." (USAF)

This planform view of the YF-23A PAV-1 (t/n 800) shows the tandem wing arrangement, with a 40-degree swept wing and the aft ruddervators canted outward at 50 degrees. Also visible are the engine nozzles placed well ahead of the serrated aft section. (USAF)

YF-23 PAV-1 with test pilot Bill Lowe aboard awaits runway clearance as a Northrop B-2A Spirit stealth bomber approaches for landing. This is test pilot Jim Sandberg's favorite photo, but it was not easy to pull off. The B-2 team was not allowed to share flight schedules with the YF-23 team. Through a series of nonofficial contacts, the YF-23 team was able to guess roughly when the B-2 might be landing. Bill Lowe was instructed to wait a few minutes, and Northrop photographer and B-2 Flight Test Engineer Bill Flanagan captured both exotic aircraft. (Northrop Grumman Corporation)

Black Widow II: It's All in the Name

At a secret location early in the YF-23A's development, Northrop engineers noticed that during RCS testing the computerized return pattern of the aircraft resembled a spider. Later at Edwards, a technician working under the aircraft hit his head on an open access door. For safety reasons he painted it bright red; with the opposing door also painted red, it looked like the hourglass pattern on the belly of a black widow spider. This was too many coincidences. Northrop's P-61 Black Widow piston-powered twin-engine night fighter had achieved great success during World War II. Thus, the YF-23A picked up the unofficial name "Black Widow II." However, when a first flight YF-23A photo appeared on the cover of *Aviation Week* on 17 September 1990, a left bank revealed the aircraft's underside and the bright red hourglass. Shortly afterward, senior Northrop officials ordered it immediately removed. "Gray Ghost" was another nickname, and PAV-2 had "Spider" painted on the inside of its nose landing-gear door. Many aviation historians wonder if Black Widow II would have stuck if Northrop's YF-23A had won the ATF contract. After all, the Air Force rejected Lockheed's Lightning II for the F-22 and named it the Raptor.

The Lockheed YF-22A looks on as the Northrop YF-23A PAV-2 (t/n 801) Gray Ghost takes on fuel from a KC-135. According to Northrop test pilot Jim Sandberg, the General Electric YF120-100 dual-cycle engine in PAV-2 was a higher performer on both competing platforms, resulting in a higher maximum speed. However, the YF120-100 was more difficult to throttle precisely, and during aerial refueling Sandberg placed one engine in a high-power setting, and varied the throttle on the other to keep in contact with the tanker. (USAF)

YF-23A PAV-1 with landing gear extended approaches the runway at Edwards AFB. The leading-edge slats, flaps, and ailerons are visible. (AFFTC History Office)

Lockheed YF-22A

On the YF-22 Team, Lockheed was the prime and had previously specialized in stealth technology. The company was enthusiastic about the ATF prototype that would utilize this expertise. During the late 1970s, Lockheed's Skunk Works Division had produced the Have Blue subscale demonstrators and the F-117 Nighthawk in complete secrecy. The aircraft's faceted design to obtain a very-low RCS proved successful. However, the F-117 was a subsonic attack aircraft with nonafterburning engines. The ATF would be designed for Beyond Visual Range (BVR) intercepts, maneuverability, supercruise, and attaining Mach 2 plus with afterburner. Of primary importance was to produce an agile air dominance fighter that must also maintain stealth. A challenging task indeed.

Team member Boeing was experienced in mass production techniques, and General Dynamics had recently produced the F-111 and F-16. Work was divided between the team members: Lockheed Skunk

A USAF F-22A climbs in afterburner. (Author Photo/Illustration)

Works assumed overall design responsibility including RCS work, and would build the forward fuselage and cockpit in their Burbank, California, facility. Boeing would tackle the wings and aft fuselage while General Dynamics would produce the center fuselage, weapons bay, and undercarriage. Final assembly would take place at Lockheed's Palmdale, California, facility.[15]

Rollout and First Flight

Air Force Plant 42 in Palmdale once again took its place in aviation history as the first YF-22A (t/n N22YF) PAV-1 was unveiled inside Lockheed's Plant 10 facility on 29 August 1990. Through special effects lighting, a first view of the aircraft depicted a very different design solution to the ATF requirements. The twin vertical stabilizers were rather adequate compared to the entire airframe and were only slightly canted outward. A compromise had been made, sacrificing some stealth for maneuverability. In fact, when the Northrop team finally had a look at the competing YF-22, they thought they had achieved a superior stealth solution.

It was an ideal photo op when both the YF-23A PAV-1, dark gray, and the PAV-2, painted light gray, flew in formation. (USAF)

YF-23 Parts Commonality

Early in the YF-23A flight test program, Paul Metz provided some insight and lessons learned on parts commonality in a paper for the SETP. Metz's initially stated: "First, off-the-shelf does not equal trouble free."

- The nose gear was from an F-15C, with an F-15 STOL/MTD (Short Takeoff and Landing/Maneuver Technology Demonstrator) steering actuator. During the first taxi test we encountered a heavy shimmy. Inspection of the nose gear found no obvious culprits such as free-play. By reducing damping of the steering actuator, we could analytically replicate the shimmy, but the steering actuator was identical to the SMTD, where no shimmy was encountered. McDonnell Douglas engineering suggested a mass balance, which was fabricated and installed forward of the strut axis. The next taxi run showed a virtual elimination of the problem.
- Aircraft brakes were an accepted design compromise for the YF-23A. Again, for cost savings we used the F/A-18's main landing gear, wheels and brakes. They had less energy capacity than required for the heavier YF-23A. During landing we routinely used aero-braking, and didn't touch the brakes until about 80 mph—we rolled out the entire length of the runway to save tires. Obviously, production aircraft will have custom landing gear, but for the purpose of the Dem/Val program the F/A-18 brakes were adequate.

Another lesson learned was that ground effects remain hard to predict. We were concerned that the aircraft would require speeds well above flying speed to rotate and fly. The taxi tests suggested that we had considerably more pitch than predicted, and first flight confirmed this. The aircraft rotated nicely at 120 KCAS (138 mph) and flew off at about 20 knots (23 mph) less than the simulator predicted. Up and away and out of ground effect, the aero data was very close to predictions.

- Our final lesson has been the reaffirmation of the value of the CALSPAN TIFS (Total Inflight Simulator). Testing had suggested that formation handling qualities were excellent. The aircraft is nimble and easily moved around on the wing, but is stable and "locks in" to any position desired. Pilot workload was very low and this was further validated during aerial refueling. The airplane is the easiest refueler I have ever flown; and I never thought anything could beat the F-105 Thud.
- Similarly, the TIFS gave us real insight into the landing phase. The importance of positive speed stability was proven, and the flight controls were thoroughly stressed in the power approach phase. The YF-23A proved to mimic the TIFS results quite accurately. Landings are "no brainers." Speed on final can be controlled to within plus or minus two knots with little effort. Similar to the F-15 the airplane floats onto the concrete and actual touchdowns are difficult to detect.[14]

The sleek YF-23A PAV-2 moving up behind a KC-135 tanker. During the Dem/Val, actual missile launches were not required, but PAV-1 carried an instrumented AIM-120 AMRAAM mounted to an advanced launcher in its weapons bay. (USAF)

The number-one YF-22A (t/n N22YF) in April 1991, just outside the ATF Combined Test Force hangar at Edwards AFB. (Author)

The YF-22A was 62.1 feet long, 5.4 feet shorter than the YF-23A; its wingspan of 44.5 feet had a 30-degree sweep. Rather large trapezoidal inlets were located on each side of the forward fuselage. The cockpit design appeared to provide excellent all-around visibility for the pilot, and following the successful F-16 program, the cockpit was equipped with a side-stick controller. The YF-22A airframe was composed of 39 percent titanium, primarily in the bulkheads and in the aircraft's hot sections. Another 24 percent was carbon-fiber composites, such as the access doors and the honeycomb sandwich skin sections. Although the Air Force had dropped its thrust vectoring requirement, Lockheed opted to retain the system on the aft nozzles of the YF-22A. This area was, in fact, off-limits to photographers for an extended period of time. Later during flight evaluations, the YF-22A used vectoring to enhance its turning radius at Mach 1 without speed bleed-off.

Lockheed Chief Test Pilot David Ferguson took the number-one YF-22A PAV-1 into the air at Palmdale on 29 September 1990 and made the short flight to Edwards AFB. No anomalies were reported and Ferguson was impressed with the aircraft's handling qualities. The first YF-22A was powered by the Pratt & Whitney YF119-100, and the second prototype (PAV-2) would be powered by the General Electric YF120-100. As with the Northrop YF-23A prototypes, this allowed the two competing engine types to be evaluated in two identical aircraft. The quick-paced program followed with a supersonic flight on 25 October. On the 11th flight on 26 October, the first

On 29 August 1990, the YF-22A's rollout ceremony was held at Lockheed's Plant 10 at Air Force Plant 42 in Palmdale, California. (Lockheed Martin)

The Lockheed F-117A was first unveiled in 1981 and featured a faceted design to achieve a low observable signature. The YF-22A utilized this technique along with some curvilinear aspects. In this image the lead conceptual F-117A is testing an experimental embedded light-manipulation camouflage system, for switching from night to daylight missions. Although officially retired into flyable storage in 2008, at least two F-117As are reported to be conducting test flights. (Author Photo/Illustration)

The Lockheed YF-22A PAV-1 (N22YF) parked at the ATF Combined Test Force hangar during April 1991. Overall design attributes of the YF-22A sacrificed some stealth for maneuverability. The canopy shape and positioning provides excellent pilot visibility during all flight regimes. (Author)

Just prior to pulling the wheel chocks, Lockheed chief test pilot Dave Ferguson prepares to conduct the first YF-22A taxi tests at Lockheed's Air Force Plant 42 Palmdale facility. (Lockheed Martin)

aerial refueling was completed. Supercruise was achieved in early November with an outstanding Mach 1.58 on the Mach meter.[16]

Number-two YF-22A (t/n N22YX-AF s/n 87-0701) piloted by Lockheed test pilot Tom Morganfield first flew on 30 October 1990. For the first time the weapons bay doors were opened in flight on 20 November. Although the firing of missiles was not required for the Dem/Val, later that month, Jon Beesly, piloting PAV-2, fired the first live air-to-air missile from an ATF: an AIM-9 Sidewinder over the Naval Weapons Center at China Lake, California. On 20 December, Tom Morganfield in PAV-2 launched an inert AIM-120 AMRAAM on the NAS Point Mugu Pacific Missile Test Range. For the launch sequence, both missiles were extended from the weapons bay on its launcher and pyrotechnically ejected to clear the aircraft; the weapons bay door is equipped with a spoiler to control the airflow.[17] This completed the YF-22A missile-testing phase. Concurrently, during the Dem/Val phase, the Northrop YF-23A PAV-1 carried an instrumented AIM-120 AMRAAM mounted to an advanced launcher in its weapons bay. Northrup opted to not fire a missile, and this technique simulated an actual launch.

The first YF-22A tested the thrust-vectoring system on 15 November 1990 and successfully completed rapid supersonic roll and pitch rates. The resulting data proved superior to contemporary fighters operating at subsonic speeds. The actual turning radius was improved by 35 percent at Mach 1.4. Additionally, there was minimum speed bleed-off during these turns. The decision to retain the thrust-vectoring system seemed to pay off. On 17 September, the number-two[18] F-22A successfully flew at 60-degrees angle-of-attack and demonstrated post-stall flight with thrust vectoring. Near the close of testing on 28 December 1990, Morganfield accelerated PAV-1 to a maximum speed of Mach 2. One issue that could affect future performance that Lockheed engineers were examining was

On 29 September 1990, Dave Ferguson took the number-one YF-22A PAV-1 into the air at Palmdale and made the short flight to Edwards AFB. No anomalies were reported, and Ferguson was impressed with the aircraft's handling qualities. The first YF-22A was powered by the Pratt & Whitney YF119-100, and the second prototype (PAV-2) would be powered by the General Electric YF120-100. (Author Photo/Illustration)

During the Dem/Val the YF-22A PAV-1 is pulling up to go vertical during a climb test. (Author Photo/Illustration)

the weight of the YF-22A. The takeoff combat weight had increased to 58,000 pounds; conversely, although appearing larger, the YF-23A at maximum weight was 54,000 pounds.

During a December 1990 press conference, Lockheed Chief Test Pilot Dave Ferguson remarked, "We have engaged the thrust vectoring on both aircraft, and this roughly gives you twice the amount of roll power at slow speeds. It's kind of an indirect thing in that vectoring does not directly increase the roll power. It controls the pitch of the aircraft so it allows more of the differential tail and other roll devices to be used for rolling the airplane. We've had the airplane as slow as 120 knots mph with maximum stick rolls and we found that the aircraft will roll in excess of 100 degrees per second."[19]

Decision Time and a Precursor for Future Production

Similar to the unveiling of the Northrop YA-9A and Fairchild YA-10A, when the ATF demonstrators were shown for the first time, it was evident that both contractors had come up with completely different design solutions. Despite the excruciating cost increases on the B-2 program due to draconian cuts in production numbers, there were individuals who immediately sought to reduce the F-22 procurement. The first reduction was an adjustment due to the end of the Cold War. Although it was announced just prior to contractor selection, at the time it made sense; unfortunately it turned into a slippery slope. Major reductions instituted after the financial calculations for a production run have been carefully established by contractors gradually led to a unit-cost disaster. This first cut turned out to be only one of a series of ATF number reductions that seemed to be, once again, designed to raise the unit cost.

One day before the selection of a winner of the ATF contract, Sec. of Defense Dick Cheney announced that the number of ATFs would be reduced from 750 to 648. The next day, on 23 April 1991, Sec. of the Air Force Donald B. Rice announced that the Lockheed/Boe-

The Gray Ghost Northrop YF-23A PAV-2 flies with the Lockheed YF-22A PAV-1 over the Edwards test range. (USAF)

ing/General Dynamics YF-22A Team had been selected to develop the ATF. Dr. Rice commented, "[This aircraft] clearly offered better capability and lower cost." Rice later said that "neither aircraft was noticeably more stealthy or maneuverable than the other." It was also stated that the Pratt & Whitney YF119-100 engine was selected because it was better integrated and "benefitted from the organization of Lockheed's offering." The Air Force judged both candidates as outstanding, but commented that the YF-22A was more balanced and they preferred the Lockheed industrial team.[20] This had to be a tough choice because the YF-23A was reportedly faster and had a lower RCS. But the YF-22A was more maneuverable.

Would the YF-22A's maneuverability prove more effective in the long run? At the time a Pentagon spokesperson emphasized that Northrop's proposal met or exceeded all requirements and "we would have gone with it with full confidence if there wasn't another plane in it. We had two really super planes, but the better plane won. It's too bad we can't have them both."[21]

On 2 August 1991, the initial engineering and manufacturing development (EMD) phase contract for $9.55 billion was awarded by the Air Force. This would include the delivery of 11 F-22A FSD aircraft. Two of these aircraft would be F-22B two-seat aircraft; however, this variant was later canceled to save costs. Lockheed would also produce two fatigue/static testbed aircraft. Pratt & Whitney received a contract for $9.5 billion to supply 33 F119-100 engines.

On 15 August 2015, during a 25th YF-23A First Flight Anniversary event at the Western Museum of Flight, Torrance, California, Paul Metz commented on the program. He emphasized that Northrop had the finest engineers anywhere and they had created an aircraft that surpassed requirements. "Both

Lockheed YF-22A PAV-1 and PAV-2 flying together over the Edwards compass rose. PAV-1 has the spin-chute device mounted to its aft section. (USAF)

Lockheed's proposed U.S. Navy F-22N for the NATF program. The carrier-based two-seat aircraft would have utilized a variable-geometry swing wing to slow landing-approach speed. Designed for the Navy as an effective, surviv-able, and affordable multirole aircraft, it featured slight iterations from the AX and F/A-X programs that all materialized at the time. (Lockheed Martin)

Two conceptual U.S. Navy/Northrop F-23Ns on a sortie near the carrier strike force. The Northrop proposal for the F-23N NATF featured canards for maneuverability and for slower approach speeds for carrier ops. The design also featured slightly canted twin vertical tails with ser-rated trailing edges that replaced the YF-23A ruddervator arrangement. This change was to achieve slow speed aerodynamic control, while retaining a low RCS. (Author Photo/Illustration)

the YF-22A and YF-23A were green-lit—in other words, both compet-itors passed all the technical requirements of the ATF program." Metz continued that "the decision between the YF-22A and YF-23A was based on non-technical issues, as related in the announcement."

Metz also hinted that not everyone involved in the decision had an engineering background and that they may have been influenced by better marketing. For example, there were released photos of the YF-22A at 60-degrees AOA, which the YF-23A could have easily performed, but it wasn't part of the flight test program. Additional-ly, photos showing the competitor YF-22A firing an AIM-9M and AIM-120 were released. Metz pointed out that was "again, something the YF-23A could do but that was not required in the test program. In retrospect, Northrop could have done a better job of marketing to nontechnical persons rather than rely on fantastic, but occasionally opaque, engineering specifications and results."

YF-23A program managers and test pilots were unanimous on one thing: "We can't give any details, but the YF-23A was really fast; really fast." Immediately after the loss, Northrop CEO and chairman Kent Kresa wrote a cover letter to Northrop shareholders: "In the wake of losing ATF, the Company will work better to document its ability to reduce risk and manage programs." Many years later in a documentary on the YF-23A's history, Kresa said, "To this day I felt they made the wrong decision, if the criteria was for the best possi-ble airplane for the mission. You ask me how I felt, that's how I felt."

The winning Lockheed F-22A Raptor program was headed into unknown territory. A minefield of escalating costs and delays and

unrelenting budget crunchers whose single skill is to reduce aircraft production numbers. It is interesting to note that after the USAF LWF YF-16 versus the YF-17 contest, the Navy opted not to embrace the USAF YF-16 winner and chose the twin-engine YF-17; it evolved into the F/A-18 Hornet. In 1988, the Navy began reviewing the spec-ifications for a navalized F-22N, known as the NATF. A concurrent F-22N production line could have reduced unit cost early on. The NATF program was dropped in 1991.

Nip and Tuck

The Lockheed YF-22A was judged to be the lower risk because of necessary structural changes that would be required to bring the Northrop YF-23A configuration up to FSD standards. In fact, both aircraft would require such modifications. Northrop would have revised the upper aft fuselage bread-loafs section to a lower and smoother design with the aft nozzles moved slightly closer together. There were rumors that Northrop would have added separate rud-ders to the large ruddervators. However, it is believed that only the contour would have been altered slightly. Conversely, after the con-tract award there were alterations to the original YF-22A to attain the FSD F-22A configuration.

The F-22A's air intakes were moved slightly aft, and the canopy was moved a few inches forward for better pilot visibility, which changed the contour of the nose. In addition, the main landing-gear doors' angle toward the fuselage was altered, and more noticeably

The first flight of the Lockheed /Martin F-22A Raptor 01 (s/n 4001) Spirit of America occurred at 10:18 a.m. EST on 7 September 1997 from Dobbins Air Reserve Base, Georgia, adjacent to Lockheed Martin's Marietta plant. In the cockpit was Paul Metz, who had left Northrop and joined Lockheed Martin as its chief test pilot. (Lockheed Martin)

Two conceptual operational USAF/Northrop Grumman F-23As. Stealth and high Mach speed were the YF-23A's outstanding attributes. The operational version would have featured a slight shape modification on the ruddervators configuration, the aft engine section is shallower and less squared off, and part of the aft section is straight-edged. To accommodate the tandem weapons bays, the operational F-23's forebody was stretched approximately 2.5 feet. (Author Photo/Illustration)

the area of both the twin vertical fins and horizontal stabilizers was reduced by 10 percent. The contour of the horizontal stabilizers was also changed. On 4 March 1994, new computer modeling techniques discovered shortfalls in the F-22's RCS measurements. Drain holes on the aircraft's underside were reduced, and access panels were combined. Northrop test pilot Paul Metz would later comment, "The YF-23A was not the FSD F-23A; the prototype is only a definition of what could have been. As noted, after the YF-22A won the competition there were a series of refinements that took place to evolve the aircraft into a production F-22 Raptor. The YF-23A was a fine aircraft, but never had the opportunity to evolve."[22]

F-22 Production Cuts

In an editorial in *Air Force* magazine, Editor-in-Chief Robert S. Dudney wrote, "If the first three cuts were damaging, the next one could be fatal if it drops the goal to anything like 180 fighters.

This might drive the cost of each F-22 beyond a politically sensitive threshold. At that point, it probably would fall into what Sen. Daniel Y. Inouye (D-HI), chairman of the Senate defense appropriations subcommittee, calls 'the B-2 Syndrome.'" Dudney continued, "Inouye, a staunch airpower advocate, notes DoD first wanted to buy several hundred B-2 stealth bombers but reduced the goal to 132 aircraft. Then it was cut to 75 for budget reasons and cut again to 20,[29] again for budget reasons. Each time, the program's sunk costs were spread over fewer airplanes and unit cost grew dramatically. It wasn't long before critics could assail the B-2 as the $2 billion bomber. The B-2 never recovered from that political disaster. Few believe the F-22 would fare any better under similar circumstances."[30]

Another hypothetical USAF/Northrop F-23A air dominance fighter from the 422nd Test & Evaluation Squadron. The sleek F-23 silhouette provides a good indication of its low radar signature. (Author Photo/Illustration)

An F-22A (t/n 005) from the 412th Test Wing (t/n 005) taxis on the runway at Edwards AFB during October 2003. (Author)

Exporting the Raptor

In essence, exporting the F-22 was forbidden. U.S. legislation was passed after the rollout of the first EMD F-22 that forbade export of the aircraft with its radar-evading stealth features and state-of-the-art software. Officially it was called the Obey Amendment of 1997 to the Appropriations Bill Public Law 106-79, Section 8092.[23] At the start of the F-22 program, Lockheed had calculated exports into its financial calculus. Allies such as Japan, Israel, the Republic of Korea, and Australia were considered prospects. Early on, the Japanese government showed a keen interest in acquiring the F-22 and even offered to cover the cost to reengineer sensitive systems to meet export restrictions.[24] This would create a very capable F-22, less some of the most sensitive technical data. Australia, a close ally, is in excellent geographical position to counter China's push into the South China Sea. In a political sense, introduction of the sophisticated F-22 in Israel and the Republic of Korea could have posed problems. However, Israel would feel more secure with the F-22's capabilities in the event it had to defend itself against a more sophisticated Iranian military. Israel is an F-35 JSF partner with an order for 33 F-35As. Two jets will be delivered in 2016 and the remaining by 2021; that is over 10 years after the F-22 export denial.

The United States already had close multifaceted military cooperation efforts with Japan. Mitsubishi Heavy Industries built the F-4EJ Phantom II and F-15C/DJ Eagle under license. During June 2009, as chairman of the Senate Appropriations Committee, Sen. Daniel Inouye (D-HI) actually forwarded a proposal to Japan's ambassador to the United States, offering 40 F-22s to be delivered in 2017. What was not known was the amount of Japan's offer to finance U.S. reengineering of systems to make them less sensitive. This would hopefully lower the unit cost estimated to be approximately $290 million; this amount was spread out over all incurring costs. Despite the aircraft unit cost, Japan remained interested. Congress was behind the deal, which would increase the number of F-22s produced and possibly lower the cost of the U.S. version. Although the cost was high, this could be balanced out in Japan's defense budget. With the F-22 being an overwhelming force multiplier, the JASDF could retire their older F-4 Phantoms earlier and operate fewer F-15J Eagles.[25] As it turned out, Secretary Gates disagreed with the proposal, as it interfered with his F-22 reduction plans already in place. Gates offered the F-35 JSF instead, but at the time JASDF experts knew the F-35 was no match for the F-22's capabilities; plus, the F-35 delivery schedule was nebulous. Additionally, the JASDF needed to project its defense posture over the Sea of Japan, East China Sea, Sea of Okhotsk, and the Pacific Ocean to the east—and the twin-engine air-dominance

A hypothetical view of two JASDF F-22AJs in a near-vertical climb. Export of the F-22 was forbidden by U.S. legislation enacted in 1997. In 2005, several Air Force senior officers and congressmen with a forward vision wanted that bill reviewed from a technical point of view. It was never overturned and, adding to the misjudgment, the F-22 production number was also capped. Today, China is projecting its power in the region, and the force-multiplier F-22 would be a viable deterrent. A modified but highly capable F-22 for the JASDF would have also continued a close high-technology aircraft relationship with Japan. (Author Photo/Illustration)

A conceptual Israel Air Force F-22I flying a current operational F-16I over desert terrain. Israel was considering the F-22 and, to avoid potential political problems, even a small number of F-22s would have provided substantial security and deterrence well into the future. Today, 10 years later, there are numerous threats and a more sophisticated Iranian military. (Author Photo/Illustration)

F-22 fit the mission. JASDF fighters/interceptors consisted of the twin-engine F-4EJ and F-15C/DJ, and only the indigenous F-2 was a single-engine jet. Today, Japan is grappling with long-range air-defense issues as it faces an increasingly aggressive China. It was during February 2005 when Air Force Chief of Staff Gen. John Jumper stated that this restricted export policy banning foreign sales of the F/A-22[26] should be reexamined. General Jumper's successor, Gen. T. Michael Moseley, was also in favor of exporting the F-22. Apparently, the next chief of staff, Gen. Norton Schwartz, did not push the idea any further.[27]

Another negative side effect of not working on this issue more closely with Japan was that it disrupted the close high-technology relationship the United States and Japan have shared for many decades. In addition, the U.S. balance of trade is affected. Japan is now developing a stealth fighter on its own, or it could still obtain an aircraft from other country. The United States no longer has a monopoly on advanced fighter aircraft. There would most likely be no F-35 JSF program without the partner nations participating and purchasing the airplane to increase production. The F-35 has stealth coatings and other advanced features, including the special helmet cueing system with all-aspect viewing. The F-35 can not only be exported but is now being built outside the United States.[28] Despite ongoing problems, the F-35 enjoys unwavering DoD support. Yet at the time, with its production numbers being so critical to its survival, the F-22 was not reviewed again for possible export.

Pure power is demonstrated as a conceptual RAAF (Royal Australian Air Force) F-22A pulls toward vertical. Australia also considered the F-22 because it's geographically positioned to counter China's continuing power projection into the South China Sea. With the F-22 export denied, the RAAF acquired the F/A-18F Super Hornet and later the EA-18G Growler. (Author Photo/Illustration)

Air Force officials in the Pentagon listed basic mistakes F-22A critics were making:

The threats: In 2005, Sec. of Defense Donald H. Rumsfeld's reduction decision was based on the premise that big weapon systems are no longer needed in an era of "irregular, catastrophic, and disruptive" forms of conflict. Air Force officials emphasized that it is not about today, but about the period of 2015–2020.[31] Additionally, most critics disparage the Raptor as a mere dogfighter. Essentially, they had no concept of its electronic capabilities, such as precision ground attack, surveillance, electronic attack, and data collection for networked warfare.

Required numbers: Some critics argue the USAF could get by with a silver-bullet force, a relative handful of highly capable F/A-22As. To these analysts, a total of 180 Raptors would be more than sufficient to prevail in any combat scenario. True, but irrelevant, said USAF officials, because that is not the basis for determining force structure. What is needed is a sufficient number of F/A-22As to maintain an adequate rotation base and keep the operational tempo of the force within bounds. The Air Force said the minimum requirement is one F/A-22A squadron (24 combat-coded Raptors) for each of its 10 Air and Space Expeditionary Forces. That would enable USAF to forward deploy, at all times, two F/A-22A squadrons without breaking

An F-22A Raptor going vertical at high altitude during a 2003 test-flight evaluation. (Author Photo/Illustration)

An F-22A makes a high-speed pass with its weapons bay open. The F-22A is capable of carrying four AIM-120 AMRRAMs, two AIM-9 Sidewinders, and/or a mix of PGMs in its internal weapons bay. (Author)

During January 2005 Lockheed Martin's Advanced Development Projects Division revealed the latest configuration of its FB-22, a proposed affordable F-22A derivative. The two-seat stealthy deep-strike aircraft, powered by two derivative F119 engines, would have Mach 1.9 penetration capability for time-critical targets. Designed with three times the range as the F-22A, other enhancements included an expanded weapons bay, underwing conformal stores, network warfare enabled, and multimission capability. The FB-22's wingspan is 73.6 feet and its overall length is 64.3 feet. Weapons payload would be 30,000 pounds, and to reduce tanker support, internal fuel capacity would be a respectable 43,745 pounds. The FB-22 concept was not funded. (Author Photo/Illustration)

rotation cycles. According to Air Force officials, this requires a fleet of 381 Raptors, more than twice the 180 fighters now in the plan. In early 2005, USAF Chief of Staff Gen. John Jumper offered to defer some purchases of the impending F-35 JSF instead, but the Pentagon rebuffed this idea.[32]

Former commander of Air Combat Command Gen. John M. Loh recently commented on this critical subject. "From 1997 onward, the numbers of F-22s were reduced from 750 to 339 in 1997, to 277 in 2003. Then, in April 2009, reduced to 187 when Secretary Gates terminated the production. As these reductions took place, I was furious that the Congress and the DoD were overlooking a most fundamental business principle, return on investment, that no business spends $28 billion to develop a product expecting a handsome return over a long production cycle, then terminates the program after only a few hundred." General Loh continued, "That's corporate negligence. I had just endured this 'graveyard spiral' of dwindling numbers causing increased unit costs on the B-2 Spirit stealth bomber, to the point that we spent as much to develop it (about $25 billion) as we spent on production (about $24 billion) for only 21 B-2s. The B-2 cycle was a gross violation of return on investment."[33] It is also vital to note that during ATF Dem/Val, both the Lockheed and Northrop ATF teams each funded approximately $1.1 billion of internal funding on their prototypes before F-22 EMD production even started.

Secretary Gates Takes Action

On 6 April 2009, Sec. of Defense Robert Gates staged a preemptive budget attack. He announced cuts of $78 billion to the U.S. military and defense department over five years. Among the 32 Pentagon program casualties was the F-22. Gates later stated that other defense secretaries had cut the program, and he was just delivering the coup de grace.[34] Unfortunately, perpetuating an incorrect initial decision is not the best way to proceed.

Gates commented on high-tech wars against peers, "I was convinced they were far less likely to occur than messy, smaller unconventional military endeavors." As a result Gates moved to quash any programs like the F-22 that were meant to counter a world-class threat.[35] No one would dispute that the United States must be prepared for the type of asymmetric warfare that Secretary Gates mentioned, but we need to be prepared for both. Not producing enough F-22As that can guarantee air superiority over the next future conflict is a questionable strategy.

Did Secretary Gates forget about the U.S. Cold War strategy to preserve peace? During that period the United States established a triad of nuclear forces comprised of long-range bombers, submarines with SLBMs, and land-based ICBMs—a buildup far superior to the Soviet Union. This triad, plus the initial development President Reagan's Strategic Defense Initiative (SDI) that could negate the Soviet

A conceptual USAF/Northrop Grumman FB-23 during a high-speed dash. During the fall of 2005, Northrop Grumman released limited information regarding their FB-23 design, a stealthy deep-strike derivative of the YF-23A. Although drastically improving its range and payload, the FB-23 retained the tandem-wing low-observable attributes of the original YF-23A. The fuselage was lengthened to accommodate a larger weapons bay, and the cockpit was now a two-seat arrangement redesigned for sustained flight above Mach 2. The FB-23 concept was not funded. (Author Photo/Illustration)

An F-22A Raptor (t/n 013) from the 422nd Test & Evaluation Squadron taxis at Nellis AFB. (Author)

An F-22A Raptor (t/n 015) from the 422nd Test & Evaluation Squadron at rest in the shade from the desert sun at Nellis AFB in March 2004. (Author)

The X-44A MANTA (multiaxis no-tail aircraft) concept was first disclosed in 1999 with a goal to fly in 2007. The X-44A was a cooperative effort by NASA Dryden Flight Research Center, Lockheed Martin, Pratt & Whitney, and the USAF Research Laboratory. The concept would utilize an F-22 fuselage, a delta wing with rounded edges, no verticals tails, and be powered by two P&W F119-100 engines with new control systems. The X-44A would use thrust vectoring (TV) only with low-observable three-dimensional nozzles. Conventional flight-control surfaces would be eliminated. The flight-test study would benefit future military and commercial aircraft. However, due to cuts in F-22 production numbers and lack of funding, the program was canceled in 2000. (Author Photo/Illustration)

Union's ICBMs aimed at the United States, gradually achieved a U.S. Cold War victory. Technically and economically, the Soviets could not keep up. These DoD programs ultimately prevented the unthinkable, securing the idea that no rational nation would challenge us with nuclear weapons. As soon as you begin to relax those standards, your adversaries will be looking for opportunities. Instituting major defense cuts with a weak foreign policy is a terrible combination. In viewing today's international U.S. leadership vacuum, Russia has been active during President Obama's two terms in office: the invasion of eastern Ukraine, the annexation of Crimea, and military expansion into the Arctic regions. A major blunder[36] was failing to act to prevent Syria's civil war from spiraling out of control, which gave Vladimir Putin a green light for adventurism.

Meanwhile, China has continued to shift its military posture from mostly a defensive mode to the development of sophisticated aircraft for the People's Liberation Army Air Force (PLAAF) and naval assets to project power. China continues to violate international law by building artificial islands on reefs in the South China Sea that are claimed by the Philippines. At least one 10,000-foot runway is under construction that could handle bombers, fighters, and maritime

An F-22A Raptor from the 422nd Test & Evaluation Squadron at Nellis AFB with its weapons bay open. The EDO Corporation's dedicated launcher will extend into the airstream, and the missile is ejected forcefully away from the aircraft. The F-22A is capable of carrying up to eight air-to-air missiles and/or PGMs. (Author Photo/Illustration)

A Raptor's tight turning capability is demonstrated in afterburner. The author notes that while observing take-offs at Edwards AFB, the superior acceleration of the F-22A over the F-16 and F-15 is readily apparent to the naked eye. (Author)

A USAF F-22A Raptor in full afterburner demonstrates its rapid-climb capability. (Author)

A conceptual Northrop Grumman ASTRA (advanced stealth-technology reconnaissance aircraft): An advanced two-seat strike-reconnaissance concept based on YF-23 technology. The stealth and speed advantages were certainly aspects that could be incorporated into such a YF-23A derivative aircraft. (Author Photo/Illustration)

patrol aircraft. This is China's first serious attempt to artificially project new territorial waters and challenge U.S. dominance in the Pacific.

Behind-the-Scenes Maneuvering

On the following 22 July, the U.S. Congress approved all defense cuts proposed by Secretary Gates, including the F-22 production cap.[37] Most members of Congress viewed this as an opportunity to trim the budget, and they trusted the opinion of the Secretary of Defense. Some of the cuts were probably justified, but not all. This should have been a warning to keep Congress properly informed on defense matters. The vote was no coincidence. For a long time Secretary Gates had been working hard and maneuvering behind the scenes. He sacked Sec. of the Air Force Michael W. Wynne and Chief of Staff Gen. T. Michael Moseley. His rationale was never publicly released, but Wynne and General Moseley were fervent F-22 supporters.

During Gates's consensus-building effort, he had bluntly warned Lockheed Martin not to promote the F-22 or face funding cuts to their F-35 JSF program. Lockheed Martin was unquestionably boxed in—a definite downside of holding too many similar contracts, in this case fighter jets. What was truly astounding was a Gates statement comparing the F-22 and F-35 programs. Gates justified the ending of production by noting, "The F-35 was coming along and was comparable to the F-22 in the air-to-air mission." Even the F-35's prime contractor Lockheed Martin has never claimed this.[38] Gen. Mark Welch, the Air Force chief of staff, stated in September 2015 that "the F-35 was never designed to be the next dogfighting machine. It was designed to be the multipurpose, data-integration platform that could do all kinds of things in the air-to-ground arena including dismantling integrated air defenses. It has an air-to-air capability, but it was not intended to be an air superiority fighter. That was the F-22."[39]

Due to the low production number, during late 2015 the Air Force released its plans to retain the F-22 Raptor fleet into the 2040s. The design life of the F-22 is 8,000 hours—which roughly equates to a service life of about 22 years, at 360 hours of flying per year. (USAF)

A conceptual view of an F-22A escorting a RuAF Tupolev Tu-160 Blackjack bomber. Reminiscent of the Cold War, these type of intercepts are becoming common once again. For long-range intercepts, or ferry fights, where stealth is not needed, the F-22A utilizes jettisonable drop tanks. (Author Photo/Illustration)

An emerging Russian stealth fighter, the Sukhoi PAK FA T-50 first flew on 29 January 2010. Destined for deployment with the Russian Air Force (RuAF), the stealthy single-seat twin-engine fighter has demonstrated excellent maneuverability. The T-50 design features low RCS, but would recommend embedding the IRST system, which is located just ahead of the canopy. Capable of supercruise, within five years the T-50 will have an uprated engine. A cooperative effort with India is underway to increase production. (Author Photo/Illustration)

Following a Flawed Strategy

Secretary Gates specified that in the event of a conflict with China, the F-22's potential Pacific bases in Japan and elsewhere would be destroyed, leaving nowhere to base a short-range aircraft like the F-22.[40] This implies that the USAF would permit its entire Far East–based F-22 fleet to get caught on the ground. That statement probably had many senior Air Force officers wondering about the type of logic and attitude they were actually dealing with. As far as range, the F-22 has a combat radius comparable to contemporary fighters and is equipped with jettisonable drop tanks for long-range sorties. Gates also indicated the F-22 "would not play a role in any of the wars we were already in."[41, 42] It should be noted that many Cold War aircraft and missiles never entered combat, and that's what SAC had planned for—a strong deterrence.

Another serious flaw in Gates's strategy was his statement that "the Raptor would be an overkill in any fight." Any combat pilot would tell you that surprise and an overall advantage over the enemy was critical in any aerial dual. This eventually provides an advantage for our ground forces to do their job. This has worked since World War II, and now Gates wanted to change the formula. Was Gates's philosophy to lower our technical standards and tilt the playing field in favor of our adversaries? That could prove very costly in the long run. Even if China continued producing fourth-generation fighters with advanced air-to-air missiles, their strategy is to produce large numbers of aircraft. And numbers will always get you. Gates also stated that U.S. intelligence had informed him China would not have a compet-ing stealth fighter until the early 2020s at the earliest. This statement is quite illogical. It implies that if we cap the number of F-22s in 2009, when China fields a competing stealth fighter fleet in the early 2020s, the United States will be ready with a minimum fleet of F-22s.

Even our British ally was stunned by the action of the U.S. government. In the comment section of *Flight International* magazine, published in April 2012, the editors wrote, "Terminating the

An F-22A Raptor from the 1st Fighter Wing at Langley AFB on a Red Flag mission over the Nellis AFB Test and Training Range. The Groom Lake (Area 51) base is in the background. (USAF)

On 11 July 2008, an F-22A from the 411th Flight Test Squadron released the first GBU-39 small-diameter bomb (SDB) at supersonic speed. The GBU-39 with a folding X-wing is capable of destroying critical targets at standoff distances. A single F-22 can carry eight SDBs and hit that number of separate targets on a single sortie. (USAF)

China's challenge: A prototype Chengdu J-20 stealth air superiority/multirole fighter escorted by two PLAAF J-10S fighters The Chinese J-20 stealth fighter made its first flight on 11 January 2011 and is designed to carry antiship missiles to challenge the U.S. Navy in the Asia-Pacific region. Although described as a coincidence by Chinese officials, the J-20's first flight occurred during a visit by U.S. Sec. of Defense Robert Gates. Several years earlier in April 2009, Gates capped the Lockheed Martin F-22 production and predicted that China would not have a stealth fighter until the 2020s. (Author Photo/Illustration)

Lockheed Martin F-22 Raptor program after 187 production examples was shortsighted and irresponsible. Production of the F-22 met its end just when it was starting to bear the fruits of painful learning. Now the U.S. may be ill-equipped to counter threats from fast-rising rivals. The U.S. spent some $70 billion on a fighter that will have no true rival for decades but that investment was squandered amid an ideological debate over the changing nature of warfare. The USAF was allowed to buy barely enough F-22s for six squadrons while training and test units go neglected. The new fighters of China and Russia are superior to Western fourth-generation designs."[43]

Basically, capping F-22 production as the F-35 program was in its early development was a serious mistake. Even though the F-35 is not on parity with the F-22, it is the only fifth-generation fighter the United States is producing and would complement the F-22 handily. Secretary Gates won his massive budget-trimming effort as all but two of the proposed DoD program cuts were eventually agreed upon by Congress. An assessment some nine years later during late 2015 concludes that the USAF still needs more F-22s, and out of the three F-35 variants only the USMC F-35B has achieved IOC. Only history will tell who the actual winners and losers were.

During Secretary Gates visit to the People's Republic of China in January 2011, the Chinese government released photos of their new Chengdu J-20 stealth fighter in flight. This was 10 years ahead of Gates's prediction. In October 2014, the Shenyang J-31, a Chinese equivalent to the Lockheed Martin fifth-generation F-35 JSF, was

flown for the first time. So much for no peer adversaries. Although neither of these Chinese stealth fighters will ever approach F-22/F-35 capabilities, superior production numbers could pose a future threat from both China and Russia. All agree that Gates's termination of F-22 production will have a lasting negative impact on national security.

Congressional Required Reading

During early 2009, before the DoD program-cuts press conference, Lockheed Martin was bluntly informed by Secretary Gates to suspend any promotion and support activities for the F-22. However, just prior to that, several new data points were released regarding the aircraft's performance. This included an RCS that officials only characterized as "better" than what was asked for. Pentagon officials previously said privately that the desired signature from certain critical angles was -40 dBsm,[44] the equivalent radar reflection of a steel marble. By comparison, the follow-on F-35 JSF has a greater signature of -30 dBsm, about the size of a golf ball. Additionally, supercruise capability has been extensively employed during ACM operations. Indications are that F-22s flying in supercruise have attained Mach 1.78, and in full military power the Raptor is operating at slightly above 50,000 feet.

During its first joint exercise in 2008 out of Elmendorf AFB, Alaska, the F-22 initiated aerial battles at about 65,000 feet. The

During deployment in Alaska, an F-22A ejects self-defense flares. Already an electronic powerhouse, the near future may prove even more potent for the F-22A. High-power microwaves (HPM) and operational tactical lasers are in development. (Lockheed Martin/ John Dibbs)

Two F-22A Raptors bank left as the sun rises over the Atlantic Ocean. (Author Photo/Illustration)

Raptor's Northrop Grumman/Raytheon Active Electronically Scanned array (AESA) radar has a range of 5 percent greater than expected. That means a cushion of an additional 5 to 6 miles of detection range against approaching bogeys. U.S. aerospace officials agree that an AESA radar "at least doubles" the range over standard aircraft radars. When coupled with the electronic techniques generator in an aircraft, the radar can project jamming, false targets, and other deceptive information into enemy sensors. That could allow electronic attack at ranges of 150 miles or more. The ability to pick out small targets at greater ranges also permits AESA-equipped aircraft to locate and attack cruise missiles, stealth aircraft, and small UAVs. In operational combat effectiveness estimates against top dissimilar fighter aircraft such as the contemporary Sukhoi Su-27 and Mikoyan MiG-29, Lockheed Martin and USAF analysts put the loss-exchange ratio at 30:1 for the F-22; 3:1 for the F-35; and a sobering 1:1 or less for the F-15, F/A-18, and F-16.[45]

Active Raptors

Lockheed had internally nicknamed the YF-22A the Lightning II after its legendary P-38 Lightning of World War II fame. On 9 April

An F-22A Raptor on a heritage flight pass with the venerable P-38L Lightning, A-10C Warthog, and F-16C Viper. (Author)

A USAF/Lockheed F-22A Raptor creates vortices as it pulls a tight turn in the sunset. (Author)

1997, the Air Force officially named the F-22A the Raptor. The first flight of Raptor 01 (s/n 4001), *Spirit of America*, occurred at 10:18 a.m. EST on 7 September 1997 from Dobbins ARB, Georgia, adjacent to Lockheed Martin's Marietta plant. In the cockpit was Paul Metz, who had left Northrop and joined Lockheed Martin as its chief test pilot.

The first production F-22A lifted off at 140 knots mph and remained aloft for 58 minutes. All systems functioned normally as Metz cycled the landing gear, initiated power changes known as engine transients, and reached an altitude of 20,000 feet. After Raptor 01 landed Gen. Dick Hawley, commander of Air Combat Command, quipped, "The airplane will assure our nation of air dominance well into the next century."[46] On 15 December 2005, the F-22A reached IOC.

During late 2015, the Air Force released plans to retain the F-22 Raptor fleet into the 2040s. "Based upon current projected fleet flying hour programs and actual aircraft usage, the predicted service life of the Raptor fleet goes into the 2040s without a SLEP (Service Life Extension Program) of the airframe," said USAF spokesman Ed Gulick. "While the design life of the F-22 is 8,000 hours—which roughly equates to a service life of about 22 years at 360 hours of flying per year—each aircraft has data recorders measuring every stress and strain on the jet."[47] In addition, through 2020 the Air Force is procuring 10,824 upgrade kits under the Reliability and Maintainability Maturation Program (RAMMP) for the F-22A fleet. In conjunction with the Structure Retrofit Program (SRP) the fleet is upgrading to the Increment 3.2 configuration. This adds improved data link and integrates the new AIM-120D AMRAAM and AIM-9X Block II. A redesigned On-Board Oxygen Generation System (OBOGS)[48] is also included to prevent hypoxia-like symptoms.[49]

Despite being capped at 187 aircraft by former Sec. of Defense Robert Gates in April 2009, the F-22 has served with distinction. With the F-22 in combat operations for less than a year, during September 2015 Air Combat Command chief Gen. Hawk Carlisle commented to reporters, "The F-22 is even better than we thought, we won't send airplanes into certain areas of the Syria/Iraq battle zone unless they have F-22s with them." Carlisle also praised the situational awareness of the jets, saying, "Their precision attack ability and capacity enables the F-22 to serve as the quarterback of any air operation. So far in the Middle East, they've flown thousands of hours and flown hundreds of sorties and dropped hundreds of bombs with incredible accuracy. Moreover, the F-22s are turning in mission capable rates of 75–80 percent, and even better in the field, and are proving far more maintainable than originally expected." General Carlisle followed by acknowledging that the number of F-22s[50] is far too small, and when a reporter asked if the USAF should buy more, he said, "I dream about it every night." Practically, though, he said, "The budget may just be too tight to permit such a thing, although the tooling was retained when the production line closed." Carlisle concluded by professing the F-22 as extraordinary and really reaching its stride.[51]

Specifications

Lockheed YF-22 Prototype—Air Dominance Fighter
Crew: 1—pilot
Wingspan: 44 ft. 6 in. (13.5 m)
Length: 62 ft. 1 in. (18.9 m)
Height: 16 ft. 6 in. (5 m)
Maximum weight: 58,000 lb (26,308 kg)
Combat radius: 800 miles (1,482 km)
Supercruise speed: 1,059 mph (1,704 km/h) Mach 1.6
Maximum speed: 1,451 mph (2,335 km/h) Mach 2.2 (top speed classified)
Service ceiling: 50,000 ft. (13,472 m)
Powerplant: PAV-1, 2 Pratt & Whitney YF119-PW-100 turbofans—35,000 lb (155.6 kN) thrust each; PAV-2, 2 General Electric YF120-GE-100 turbofans—35,000 lb (155.6 kN) thrust each
Armament: Test launch, AIM-9M Sidewinder and AIM-120 AMRAAM

Northrop YF-23 Black Widow II Prototype—Air Dominance Fighter
Crew: 1—pilot
Wingspan: 43 ft. 7 in. (13.3 m)
Length: 67 ft. 5 in. (20.5 m)
Height: 13 ft. 11 in. (4.2 m)
Maximum weight: 54,000 lb (24,493 kg)
Ferry range: 2,800 miles (4,506 km)
Combat radius: 900 miles (1,448 km)
Supercruise speed: 1,381 mph (2,222.5 km/h) Mach 1.8
Maximum speed: 1,522 mph+ (2,449 km/h) Mach 2+ (top speed classified)

Service ceiling: 50,050 ft. (15,255 m)
Maximum ceiling: 65,000 ft. (19,812 m)
Powerplant: PAV-1, 2 Pratt & Whitney YF119-PW-100 turbofans—35,000 lb (155.6 kN) thrust each; PAV-2, 2 General Electric YF120-GE-100 turbofans—35,000 lb (155.6 kN) thrust each
Armament: PAV-1, instrumented AMRAAM mounted to an advanced launcher in weapons bay

Lockheed Martin F-22 Raptor—Air Dominance Fighter
Crew: 1—pilot
Wingspan: 44 ft. 5 in. (13.5 m)
Length: 62 ft. (18.8 m)
Height: 16 ft. 6 in. (5 m)
Maximum weight: 83,500 lb (37,874 kg)
Ferry range: 1,850 miles+ (2,977 km+) with drop tanks
Combat radius: 800 miles (1,481 km)
Supercruise speed: 1,212 mph (1,950 km/h) Mach 1.58
Maximum speed: 1,522 mph+ (2,449 km/h) Mach 2+ (top speed classified)
Service ceiling: 50,000 ft.+ (15,240 m+)
Maximum ceiling: 65,000 ft. (19,812 m)
Powerplant: 2 Pratt & Whitney F119-100 turbofans—35,000 lb (155.6 kN) thrust each with afterburner
Payload: 17,000 lb (7,711 kg) mixed ordnance of air-to-air/air-to-ground
Armament: 1 General Electric Vulcan M-61A2 20mm rotary cannon

Chapter 10

COMPETITION OF THE CENTURY THE JOINT STRIKE FIGHTER
BOEING X-32 VERSUS LOCKHEED MARTIN X-35

The formation that never occurred: a conceptual USAF/Boeing F-32A with a USAF/Lockheed Martin F-35A. (Author Photo/Illustration)

Beginning in 1986, the Defense Advanced Research Projects Agency (DARPA) began a cooperative effort with the British Ministry of Defence (MoD) to test the feasibility of a replacement for the RAF/RN Harrier but with increased performance. The more advanced jet fighter program was designated Advanced Short Takeoff and Vertical Landing (ASTOVL). Funding was allocated to General Dynamics, Lockheed, McDonnell Douglas, Pratt & Whitney, and General Electric.[1] Before the entire DARPA test plan could evolve, it was determined that its data could benefit future Short Takeoff and Vertical Land (STOVL) requirements of the USMC as well as attack aircraft for the USAF/USN. A commonality could be formed using a more technically precise method than the previously flawed TFX (F-111) program. With this, the ASTOVL program was changed to the Common Affordable Lightweight Fighter (CALF). Boeing, Lockheed, McDonnell Douglas, and Northrop were invited to submit proposals to design and build two demonstrator aircraft: one STOVL and one Conventional Takeoff and Landing (CTOL).[2]

Joint Advanced Strike Technology

The CALF program continued, but by the early 1990s general consensus in the Pentagon was that the DoD could not afford parallel Air Force/Navy tactical aircraft programs. In 1993, a bottom-up review of Air Force/Navy tactical aircraft development programs was concluded. As a result, both the Air Force Multirole Fighter (MRF) and the A/F-X Air Force/Navy joint deep-strike penetration fighter program were canceled and a new program called Joint Advanced Strike Technology (JAST) was created. The JAST office, officially opened on 27 January 1994, was assigned the task of defining and developing aircraft, weapon systems, and advanced sensor technologies.[3]

Essentially, JAST would demarcate the design and procurement goals for future tactical fighters for many decades. JAST's first program director was Maj. Gen. George K. Muellner, USAF, a veteran command/fighter pilot with 690 combat missions during the Vietnam War and more than 5,300 hours flying advanced aircraft. Gen. Muellner knew what advanced aircraft were supposed to do and how to develop them. As CALF was absorbed by JAST in late 1994, Muellner sought to retain the affordability part of CALF and the mission part of MRF and A/F-X. In addition to producing a family of aircraft

Joint Strike Fighter contenders face-to-face: The Boeing X-32A and the Lockheed Martin X-35A on the tarmac at Edwards AFB. (AFFTC History Office)

a potential operational scenario at sea, the USMC/RN variant required vertical-landing mode to recover on the small-deck carriers. If the second lift-fan engine didn't start, the aircraft would be lost.

Transition to Joint Strike Fighter

to perform multiservice missions, the overall goal was to produce a high-performance fighter but at a low enough cost to gradually replace F-16s in USAF and allied air forces. Gen. Muellner was adamant that whatever aircraft was produced would satisfy more than just one U.S. military service.[4]

There would be data applied to JAST from the positive lessons learned on the TFX (F-111). The F-111B variant proved unsuitable for Navy carrier operations, although the USAF F-111/FB-111 variants eventually achieved success in service. Muellner pointed out that the "A" in JAST should stand for *affordability*, since cost control is considered the core mission of the JAST program. "Our focus is to drive down significantly the cost of the next-generation weapon system," said Muellner.[5] At the time (1994), the cost target for JAST was to remain below the canceled A/F-X, which was estimated at approximately $90 to $110 million per aircraft. Within the process of keeping cost down, the aircraft's performance was not designed to be cutting edge. According to Gen. Muellner, "JAST would be an evolutionary, rather than a revolutionary aircraft. We are developing an aircraft with an incremental increase in performance at a reasonable cost."[6] In addition to the U.S. tri-services, the JAST was seeking international participation with the UK, France, and Germany. The UK MoD was already participating with ARPA[7] as a partner in the ASTOVL research area. Another goal of JAST was to produce concept demonstrator aircraft to prove technologies at minimum cost. The plan closely resembled the classified Lockheed Have Blue program, which produced two subscale aircraft to flight test low observable (LO) techniques for the F-117A stealth attack aircraft.

Under this effort, Lockheed's design utilized a shaft from the main Pratt & Whitney F119 connected to a forward driveshaft which drove the lift fan located just aft of the cockpit. Boeing's design was a direct-lift solution, with no separate lift fan; this was similar to the AV-8B Harrier II. McDonnell Douglas's unique design would bleed high-pressure air from the main powerplant compressor and then join that with a second forward-located turbine engine.[8] When needed for vertical landing, the smaller forward engine would be started. The high-risk side of this design was that the aircraft in conventional mode would be carrying the dead weight of the forward engine. In

The time had arrived to move from technology demonstrators to production aircraft needed to replace aging F-16s in the USAF and allied air forces. In early 1996, JAST was redesignated the Joint Strike Fighter (JSF) program. It was a new direction in which full-scale demonstrators would be built by competing contractors and would be configured as close as possible to production aircraft. JSF RFPs were issued during March 1996, and on 16 November, Sec. of Defense Dr. William Perry announced that Boeing and Lockheed Martin were selected to build and fly prototypes.[9]

Following the ATF program (YF-22 and YF-23), in the natural scheme of designations, the JSF demonstrators should have been YF-24 and YF-25. However, since the original CALF part of the equation was not a production aircraft, but a technology demonstrator, the YF or XF designations would not be used. Instead the JSF demonstrators were assigned X designations. At the time, the last X-plane was the Rockwell International/MBB X-31A EFM (Enhanced Fighter Maneuverability) and the Boeing JSF demonstrator was assigned

The unmanned subscale Boeing Phantom Works X-36 Tailless Fighter Agility Research Aircraft made in cooperation with NASA Ames Research Center. The theoretical advanced concept is about one-fourth the size of an actual fighter. The X-36 was 19 feet long, had a 10.4-foot wingspan, and reached a speed of 234 mph at 20,000 feet. Begun in 1994 by McDonnell Douglas, the X-36 explored superior agility, low-speed agility, and high angle-of-attack flight up to 40 degrees. Boeing inherited the program after the merger with McDonnell Douglas. The X-36 completed its 31-flight research program on 12 November 1997. (Author Photo/Illustration)

A conceptual USAF/McDonnell Douglas CTOL variant from the Operational Test & Evaluation squadron at Nellis AFB. Unfortunately, the stealthy McDonnell Douglas JSF design was eliminated prior to the fly-off. The configuration featured an unusual lambda wing shape influenced by the X-36 UAV and a control philosophy and stealth characteristics reminiscent of the YF-23A ATF. Utilizing experience from the X-36, basic control and stability would be provided by split air brake rudder surfaces on the wing trailing edge, and combat agility would be provided by a lightweight all-axis thrust-vectoring nozzle. (Author Photo/Illustration)

X-32. The next two X slots were NASA unmanned space projects: the Lockheed Martin X-33 RLV and the Orbital Sciences air-launched X-34. Subsequently, the Lockheed Martin JSF prototype received the X-35 designation.

Boeing X-32 JSF One Team

On 14 December 1999, at the Boeing Palmdale facility at Air Force Plant 42, thousands of Boeing employees and, via satellite link, subcontractors and customers, witnessed the unveiling of the X-32A and X-32B JSF prototypes. Although work on the X-32B variant was begun three months after the A model, both aircraft were ready for the rollout. Boeing officials credited the JSF One Team's financial and technical performance throughout the process for keeping the X-32 on track. Boeing Chairman and Chief Executive Officer Philip M. Condit commented as the two prototypes were unveiled, "This is a great day. It's about people and processes. The JSF One Team is the future. This is a day that's about a design more efficient than anything done before. It's about international cooperation. It's about affordable products, lean manufacturing and first-time quality. It's about complete solutions. The Boeing JSF is the 21st Century tactical fighter." Boeing Vice President and JSF General Manager Frank Statkus added, "We have made lean design and manufacturing a reality on the JSF program. Our One Team members have used inno-

vation and dedication to demonstrate the benefits of being lean."[10] Col. Michael Poore, Joint Program Office (JPO) X-32 program manager, said, "The Joint Strike Fighter will help America and its allies continue to hear the sound of freedom well into the next century." Commending the JSF One Team, Colonel Poore added, "The program has validated affordability."

The Strategy Behind the Contour

Initially and throughout the competition, there were many negative comments about the X-32's configuration. First and foremost,

The Boeing X-32A CTOL is strapped down testing the afterburner of the Pratt & Whitney F120-100. The unique two-dimensional exhaust nozzle is in the full-open position. (USAF)

The Boeing Bird of Prey demonstrator was a classified very-low-observable technology program. The proprietary program was initiated by McDonnell Douglas Phantom Works and continued by Boeing after the mid-1997 merger. Boeing applied manufacturing and stealth technologies to its JSF concept, including large-piece composite structure and three-dimensional virtual-reality design and assembly. While testing all-aspect VL RCS and other stealth technologies between 1996 and 1999, the demonstrator completed 38 flights in secret and was not declassified for public view until its 18 October 2002 rollout. Because of its unusual contour, the Bird of Prey was named after the Star Trek series' Klingon spacecraft and is currently on display at the National Museum of the USAF. (Author Photo/Illustration)

The Boeing X-32A CTOL and conceptual operational F-32A CTOL have substantial differences in configuration. The X-32A demonstrator featured a delta wing and v-tails. The proposed version to be built, if Boeing had been selected, has a more conventional swept wing, canted vertical tails, and horizontal stabilizers. (Author Photo/Illustration)

aircraft are designed with a purpose in mind, and that is to meet and/or exceed the customer's requirements. Preserving variant commonality, while still achieving stealth characteristics, supersonic capability, substantial combat radius, advanced avionics/electronic attack, low-cost efficient manufacturing, and unit cost control, are difficult goals. The X-32 design was the result of thousands of hours of 3-D solid modeling, virtual reality, and digital simulation of assembly processes. Boeing had initiated a process in the Dem/Val phase to minimize costs, enhance supportability, and improve overall performance. This maintained the original research and planning for its weapon-system concept.

As in the previous A-X and ATF competitions, there were wide-ranging requirements, and the two competitors came up with completely different designs. The same applied to the JSF competition, in which the X-32A contour was the result of overall conflicting requirements. During the design and simulation-process, commonality was primary. The X-32B STOVL variant was the most complex, and to accommodate its direct-lift systems, the engine was mounted in the forward fuselage. The thrust nozzles became the CG, which resulted in a shortened forward section ahead of the cockpit. This was compatible with the carrier variant (CV) to meet over-the-nose visibility for carrier approach requirements. Simulations proved the configuration would also work well for the CTOL and STOVL variants. Boeing's Phantom Works design team developed a thick one-piece delta wing, which could hold maximum fuel to avoid the use of drop tanks except for ferry flights. The wing design would also perform well in the high-alpha regime. To save costs in manufacturing, the X-32 wing skin was a single-mold lightweight composite piece for all three variants. In addition, the wingspan was compatible with U.S. Navy, USMC, and allied aircraft carrier decks and elevators and did not require folding wingtips. Aft of the delta wing were V-tails and a two-dimensional flat exhaust nozzle similar to the F-22.

The X-32's fuselage was widened for maximum space in the internal weapons bay to avoid using external wing hardpoints and preserve the low RCS. The large inlet was located under the nose, similar to the F-16 and X-31A, to direct air into the intake during tight turns. This inlet featured an additional device to shield the engine's fan blades from radar, a unique solution incorporating inlet guide vanes that fully opened for maximum thrust at takeoff or for hovering (X-32B). When full airflow was not needed, these vanes would close slightly to preserve a low RCS. Boeing's demonstrators would be powered by the Pratt & Whitney F135 turbojet that generated 40,000 pounds of thrust with afterburner.

The X-32A was tasked to demonstrate conventional takeoff and landing for the USAF and would be modified for carrier-approach flying qualities for the U.S. Navy. The X-32B also demonstrated STOVL requirements for the USMC, Royal Air Force/Royal Navy, and Italian navy.

Additional Boeing goals for the JSF Program:

- Demonstrate commonality across the variants, including design/build processes
- Demonstrate the Boeing direct-lift propulsion concept for STOVL hover and transition
- Demonstrate low-speed carrier-approach flying qualities

Refining the Design

In early 1999, Boeing announced a series of steps to mature its JSF design. This effort was intended to minimize costs and improve

The Boeing X-32A CTOL accompanied by an F/A-18D chase aircraft. The X-32A's wide intake featured an additional device to shield the fan blades from radar. The unique solution incorporated inlet guide vanes, which fully opened for maximum thrust at takeoff or for hovering (X-32B). When full airflow was not needed, these vanes would close slightly to enhance low observability. (USAF)

An excellent view of the Boeing X-32A CTOL variant's single-piece delta wing and V-tail configuration. (USAF)

delta wing. This maintained the necessary approach speed and stealth advantages. The aircraft's wing remained a single-piece over-the-fuselage structure, thereby preserving the low-cost highly modular approach and high-fuel capacity. The forward fuselage remained virtually intact, except for the chin inlet, which was modified with additional sweep. Boeing indicated that it would be lighter and stealthier and that it would enable better aerodynamic performance at all angles-of-attack.

Shortly after the announced changes, new Boeing advertisements appeared featuring the modified production configuration. Boeing was gambling that the change in their final product would not prove to be a negative in the competition. The flight evaluation, however, would be conducted with the original X-32 contour. The positive side was that Boeing was already reducing cost and risk for the next EMD phase. Lockheed Martin also gambled on their more complex lift-fan design for the X-35B STOVL variant.

performance capabilities while preserving the fundamentals of Boeing's Preferred Weapon-System Concept (PWSC): the operational JSF. "This is part of our long-term weapon-system maturation plan," said Frank Statkus. "We're reducing risk by refining our configuration now rather than later. This upgrade brings us closer to our final design for a truly affordable operational JSF."[11] Additional studies had concluded that the combination of two-dimensional vectoring nozzle and trailing-edge elevons did not provide sufficient pitch authority to meet the rigorous demands of the U.S. Navy carrier-approach requirements. To meet these requirements, a modified configuration close to Boeing's PWSC configuration was undertaken. This included changing the delta wing to a swept wing and adding horizontal stabilizers for additional control power. The update also included a refined empennage and a modification to the wing's trailing edge, while retaining the same high leading-edge sweep of the original

First Flight of Boeing's JSF Candidate

The Boeing X-32A CTOL came to life in May 2000, as first taxi tests took place at Air Force Plant 42 in Palmdale. Chief Test Pilot Fred Knox maneuvered near Boeing's hangar, conducting several slow-speed turns, braking tests, and rudder controls tests. Top speed attained was 63 mph, as verification of aircraft systems, steering, engine controls, and flight-control surfaces were confirmed. Knox quipped, "We accomplished everything we set out to do. The aircraft taxies as well as it's going to fly." Shortly after receiving engine flight certification from Pratt & Whitney, high-speed taxi tests commenced.[12]

Looking up into the weapons bay of the Boeing X-32A from a chase plane. An AIM-120 AMRAAM is visible, with a 1,000-pound-bomb shape in shadow in the upper bay. (USAF)

The canopy-bubble design of the Boeing X-32A CTOL provides good pilot visibility. (USAF)

The Boeing X-32A moves in behind a USAF KC-10A Extender aerial tanker to test the Navy-type hose-and-drogue system. The X-32A also tested the X-32C CV flight characteristics and systems for the U.S. Navy requirements. (USAF)

The Boeing X-32 simulating a carrier approach on Runway 22 at Edwards AFB equipped with an Optical Landing System (OLS), known as "the meatball" or "the ball." To simulate the carrier variant, the X-32A was equipped with upper-wing vortex slats that worked in conjunction with trailing-edge flaps. This increased lift and controllability during low-speed carrier approaches. (AFFTC History Office)

It was 7:53 a.m. PDT on 18 September when Fred Knox[13] took the X-32A aloft from Air Force Plant 42. Rotation occurred at approximately 149 mph and liftoff followed at 172 to 178 mph after a takeoff roll of 2,200 to 2,500 feet. Knox checked the aircraft's airworthiness and various systems. The landing gear was not retracted, and the X-32A reached 10,000 feet and maintained 230 mph.[14] During initial climb out, the F/A-18 chase plane required a lot of afterburner to keep in position.

Knox also noted the X-32A's handling was very similar to the Hornet because it was designed that way.[15] Originally, the flight plan called for 30 to 40 minutes and landing at the AFFTC at Edwards AFB. However, the flight was cut to 20 minutes because of a minor hydraulic fluid leak caused by a loose O-ring forward of the weapons bay. Despite the shortened flight, 80 percent of test card objectives were completed. During the debrief, Knox commented, "Very shortly after liftoff, it was absolutely clear to me that I was flying the airplane we had designed and built, and that I had been simulating for several years."[16] Boeing officials were excited, although experience had shown that the company making the first flight during a competition did not necessarily have an advantage. The first flight initiated a five-month test program for the number-one aircraft that totaled approximately 100 hours. The next six flights would verify the flight envelope for airworthiness. At 8:30 a.m. PST on 21 December 2000, Air Force lead test pilot Lt. Col. Edward Cabrera exceeded Mach 1 in the X-32A at an altitude of 30,000 feet on the 49th flight of the aircraft.

The modified X-32A was also used to conduct Navy aircraft-carrier approaches to confirm the CV requirements. Runway 22 at Edwards AFB was outfitted with special gear. Both Fred Knox and Navy Cmdr. Phillip Yates utilized an Optical Landing System (OLS) known as "the meatball" or "the ball" to receive glidepath cues that simulated carrier landings. Approaches would begin at altitudes between 10,000 to 15,000 feet and descend in carrier-approach configuration. The X-32A's upper wing was fitted with vortex flaps just behind the leading edges working in conjunction with the trailing-edge elevons, which allowed for slow approaches without an excessively high angle-of-attack. Rapid acceleration during a simulated "bolter" was also demonstrated. In total, the modified X-32A simulated 97 carrier approaches and 74 touchdowns were accomplished. In-flight refueling with KC-135 tankers with both the boom/receptacle and hose-and-drogue systems were also conducted. Additionally, proprietary X-32A CTOL weapons bay tests, avionics, and supersonic flights were all carried out successfully, and a total of 66 flights were amassed during the four months of flight-testing.

X-32B STOVL Variant

On 29 March 2001, the X-32B STOVL variant took to the air with Boeing test pilot Dennis O'Donoghue in the cockpit. During the 50-minute flight from Palmdale to Edwards, the aircraft's handling characteristics in the conventional mode were checked out.[17] Shortly thereafter, the X-32B flew a transcontinental ferry flight from Edwards to NAS Patuxent River. In the Navy's test area at Pax River, vertical takeoffs were accomplished, with the first vertical landing occurring on 3 July 2001. The aircraft also successfully transitioned to and from STOVL flight mode, confirming the

The Boeing X-32B STOVL variant overflies NAS Patuxent River. The X-32B STOVL did not have leading-edge slats as the X-32A, and the width of the wing was narrower. Pax River has been the home for numerous Navy aircraft undergoing test flights. (U.S. Navy)

The Boeing X-32B STOVL variant undergoing vertical lift testing at NAS Patuxent River. The direct-lift system on the X-32B was designed not to damage the landing surface with heat. (U.S. Navy)

Boeing Advanced Program Manufacturing Experience

- Northrop Grumman B-2A Spirit: Outboard wing segment, aft center fuselage, landing gear, fuel system and weapons delivery system manufacturing, and low-observable techniques.
- Lockheed Martin F-22 Raptor: Wings, aft fuselage, engine/ nozzle integration, life support systems, radar, avionics integration, 70 percent of mission software, laboratories and training systems.
- Boeing F/A-18E/F Super Hornet: All aspects of production (inherited from McDonnell Douglas).
- Boeing X-36 Tailless Agility Research Aircraft: Two unmanned demonstrators flight tested (inherited from McDonnell Douglas).
- Boeing AV-8B Harrier II: Vertical lift techniques and all production aspects (inherited from McDonnell Douglas).
- Phantom Works Bold Strokes: Open systems architecture.
- Bird of Prey: This proprietary aircraft demonstrator was classified throughout its development and flight-test program (1992–1999). Boeing assumed the program after its merger with McDonnell Douglas in 1997 and inherited the Very Low Observable (VLO) data.
- Lockheed Martin/Boeing RQ-3 Tier III Minus DarkStar UAV: Teamed with Lockheed Martin on the stealthy UAV.
- Boeing Delta IV Expendable Launch Vehicle (ELV): Factory design and procedure experience (inherited from McDonnell Douglas).

- Boeing 777 and Next-Gen 737 airliners: Lean design and manufacturing experience.

Post X-32 JSF experience applied to the following:

- Boeing X-45A UCAV: Phantom Works developed the X-45A Unmanned Combat Aerial Vehicle (UCAV), an autonomous jet-powered vehicle that would far surpass any unmanned combat aircraft flying. Capable of speeds up to 500 mph at 40,000 feet altitude, the UCAV program eventually led to the larger X-45C Phantom Ray UAV.
- Boeing 7E7 Dreamliner: Evolved into the Boeing 787 Dreamliner; manufacturing lightweight composites.
- Boeing X-37B Orbital Test Vehicle (OTV): Materials development for the unmanned autonomous reusable space vehicle.

A future Red Flag exercise: A conceptual view of a USAF/ Boeing F-32A in lizard camouflage from the 64th AGRS at Nellis AFB. The Aggressor is operating over the Nellis range with two F-32As visiting from Hill AFB. (Author Photo/Illustration)

effectiveness of the direct-lift system as the aircraft transitioned from cruise nozzles to the lift nozzles. The X-32B test flights ended in July 2000 and matched flight performance with computer predictions based on years of simulation. In an operational sense, vertical take-offs are not critical, since the USMC, Royal Navy, and Italian Navy STOVL aircraft will primarily conduct ski-jump takeoffs.

Lockheed Martin X-35

Although bearing a slight resemblance to the F-22 Raptor, the X-35 JSF was in a class of its own. The X-35 design had conventional swept wings and horizontal stabilizers with outwardly canted vertical tails. The fuselage was rather sleek despite having internal weapons bays to preserve a low RCS. Two side-positioned serpentine intake ducts concealed the fan blades and allowed the X-35's nose to accommodate a larger radar dish. Although not a faceted stealth-technique design, the aircraft skin eliminated seams based on Lockheed's experience with the F-117A Nighthawk program.

The cockpit featured a bubble canopy positioned in front of a humped spine that created space for the lift fan. The shaft-driven counter-rotating lift fan would be installed in the X-35A CTOL to convert it to the X-35B STOVL variant. However, this required commonality worked against the other variants by limiting six o'clock (rearward) visibility. Additionally, to further accommodate the lift-fan mechanism, all the X-35 variants featured a forward-hinged

The Lockheed Martin X-35A overflies Edwards AFB with Rogers Dry Lake ahead of the aircraft and NASA's Dryden Flight Research Center in the lower left. (USAF)

canopy. This was done to prevent lift-fan integration problems just aft of the cockpit. Lockheed Martin's design team reported that the forward hinge is lighter with significant maintainability advantages over a typical legacy fighter's aft-hinged canopy. In addition, the ejection seat can be removed and reinstalled without having to remove the canopy. From the onset, the plan would be to test fly and complete the X-35A's evaluation, after which the aircraft would be grounded and modified to the X-35B STOVL configuration. This included adding a shaft-driven lift fan with counter-rotating fans, two roll-control ducts, and a swiveling main-engine exhaust nozzle to provide STOVL capabilities. The system had been previously tested at NASA Ames Research Center in Palo Alto, California.

The X-35C CV for the Navy had a larger wing area due to larger outboard sections and control surfaces. All variants would use tough Northrop Grumman A-6 main gear and Boeing F-15E nose gear. Later, in production F-35s, wing hardpoints were necessary to

Two USMC/Lockheed Martin F-35Bs from VFMA-121 climbing in formation. (Author Photo/Illustration)

Borrowing Parts to Cut Costs

The Lockheed Martin X-35A/B/C air vehicles utilized the following parts/subsystems from existing aircraft:

- Northrop Grumman A-6E Intruder: Main landing gear
- Boeing F-15E Strike Eagle: Nose gear
- Boeing F/A-18E/F Super Hornet: Environmental cooling system
- Lockheed Martin F-22 Raptor: Auxiliary power system
- Northrop Grumman B-2A Spirit: Airframe-mounted accessory drive
- Boeing AV-8B Harrier: UPCo ejection seat
- Lockheed Martin C-130J Hercules: Two cockpit color multifunction displays
- Lockheed Martin F-16 Viper: Several subsystems and controls

The X-35A has sleek contour with its air-refueling receptacle aft of the cockpit and serpentine intake design. (USAF)

The Lockheed Martin X-35A photographed over the Edwards range during flight evaluations. The A variant was later converted into the STOVL B variant. (USAF)

increase payload capability. These could be used when stealth was not needed or for standoff weapons. Once in close for ACM, the hardpoints would have to be jettisoned.

X-35A First Flight

Unlike the Boeing simultaneous debut of the X-32A and X-32B, there was no official rollout of the X-35A at Lockheed Martin's Palmdale facility. Time was of the essence as the aircraft was checked out, and during the second week of October 2000 the first low-speed taxi tests commenced. High-speed tests were run on 18 October. First flight of the X-35A CTOL occurred on 24 October with Lockheed Martin JSF Chief Test Pilot Tom Morganfield in the cockpit. Accompanied by two F-16 chase aircraft, the routine quick hop from Air Force Plant 42 to Edwards AFB took approximately 20 minutes. The reason for the truncated test flight was the failure of a nose-gear sensor that prevented the doors from closing, and Morganfield elected

The X-35C CV had a larger wing area and control surfaces. Here the X-35C catches the "meatball" on the portable OLS for guidance, while simulating carrier approaches and landings at Edwards AFB. (AFFTC History Office)

to cut the flight short. With the landing gear left extended, the intended goals of 310 mph and 40,000 feet altitude were not carried out on this flight. With the shift of focus to the AFFTC at Edwards, approximately 150 government and industry personnel moved from Palmdale to Edwards. By 22 November 2000, the X-35A had completed 27 flights in 30 days, making good progress on the performance cards.[18] Within a couple of days, the X-35A was ferried back to the Palmdale facility to undergo conversion to the X-35B STOVL variant. The modifications would take two months. If needed as a backup, the X-35C CV could also be modified to the STOVL variant.

On 16 December 2000, with Lockheed test pilot Joe Sweeny in command, the X-35C CV took off from Palmdale and landed safely at Edwards after approximately 27 minutes. The X-35C CV had a larger wing surface, due to larger outboard sections and control surfaces. During the transfer flight, the aircraft reached 10,000 feet and a speed of 288 mph. A former Navy pilot, Sweeny evaluated handling characteristics that included rolls and primary systems check.[19] The X-35C also employed the Runway 22 OLS setup used by the Boeing X-32 at Edwards AFB. The X-35C successfully conducted glidepath carrier approach and landing tests. Both the X-35B and X-35C were equipped with folding wingtips. In all, six company and military test pilots were assigned to fly the X-35 demonstrators during evaluations.

Ups and Downs

After conversion of the X-35A to the X-35B STOVL, the aircraft was ferried from Palmdale to NAS Patuxent River. On 12 May 2001, hover pit tests commenced. The first pilot was British Aerospace and former Harrier test pilot Simon Hargreaves, who checked out the aircraft's systems on 24 May. A critical test took place on 23 June when the lift-fan shaft was engaged, and the X-35B lifted off the ground to approximately 15 to 20 feet. It then conducted a vertical landing. On the next day an altitude of 25 feet was reached, and a stabilized hover with flight-control tests was achieved.[20] Lockheed Martin and USMC test pilots also flew the X-35B STOVL variant. Its flight test

The Lockheed Martin X-35C Carrier Variant with its colorful logo on the vertical tails. Having learned lessons from their YF-22 ATF contract win, Lockheed continued a similar marketing strategy on the JSF competition. Aircraft appearance can pay off to a certain degree. (USAF)

program was one of the shortest and most effective in history, lasting from 23 June 2001 to 6 August 2001.

Recalling the success of clever marketing on the F-22 ATF program, Lockheed Martin pushed the go-ahead button early in the competition. The company capitalized on the F-35's sleek contour and promoted its similar look to the F-22. During the flight evaluations, the X-35 variants were painted with two shades of gray that closely mimicked operational camouflage patterns. This marketing strategy was capped off with the X-32B, which, after conversion, sported a lively "Hat Trick" drawing and "X-32B STOVL" painted on the tails. This continued with the X-35C CV, appearing very Navy-like, with vertical tails painted black with a bright X-35C logo.

Announcement Day

Selection day for the JSF contract award was a major event for the entire aerospace industry. It was 26 October 2001, and hundreds of employees and program officials from both Boeing and Lockheed

The Lockheed Martin X-35B after conversion from the A CTOL configuration. The aircraft now featured a colorful "Hat Trick" tail logo. Among its many test records, this aircraft was the first in history to achieve a STOVL takeoff/landing and level supersonic dash during a single flight. In addition, it is the first aircraft to fly using a shaft-driven lift-fan propulsion system. (USAF)

The X-35B undergoes STOVL testing at Lockheed Martin's Palmdale facility. Its nozzle is positioned in a downward position to produce vertical lift. The F135 engine with the shaft-driven lift-fan generates 42,000 pounds of thrust in the STOVL mode. (Lockheed Martin)

The X-35B shaft-driven lift-fan area. Additionally, two roll ducts and a swiveling main engine exhaust nozzle provide the vertical lift for the USMC F-35B and RAF/RN variant. The system was thoroughly tested at NASA Ames Research Center in Palo Alto, California. (Lockheed Martin)

The Lockheed Martin X-35C with two-tone gray camouflage and Navy-style tail colors. (Lockheed Martin)

Martin were linked via satellite to the Pentagon. Under Secretary of Defense for Acquisition, Technology and Logistics Edward C. "Pete" Aldridge Jr. announced that the Joint Strike Fighter program would proceed into the System Development and Demonstration (SDD) phase. This was followed by Sec. of the Air Force Dr. James G. Roche, who had the final judgment on the selection. "Lockheed Martin, teamed with Northrop Grumman and BAE, will develop and produce the Joint Strike Fighter aircraft.

This initial contract for $18.9 billion will produce aircraft to be used by the U.S. Air Force, Navy, and Marines, as well as the United Kingdom's Royal Air Force and Navy." Then in almost the exact words that declared the Lockheed Martin F-22 Advanced Tactical Fighter contract win some ten years earlier, Secretary Roche added,

"The F-35 emerged as the clear winner, and noted that program risk was key to the decision."[21] Naturally there were rousing cheers from the Lockheed Martin gatherings and disbelief and silence from the Boeing groups. This had been a winner-takes-all competition, and in their thoughts was the fact that the JSF could very well be the last manned combat fighter competition.

At Boeing there was hope that perhaps work on some part of the massive JSF program would materialize. However, the quote that would resonate for years was that Lockheed Martin won because of "low risk." Harry C. Stonecipher was president and CEO of McDonnell Douglas when their JSF design was dropped from the competition prior to the fly-off. This was one of the factors that led to the 1997 merger of Boeing and McDonnell Douglas. In August of that year, Stonecipher joined Boeing as President and CEO, along with Chairman Phil Condit. After the October 2001 JSF announcement that Lockheed Martin had been selected over Boeing, Stonecipher was reported to have quipped, "I am the only company CEO to have lost the JSF competition twice."

Secretary Roche also mentioned that Pratt & Whitney Military Engines had been awarded a contract for more than $4 billion to develop the F135 propulsion system. The JSF acquisition strategy also called for the development of two engine types. Eventually, Pratt & Whitney will compete with the F120 engine developed by a General Electric/Rolls Royce team. This team would receive a next-phase development contract within a few weeks. The F-35 is a single engine aircraft, and the prudent strategy is to have both engine types interchangeable on all variants.

In the interim, both contractors had suffered setbacks, and the government warned Lockheed Martin about cost overruns early on. Then in September 2000, there was a shakeup of the staff, which made the Marines particularly nervous. X-35B STOVL variant Program Manager Harold Blot, a retired general and USMC expert on vertical flight, was taken off day-to-day operations just weeks prior to first flight. Blot returned to an assistant role for Frank Cappuccio, vice president and JSF program manager at Fort Worth. For the

Two USAF/Lockheed Martin F-35A Lightning II CTOL variants. (Author Photo/Illustration)

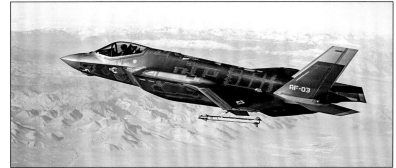

The third F-35A CTOL (AF-03) carries an AIM-9 Sidewinder on a hardpoint to test the air-to-air missile. From NAS Fort Worth Joint Reserve Base, Texas, Lockheed Martin test pilot Bill Gigliotti took AF-03 on its first flight on 6 July 2010. (USAF)

Crossing the Florida coastline from the Gulf of Mexico, an F-35A is escorted by an F-16C. Both aircraft are assigned to Eglin AFB for weapons evaluations. (USAF)

Two F-35A Lightning IIs from the Operational Test & Evaluation (OT&E) at Nellis AFB on a test sortie. (Author Photo/Illustration)

Four F-35A Lightning IIs together near Edwards AFB during early flight evaluations. (Lockheed Martin)

Marines, the STOVL variant was their entire future of air operations. JSF Air Vehicle integrated product team leader John Fuller was given the task of providing new oversight for the Skunk Works and their JSF operations.[22] It was reported that one of the reasons Lockheed Martin won the F-22 ATF contract was that the Air Force was comfortable with the company's management. A senior industry official tied to the JSF program said, "On the JSF program, the customer is comfortable with Boeing and not with Lockheed Martin." Lockheed Martin had been previously warned by the Joint Program Office (JPO) not to meddle with the management structure, but to increase funding for the flight demonstration phase. The old adage of "listening to the customer" was not adhered to. Some officials disclosed that Lockheed officials were upset because Boeing was flying and they were not. Fuller was sent in "to kick butt."[23]

An Immense Task for a Single Prime Contractor

As touted, this was certainly the $200 billion-plus contract win of the century, with a projected 3,000 aircraft for the United States and the UK; other estimates predicted international orders could

An F-35A Lightning II from Luke AFB, Arizona. Luke is the primary base for F-35A pilot training for international JSF partner nations. (USAF)

double that number. The Air Force had signed up for 1,763 F-35A CTOL variants that would eventually replace the F-16 and A-10 fleets. A total of 609 STOVL variants were headed for the Marine Corps to replace F/A-18C/D and AV-8B Harriers. The U.S. Navy was slated to purchase 480 F-35C CVs for big-deck carrier ops. The Royal Air Force and Royal Navy would receive a combined 150 STOVL variants. Other allies were to follow as contributing partners with F-35A orders. Cost projections in 2001 dollars were estimated at $40 million for the CTOL variant and $50 million for the STOVL variant. Initially, 21 aircraft would be built for the SDD phase.

The Government Accounting Office (GAO) warned that the JSF program was at risk of not meeting its affordability objective because critical technologies were not mature enough to be a low-risk program. The Pratt & Whitney F119 that powered the X-35 prototype was modified and redesignated F135. P&W received a $4 billion contract for the SDD phase. Meanwhile, to keep the propulsion industrial base intact, the DoD authorized funding to General Electric/ Rolls-Royce to concurrently develop the F120 engine.[24] The other part of the equation in this propulsion strategy was the ability to install either engine in any JSF variant. Of critical importance, the single-engine F-35 would be replacing the majority of fighter aircraft fleets within 20 years. Any fleet-wide grounding due to an engine anomaly would be catastrophic.[25]

The goal for stealth was set at -30dBsm in the majority of aspects. The X-35 performed well, as did the X-32. However, Boeing was offering a different configuration for the production version (F-32) that featured a more conventional swept wing in place of the delta wing, plus added horizontal stabilizers with canted vertical stabilizers. Boeing relied on extensive simulation data and aircraft-contour pole models to establish the new configuration's RCS.

A conceptual operational People's Liberation Army Air Force (PLAAF) Shenyang FC-31 Gyrfalcon (Falcon Hawk). After introducing the Chengdu J-20 in 2011, a second Chinese stealth fighter, the J-31 (FC-31), made its first flight on 31 October 2012. This was well ahead of U.S. expectations. The airframe is reminiscent of the F-22, but sized in the F-35 JSF class. However, unlike the single-engine F-35 Lightning II, the J-31 is powered by twin engines (Russian designed RD-93s). The Mach 1.8 capable J-31's internal weapons bay can accommodate four air-to-air missiles and could operate from PLAAF land bases or from Chinese navy aircraft carriers. Chinese officials have hinted that the J-31 (FC-31) could compete with the Lockheed Martin F-35 in the international marketplace. (Author Photo/Illustration)

Keeping Cost Down: No Easy Solution

Despite all the public confidence in the winner-takes-all JSF contract award, there was concern with a single contractor team handling the entire JSF production. Prior to the award, an independent Pentagon panel had been assembled to examine the concerns. The panel looked at what would be required to keep both contractors healthy and competitive and preserve the tactical aircraft industrial base. That included the future of the losing contractor and cost impact with all further competition removed. The idea of a split contract and how to execute the process was discussed. Congressional representatives from both of the companies' locations preferred obtaining part of a split rather than nothing at all. Three options were covered.

Option I: Similar to the F-22 program, Lockheed Martin was responsible for 60 percent and Boeing for the remainder. For JSF, the winning contractor would be forced to include the team members from the losing bidder as major subcontractors. It was felt that this could work if the government permitted the winning contractors to determine how the work would be split.

A USMC F-35B from VMFA-121 conducts a hover in STOVL mode. With the F-35B stationary, there is no airflow over the top of the aircraft. The large open door on top of the aircraft scoops up air and funnels it into the lift fan. The thrust on the F135 engine was fixed at just over 41,000 pounds, so one way to reduce weight on the F-35B STOVL variant was to delete the attached retractable cockpit ladder for ingress/egress. (Author)

For the F-35B to convert from conventional flight to STOVL, the pilot pushes a button. The sequence opens all the exterior doors and prepares to engage the lift-fan clutch. Once the propulsion system engages the clutch, the counter-rotating blades spin up to full thrust. The sequence is completed in 15 seconds, and in STOVL mode the aircraft responds to normal side-stick control inputs. (Author)

A USN/Boeing F/A-18F Super Hornet escorts the No. 1 RAF F-35B Lightning II STOVL variant on a test-flight sortie. Operating out of NAS Patuxent River, the F-35B made its first supersonic flight (Mach 1.07) on 10 June 2010. The RAF and RN will both operate 138 F-35Bs. Primary training will occur at MCAS Beaufort, South Carolina, where British pilots will co-locate with USMC crews and their F-35Bs. Operational test and evaluation of the initial RAF/RN F-35s will operate out of Edwards AFB, California. (U.S. Navy)

Option II: One company would build certain versions of the JSF, such as the USAF CTOL variant, and the other would build the remaining models, the CV and STOVL. Companies would still compete for international production and aircraft upgrades. This may cost more up front, but in the long term there would be savings from the competition. Other panel members disagreed with this method, declaring that with such a split no company would have full control over the entire program, so how would costs be kept down?

Option III: A suggestion by the Defense Science Board would have Boeing and Lockheed Martin compete for each lot of production of the winning JSF. This approach was similar to the AIM-120 AMRAAM air-to-air missile program between Hughes and Raytheon. An annual competition between Boeing and Lockheed Martin to determine the split would keep the unit cost down. On the other side, detractors indicated that the cost could rise, since both companies would have to retain the capability to build all three variants. Additionally, securing a multiyear block buy procurement would be difficult under this process.

Recall that the year was 2000, and cost targets for JSF variants were $28 million for the USAF CTOL, $35 million for the USMC STOVL, and $38 million for the Navy carrier variant. During late

Sunset clouds frame a USMC F-35B Lightning II from VMFA-121 as it takes off in afterburner from MCAS Miramar, California. Marine Fighter Attack Squadron VMFA-121 based at MCAS Yuma, Arizona, was declared operational on 31 July 2015. (Author Photo/Illustration)

After an F-35C CV (CF-02) on a test flight jettisons an AIM-120 AMRAAM out of its weapons bay, motor ignition soon follows. The circular spots on the aircraft and missile are for long-range photo tracking. (U.S. Navy)

2001 Pete Aldridge Jr. commented, "We would not discourage Lockheed Martin from taking advantage of Boeing's talents." But Aldridge remained neutral on any Pentagon initiative.

Boeing Chairman Phil Condit said the company was ready to work with Lockheed Martin if asked. There was a warning that Boeing risked losing special skills if it didn't receive some work on the F-35. Congress seemed willing to assist. "Two production lines represent an insurance policy without which this nation cannot live," said Sen. Christopher Bond (R-MO), who happened to be a member of the Senate Defense Appropriations Subcommittee.

Those Shifting Cost Estimates

When the JSF contract was awarded to Lockheed Martin in 2001, the program was worth approximately $18.9 billion. In 2009, the cost of the program was estimated by the Pentagon to be approximately $300 billion. Today (2015), to those interested in projecting shock value, JSF is estimated to be a $1 trillion program. Breaking this down, the cost of acquiring 2,456 aircraft is approximately $300 billion. If life-cycle operating and support cost of $760 billion is added in, this is about $1 trillion. Basically, three-fourths of that $1 trillion is the cost of ownership. But there are those individuals who, for personal agendas, cast a wide net and mesh all costs together.[29]

Six Basic Cost Categories
- Recurring Flyaway Cost: This is the sticker price representing the cost of what you actually fly away with. Includes sunk costs such as R&D and testing.
- Flyaway Cost: This cost is slightly larger than recurring flyaway cost by averaging in some nonrecurring expenses such as line startup cost.
- Weapon System Cost: This level includes weapon system cost, publications, technical data, support and training equipment, and contractor services.
- Procurement Cost: Adds in initial spare parts and deployable spares package. Captures expenses directly related to buying and initially operating the aircraft.

- Program Acquisition Cost: Includes military construction for new facilities, engineering manufacturing development, and RDT&E costs.
- Life-cycle Cost: Adds in the cost over the entire life of the program, including operations, maintenance, support, fuel, and military personnel expenses.

There are also three methods used to compute the cost. To hold costs steady a baseline year can be used. Sometimes F-35 costs are presented in Fiscal 2002 dollars. Current-year costs are greater and are achieved by converting costs over a lengthy program to an understandable financial terminology in today's dollars. Then-year dollars include inflation and therefore yield the greater figures. The difference is massive since a program like the F-35 will still be active way out in 2034. For example, an aircraft program that costs $100 million today will increase to $200 million in 20 years merely due to inflation. Essentially, those that tout the $1 trillion JSF cost are off by a factor of four.[30]

A U.S. Navy F-35C CV (CF-01) during a test of the hose-and-drogue system. Note the colorful tail markings similar to the earlier X-35C during the flight-testing evaluation. (U.S. Navy)

The underwing detachable weapons/stores hardpoints of U.S. Navy F-35C (CF-01) can be installed when full stealth mode is not required. (U.S. Navy)

The president of Lockheed Martin's Aeronautics Division, Dain M. Hancock, responded, "We'll do what the government would like us to do." However, according to Tom Burbage, Lockheed Martin JSF general manager, this task would not be easy. "After giving 18 percent of the production to Northrop Grumman and 12 percent to BAE Systems there isn't much we can do for Boeing without hurting ourselves." Secretary Roche indicated that the Pentagon would work with Lockheed to preserve competition on the avionics side, which meant carving out a place for Raytheon. Northrop Grumman was the selected radar supplier, but the Pentagon wanted to retain those skills at both companies.[26] Lockheed wanted the prime radar supplier to engage the second with adequate work. In the end nothing was done for Boeing, which reduced its projected 2002 revenues by $1 billion. Condit felt the impact would be more long term.

There was confidence in the new unmanned program that Boeing Phantom Works was working on in the tactical aircraft realm: the X-45A UCAV.[27] At the time Pete Aldridge saw a bright future for unmanned air vehicles. "We're going to continue to look at unmanned combat air vehicles and the JSF design teams and would be very appropriate to work on those problems," and added that Boeing has plenty of other Defense Department contracts. Aldridge continued, "In the 2002 budget we've put in $30 million for a new long-range strike platform. And when you get to 2025 or 2040, it's not clear that manned aircraft competitions will exist at all." As it turned out, Boeing's high-performance autonomous X-45A UCAV[28] was extremely successful during flight test, but for unknown reasons the Air Force never ordered it into production. This was a major setback for the long-term future of Boeing tactical aircraft.

Program Setbacks: Options

Lockheed veterans finally witnessed their famed World War II fighter, the P-38 Lightning, commemorated on 7 July 2006. The pro-

An F-35C Lightning II Carrier Variant (CV) at Edwards AFB AFFTC. The CV has a strengthened fuselage and landing gear. Note the twin nose wheels. The F-35A and F-35B have a single nose-wheel bogie. (Lockheed Martin)

duction model F-35 was officially named Lightning II by Air Force Chief of Staff Gen. Michael T. Moseley. Meanwhile, despite delays in the JSF program and cost increases that generated many rumors of impending cancellations, the program proceeded. News reports emerged regarding the high aerodynamic penalties paid to achieve STOVL capability. Some suggested that the USMC should buy the F-35A variant or gradually retire their F/A-18 Hornets and procure the newer F/A-18E/F Super Hornet. Due to performance problems and delays, on 6 January 2011 Secretary Gates placed the F-35B STOVL variant on probation for two years. Gates commented, "If we cannot fix this variant during this time frame, and get it back on track in terms of performance, cost, and schedule, then I believe it should be canceled."[31] In response, Lockheed Martin CEO Robert Stevens said, "The company is determined to meet its commitments. We recognize our role and responsibility to deliver extraordinary fighters in three variants. We're committed to doing that, and we're confident that we'll succeed, including delivering the STOVL variant."

Just over one year later in February 2012, Sec. of Defense Leon Panetta lifted the F-35B probation. This drew congressional criticism from both Senate Armed Services Committee Chairman Carl Levin (D-MI) and Sen. John McCain (R-AZ). They informed Secretary Panetta in a letter that "in the intervening time since probation was imposed, more problems with the F-35B's structure and propulsion, potentially as serious as those that were originally identified a year ago, have been found." The letter also pointed out that "the F-35B[32] had completed only 20 percent of its developmental test plan to date. Your decision, therefore, appears at least premature."[33]

Scrap the CTOL Variant

A most unusual press account zeroed in on the F-35A Lightning II CTOL variant. During April 2013, former Chief of Naval Operations Adm. Gary Roughead stated that the Pentagon should consider eliminating the F-35A CTOL variant in favor of the F-35C CV. The Pentagon's office of Cost Assessment and Program Evaluation (CAPE) had been studying the idea. "The question must be asked as to whether it is better to reduce the number of F-35 variants to two: the STOVL and one CTOL version. My simple logic says it probably is, but there are a lot of factors that go into it," said Admiral Roughead. "It makes sense to have the USAF adopt the 'C' variant because it can operate from land bases as well as from the Navy's 11 big-deck aircraft carriers, whereas the 'A' variant cannot. The reason that I said to go with the 'C' is because you will still want to be able to use the JSF from aircraft carriers."[34]

This concept to eliminate the A variant contained many unanswered variables. First, there is a host of specified requirements for the JSF variants. The USAF F-35A CTOL variant is built to sustain 9 Gs during maneuvers. The F-35B STOVL and F-35C CV are designed for 7.5 Gs. The C variant also has larger wing and control surfaces to provide increased range and controllability for carrier ops, plus a strengthened airframe and landing gear not required by the Air Force. Additionally, both the CV and STOVL variants have no internal 25mm gun; when missions required it, the gun would be carried in an external pod. The Air Force was not interested in this inefficient arrangement. Installing the external gun pod on the CV and STOVL variants brings the aircraft two penalties: weight and aerodynamic drag. The Air Force learned the lessons of external gun pods on the F-4 Phantom II during the Vietnam War. Summarily, the idea to scrap the A variant never gained any traction.

Sticker Shock

Another report stated that the U.S. Navy was not pleased with the projected price tag of the F-35C CV. Naval officials were concerned with the capability and unit-cost ratio when the Boeing F/A-18E/F Super Hornet was being offered at favorable rates. During October 2015, a new Boeing F/A-18E/F Super Hornet proposal for the Navy was revealed. Since the Navy can afford to purchase only 20 F-35Cs a year or less, a dramatic fighter shortfall will hit the fleet. Boeing's offer includes an F/A-18E/F Service-Life Extension Program (SLEP), upgrades, and new aircraft production. Boeing hopes this plan will go through as DoD budget limitations are hurting the Navy's acquisition of F-35Cs, which cost 80 percent more to procure and operate than the F/A-18. The original plan to extend production with upgraded Super Hornets was named the "Advanced Super Hornet." The new program, which includes conformal fuel tanks, uprated engine, and widescreen cockpit instruments, has been dubbed "Enhanced Hornet Flightpath."[35]

An F-35A Lightning II from the 419th FW makes an arrival pass over Hill AFB. The pilot's HMD system is binocular, as opposed to the standard monocular type. This provides the pilot with actual representation of the outside view, including a view through the underside of the aircraft. The F-35A's 25mm GAU-22/A rotary cannon is located above the left inlet. To preserve stealth, the barrel is hidden behind a retractable door until the trigger is depressed. The F-35A internal gun is slated to be operational by 2017. (USAF)

Hill AFB received its first F-35A Lightning IIs on 2 September 2015. They are assigned to the 388th Fighter Wing and Air Force Reserve Command associate 419th FW. Hill will eventually receive 72 F-35s by 2019. (USAF)

On 8 August 2014, the first two RAAF F-35As (AU-1, AU-2) were rolled out at Lockheed Martin's Fort Worth, Texas, facility. The aircraft are the first two of a total order for 72 F-35As. AU-1 made its first flight on 29 September 2014 from Fort Worth with test pilot Al Norman in the cockpit. Pilot training is slated for Luke AFB, and the F-35As will be delivered to RAAF 3 Squadron in 2017. IOC is slated for late 2020. (Lockheed Martin)

An F-35C carrier variant from VX-23 Salty Dogs flies a sortie testing underwing hardpoints, including AIM-9 Sidewinder missiles. The various-shaped marks on the hardpoints are for long-range photo tracking. Lockheed Martin is developing a special all-aspect turret for solid-state high-power laser systems that are being developed. The quick-reacting laser will be able to take out missiles and airborne threats. (U.S. Navy)

F-35C (CF-05) from VX-23 just seconds away from a trap landing aboard the USS Nimitz. (U.S. Navy)

Looking Back

After 12 years of working on the JSF program, retiring Lockheed Martin Executive Vice President Tom Burbage looked back in hindsight on key lessons learned. "We could have spared the program a costly redesign and a troubled relationship with international partners. The F-35 team initially did not fully understand the challenges of sharing information between hundreds of suppliers spanning across multiple countries." Another lesson Burbage related was that all of the companies involved in a project the size and scope of the F-35 need to be on the same information technology system to share data seamlessly. "You want them all on the same set of tools when you start."[36] These JSF problems are certainly reminiscent of

A F-35C (CF-05) from VX-23 Salty Dogs about to catch the third wire aboard the USS Nimitz. (U.S. Navy)

A USN/Lockheed Martin F-35C (CF-03) Lightning II from VX-23 Salty Dogs turns on final approach to the USS Nimitz (CVN-68). After performing a low fly-by and touch-and-go, the first trap was conducted at 12:58 p.m. PDT on 3 November 2014. The Nimitz was operating approximately 46 miles off the coast of San Diego. (U.S. Navy)

early Boeing 787 Dreamliner difficulties with outsourcing worldwide suppliers for aircraft assembly.

Another problem that could not have been foreseen was how to avoid the weight issues lurking in the models. Burbage continued, "During the early years between 2004 and 2005, engineering models began to show that the weight of the F-35B STOVL was getting too high. Somewhere along the way we made an error in our parametric engineering models," Burbage said. "Things we knew about were predicted pretty close; what wasn't predicted by the model was the stealth and internal weapons bays because the airplanes that had those capabilities weren't part of the database."[37]

The first catapult launch of an F-35C (CF-05) from VX-23 Salty Dogs during November 2014 aboard the USS Nimitz. (U.S. Navy)

Electrons Rule

Well beyond being just another fighter, the F-35's elaborate electronic capabilities—with 8.6 million lines of code—places it well ahead of potential adversaries. In fact, the aircraft and its ground systems undergo two full-scale cyber penetration resiliency tests a year.[38] Although antihack penetration tests have been successful, during late May 2015, Maj. Gen. Jeffrey Harrigian, director of the Air Force F-35 Integration Office, indicated that "there are hardware and software items (some classified), that are running late and IOC dates may have to be amended."[39] The F-35 variants are all software dependent, and even operating the gun requires software development. A concern is the USMC F-35B variant is specifically designed for CAS, and the software to operate the external 25mm cannon will not be operational until 2017. In the past a mechanical solution would be in order, but today it's software code.

Off-loading fuel from a tanker is also a mid-2015 hiccup, as software is consistently slowing transfer of the last 1,000 pounds

During ceremonies on 22 September 2015, attended by the Norwegian Minister of Defence Ine Eriksen Soreide, the first RNoAF F-35A was rolled out at Lockheed Martin's Fort Worth facility. This was quickly followed the next month on 6 October by the maiden flight. Similar to the RNoAF F-16s in the fleet, the new F-35As are fitted with a drag chute for landing on icy runways. The RNoAF has a firm order of 52 Lightning IIs and is also developing the Joint Strike Missile for its own and allied F-35s. Flight training will take place at Luke AFB, with combat readiness expected in 2019. (Lockheed Martin)

The Future with Sensor Fusion

Once fielded, the multirole F-35 will represent a quantum leap in capability with enhanced lethality and survivability in denied air space. Utilizing new-generation stealth techniques, integrated avionics, sensor fusion, and superior logistics support, the F-35 family represents the most powerful and comprehensive integrated sensor package of any fighter aircraft in history. Designed with the entire battlespace in mind, the F-35 will introduce increased flexibility and capability for the United States and its allies. Reliance on any single capability (electronic attack, stealth, etc.) is not sufficient for success and survivability in the future. Missions traditionally performed by specialized aircraft (air-to-air combat, air-to-ground strikes, electronic attack, intelligence, surveillance and reconnaissance) can now be executed by a squadron of F-35s.

Advanced Stealth

To achieve VLO characteristics, the F-35 utilizes an integrated airframe design, radar-absorbent material, and additional features, making it virtually undetectable by enemy radar systems. Throughout the JSF development program, extensive testing was conducted to confirm that the combination of stealth, advanced sensors, data fusion, sophisticated ECMs, and electronic attack provided superiority. The original strategy created a high-low mix of F-22s and F-35s, with both sophisticated stealth aircraft working together in theater. Previously, stealth aircraft such as the F-117 Nighthawk and B-2 Spirit were on their own. However, capping of F-22 production at 187 aircraft has threatened that strategy, and military planners are struggling with this. One solution is to enhance and upgrade the F-15C Eagle, which has an average fleet age of 28 years. Under the designation "Talon Hate," Boeing has offered the F-15C (2040C) with twice the air-to-air missile capacity to complement the high segment (F-22) of the mix.

Electronic Attack: Advanced EW capabilities enable the F-35 to locate and track enemy forces, suppress and jam radar systems, and disrupt attacks. The F-35's advanced avionics provide the pilot real-time access to battlespace information in a 360-degree realm.

Air-to-Surface: The F-35's VLO stealth technology and AESA radar will allow for launching standoff PGMs without detection. If the sortie proceeds and penetration of denied airspace is required, the external hardpoints will be jettisoned. The F-35 in a clean configuration will be in stealth mode.

Air-to-Air: Integrated sensors and information and weapons systems provide pilots an advantage over adversarial frontline fighters. Until our potential adversaries field fifth-generation aircraft, the F-22 and F-35 will have an advantage with VLO. In the not-too-distant future, directed-energy solid-state tactical lasers and/or High-Power Microwave (HPM) weapons will be operational on fighter aircraft.

Intelligence, Surveillance, and Reconnaissance (ISR): At the center of the electronic-powerhouse F-35 is its core processor capable of performing 400 billion operations per second. The electronic suite developed by BAE Systems is classified, but will be able to pinpoint enemy radar and EW emissions. The eight-point Electro-Optical Targeting System (EOTS) provides the pilot 360-degree coverage at adequate range to determine the type of countermeasures to be used: kinetic PGMs or electronic. Utilizing stealth, advanced sensors plus data fusion, F-35 pilots will have enhanced situational awareness. Critical ISR missions can be carried out by the F-35 with the most powerful and comprehensive sensor package on any fighter aircraft ever produced.

Interoperability: The F-35 was designed to share all the data it sees and collects; this includes legacy aircraft as well as other F-35s in the mission scenario. Sharing of data with commanders will be particularly useful. This unique capability will provide situational awareness to the entire network to ensure mission success.

Full Mission-Systems Coverage: Mission systems are the avionic, integrated electronic sensors, displays, and communications systems that collect and share data with the pilot and other friendly aircraft and control centers on aircraft carriers or on the ground. The F-35 features a very robust communications suite that includes AESA radar, EOTS, Distributed Aperture System (DAS), Helmet-Mounted Display (HMD), and Communications, Navigation, and Identification (CNI) avionics.

Two USMC F-35B Lightning IIs from VMFA-121 Green Knights approaching the coastline. VMFA-121 based at MCAS Yuma, Arizona, was declared IOC on 31 July 2015. (Author Photo/Illustration)

Two conceptual Japan Air Self Defense Force (JASDF) F-35AJs take to the skies after initial deliveries during late 2016. One F-35A is carrying AIM-9 Sidewinders on hardpoints and the other is in a clean stealth configuration. On 9 December 2011, Japan's Ministry of Defense selected the F-35A Lightning II CTOL and ordered 42 aircraft. F-35As will gradually replace JASDF F-4EJs and also F-15CJs that are not upgraded. (Author Photo/Illustration)

The latest additions to the USAF fleet: A Boeing KC-46A Pegasus next-generation aerial tanker prepares to refuel a Lockheed Martin F-35A Lightning II. (Author Photo/Illustration)

of fuel into the F-35. JSF Program executive officer Lt. Gen. Christopher C. Bogdan explained that a software patch will be applied to the F-35 fleet to enable quicker opening and closing of valves. "It may become operationally relevant, because as the fuel flows, the fighter continues to burn fuel. This is exacerbated, particularly if the mission calls for the fighter to depart the tanker with completely full tanks," said Gen. Bogdan. As of November 2015, the aerial refueling problem was being worked on.

Meanwhile, the Pentagon is striving to adhere to the IOC goals for the F-35A CTOL and F-35C CV Lightning IIs. The first post-IOC upgrade is Block 4, but it has changed twice within two years. The original plan was to roll out numbered block upgrades in two-year intervals. However, in early 2014 Gen. Bogdan revealed that Block 4 would be spilt into Block 4A and 4B—and they would reach IOC in 2024. The bad news was that anything post–Block 4 would have to wait until 2026. The feedback from customers was not positive, so a new plan was developed that will divide Block 4 into four segments and that speeds up the first installment to 2019. Still, common operating items will take precedence over customer-unique upgrades.[40]

In June 2015, Gen. Carlisle asserted that "upgrading the Lockheed Electro-Optical Targeting System and the wide-area high-resolution Synthetic Aperture Radar (SAR) mode (Big SAR), are vital. Big SAR integrates with the Northrop Grumman APG-81 AESA radar. As we look to the future, the Big SAR and advanced EOTS are the things we have to have on the sensor side." These upgrades were originally planned for Block 3 standard, but have been delayed to Block 4. Gen. Carlisle emphasized, "Improved air-to-air capabilities for the F-35 are vitally important, because the USAF did not buy enough Lockheed F-22 air superiority fighters.

"Probably one of the greatest mistakes was the lack of more F-22s, and the decision to end Raptor production early.[41] Out of the original acquisition plan for 750 F-22 air dominance fighters, the USAF has only 180." The software for weapons integration (air-to-ground/air-to-air) for both U.S. services and international partners is still an issue that hopefully will not fall behind schedule. The sooner these difficulties are corrected, the better chances for a multiyear block buy. That, of course, means lower unit prices in the long run.[42]

A future aircraft for the USAF Ambassadors in Blue. A current F-16C Thunderbird joins up with a conceptual F-35A in new Thunderbirds markings. The F-35A would be the eighth aircraft type operated by the USAF Aerial Demonstration Team. (Author Photo/ Illustration)

A large part of the success of the JSF program is the international cooperation and partnership team. As envisioned during the inception of the original JAST Program, the international partners contribute monetarily. Some partners also share in production and others provide major component assembly. International sales and subsequent increased production numbers contribute to unit cost reduction. As of late 2015, the Lockheed Martin F-35 international partner/customer team included Australia, Canada,[43] Denmark,[44] Israel, Italy, Japan, Netherlands, Norway, Turkey, the United Kingdom, and the Republic Of Korea.

Variants Getting up to Speed: F-35C CV

It was a sight the U.S. Navy had been waiting a long time to see. In the Pacific Ocean, approximately 90 miles off the coast of Southern California, a small outline of a jet fighter was turning toward the USS *Nimitz* (CVN-68). It was 3 November 2014, and the first F-35C Lightning II trap landing was successful. The F-35C from Navy Air Test and Evaluation Squadron (VX-23) was flown by Navy test pilot CDR Tony "Brick" Wilson, who caught the preferred number-three arrestor wire. During the 10-day-at-sea trial, two F-35Cs continued a series of successful catapult launches and traps aboard the *Nimitz*. Navy pilots noted that the preferred number-three wire was caught in the majority of traps.

A second series of F-35C Lightning II at-sea test flights was conducted during October 2015 aboard the USS *Dwight D. Eisenhower* (CVN-69). The *"Ike"* was operating in the Atlantic about 100 miles off Norfolk, Virginia, and according to the Navy, F-35C flight-ops were very successful. The F-35Cs carried different weapons loads to establish standards for catapult settings at different aircraft weights. Pilots also tested the redesigned all-aspect cueing Rockwell Collins helmet during night carrier ops. Rear Adm. John Haley, commander of Naval Air Force Atlantic said, "Development testing of the F-35C, the carrier variant of the new stealthy fighter jet, had been 'pretty doggone good' compared with earlier aircraft." Haley added, "We're basically two years from being operational." As of October 2015, developmental testing of the F-35C CV is approximately 80 percent complete, and it will be the last variant to enter service. The first combat-ready squadron will be operational in 2018. The F-35's ability to fuse data from a variety of radars and other sensors and then share it with ships and other aircraft will change the way the Navy fights wars. Haley commented, "The F-35C will provide a huge

A conceptual U.S. Navy F-35C Lighting II as a member of the famed U.S. Navy Blue Angels. However, in January 2016 the Navy announced that it was transitioning to the F/A-18E/F Super Hornet. The F-35C will have to wait a little longer. (Author Photo/Illustration)

A future dissimilar aircraft program: An F-35A Lightning II Aggressor flies over the Nellis AFB range with a special U.S.-acquired advanced Sukhoi Su-35S Flanker-E. This is a hypothetical continuation of the Red Eagles 4477th TEF/Red Hats 6513th TS dissimilar aircraft familiarization and evaluation programs of the 1970–1980s. During that time, the specialized squadrons operated foreign MiG-15, MiG-17, MiG-21, MiG-23, MiG-29, and Su-22 aircraft. (Author Photo/Illustration)

On 30 October 2015, USAF F-35A (AF-02) successfully fired the four-barrel internal GAU-22/A 25mm rotary cannon for the first time while airborne. A single one-second burst fired 30 rounds and was quickly followed by two additional two-second 60-round bursts. (USAF)

benefit to U.S. military commanders in coming years, working in tandem with the Boeing F/A-18F/F Super Hornet and EA-18G Growlers."[45]

F-35B STOVL

The USMC F-35B Lightning II STOVL variant underwent successful at-sea trials aboard the L-Class carrier USS *Wasp* off the coast of Virginia during May 2015. Successful ski-jump takeoffs and vertical landings were carried out. On 31 July 2015, Gen. Joseph F. Dunford,[46] commandant of the U.S. Marine Corps, declared, "I am pleased to announce that VMFA-121 has achieved IOC in the F-35B, as defined by requirements outlined in the June 2014 Joint Report to Congressional Defense Committees." Technically, VMFA-121 could be called upon for emergency operations at any time.

F-35A CTOL

As of late summer 2015, Lockheed Martin, with its partner BAE Systems, was preparing for F-35 full-rate production. The aggressive schedule called for a $1.2 billion upgrade to add additional assembly areas, refurbish hangars, and possibly double the workforce. On 14 October 2015, the 388th Fighter Wing and 419th Fighter Wing at Hill AFB welcomed their first three F-35A Lightning IIs. The formal cere-

A USMC F-35B Lightning II climbs out at sunrise. (Author Photo/Illustration)

mony provided elected officials and base personnel an opportunity to view the aircraft. Sen. Orin Hatch, (R-UT) president pro tempore of the U.S. Senate, declared the F-35 "a groundbreaking weapons system that will play a critical role in our national defense." The Fighter Wings at Hill AFB were the first to fly combat-coded F-16s and will also be the first to fly operational new-generation F-35As.

During September 2015, Gen. Bogdan stated, "The F-35 program has shifted from 'slow and steady' to 'rapidly growing and accelerating.' The program is ramping up from a three-year period where production was '30-40 a year' to next year, when production will nearly triple to 120." Bogdan then added, "USAF IOC will indeed be declared 1 August 2016."[47]

Specifications

Boeing X-32A—Joint Strike Fighter Concept Demonstrator
Crew: 1—pilot
Wingspan: 36 ft. (10.9 m)
Length: 47 ft. (14.3 m)
Height: 13 ft. (3.9 m)
Maximum weight: 50,000 lb (22,679.6 kg)
Range: 1,000 miles (1,609 km)—internal fuel only
Maximum speed: 1,200 mph (1,931 km/h) Mach 1.6
Maximum ceiling: 50,000 ft. (15,240 m)
Powerplant: 1 Pratt & Whitney F-119-PW-114 turbofan—40,000 lb (178 kN) thrust with afterburner
Payload: Mixed ordnance of air-to-air/air-to-ground
Armament: None

Lockheed Martin X-35A—Joint Strike Fighter Concept Demonstrator
Crew: 1—pilot
Wingspan: 35 ft. (10.67 m)
Length: 51 ft. 4 in. (15.67 m)
Height: 17 ft. (5.2 m)
Loaded weight: 44,400 lb (19,960 kg)
Range: 1,100 miles+ (1,770 km+)
Maximum speed: 1,200 mph (1,930 km/h) Mach 1.6
Maximum ceiling: 50,000 ft. (15,240 m)

Powerplant: 1 Pratt & Whitney F119-PW-611 turbofan—40,000 lb (178 kN) thrust with afterburner
Payload: Mixed ordnance of air-to-air/air-to-ground
Armament: None

Lockheed Martin F-35A Lightning II—Next Generation Strike Aircraft
Crew: 1—pilot
Wingspan: 35 ft. (10.6 m)
Length: 51 ft. 4 in. (15.6 m)
Height: 14 ft. 4 in. (4.3 m)
Maximum weight: 70,000 lb (31,751 kg)
Empty weight: 29,036 lb (13,179 kg)
Range: 1,380 miles (2,220.8 km)
Combat radius: 690 miles (1,110 km)
Maximum speed: 1,200+ mph (1,931+ km/h) Mach 1.6+
Maximum ceiling: 50,000 ft. (15,240 m)
Powerplant: 1 Pratt & Whitney F135-100 turbofan—40,000 lb (178 kN) thrust with afterburner; F-35B STOVL variant—42,075 lb (187 kN) thrust with lift fan
Payload: Up to 18,000 lb (8,164.6 kg) mixed ordnance of air-to-air/air-to-ground
Armament: 1 General Dynamics GAU-22/A 25mm rotary cannon

A

AAA: Anti Aircraft Artillery
ABL: Airborne Laser
ACC: Air Combat Command
ACF: Air Combat Fighter
ACM: Air Combat Maneuvering
ADC: Air Defense Command
ADIZ: Air Defense Identification Zone
ADP: Advanced Development Projects
ADV: Air Defense Variant
AESA: Active Electronically Scanned Array
AFA: Air Force Association
AFAC: Airborne Forward Air Controller
AFFTC: Air Force Flight Test Center
AFGSC: Air Force Global Strike Command
AFRL: Air Force Research Laboratory
AFSC: Air Force Systems Command
AIAA: American Institute of Aeronautics and
  Astronautics
AIM: Air Intercept Missile
ALBM: Air Launched Ballistic Missile
ALCM: Air Launched Cruise Missile
AMC: Air Materiel Command
AMRAAM: Advanced Medium Range
  Air-to-Air Missile
ANG: Air National Guard
AOA: Angle Of Attack
ARDC: Air Research and Development
  Command
ARPA: Advanced Research Projects Agency
ASAT: Anti-Satellite
ASD: Aeronautical Systems Division
ASTOVL: Advanced Short Takeoff and Vertical
  Landing
ATB: Advanced Technology Bomber
ATF: Advanced Tactical Fighter
ATB: Advanced Technology Bomber
A-X: Attack-Experimental

B

BAC: British Aircraft Corporation
BOMARC: Boeing and the Michigan Aeronau-
  tical Research Center
BSAX: Battlefield Surveillance Aircraft
  Experimental
BuAer: Bureau of Aeronautics
BVR: Beyond Visual Range

C

CALF: Common Affordable Lightweight Fighter
CAPE: Cost Assessment and Program
  Evaluation
CAS: Close Air Support
CDI: Concept Definition Investigation
CG: Center-of-Gravity
CGI: Computer Generated Imagery
CIA: Central Intelligence Agency
CINC: Commander-In-Chief
CMUP: Conventional Mission Upgrade
  Program
CNO: Chief of Naval Operations
CONECT: Combat Network Communications
  Technology
CSAR: Combat Search And Rescue
CTOL: Conventional Takeoff and Landing
CV: Carrier Variant

D

DARPA: Defense Advanced Research Projects
  Agency
Dem/Val: Demonstration/Validation
DEW Line: Distant Early Warning Line
DFRC: Dryden Flight Research Center
DFE: Derivative Fighter Engine
DoD: Department of Defense
DSB: Defense Science Board
DSO: Defensive Systems Operator
DU: Depleted Uranium
DVA: Design Verification Article

E

ECM: Electronic Countermeasures
EFA: European Fighter Aircraft
EFM: Enhanced Fighter Maneuverability
ELINT: Electronic Listening Intelligence
EMD: Engineering and Manufacturing
  Development
EMP: Electromagnetic Pulse
EOTS: Electro-Optical Targeting System
ETF: Enhanced Tactical Fighter
EW: Electronic Warfare

F

FAC: Forward Air Controller
FBX: Fighter Bomber Experimental
FIS: Fighter Interceptor Squadron
FLIR: Forward Looking Infrared
FOB: Forward Operating Base
FOD: Foreign Object Damage
FSD: Full-Scale Development
FX: Fighter Experimental

G

GAO: Government Accounting Office
G-LOC: G-induced Loss of Consciousness
GOR: General Operational Requirements
GPS: Global Positioning System

H

HASC: House Armed Services Committee
HEF: High Energy Fuel
HEI: High Explosive Incendiary
HMD: Helmet Mounted Display
HPM: High Power Microwaves
HUD: Head-Up Display

I

ICBM: Intercontinental Ballistic Missile
IMINT: Imagery Intelligence
INS: Inertial Navigation System
IOC: Initial Operational Capability
IRBM: Intermediate Range Ballistic Missile
IR&D: Internal Research and Development
IRST: Infrared Search and Track
ISR: Intelligence, Surveillance, Reconnaissance
IRBM: Intermediate Range Ballistic Missile

J

JASDF: Japan Air Self Defense Force
JAST: Joint Advanced Strike Technology
JDAM: Joint Direct Attack Munition
JHMCS: Joint Helmet Mounted Cueing
  System
JPO: Joint Program Office
JSF: Joint Strike Fighter
JSTARS: Joint Surveillance Target Attack Radar
JTAC: Joint Tactical Air Controllers

L

LABS: Low Altitude Bombing System
LEX: Leading Edge Extensions
LO: Low Observable
LMSI: Lockheed Martin Systems Integration
LRC: Langley Research Center
LRI: Long Range Interceptor
LRIX: Long Range Interceptor Experimental
LRS-B: Long Range Strike-Bomber
LTV: Ling-Temco-Vought
LUSTY: Luftwaffe Secret Technology
LWF: Lightweight Fighter

M

MAD: Mutually Assured Destruction
MANTA: Multi-Axis No-Tail Aircraft
MAP: Military Assistance Program
MER: Multiple Ejection Rack
MoD: Ministry of Defence
MRF: Multirole Fighter
MYP: Multi-Year Purchase

N

NAA: North American Aviation
NACA: National Advisory Committee for
  Aeronautics
NACF: Navy Air Combat Fighter
NAS: Naval Air Station
NASA: National Aeronautics and Space
  Administration
NATC: Naval Flight Test Center
NATF: Navy Advanced Tactical Fighter
NATO: North Atlantic Treaty Organization
NGB: Next Generation Bomber
NORAD: North American Air Defense
NRL: Naval Research Laboratory
NSAM: National Security Action
  Memorandum
NWC: Naval Weapons Center

O

OBOGS: On-Board Oxygen Generation System
OLS: Optical Landing System
OMS: Orbital Maneuvering System
OR: Operational Requirements

P

PAV: Prototype Air Vehicle
PGM: Precision Guided Munition
PLAAF: People's Liberation Army Air Force
PRC: People's Republic of China
PWSC: Preferred Weapon System Concept

R

RAAF: Royal Australian Air Force
RAF: Royal Air Force
RAM: Radar Absorbent Materials
RAMMP: Reliability and Maintainability
  Retrofit Program
RATO: Rocket Assisted Takeoff
RCAF: Royal Canadian Air Force
RCS: Radar Cross Section
RDAF: Royal Danish Air Force
R&D: Research and Development
RDT&E: Research Development Test &
  Evaluation
RFI: Request for Information
RFP: Request for Proposal
RIO: Radar Intercept Operator
RN: Royal Navy
RNLAF: Royal Netherlands Air Force

RNoAF: Royal Norwegian Air Force
ROKAF: Republic of Korea Air Force
RSO: Reconnaissance Systems Officer
RuAF: Russian Air Force

S

SAC: Strategic Air Command
SALT: Strategic Arms Limitation Treaty
SAM: Surface to Air Missile
SAR: Synthetic Aperture Radar
SASC: Senate Armed Services Committee
SCRAM: Short Range Attack Missile
SDD: System Development and
  Demonstration
SDI: Strategic Defense Initiative
SEAD: Suppression of Enemy Air Defenses
SECDEF: Secretary of Defense
SETP: Society of Experimental Test Pilots
SFC: Side Force Control
SHORAN: Short Range Navigation
SLAR: Side-Looking Airborne Radar
SLBM: Submarine Launched Ballistic Missile
SLCM: Sea Launched Cruise Missile
SLEP: Service Life Extension Program
SMCS: Structural Mode Control System
SRP: Structure Retrofit Program
SRW: Strategic Reconnaissance Wing
START: Strategic Arms Reduction Treaty
STEMS: Structural Test Engine Monitoring
  system
STOL: Short Takeoff and Landing
STOL/MTD: Short Takeoff and Landing/
  Maneuver Technology Demonstrator
STOVL: Short Takeoff and Vertical Landing

T

TAC: Tactical Air Command
TFR: Terrain Following Radar
TFW: Tactical Fighter Wing
TFX: Tactical Fighter Experimental
TGP: Targeting Pod
TIFS: Total Inflight Simulator
TRL: Technology Readiness Level
TRW: Tactical Reconnaissance Wing

U

UAV: Unmanned Aerial Vehicle
UCAV: Unmanned Combat Air Vehicle
USAAC: United States Army Air Corps
USAAF: United States Army Air Forces
USAF: United States Air Force
USAFE: United States Air Force Europe
USMC: United States Marine Corps
USN: United States Navy
USSR: Union of Soviet Socialist Republics

V

VAID: Variable-Area Inlet Duct
VFAX: Vertical Fighter Attack Experimental
VLO: Very Low Observable
VPAF: Vietnamese People's Air Force
V/STOL: Vertical and/or Short Takeoff and
  Landing
VTOL: Vertical Takeoff and Landing

W

WADC: Wright Air Development Center
WMD: Weapons of Mass Destruction
WS: Weapon System
WSO: Weapon Systems Operator

Prologue

1 At 437-mph combat speed, the P-51 was the fastest AAF fighter; the Luftwaffe Me 262 was about 100-mph faster.

2 The unstable liquid fuel for the Me 163B Komet's Walter HWK 509A-2 rocket engine, proved to be extremely hazardous during transport and fueling operations.

3 Gen. Jimmy Doolittle, considered the P-51's performance superior to the P-38. Gen. Doolittle gradually increased P-51 numbers for bomber escort duty, and assigned the P-38 to reconnaissance sorties.

4 The Goering Aeronautical Research Center was also referred to as the Luftfahrtforschungsanstalt (LFA).

5 Wolfgang Samuel, *American Raiders*, University Press of Mississippi/ Jackson 2004, page 148.

6 ibid

7 German aerospace engineer Dr. Adolf Busemann presented the first research paper on the concept of swept wings at the Volta Conference in Rome in 1935. Under the auspices of Operation Paper Clip, Dr. Busemann emigrated to the United States in 1947.

8 In 1944, at the urging of Gen. Hap Arnold, Theodore von Karman left Cal Tech to become head of the AAF Scientific Advisory Board. During his illustrious career he received numerous prestigious scientific awards. In his honor, each year the California Institute of Technology presents the International Von Karman Wings Award to a selected individual.

9 Although George Shairer was Boeing's chief aerodynamicist, he was primarily onsite at Volkenrode as a member of the AAF Scientific Advisory Board.

10 ibid

11 The original letter referring to the German wind-tunnel data written by George Schairer no longer exists, but a replica resides in the Boeing archives.

12 Eugene E. Bauer, *Boeing: The First Century*, TABA Publishing, Inc., Enumclaw, Washington 2000, page 121.

13 Prior to and during World War II, the California Institute of Technology (Caltech) 10-foot wind tunnel was routinely used by major aircraft manufacturers. Aircraft wind-tunnel models, including the AT-6, B-25, B-17, B-24, B-29, P-38, and P-51 were tested there.

14 Eugene Rogers, *Flying High: The Story of Boeing and the Rise of The Jetliner Industry*, page 94.

15 Robert Young, "Operation Lusty," *Air Force Magazine*, January 2005, page 62.

16 Although examples of the Me 163B Komet were captured, its rocket engine was considered too dangerous to ignite. It was flight tested in the glide mode only.

17 NAA engineers were able to examine a captured Me 262, and also replicate its leading-edge slats.

18 Wright Field was renamed Wright-Patterson AFB on 13 January 1948.

19 During World War II, NAA's Kansas City Plant turned out thousands of B-25 Mitchell bombers and P-51 Mustang fighters.

20 Ray Wagner, *Mustang Designer*, Orion Books, Division of Crown Publishers Inc., 201 East 50th Street, New York, NY 10022, 1990 page 170.

21 Erik Simonsen interview with former NAA President John Leland "Lee" Atwood, 1997.

22 Ray Wagner, *Mustang Designer*, Orion Books, Division of Crown Publishers Inc., 201 East 50th Street, New York, NY 10022, 1990 page 170.

23 Erik Simonsen interview with former NAA President John Leland "Lee" Atwood, 1997.

24 Col. Kenneth Chilstrom's USAF career was impressive. He was the first USAF pilot to fly the XP-86 Sabre Jet, became chief test pilot at Wright Field, band was Commander of the USAF Test Pilots School. Chilstrom later served as a USAF manger on the NAA F-108 Rapier Mach 3 interceptor, and also the Lockheed YF-12A Mach 3 interceptor programs.

25 In June 1948 the USAF changed its aircraft designation "P" for Pursuit to "F" for Fighter.

26 Norm Avery, *North American Aircraft 1934 -1998 Vol. 1*, Greens Inc. Printers & Lithographers 1998.

27 The Navy FJ-2's four 20mm cannons carried a greater punch than the standard six .50-cal. machines guns of the USAF F-86.

Chapter 1

1 U.S. engine manufacturers were all heavily burdened supporting the war effort. General Electric, although not producing engines at the time, was selected because it had available capacity. Initially Allison co-produced GE engines. The early days witnessed GE, Allison, and Westinghouse grow in importance, with GE outlasting the trio in the propulsion business.

2 Marcelle C. Knaack, *Post-World War II Bombers: 1945-1973*, Office of Air Force History, Washington, DC, 1988

3 Special missions could involve the British 22,000-lb bunker-buster penetrator bomb.

4 ibid

5 At the time the medium-bomber requirements were issued, Consolidated-Vultee (Convair) was already heavily committed to the B-36 heavy bomber. It received that contract two and a half years prior, on 15 November 1941. Note that on 17 March 1943, Consolidated Aircraft Corporation merged with Vultee Aircraft Corporation, forming Consolidated-Vultee. The shortened name Convair was openly used, but didn't become official until April 1954.

6 Strategic Air Command (SAC) was established on 12 March 1946, and on 21 March Gen. George Kenney became the first commander in chief of SAC (CINCSAC).

7 ibid Norm Avery, *North American Aircraft 1934 -1998 Vol. 1*, Narkiewicz//Thompson Santa Ana, California, 1998

8 Marcelle C. Knaack, *Post-World War II Bombers: 1945-1973*, Office of Air Force History, Washington, DC, 1988

9 On the previous 18 September 1947, the U.S.AAF was designated a separate military branch and redesignated United States Air Force (USAF).

10 Also during the previous September 1947, the USAF reclassified the B-45A from a medium to a light bomber and assigned it to Tactical Air Command (TAC).

11 On 9 November 1948, SAC headquarters was established in Omaha, and on 19 November Gen. Curtiss LeMay became the second CINCSAC.

12 Norm Avery, *North American Aircraft 1934 -1998 Vol. 1*, Narkiewicz//Thompson, Santa Ana, California, 1998

13 ibid

14 On 19 October 1948, Gen. Lemay started his command of SAC. He inherited a mostly obsolete USAF inventory of 837 aircraft. By the time he departed in mid-1957 to become vice chief of staff, there were 3,040 much-more capable aircraft in the fleet.

15 A total of 96 B-45As were delivered to the USAF. Additionally, the B-45B never reached production, and only 10 B-45Cs were delivered, before production was converted to the RB-45C reconnaissance variant; 33 RB-45Cs were built.

16 Walter Boyne, "Watching China," *Air Force Magazine*, Vol. 84, No. 6, June 2001

17 Prior to the introduction of the Boeing KC-97, the Boeing B-50—which was an improved and uprated B-29—was also converted into an aerial tanker. KB-50s were equipped with the probe-and-drogue system for refueling tactical fighters, up to three at a time. For improved performance, the KB-50J was modified with two added J47 turbojets; a total of 112 were converted.

18 RB-45C night missions over denied airspace only lasted for five months. A problem occurred with the forward bomb bay doors, which caused severe buffeting when opened to drop flash bombs. This interfered with the quality of ground-target camera imagery.

19 ibid

20 The 1951 agreement to conduct covert overflights was in stark contrast to Attlee's past conduct. When Attlee's new Labour government came into office in 1945, he was open in his relations with the Soviets. Attlee even agreed to sell Rolls-Royce Nene jet engines, along with a licensing agreement for production, to the Soviet Union. This serious error in judgment by the British even surprised Soviet leader Joseph Stalin, who ordered aircraft propulsion engineer Vladimir Klimov to immediately begin reverse-engineering the design. The result was the Klimov RD-45, which provided the engine technology for the MiG-15. This had serious consequences during the Korean War.

21 L. Parker Temple III, *Shades of Grey*, American Institute of Aeronautics and Astronautics (AIAA) Inc., Reston, Virginia, 2005

22 The Convair XA-44 attack aircraft evolved into a unique XB-53 forward-swept wing (FSW) medium-bomber design. Unfortunately, the Convair XB-53 only reached the conceptual stage.

23 Charles Lindbergh took off from San Diego on 10 May 1927 headed for St. Louis to begin his trek to the east coast, and on to his record nonstop flight to Paris. He agreed to lend his name to the new San Diego Municipal Airport, thus Lindbergh Field. During the ensuing decades, the airport hosted many historic Consolidated-Vultee (Convair) aircraft. Today, it is the San Diego International Airport with a single 9,400-foot runway.

24 XB-46 test pilot Sam Shannon also made the first flights in the XF-92A and XF2Y-1 Sea Dart, and he participated in the F-102 Delta Dagger program, all classic Convair delta-wing aircraft.

25 Joe Mizrahi, *The Last Great Bomber Fly Off, Wings, Vol. 29, No. 3*, June 1999

26 Walter Boyne, *Convair's Needle Nose Orphan*, Air Force Flight Test Center Archives

27 ibid

28 The Air Force Museum was renamed the National Museum of the United States Air Force in October 2004.

29 *American X & Y Planes: Kev Darling Vol. 2, Experimental Aircraft Since 1945*, Crowood Aviation Series, The Crowood Press 2012, p 14-1

30 ibid

31 Marcelle C. Knaack, *Post-World War II Bombers: 1945-1973*, Office of Air Force History, Washington, DC, 1988

32 *American X & Y Planes: Kev Darling Vol. 2, Experimental Aircraft Since 1945*, Crowood Aviation Series, The Crowood Press 2012, p 14-1

33 Marcelle C. Knaack, *Post-World War II Bombers: 1945-1973*, Office of Air Force History, Washington, DC, 1988

34 ibid

35 ibid

36 Author Erik Simonsen, Interview with Walter J. Boyne, Dec. 2014

37 Walter J. Boyne, *Beyond the Wild Blue: A History of the U.S. Air Force 1947-1997*, A Thomas Dune Book, St. Martin's Press, New York, NY, 1997

38 The Boeing KC-97 aerial tanker entered service in 1950 and gradually replaced the KB-29 tankers.

39 ibid

40 Marcelle C. Knaack, *Post-World War II Bombers: 1945-1973*, Office of Air Force History, Washington, DC, 1988

41 The B-47E that entered service beginning in 1953 produced an improved 43,000 pounds of thrust with its six engines. The total of 1,341 B-47Es were produced by Boeing (691), Douglas (264), and Lockheed (386).

42 Walter J. Boyne, "Reconnaissance on the Wing," *Air Force Magazine*, October 1999, page 77

43 ibid

44 The air-launched Ryan BQM-34 Firebee was capable of Mach .95 and 60,000 feet altitude.

Chapter 2

1 Although technically replaced by the B-57 as a light bomber, the piston-powered A-26 Invader also later served during the Vietnam War

2 The more advanced Convair B-36 heavy bomber was in USAF service; however, President Harry S. Truman did not order it into action in a conventional bomber role in Korea.

3 Marcelle C. Knaack, *Post-World War II Bombers: 1945-1973*, Office of Air Force History, Washington, DC, 1988

4 ibid

5 Norm Avery, *North American Aircraft 1934 -1998 Vol. 1*, Narkiewicz/ Thompson Santa Ana, California, 1998

6 James V. Forrestal was the first U.S. Secretary of Defense.

7 Robert C. Mikesh, *Martin B-57 Canberra: The Complete Record*, Schiffer Publishing Ltd., Atglen, PA, 1995

8 In March 1981, NORAD was renamed North American Aerospace Defense Command.

9 An unguided rocket really means unguided: Both the United States and Canada were very fortunate in the early days of the Cold War that Soviet jet bombers did not attempt to overwhelm their airspace. The unguided Mighty Mouse rockets were relatively ineffective. As demonstrated on 16 August 1956, when two F-89D Scorpion interceptors were scrambled to intercept a NAS Point

Mugu, California–based drone. The wayward vintage World War II U.S. Navy F6F-5K Hellcat was headed for populated areas near Los Angeles. The F-89Ds fired a total of 208 Mighty Mouse rockets, but failed to shoot down the piston-powered Hellcat, which eventually ran out of fuel and crashed near Palmdale, California.

[10] Jan Zurakowski later became the chief test pilot for the Avro CF-105 Arrow prototype program

[11] The RCAF acquired 56 McDonnell F-101Bs and 10 F-101F trainers, designated CF-101B and CF-101F.

[12] On 4 February 2015, test pilot Fitz Fulton (Lt. Col. USAF Ret.) passed away at the age of 89. In his flying career Fulton logged more than 16,000 hours in 240 aircraft types. This included flying 53 combat missions in Korea in the A-26 Invader, motherships that launched every X-Plane, and the Boeing 747 Shuttle Carrier Aircraft. Fulton also tested the B-36, B-45, B-47, XB-51, RAF Canberra, B-57, YB-60, B-52, B-58, XB-70, and YF-12A/C.

[13] Lt. Col. Fitzhugh "Fitz" Fulton, Jr., *Father of the Mother Planes: The Story of USAF and NASA Test Pilot Lt. Col. Fitzhugh "Fitz" Fulton, Jr.*, An Autobiography, Published by Fitz Fulton, Los Angeles, CA, 2013.

[14] ibid

[15] Marcelle C. Knaack, *Post-World War II Bombers: 1945-1973,* Office of Air Force History, Washington, DC, 1988

[16] ibid

[17] Scott Libis, *The Martin XB-51, Air Force Legends Number 201*

[18] The XB-51's unique T-tail arrangement would soon emerge in commercial aircraft designs such as the Boeing 727, Hawker Siddeley Trident, and Tupolev Tu-154.

[19] The original title for *Toward the Unknown* was *Flight Test Center*, and when the film was released in Great Britain the title was *Brink of Hell*.

[20] ibid

[21] Marcelle C. Knaack, *Post-World War II Bombers: 1945-1973,* Office of Air Force History, Washington, DC, 1988

[22] Scott Libis, *The Martin XB-51, Air Force Legends Number 201*

[23] Lt. Col. Fitzhugh "Fitz" Fulton, Jr., *Father of the Mother Planes: The Story of USAF and NASA Test Pilot Lt. Col. Fitzhugh "Fitz" Fulton, Jr., An Autobiography.* Published by Fitz Fulton, Los Angeles, CA, 2013

[24] Scott Libis, *The Martin XB-51, Air Force Legends Number 201*

[25] Marcelle C. Knaack, *Post-World War II Bombers: 1945-1973,* Office of Air Force History, Washington, DC, 1988

[26] Scott Libis, *The Martin XB-51, Air Force Legends Number 201*

[27] Total cost of the two XB-51 prototype experimental program over four years was $12.6 million, approximately $2.4 million greater than planned.

[28] The Martin Company was building the P6M Seamaster for the U.S. Navy, a high-speed (Mach .89) jet-powered seaplane bomber.

[29] Robert F. Dorr, *The Martin XB-51 Bomber: Martin's Marvelous Might-Have-Been Bomber,* Defense Media Network, October 6, 2012

[30] Lt. Col. Fitzhugh "Fitz" Fulton, Jr., *Father of the Mother Planes: The Story of USAF and NASA Test Pilot Lt. Col. Fitzhugh "Fitz" Fulton, Jr., An Autobiography.* Published by Fitz Fulton, Los Angeles, CA, 2013

[31] ibid

[32] The production of the British-designed Canberra by the Martin Company was anything but easy.

[33] Marcelle C. Knaack, *Post-World War II Bombers: 1945-1973,* Office of Air Force History, Washington, DC, 1988

[34] Specifications and capabilities of the NAA B-45C Tornado are thoroughly covered in Chapter 1.

[35] ibid

[36] Early English Electric RAF Canberras were designated B2. The USAF would designate it the B-57A.

[37] ibid

[38] Over the duration of the USAF/Martin B-57 Canberra's 403-aircraft production run, English Electric received over $3.5 million in royalty payments.

[39] The Canberra originally received high marks for its range/loiter time from the selection committee.

[40] ibid

[41] Robert C. Mikesh, *Martin B-57 Canberra: The Complete Record,* Schiffer Publishing Ltd., Atglen, PA, 1995

[42] Guy Martin, *The American Canberra, Combat Aircraft,* December 2006

[43] With its wide-ranging experience as the B-57 maintenance contractor, General Dynamics proposed major modifications to the wings. They were awarded an Air Force contract to develop the RB-57D. This variant was followed by the RB-57F/WB-57F.

[44] In 1961 the Glenn L. Martin Company merged with American-Marietta Corp., forming Martin Marietta. Martin Marietta merged with Lockheed in 1995, forming Lockheed Martin.

Chapter 3

[1] A possible alternate to escorts was the parasite fighter. McDonnell Aircraft responded to the parasite fighter request for proposal (RFP) with its XF-85 Goblin. The ultra-small jet would be carried into denied airspace by the host B-36 long-range bomber and released in the target area to defend the bomber formation. The program encountered severe airborne capture/release difficulties and was canceled.

[2] Dennis R. Jenkins & Tony Landis, *Experimental & Prototype U.S. Air Force Fighters,* Specialty Press, 838 Lake Street South, Forest Lake, MN, 55025, 2008

[3] Note that no air-to-air missiles were listed as a requirement, since they did not exist at the time.

[4] ibid

[5] Republic Aviation's XP-91 penetration-fighter entry was directed to switch to a point-defense interceptor.

[6] ibid

[7] On 18 September 1947 the United States Army Air Forces became a separate service and was designated the United States Air Force (USAF).

[8] Company founder James McDonnell had a fascination with the occult and started a tradition of naming new McDonnell fighter aircraft to reflect this: Voodoo, Banshee, Goblin, Demon, and Phantom.

[9] Republic Aviation actually flight-tested a V-tail configuration on its XF-91 point-defense fighter.

[10] Tony Butler, *Early U.S. Jet Fighters Proposals, Projects and Prototypes,* Hiloki Publications, Manchester, UK, 2013

[11] Dennis R. Jenkins & Tony Landis, *Experimental & Prototype U.S. Air Force Fighters*, Specialty Press, 838 Lake Street South, Forest Lake, MN, 55025, 2008

[12] During June 1948, the Air Force aircraft designation of *P* for *Pursuit* was changed to *F* for *Fighter*.

[13] ibid

[14] Internal fuel capacity was increased in the prototype, but the wingtip tanks as envisioned in early artwork were never added to the aircraft during the fly-off.

[15] Our adversaries were closely watching the effects of the greatly reduced military budgets that the Truman administration was instituting. Within two years the Korean War broke out.

[16] ibid

[17] The number-one XF-88 was modified to flight-test a turboprop engine; it was redesignated XF-88B.

[18] Although the XP-90 was an innovative design for its era, Lockheed chief designer Kelly Johnson was not pleased with the prototype assembly process, which took place in the standard assembly factory. In retrospect, the successful XP-80 Shooting Star prototype had been built within the confines of the Skunk Works. Many lessons were learned.

[19] Warren M. Bodie and Cory C. Jordan, *Lockheed's Supersonic Gamble: XF-90, Flight Journal,* Pg. 78, Air Age Inc., Ridgefield, CT, Aug. 2001

[20] The Saab A32 Lansen all-weather fighter, produced for the Swedish Air Force beginning in 1955, features a forward fuselage, intakes, and 35-degree-sweep wing configuration remarkably similar to the Lockheed XF-90.

[21] ibid

[22] ibid

[23] Previously published accounts have stated that NAA test pilot George Welch broke the sound barrier in level flight in the XP-86, prior to Chuck Yeager's 14 October 1947 Mach 1 flight in the rocket-powered Bell X-1. According to Bob Hoover (P-80 chase pilot), the XP-86 was equipped with the J35-C-3 engine and was not capable of Mach 1. During December 1947 the XP-86 with the uprated J35-A-5, exceeded Mach 1 in a shallow dive.

[24] Had Convair engineers noticed this feature on the YF-93A wing root, they could have avoided a lot of delays and cost on the original Convair YF-102 Delta Dagger. The YF-102 could not exceed Mach 1 during flight-testing in 1953. The mid-fuselage Coke-bottle shape was added later and solved the problem.

[25] Bill Yenne, *Rockwell: The Heritage of North American,* Crescent Books, New York, NY, 1989

[26] Dennis R. Jenkins & Tony Landis, *Experimental & Prototype U.S. Air Force Fighters,* Specialty Press, 838 Lake Street South, Forest Lake, MN, 55025, 2008

[27] Another aspect of the Truman FY1950 budget doctrine was the stipulation to use up reserves of World War II aircraft in the inventory prior to requesting funding for new aircraft types. This can only be categorized as a naïve strategy resulting from not being aware of, or understanding, the emerging Soviet threat.

[28] The U.S. also canceled the advanced NAA F-108 Rapier interceptor in 1959 and wanted to sell the SAM to Canada.

[29] Canada did procure the Boeing BOMARC IM-99 (Canada designation CIM-10B) air defense missile in 1962, becoming operational in December 1963. The Canadian government did not want to arm the missiles with nuclear warheads, and this disagreement wound up dissolving Prime Minister Diefenbaker's Cabinet. Conventionally armed BOMARCs could not guarantee a direct hit or a near miss to down the target (presumably a Soviet bomber). The Canadian BOMARC fleet was retired early in 1972. The idea of relying only on missiles with no plan for the warhead type (conventional or nuclear) and with no means to positively identify a potential intruder (IFF—identification, friend or foe) was indeed a flawed strategy.

Chapter 4

[1] A follow-on B-47Z variant would have been powered by J57 engines. However, even with increased thrust, the B-47 airframe had limited growth potential, especially for the later hydrogen bomb. SAC would push to proceed with the larger YB-52.

[2] Marcelle C. Knaack, *Post-World War II Bombers: 1945-1973,* Office of Air Force History, Washington, DC, 1988

[3] Bill Yenne, *B-52 Stratofortress: The Complete History of the World's longest Serving and Best Known Bomber,* Zenith Press, Minneapolis, MN, 2012

[4] Holden Withington, the last surviving B-52 designer, passed away on 9 December 2011 at the age of 94. Withington participated in the Dayton hotel room weekend marathon that produced a modified B-52 design including a scale model.

[5] Walter J. Boyne, *Beyond the Wild Blue: A History of the U.S. Air Force 1947-1997,* A Thomas Dune Book, St. Martin's Press, New York, NY, 1997

[6] The balsa-wood scale model was eventually returned to Boeing and now resides in the archives.

[7] Bill Yenne, *B-52 Stratofortress: The Complete History of the World's longest Serving and Best Known Bomber,* Zenith Press, Minneapolis, MN, 2012

[8] Three days later on April 18th, the competing Convair YB-60 made its first flight at Carswell AFB, Texas, adjacent to the Convair Fort Worth facility.

[9] Marcelle C. Knaack, *Post-World War II Bombers: 1945-1973,* Office of Air Force History, Washington, DC, 1988

[10] ibid

[11] The Convair proposal also included a plan that the B-36G could be converted into a turboprop airplane. The existing B-36 fleet could also be modified if required. As a cover for any potential setbacks with turbojet engine development, the Air Force agreed.

[12] ibid

[13] The designation Y was applied to the engine designation identifying it as a prototype.

[14] ibid

[15] Don Pyeatt and Dennis Jenkins, *Cold War Peacemaker: The Story of Cowtown and the Convair B-36,* Specialty Press, 838 Lake Street South, Forest Lake, MN, 55025, 2010

[16] ibid

[17] When the pusher-prop Northrop XB-35 with no vertical tail was converted to the all-jet YB-49A configuration, small vertical and ventral fins had to be added. It was confirmed that the XB-35 propellers did offer some lateral stability.

[18] ibid

[19] Marcelle C. Knaack, *Post-World War II Bombers: 1945-1973,* Office of Air Force History, Washington, DC, 1988

[20] Don Pyeatt and Dennis Jenkins, *Cold War Peacemaker: The Story of Cowtown and the Convair B-36,* Specialty Press, 838 Lake Street South, Forest Lake, MN, 55025, 2010

[21] Had the Convair B-60 gone into service, this feature could have caused a serious runway foreign-object damage (FOD) problem for SAC, which continually practiced Minimum Interval Takeoff drills to scramble all bombers and tankers. The exercise was designed to send up the maximum number of bombers up in the minimum amount of time in the event of a nuclear attack on the United States.

[22] Lt. Col. Fitzhugh "Fitz" Fulton, Jr., *Father of the Mother Planes: The Story of USAF and NASA Test Pilot Lt. Col. Fitzhugh "Fitz" Fulton, Jr., An Autobiography,* published by Fitz Fulton, Los Angeles, CA, 2013

[23] Don Pyeatt and Dennis Jenkins, *Cold War Peacemaker: The Story of Cowtown and the Convair B-36,* Specialty Press, 838 Lake Street South, Forest Lake, MN, 55025, 2010

[24] Don Pyeatt and Dennis Jenkins, *Cold War Peacemaker: The Story of Cowtown and the Convair B-36,* Specialty Press, 838 Lake Street South, Forest Lake, MN, 55025, 2010

[25] Marcelle C. Knaack, *Post-World War II Bombers: 1945-1973,* Office of Air Force History, Washington, DC, 1988

[26] Only three B-52As were built. The remaining 10 aircraft were converted into B-52B models.

[27] ibid

[28] ibid

[29] On 29 June 1985, 30 years later to the day, the Rockwell B-1B Lancer was delivered to SAC at Dyess AFB, Texas.

[30] Katherine Johnsen, "House Committee Adds Bombers to Budget," *Aviation Week & Space Technology,* Hightstown, NJ, May 8, 1961, page 26,

[31] Katherine Johnsen, Senate Group Joins Bomber Drive, Adding $525 Million to Budget, Aviation Week & Space Technology, Hightstown, NJ, May 15, 1961, page 27-28

[32] The following year McNamara canceled the Skybolt and reduced the XB-70 to a supersonic test platform.

[33] ibid

[34] In 2016, 55 years later, the B-52H is still in service.

[35] During the 1970s, the B-52D and B-52F were called upon during the Vietnam War. It is fortunate that these bombers had not been phased-out and the USAF had adequate numbers to carry out this new conventional mission as well as maintaining SAC's deterrence fleet.

[36] Secretary McNamara was growing impatient with several launch failures of the Douglas AGM-48A Skybolt ALBM during testing. The missile was a challenge, attempting to operate at Mach 12.4 (9,500 mph). Ironically, there was a successful test three days after the cancellation announcement. During the previous Eisenhower administration, the Corona reconnaissance satellite program suffered 14 failures prior to successfully gathering imagery of the Soviet Union. In the face of potential failure, having sufficient patience can be a virtue.

[37] Headquartered at Barksdale AFB, Louisiana, AFGSC was formed on 7 August 2009. AFGSC is responsible for the U.S. land-based ICBM force, two B-52H Wings, and the single B-2A Wing.

[38] John Tirpak, Daily Report, *Air Force Magazine,* October 10, 2014

[39] Arie Church, End of the Smoke Trail, Daily Report, *Air Force Magazine,* April 22, 2015

[40] In compliance with the Strategic Arms Limitation Talks (SALT) agreement with the Soviet Union, the B-1B Lancer was decertified from carrying nuclear-armed ALCMs and nuclear gravity bombs, and designated a conventionally armed bomber. This involved removing the bombers' hardware necessary to carry ALCMS, which was verified by Russian onsite observers. In hindsight, when the conventionally armed CALCM was developed, having the B-1B available to carry CALCMs would have been a tremendous asset in several major operations.

[41] The AGM-129B ACM was retired from active service during 2012.

[42] Marcelle C. Knaack, *Post-World War II Bombers: 1945-1973,* Office of Air Force History, Washington, DC, 1988

Chapter 5

[1] Dennis R. Jenkins & Tony R. Landis, *Experimental & Prototype U.S. Air Force Fighters,* Specialty Press, 838 Lake Street South, Forest Lake, MN, 55025, 2008

[2] The Republic Aviation F-105 contract was one of the initial weapon system (WS) designated contracts that would follow for many decades. In this realm, the contractor is responsible for development and all integration.

[3] Instituted during the late 1940s, the Cook-Craigie concurrency plan was designed to dramatically reduce development time by eliminating the prototype stage. The F-105/F-107 programs did not completely eliminate prototypes, but attempted to speed up production. As aircraft became increasingly complex, this concept proved more analogous to Russian roulette.

[4] If produced, the RF-105 would feature nose-mounted camera ports similar to McDonnell's RF-101C Voodoo configuration.

[5] ibid

[6] Requirements creep is the continued addition of modifications, tasking, and upgrades to an aircraft after the program goals and schedule are established and the contract has been signed.

[7] ibid

[8] ibid

[9] ibid

[10] These aircraft names included the legendary World War II P-47 Thunderbolt; F-84 Thunderjet; F-84F Thunderstreak; RF-84F Thunderflash; XF-91 Thunderceptor; and, later during the 1970s, the A-10 Thunderbolt II. Republic's post–World War II RC-3 Seabee seaplane was originally the Thunderbolt Amphibian.

[11] During September 1956, Republic Aviation began retrofitting 1,500 F-84F Thunderstreaks with a dual-actuator control system. An advanced version of the system was planned for the F-105. It was basically a tandem actuator system with two systems operating side by side on the same control surfaces. In the event of an engine malfunction or seizure, an emergency ram-air turbine (RAT) was activated by the pilot and extended into the airstream to run the emergency pump. The F-105 would also be equipped with two separate power circuits.

[12] ibid

[13] William J. Simone, *North American F-107A,* Published by Steve Ginter, 1754 Warfield Circle Simi Valley, CA 93063, 2002

[14] ibid

[15] In *North American Aviation F-107A,* author William Simone commented that "a more advanced F-105 was anything but true."

[16] ibid

[17] Because certain segments of the designs were shared, Harold Dale was the NAA project engineer on both the F-100B fighter-bomber variant and the interceptor variant. This included the wing, empennage, and engine type. About a dozen NAA engineers were assigned to the F-100B Interceptor, which later became the group that designed the Mach-2 capable F-107A.

[18] ibid

[19] As designed, the Convair B-58 Hustler medium bomber incorporated a greatly extended and complex landing gear arrangement in order to house a large external centerline weapon pod.

[20] The NAA F-108 Rapier and XB-70 Valkyrie programs were also equipped with these complicated variable inlets for high-Mach flight; both were canceled prior to reaching operational status. Within the customer ranks (secretary of defense/DoD), numerous budget battles, arrogance, and a lack of technical understanding by various bureaus quite often entered the fray.

[21] At an early design stage, Dave Wisted related that he thought a twin-engine design was the best course to pursue. Project Engineer Harold Dale told him that the Air Force would never buy a twin-engine fighter. Six years later in January 1962, the Air Force signed on for the twin-engine F-110 Spectre, an Air Force version of the Navy's McDonnell F-4C Phantom II.

[22] ibid

[23] The T-171 (M61) is the identical 20mm cannon system selected for the Republic YF-105A.

[24] When the F-107A was canceled, the operational NAA Autonetics MA-12 fire-control system was transferred to the F-105 program.

[25] ibid

[26] Through the years the author has been continually astonished regarding the numerous theories about the location of the F-107A's upper fuselage intake, as if NAA engineers had just placed it there arbitrarily and suggesting that ejecting from the F-107A meant certain death and the design should have been immediately changed. There were critical design-requirement parameters resulting in that unique configuration, and it was far from being a random decision.

[27] ibid

[28] ibid

[29] ibid

[30] The VAID system was used in the manual mode, and not the production automated mode.

[31] The centerline tank was instrumented to provide data for the production tactical configuration.

[32] Al White later flight-tested the North American Rockwell XB-70 Valkyrie. White survived the 8 June 1966 midair collision between the XB-70 and a F-104N. During his career White accumulated 8,500 hours in 125 types of aircraft.

[33] The third F-107A (t/n 55120), with NAA test pilot Scott Crossfield at the controls, was damaged during a takeoff attempt. Contrary to many accounts of the aircraft being written off, that F-107A was quickly repaired. Shortly afterward, it appeared on static display at an Edwards AFB open house.

[34] ibid

[35] This event sounds very familiar to a strange occurrence involving Sec. of Defense Robert McNamara. McNamara visited NAA at a critical period during the development of the XB-70 Valkyrie. NAA personnel had worked for several days to prepare to answer questions. McNamara exited his limousine, walked around the massive Mach 3+ bomber, and quickly departed without asking any questions. I guess if you are "all-knowing" you don't need a briefing.

[36] ibid

[37] One difficult situation follows another. Unfortunately for North American, not too long after the F-107A debacle, the Eisenhower administration canceled the brilliantly designed Mach 3+ NAA F-108 Rapier interceptor to balance the budget.

[38] ibid

[39] Robert F. Dorr, North American's F-107 was the "Ultra Sabre," and Perhaps the "Ultra What Might Have Been", Defense Media Network, 4 January 2012

[40] William J. Simone, *North American F-107A,* Published by Steve Ginter, 1754 Warfield Circle Simi Valley, CA 93063, [2002]

[41] ibid

[42] The RF-105B variant was canceled, and the RF-101C Voodoo proceeded into production. The three RF-105Bs were completed in the factory as JF-105Bs, with a camera-housing shape in the nose, although no photographic equipment was ever installed.

[43] Robert Cushman, *Aviation Week,* 36-330 New York, NY, [25] November 1957, page 66-67

[44] The inlet on the Lockheed SR-71 Blackbird, built during the 1960s, produced most of the thrust while operating at high-Mach cruise.

[45] ibid

[46] Reacting to criticism of the use of expensive high-performance fighter-bombers in the close air support (CAS) role, during April 1961 the Air Force and Army conducted a live-fire demonstration at Nellis AFB. Both the Republic F-105 and NAA F-100 participated in the exercises.

[47] A projection of U.S. airpower capability was demonstrated at the June 1961 Paris Air Show. The F-105D, McDonnell F4H-1 Phantom II, North American Rockwell A3J Vigilante, and Convair B-58 Hustler all performed aerial demonstrations. Such performances exemplify international technical prowess and prestige, and are also critical to the U.S. balance of trade. By contrast, not one U.S. military aircraft performed at the June 2015 Paris Air Show.

[48] Better late than never: Because of combat losses from AAA, the Air Force ordered improvements to the F-105's vulnerable dual hydraulic systems that were located too close together. In-theater corrections were carried out, including the addition of a third hydraulic system in the upper fuselage.

[49] One MiG-17 kill was shared with a USAF F-4D Phantom II.

[50] John T. Correll, "How Rolling Thunder Began," *Air Force Magazine,* pages 68-72, 1501 Lee Highway, Arlington, VA 22209, March 2015

[51] Air Force Chief of Staff Gen. Curtis LeMay had continually warned President Johnson and Secretary McNamara about the traps waiting by pursuing a gradual escalation. His warnings went unheeded.

[52] ibid

[53] Perhaps history may have been different. The author believes that if President Kennedy had not been assassinated, he could have eventually determined that his choice of Secretary McNamara was not working out. Under the circumstances in which President Johnson took office, most of Kennedy's appointees were retained to maintain continuity. Unfortunately, this included Secretary McNamara. President Johnson was strictly domestic-policy oriented, focused on the Great Society. Johnson elected to "leave those technical items to the whiz kids" (McNamara's team). Thus, McNamara's dysfunctional budget-only focus on the Pentagon would continue. Under McNamara critical DoD programs had already been mangled, and the Vietnam debacle was just getting started.

[54] This scenario is strikingly similar to the recent mishandling of U.S. foreign policy in the Middle East and the asymmetric threat of terrorism that continued between 2009–2016. Examples include providing the enemy data on your strategic/tactical timetables and what restrictions you will adhere to, broadcasting a policy of no boots on the ground, and most importantly, drawing a redline and then backing down. Basic military strategy 101: your adversaries need to be kept in the dark and guessing.

[55] Dan Hampton, *The Hunter Killers: The Extraordinary Story of the First Wild Weasels,* HarperCollins Publishers, 195 Broadway, New York, NY 10007, 2015

[56] ibid

Chapter 6

[1] Note the F3H part of the designation. This was the same as the F3H Demon and continued a Navy practice of retaining previous designations for new aircraft starts.

[2] The Phantom II took shape in McDonnell's rather austere advanced design area that would later become its legendary Phantom Works. After the McDonnell Douglas merger with Boeing in 1997, the Phantom Works was continued under Boeing.

[3] In addition to the mix of Sparrows and Sidewinder missiles, for ground attack the Phantom II could carry up to 16,000 pounds of ordnance.

[4] Fielding the Phantom II without an internal gun was later deeply regretted when air-to-air combat commenced during the Vietnam War.

[5] One of the arguments against the F6D-1 was that it could not defend itself once it had expended its missiles. This was faulty reasoning—defend itself against what? First, the Missileer would launch its Eagle missiles from an average range of nearly 184 miles and then turn away. Second, the bombers that were not destroyed were not going to pursue the Missileer. Third, the Soviet Union did not have the large tanker fleets that would be required to constantly refuel short-range escort fighters. Even if they had the aerial tankers escorting long-range bombers over the arctic, this would have been a logistical nightmare.

[6] The following year, on 21 October 1959, during an F4H-1 record flight attempt not related to the test program, an engine access door failed and led to the loss of the aircraft and the death of test pilot Gerald "Zeke" Huelsbeck.

[7] Tommy H. Thompson, *Vought F8U-3 Crusader III Super Crusader,* Steve Ginter, 1754 Warfield Cir. Simi Valley, CA 93063, 2010

[8] Ralph Wetterhahn, "Where Have All the Phantoms Gone," *Air & Space Magazine,* MRC513, PO Box 37012, Washington, DC 62170, December 2008

[9] In 1962 Chance-Vought became LTV (Ling-Temco-Vought).

[10] Barrett Tillman, "Where Are They Now?," X-Cockpit, The Society of Experimental Test Pilots Technical Publications, SETP Headquarters, 44814 Elm Avenue, Lancaster, CA, Oct./Nov./Dec. 1990

[11] In 1972, during the attack-experimental (A-X) CAS competition between the Northrop YA-9A and Fairchild YA-10A, both aircraft featured off-center nose wheels to accommodate the GAU-8/A 30mm cannon.

[12] To make the trip to Edwards AFB in a single flight, part of the F8U-3 was in the cargo area of the C-124 and a section of the wing was attached underneath the cargo plane.

[13] Anxious to go, the F8U-3 took off briefly during high-speed taxi testing, making an unofficial takeoff. The same premature takeoff occurred with the Mach 3+ Lockheed A-12 reconnaissance aircraft in 1962 and the General Dynamics YF-16 in 1974.

[14] Tommy H. Thompson, *U.S. Naval Air Superiority – Development of Shipborne Jet Fighters 1943-1962,* Specialty Press, 838 Lake Street South, Forest Lake, MN, 55025, 2007

[15] ibid

[16] ibid

[17] ibid

[18] It is interesting to note that the current SEAD Wild Weasel aircraft is a single-seat F-16CJ Viper, taking over from the previous two-seat F-4G Phantom II and, prior to that, the two-seat F-105G Thunderchief.

[19] ibid

[20] There was one reason the Canadian government did not opt for the F8U-3. Officials were unfortunately caught up in the Eisenhower administration's misguided effort to convince them that manned aircraft were quickly becoming obsolete and missiles could handle air defense. This effort was partly to defend its action in the 1959 cancellation of the USAF F-108 Rapier interceptor. It was also thought that this U.S. effort also influenced the Canadian government's cancellation of their Avro CF-105 Arrow interceptor in the same year. Later the Canadian government had second thoughts when they learned that BOMARC air-defense missiles based in Canada would be armed with atomic warheads. Canada eventually accepted used F-101 Voodoos (CF-101). Lessons learned: be thorough in your research before making any major defense-related decisions.

[21] ibid

[22] McDonnell founded McDonnell Aircraft Company in St. Louis In 1939, located at Lambert Field. The company went on to build the Navy's first jet fighter, the FH-1 Phantom, in 1943, and later became a leading producer of military fighter aircraft.

[23] Dr. Henry T. Brownlee Jr., *A Phabulous Fighter,* Boeing Frontiers, 100 North Riverside Place MC: 5003-0983, Chicago, IL 60606, page 8-9 May 2008

[24] A total of 5,057 F-4 Phantoms were built in St. Louis, with the last being delivered in 1979. Under license, Japan's Mitsubishi Heavy Industries built an additional 127 F-4EJ Phantoms, the last completed on 20 May 1981. Subsequently, 14 additional RF-4EJs were acquired from McDonnell Douglas and served in the Japan Air Self-Defense Force (JASDF).

[25] ibid

[26] The success of the Navy's F-4 Phantom's integration into the USAF fleet reinforced Sec McNamara's thinking that many Navy and Air Force aircraft programs could be combined to save money. Unfortunately, aircraft size and weight requirements are not always so closely related. Ignoring naval aviation experts, McNamara forced the large Air Force TFX (F-111A) to be adapted by the Navy (F-111B) for carrier-based operations, which proved to be a protracted disaster.

[27] As a derivative of the F4H-1, the F-110A did not receive an XF-110A or YF-110A designation.

[28] Dennis R. Jenkins & Tony R. Landis, *Experimental & Prototype U.S. Air Force Fighters,* Specialty Press, 838 Lake Street South, Forest Lake, MN, 55025, 2008

[29] John T. Correll, "Rolling Thunder," *Air Force Magazine,* pages 58-65, 1501 Lee Highway, Arlington, VA 22209, March 2005

[30] ibid

[31] The consequences of projecting incompetence and weakness: On 23 January 1968 while operating in international waters, the "unescorted" and unarmed USS *Pueblo* electronic-intelligence ship was intercepted and captured by North Korean patrol boats resulting in the death of one crewmember. Later, it was determined that the Soviet Union most likely instigated the operation in order to examine encryption and coding equipment aboard the *Pueblo.* Soviet intelligence was confident that with the Johnson administration's basic ineptness and preoccupation with the Vietnam War, there would be no retaliation. It was no coincidence that about a week later, to distract President Johnson, the Tet Offensive was launched against most of South Vietnam. Both North Korea and North Vietnam were Soviet surrogates. As predicted, President Johnson shifted a few military assets, but there was no retaliation against North Korea. The 82-man *Pueblo* crew was subjected to extremely harsh treatment and were eventually released 11 months later. Secretary McNamara resigned from office on 29 February 1968, just over a month after the *Pueblo's* capture.

[32] Jack Broughton, "The Heart of the North," *Air Force Magazine,* pages 70-74, 1501 Lee Highway, Arlington, VA 22209, April 2014

[33] ibid

[34] ibid

[35] Some procurement anomalies don't change. Just prior to the F-4 being fielded in 1960 (without an internal gun), it was declared that "the day of the close-in dog fighting mix is over—targets will be tracked and destroyed with missiles before visual ID." Since that time, including the air war over North Vietnam and numerous other conflicts aground the world involving both U.S. and Allied aircraft, the internal gun proved a necessity. After all these supposed lessons learned, remarkably only the USAF F–35A variant of the JSF program will have an internal 23mm gun. The U.S. Navy F-35C and U.S.MC F-35B will use gun pods. The same aerodynamic drag will affect the F-35s as it did the Phantom II when the 20mm gun pod was used as a temporary solution more than 45 years ago.

[36] Ralph Wetterhahn, "Where Have All the Phantoms Gone?," *Air & Space Magazine,* MRC513, PO Box 37012, Washington, DC 62170, December 2008

[37] This was certainly curious since every U.S. fighter aircraft developed since World War II had tracers in their gun/cannon ammunition. It certainly took too much time to get all the equipment performing correctly during the Vietnam War. One can only imagine the frustration of the pilots.

[38] On 28 April 1967, McDonnell Aircraft Company merged with Douglas Aircraft Company, forming McDonnell Douglas Corporation

[39] ibid

[40] Beginning in the mid-1970s, the J79 engines on the F-4E, F-4J, and F-4S were gradually replaced with smokeless J79-10B and J79-17C uprated engines. This would negate the ongoing problem of the "Old Smoky" Phantom being seen by enemy pilots or gunners up to 25 miles away, not good for ground attack or air-to-air combat.

Chapter 7

[1] The term "Sandy" was used to describe the SAR A-1 Skyraider, but was also a generic term for the CSAR task. Later, the A-10 adopted the descriptor "Sandy" during CSAR missions.

[2] With a specific need by the military in mind, extensive research was done to create a specialized single-mission CAS aircraft, yet today that notion is being criticized.

[3] Fairchild World, August 1973, Fairchild Industries, Inc. Century Blvd., Germantown, MD 20767

[4] ibid

[5] Fred Anderson, *Northrop: An Aeronautical History,* Lithography Overland Printers, Inc., Northrop Corporation Century City, Los Angeles, CA 90067, 1976

[6] Production quantity is always the tricky part of aircraft procurement. Past experience with the DoD has shown that after an award, like clockwork, the production number is usually reduced, resulting in unit price increase.

[7] Fairchild publicity brochures referred to the YA-10A's engine mounting as "Caravelle fashion," so named for the 1950s French airliner that introduced this configuration.

[8] Fairchild World Vol. 11 No. 3 May/June 1974, Fairchild Industries, Inc. Century Blvd., Germantown, MD 20767

[9] Fred Anderson, *Northrop: An Aeronautical History,* Lithography Overland Printers, Inc., Northrop Corporation Century City, Los Angeles, CA 90067, 1976

[10] During YA-9A weapons testing, each wing hardpoint held double ejection racks for carrying multiple ordnance. This allowed for up to 20 Mk. 82 500-pound bombs or other ordnance to be carried.

[11] Decades later the Northrop Grumman B-2A stealth bomber would incorporate the split ailerons speed brake combination.

[12] ibid

[13] ibid

[14] During strafing, by pressing the rudder petals to produce side-slipping, the aircraft nose yaw will spread the shell dispersal; this was known as "hosing."

[15] ibid

[16] ibid

[17] The author witnessed an A-10 firepower demonstration at Nellis AFB during March 1983. Simulated Soviet tanks were the targets, and the sound of the GAU-8/A was similar to a buzz saw and pounded your chest from more than 1.5 miles away.

[18] Although extremely accurate, the latest software upgrades on the A-10C have further improved strafing accuracy.

[19] Fairchild World Vol. 10 No. 8 August 1973, Fairchild World, Fairchild Industries, Inc. Century Blvd., Germantown, MD 20767

[20] Fairchild World Vol. 11 No. 4 July/August 1974, Fairchild World, Fairchild Industries, Inc. Century Blvd., Germantown, MD 20767

[21] Fred Anderson, *Northrop: An Aeronautical History,* Lithography Overland Printers, Inc., Northrop Corporation Century City, Los Angeles, CA 900671976

[22] History can be ironic: YA-9A designer Northrop inherited the A-10 program. In 1987, all A-10 assets were acquired by Grumman from Fairchild Republic and are now part of Northrop Grumman. Northrop Grumman Aerospace Systems is partnered with Lockheed Martin Systems Integration as a member of the A-10 prime Team.

[23] Fairchild World, August 1974 Fairchild Industries, Inc. Century Blvd., Germantown, MD 20767

[24] The first fatal A-10A (s/n 75-0294) crash occurred during a flight demo on 3 June 1977 at the Paris Air Show. The aircraft completed a loop over the top, but at the end of the loop it appeared to be too low. The A-10A's sink rate increased, and it dragged its tail on the ground, the aft section departing the aircraft. As the A-10A disintegrated, the titanium bathtub separated from the aircraft and was seen tumbling down the grassy infield at Le Bourget Airport. Fairchild director of flight operations Howard "Sam" Nelson, an original A-10 first-flight pilot, was killed in the crash.

[25] Lou Drendel, *A-10 Warthog In Action,* Squadron/Signal Publications 1115 Crowley Drive, Carrollton., TX 75006-1312, 2010

[26] David A. Brown, *Aviation Week & Space Technology,* McGraw-Hill Publishing New York, NY, NATO Readiness: A-10 Crews Sharpen Air Support Skills, Cover story reprint, pages 2-4, 2 April 1979

[27] A two-year heads-up: During August 2012, U.S. intelligence had provided a warning to the Obama administration on the emergence of ISIS. A year later President Obama referred to ISIS as the "JV Team." Shortly after that, ISIS moved out of Syria and captured a vast amount of territory in Iraq.

[28] During June 2014, when the United States was slow to react to the ISIS terrorist group's advance into Iraq, Russian president Vladimir Putin requested 10 to 12 Su-25 Frogfoot attack aircraft from Iran to be sent to Iraq to assist. Iraq had operated the type under Saddam Hussein's regime, but there are few qualified pilots in the current ranks. Iran's Islamic Revolutionary Guard Corps Air Force pilots are flying the Su-25s. This development represents a major loss of U.S. influence in Iraq.

[29] Gary Wetzel, *A-10 Thunderbolt II Units of Operation Enduring Freedom 2002-07,* Osprey Publishing, Midland House, West Way, Botley, Oxford, OX2 OPH, UK, 2013

30 Aging aircraft in the fleet is nothing new. Not mentioned were other members of the geriatric aircraft lineup: the USAF B-52 is 63 years old, the KC-135 tanker is 59 years old, the F-15 is 43 years old, and the F-16 is 41 years old.

31 Department of Defense Press Release 24 Feb 2014

32 Lawmaker, and A-10 Vet Aims to Protect Warthog, Air Force Times, 30 January 2015

33 Air Force Magazine, "Building Better Warthogs," page 16, 1501 Lee Highway, Arlington, VA 22209, September 2006

34 Amy Butler, Aviation Week & Space Technology, 1166 Penton Avenue of the Americas, New York, NY, 2-12-15

35 Faulty leadership: The premature retirement of the NASA Space Shuttle in early 2011, before a new human-capable orbital system was ready, forced the U.S. human spaceflight program into disarray. A period of up to eight years or more began before the United States will be able place astronauts into LEO and dock with the ISS. Additionally, the United States pays Russia $82 million a seat on Soyuz to put a single U.S. astronaut into orbit. Prior to the shuttle's retirement the price was $22 million, and during 2014 NASA spent a total of $400 million; 2015 will cost $490 million. Not a good position for a world power to be in.

36 Early retirement misjudgment: An important USAF aircraft asset was retired just prior to the January 1991 Gulf War (Operation Desert Storm). Amid some controversy, the SR-71 Blackbird strategic reconnaissance aircraft had been retired on 22 November 1989. It was assumed that satellites could adequately provide reconnaissance coverage. But the satellites could not be retasked in a timely manner, and data that was obtained could not be dispersed to field commanders quickly enough to match the fast-paced Gulf hostilities.

37 From 2005 through 2015, the USAF has reduced its total aircraft fleet by 500 aircraft. During 2014 alone the number of airmen and women was reduced from 330,000 to just 307,000.

38 Knowledge of defense issues required for commander in chief: During the presidential debates in 2012, candidate Barack Obama while answering a question, stated that the number of U.S. Navy ships required wasn't important. Although candidate Mitt Romney did not refute it at the time, Obama had the wrong answer. The number of naval ships is critical in patrolling the millions of square miles of ocean that the Navy must keep secure—especially as China expands its influence in the western Pacific, and Russia in the North Polar regions.

Chapter 8

1 Eric Hehs, Code One, Vol. 12 No. 3, Lockheed Martin Corp. PO Box 748/Mail Zone 1224, Fort Worth , TX, pg. 22-34, July 1997

2 Ibid

3 William G. Holder and William G. Siuru, General Dynamics F-16, Aero Publishers, Inc. 329 West Aviation Road, Fallbrook, CA 92028, 1976

4 ibid

5 Ray Wagner, Mustang Designer, Orion Books, Division of Crown Publishers Inc., 201 East 50th Street, New York, NY 10022, 1990

6 Decades later this type of inlet location would be adapted by the General Dynamics F-16 Viper and Rockwell's Sabrebat FSW design.

7 Fred Anderson, Northrop: An Aeronautical History, Lithography Overland Printers, Inc., Northrop Corporation Century City, Los Angeles, CA 90067, 1976

8 ibid

9 ibid

10 Gerald Liang, "YF-17 Rollout," Air Combat Magazine, pg. 59-61 & 78, June 1974

11 Don Fink, Aviation Week & Space Technology, 1221 Avenue of the Americas, New York, NY 10020, 12 December 1974, pg. 40-46

12 Fred Anderson, Northrop: An Aeronautical History, Lithography Overland Printers, Inc., Northrop Corporation Century City, Los Angeles, CA 90067, 1976

13 Aviation Week & Space Technology, McGraw-Hill, 1221 Avenue of the Americas, New York, NY 10020, pg. 20, 17 June 1974

14 AW&ST Don Fink 16 December 1974

15 Don Fink, Inflight Refueling Helps Speed YF-17 Test Series, Aviation Week & Space Technology, McGraw-Hill, 1221 Avenue of the Americas, New York, NY 10020, 16 December 1974

16 ibid

17 Recently released F/A-18 Hornet/Super Hornet in-cockpit Go-Pro videos clearly show the pilots using these handgrips to turn to see adversaries.

18 Fred Anderson, Northrop: An Aeronautical History, Lithography Over-

land Printers, Inc., Northrop Corporation Century City, Los Angeles, CA 90067, 1976

19 ibid

20 During the 1980s, Lockheed proposed a navalized version of its USAF F-117 Nighthawk stealth fighter. Officials at DoD noted that if you change the wing area to reduce the approach speed and the canopy configuration to increase visibility, the faceted shape so carefully designed specifically for low radar cross secion (RCS) is defeated. Additionally, it was uncertain if the nonafterburning engines, specific for low IR signature, would have enough thrust for a trap landing go-around. The proposal was rejected.

21 The F-18L designation quickly disappeared as the F/A-18 designation took hold for all variants. Later disagreements on foreign sales between Northrop and McDonnell Douglas lead to lawsuits that were eventually reconciled in April 1985.

22 Eric Hehs, Code One, Vol. 12 No. 3, Lockheed Martin Corp. PO Box 748/Mail Zone 1224, Fort Worth, TX, pg. 26-27, July 1997

23 During the late 1970s, when the F-16/79 was marketed for foreign sales, President Jimmy Carter's administration stipulated a lower-thrust engine for exports to U.S. allies. Since the Soviet Union was selling their top-of-the-line fighter to Warsaw Pact countries, the de-rated engine idea on the F-16 did not sell with NATO and other international customers.

24 ibid

25 The P&W F100 engine encountered stall/stagnation problems on the twin-engine F-15 Eagle program. A YF-16 encountered the same problem during testing, but the anomaly was rectified. By 2003, there were four engine types/variants in the F-16 fleet. As the United States retires large numbers of fighters, this will not be the case in the future with the single-engine F-35 JSF, which is slated for only one engine type.

26 The first operational F-16 (t/n 80001) is on permanent display at Langley AFB.

27 Eric Hehs, Code One, Lockheed Martin Corp. PO Box 748/Mail Zone 1224, Fort Worth, TX, pg. 2-11, Third Quarter 2008

28 In 1987, Japan's MHI did reach an agreement with Lockheed Martin to coproduce the F-2 Support Fighter based on the F-16 design. Four prototypes were tested and the F-2 entered production in 1998, with first deliveries taking place in 2005. Utilizing more light-weight graphite epoxy in the airframe, the F-2's wing area is 25 percent lager, the fuselage is 17 inches longer, and the horizontal stabilizers are larger as well. The F-2 currently serves with the JASDF.

29 The EFA Team had many disagreements. France was a consortium member, but left the group in the early 1980s due to problems with EFA operational requirements.

30 Ray Whitford, Design for Air Combat, Jane's Publishing Company Ltd., 238 City Road, London EC1V 2PU, UK, 1987

31 After the ETF competition, the F-16XL was later redesignated F-16E for marketing purposes, but the program never went forward.

32 Paul Metz, "YF-23 Preliminary Flight Test Results," 1990 Report To the Aerospace Profession, The Society of Experimental Test Pilot (SETP), Headquarters, 44814 Elm Avenue, Lancaster, CA, September 29, 1990

33 One of the smartest acquisitions in decades occurred in March 1993. Lockheed purchased General Dynamics' military aircraft business. One of the greatest mysteries at the time was why Rockwell International did not opt to purchase GD's aircraft business. It would have been the perfect deal to keep Rockwell in the fighter aircraft business. Two years later in March 1995, Lockheed merged with Martin Marietta forming Lockheed Martin Company.

34 After acquiring Rockwell International's aerospace and defense businesses in December 1996, in August 1997 Boeing and McDonnell Douglas merged. The Boeing Company name was retained and the Boeing logo was modified to commemorate the merger.

Chapter 9

1 Dennis R. Jenkins & Tony R. Landis, Experimental & Prototype U.S. Air Force Jet Fighters, Specialty Press, 838 Lake Street South, Forest Lake, MN, 55025, 2008

2 ibid

3 Eric Hehs, "F-22 Design Evolution Part 1," Code One Magazine, Lockheed Martin Aeronautics Company P.O. Box 748 Mail Zone 1503, Ft. Worth, TX 76101, Vol.13 Number 2, April 1998

4 The Packard Commission was a Blue Ribbon Commission on Defense Management that issued its final report to President Ronald Reagan and Sec. of Defense Casper Weinberger on 30 June 1986. Included in the multifaceted report was the recommendation to fly competing prototypes for evaluation.

5 For Rockwell International, teaming on the ATF program would have provided an added hedge to remain in the fighter aircraft business. Even though the disappointing loss of the previous F-15 competition to McDonnell Douglas weighed heavily on the Corporation, Rockwell opted not to team for the ATF competition.

6 William B. Scott, "YF-23A Previews Design Features of Future Fighters," Aviation Week & Space Technology, 2 Penn Plaza 5th Floor New York, NY 10121, 2 July 1990

7 Smartest deal of the decade: In 1993 Lockheed purchased the aircraft businesses of General Dynamics and inherited the venerable F-16 production line.

8 Paul Metz, "YF-23 Preliminary Flight Test Results," 1990 Report To the Aerospace Profession, The Society of Experimental Test Pilot (SETP), Headquarters, 44814 Elm Avenue, Lancaster, CA, September 29, 1990

9 During the ill-fated U.S. Navy/McDonnell Douglas-General Dynamics A-12 stealth attack aircraft program, compartmentalization caused a breakdown of communications regarding vital stealth-manufacturing techniques that eventually led to the program's cancelation. The A-12 contractors wound up contacting Ben Rich at Lockheed's Skunk Works for assistance.

10 Jeffrey P. Rhodes, Air Force Magazine, 1501 Lee Highway Arlington, VA 22209-1198, Sept. 1990 pg. 116-119.

11 ibid

12 The curvilinear shape to achieve a low RCS was first introduced in 1982 on the Northrop Tacit Blue testbed. Tacit Blue tested new systems for future battlefield surveillance aircraft, plus its RCS was also measured during different flight profiles.

13 Bill Sweetman, YF-22 and YF-23: Advanced Tactical Fighters, Motorbooks International Publishers, P.O. Box 2 729 Prospect Avenue, Osceola, WI 54020, 1991

14 Paul Metz, "YF-23 Preliminary Flight Test Results," 1990 Report To the Aerospace Profession, The Society of Experimental Test Pilot (SETP), Headquarters, 44814 Elm Avenue, Lancaster, CA, September 29, 1990

15 Dennis R. Jenkins & Tony R. Landis, Experimental & Prototype U.S. Air Force Jet Fighters, Specialty Press, 838 Lake Street South, Forest Lake, MN, 55025, 2008

16 ibid

17 Michael A. Dornheim, "Lockheed ATF prototype Demonstrates Flight from Post-Stall to Above Mach 2," Aviation Week & Space Technology, 2 Penn Plaza 5th Floor New York, NY 10121, 14 January 1991

18 On 25 April 1992, Lockheed test pilot Tom Morganfield was at the controls of the number-two YF-22A. As he approached the runway to land, the aircraft entered a series of uncontrolled pitch oscillations 40 feet above the runway. Sensing an imminent ground impact, Morganfield immediately retracted the landing gear and settled onto the runway. The aircraft skidded about 8,000 feet. The cause was attributed to the computerized flight-control system, but the aircraft never flew again.

19 Aerospace Daily, "Thrust Vectoring Doubles YF-22 Roll Capability at Low Speeds," 7 December 1990

20 Mark A. Lorell - Hugh P. Levaux, The Cutting Edge, The Rand Corporation, 1333 H. Street, NW Washington, DC 20005-4707, 1998

21 Aerospace Daily, "Northrop ATF Proposal Downed by Change Risks, Documentation," 31 May 1991

22 Paul Metz, "YF-23 Preliminary Flight Test Results," 1990 Report To the Aerospace Profession, The Society of Experimental Test Pilot (SETP), Headquarters, 44814 Elm Avenue, Lancaster, CA, September 29, 1990

23 Robert F. Door, Air Power Abandoned; Robert Gates, The F-22 Raptor and the Betrayal of America's Air Force, robert.f.door@cox.net, 2015

24 James Kudes, "The F-22 Has a Future, Sell Advanced Fighter to Australia, Japanese Allies," Defense News, 20 April 2009

25 David A. Fulghum, "Japanese Officials Could Be Offered a $290 million F-22," Aviation Week & Space Technology, 2 Penn Plaza 25th Floor New York, NY 10121, 25 June 2009

26 The F-22 was redesignated F/A-22 in September 2002 to reflect a multimission capability. When IOC was achieved in December 2005, the F-22 designation was reinstated.

27 Robert F. Door, Air Power Abandoned; Robert Gates, The F-22 Raptor and the Betrayal of America's Air Force, robert.f.door@cox.net, 2015

28 The first Lockheed Martin F-35A (AL-1) built in Italy by Finmeccanica-Alenia Aermacchi made its inaugural flight on 7 September 2015.

29 Although 20 operational B-2s were built, when one aircraft was lost in an accident at Anderson AFB, Guam, the prototype demonstrator was authorized to be brought up to operational standards. Still, only 20 B-2s remain in the fleet.

30 Robert S. Dudney, "The B-2 Syndrome Rides Again," *Air Force Magazine*

31 This 2005 warning was quite accurate; as this book goes to press, we are witnessing the emergence of new Russian and Chinese high-technology stealthy fighters. 1501 Lee Highway Arlington, VA 22209-1198, July 2002, pg. 4

32 Robert S. Dudney, Editor-in-Chief, Editorial, *Air Force Magazine*, 1501 Lee Highway Arlington, VA 22209-1198, February 2005

33 Robert F. Door, *Air Power Abandoned; Robert Gates, The F-22 Raptor and the Betrayal of America's Air Force*, robert.f.door@cox.net, 2015

34 "Coup de grace" means delivering a deathblow to something that is suffering. The F-22 program was not a suffering object, but a remarkable technical achievement that only needed smart leadership in regards to production.

35 John A. Tirpak, "Gates Versus the Air Force," *Air Force Magazine*, 1501 Lee Highway Arlington, VA 22209-1198, March 2014 pg. 54-57

36 In September 2013, President Obama avoided taking firm action against President Bashar al-Assad of Syria who had crossed the president's so-called redline by using chemical weapons against his own citizens. Instead, Obama signed a surprise agreement with Putin (a supporter of al-Assad). Earlier Sec. of State John Kerry had called for the ouster of al-Assad. The agreement would have the UN dispose of all Syrian weapons of mass destruction (WMD). This flawed agreement resulted in ISIS using mustard gas on Syrian civilians in June 2015. And in September 2015, Russia flew (in An-124 cargo aircraft) troops and equipment into Syria. Russian fighter-bombers have since gone into action in that region.

37 The F-22 production cut decision was made in 2009, and six years later (mid-2015) the USAF F-35A and Navy F-35C JSF were still two years away from IOC. The F-35 is the low-end of the F-22/F-35 high-low fighter mix and will not be available in greater numbers until nearly 15 years after Secretary Gates's cut the F-22.

38 ibid

39 Defense News, online, 14 September 2015

40 Robert M. Gates, *Duty: Memoirs of a Secretary at War*, Random House LLC, New York, 2014

41 ibid

42 In 2015 the F-22 did enter combat in Syria, attacking ISIS targets with PGMs and utilizing its electronic/intelligence potency to assist other allied attack aircraft capabilities. This would have occurred much earlier, but the Obama administration was noted worldwide as always being behind the power-curve. It will take China years to fully field the J-20 and J-31 in large numbers, but they did appear nine years sooner than Gates anticipated. The Chengdu J-20 first flew on 11 January 2011, and the Shenyang J-31 flew on 31 October 2012.

43 Flight International, Comment Section, Quadrant House, The Quadrant, Sutton, Surrey, SM2 5AS, UK, 14-20, 3-9 April 2012

44 The dB term for RCS is determined in dBsm or dB relative to a 1-meter sphere (sphere with cross section of a square meter), which is the standard target for RCS measurements.

45 Dave Fulghum, "Raptor's Edge - Security and Classification Issues still bedevils efforts to sell F-22s," *Aviation Week & Space Technology*, 2 Penn Plaza 25th Floor New York, NY 10121, 9 February 2009

46 "Mission Brief – F-22 Team Newspaper, First Flight of Raptor 01 is Picture Perfect," Lockheed Martin Aeronautical Systems, 86 South Cobb Drive, Marietta, GA 30063-0264, September 1997

47 James Drew, USAF Reveals Raptor Upgrade Details, Flight International Quadrant House, The Quadrant, Sutton, Surrey, SM2 5AS, UK, 14-20 July 2015

48 The OBOGS protects pilots from chemical or biological attack. The system experienced several problems during 2011–2012, resulting in the loss of an aircraft and pilot. These problems have since been rectified.

49 John A. Tirpak, *Air Force Magazine*, Daily Update – Online, 17 September 2015

50 During September 2015, Boeing revealed a new upgrade package for its F-15C to complement the low number of F-22s in the fleet. The F-15 (C2040) would carry up to 16 air-to-air missiles and feature conformal fuel tanks, an advanced IRST sensor, and the Eagle Passive/Active Warning Survivability System (EPAWSS). The Air Force will review the proposal.

51 ibid

Chapter 10

1 Dennis R. Jenkins & Tony R. Landis, *Experimental & Prototype U.S. Air Force Jet Fighters*, Specialty Press, 838 Lake Street South, Forest Lake, MN, 55025, 2008

2 ibid

3 Bill Sweetman, *Joint Strike Fighter - Boeing X-32 vs. Lockheed Martin X-35*, MBI Publishing Company, 729 Prospect Avenue, PO Box 1, Osceola, WI 54020-0001, 1999

4 Ramon Lopez, "Operation JAST Cause," *Flight International* pg. 23 The Quadrant, Sutton, Surrey, SM2 5AS, UK, 27 April -3 May 1994

5 ibid

6 ibid

7 Government bureaucracy at work: ARPA was created in 1958. In March 1972, "defense" was added to the agency's name, changing it to DARPA. Then in February 1993, the name was changed back to ARPA; it was changed back to DARPA in March 1996.

8 Bill Sweetman, *Joint Strike Fighter: Boeing X-32 vs. Lockheed Martin X-35*, MBI Publishing Company, 729 Prospect Avenue, PO Box 1, Osceola, WI 54020-0001, 1999

9 Dennis R. Jenkins & Tony R. Landis, *Experimental & Prototype U.S. Air Force Jet Fighters*, Specialty Press, 838 Lake Street South, Forest Lake, MN, 55025, 2008

10 Boeing News Release, The Boeing Company P.O. Box 3707 Seattle, WA 98124, 14 December 1999

11 ibid

12 *Boeing News, Vol. 59 No. 21*, The Boeing Company P.O. Box 3707 Seattle, WA 98124, May 26, 2000

13 Fred Knox was a former U.S. Navy pilot with high time in the F-14 Tomcat, and he also flight-tested the Rockwell/MBB X-31A EFM aircraft.

14 Bruce A. Smith, "Boeing X-32A Flies, Begins JSF Demonstration Program," *Aviation Week & Space Technology*, 2 Penn Plaza 5th Floor New York, NY 10121, 25 September 2000

15 *Flight International*, The Quadrant, Sutton, Surrey, SM2 5AS, UK, 14-20, 29 September – 2 October 2000 pg. 5

16 Bruce A. Smith, "Boeing X-32A Flies, Begins JSF Demonstration Program," *Aviation Week & Space Technology*, 2 Penn Plaza 5th Floor New York, NY 10121, 25 September 2000

17 Dennis R. Jenkins & Tony R. Landis, *Experimental & Prototype U.S. Air Force Jet Fighters*, Specialty Press, 838 Lake Street South, Forest Lake, MN, 55025, 2008

18 Jay Miller, *The X-Planes: X-1 to X-45*, Aerofax, Inc. P.O. Box 200006 Arlington, Texas 76006, 1988

19 Dennis R. Jenkins & Tony R. Landis, *Experimental & Prototype U.S. Air Force Jet Fighters*, Specialty Press, 838 Lake Street South, Forest Lake, MN, 55025, 2008

20 ibid

21 Robert Wall & David A. Fulghum, "Lockheed Martin Strikes Out Boeing," *Aviation Week & Space Technology*, 2 Penn Plaza 25th Floor New York, NY 10121, 29 October 2001

22 David A. Fulghum, "Skunk Works Pushed To Improve JSF Effort," *Aviation Week & Space Technology*, 2 Penn Plaza 25th Floor New York, NY 10121, 29 October 2001

23 ibid

24 ibid

25 In April 2011 the U.S. Congress, in all its wisdom, canceled the JSF alternate General Electric/Rolls Royce engine, describing it as pork and a waste of money. Two years later all F-35s were grounded due to a mysterious engine fire, forcing the F-35 to miss a first appearance at the important Farnborough Air Show. Fortunately, the United States still had other tactical fighters in the fleet. Had this occurred in another 10 to 20 years it would have been very serious. Demonstrating congressional short-term memory, the F-16 worldwide fleet is flying with both P&W and GE engines to prevent the same problem.

26 Robert Wall and David A. Fulghum, "Lockheed Martin Strikes Out Boeing," *Aviation Week & Space Technology*, 2 Penn Plaza 25th Floor New York, NY 10121, 29 October 2001

27 The UCAV program was turned over to the U.S. Navy as UCAS. A competition was held between Boeing's X-45 and the Northrop Grumman X-47. The X-47 had already been funded to cover

Navy carrier ops development, and Boeing had to quickly revise its design. Eventually, the Boeing X-45 lost out to the Northrop Grumman X-47B air vehicle. Instead of the USAF having operational squadrons of Boeing X-45s (A-45) within a few years, the Navy was now developing a carrier-based UCAS-D, a far more difficult task. Many Navy officials were not that enthusiastic about unmanned aircraft operating on the carrier deck. The USAF's A-45 would have been operational by at least 2008. By the end of 2015, the Navy UCAS-D was at best ten years away from IOC.

28 During October 2015, while operating in Syria, a Russian MiG-29 Fulcrum intercepted a USAF unmanned RQ-9 Reaper and provided valuable propaganda gun-camera video to the media. This would not have happened had the high-performance Boeing A-45 (X-45) UCAV been ordered into production during the mid-2000s.

29 The author recalls working company communications on the USAF/Rockwell B-1B Lancer program during the 1980s. A favorite tactic of B-1B bomber critics was to add all the estimated life-cycle costs into the unit cost (sticker price). If this was the practice at automobile dealerships, the sticker price in the car window would include the total R&D cost prior to purchase, gasoline, insurance, maintenance costs, and any added accessories for the entire life of the car. The author believes auto sales would plummet as a result.

30 Adam J. Herbert, Executive Editor, "What Does JSF Really Cost?," *Air Force Magazine*, 1501 Lee Highway Arlington, VA 22209-1198, August 2009

31 Robert F. Dorr, "SECDEF Gates Places the F-35B on Probation," Defense Media Network, Online, 8 January 2011

32 During 2011, Great Britain decided to shift their procurement of the JSF for the RAF/RN from the F-35B STOVL to the F-35C CV. The UK obviously was not confident in the B variant's schedule. The RN aircraft carriers would have to be extensively modified to handle catapult/trap for the F-35C. This would have reduced the B-variant procure, except for the U.S.MC and Italian navy. Fortunately, for the program the UK reversed the decision a year later and will procure the F-35B.

33 Michael Bruno, "Firing Line," *Aviation Week & Space Technology*, 2 Penn Plaza 25th Floor New York, NY 10121,13 February 2012

34 Dave Majumdar, "Logic of F-35A Questioned," *Flight International*, The Quadrant, Sutton, Surrey, SM2 5AS, UK, 9-15 April 2013

35 Bill Sweetman, "Boeing Offers New, Rebuilt, Upgraded Super Hornets to U.S. Navy," *Aviation Week & Space Technology*, Online, 13 October 2015

36 Dave Majumdar, "Logic of F-35A Questioned: Flight International," The Quadrant, Sutton, Surrey, SM2 5AS, UK, 9-15 April 2013

37 ibid

38 John Tirpak, "AFM Daily Update, F-35 Routinely Passes NSA Hack Tests," Online, 2 September 2015

39 Bill Sweetman, "Plan B V.4.1?" *Aviation Week & Space Technology*, 1166 Avenue of the Americas New York, NY 10036, 8-21 June 2015

40 ibid

41 James Drew, "USAF Demands F-35 Sensor Upgrades in Block 4 Upgrade," *Flight International*, The Quadrant, Sutton, Surrey, SM2 5AS, UK, 9-15 June 2015

42 Bill Sweetman, "Plan B V.4.1?" *Aviation Week & Space Technology*, 1166 Avenue of the Americas New York, NY 10036, 8-21 June 2015

43 With the Liberal Party's victory on 20 October 2015, the new Canadian prime minister, Justin Trudeau, vowed to back away from Canada's purchase of 65 F-35As. Canada has invested $150 million in the JSF program that will not be recovered. Government officials stated that a search for alternatives would be conducted. The price for the JSF partner nations would now increase by $1 million for each F-35 ordered.

44 Although technically a JSF partner, as of late 2015 Denmark was not committed to purchase the F-35A and continues to study the Boeing F/A-18E/F Super Hornet.

45 Andrea Shalal, *Lockheed F-35s Finish At-Sea Test Flights as U.S. Navy Warms to New Jet*, Reuters, Online, 9 October 2015

46 On 29 July 2015, Gen. Dunford was confirmed by the U.S. Senate as the 19th chairman of the Joint Chiefs of Staff.

47 ibid

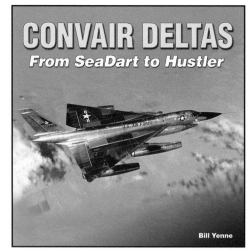
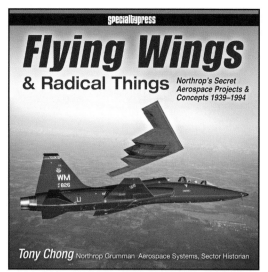
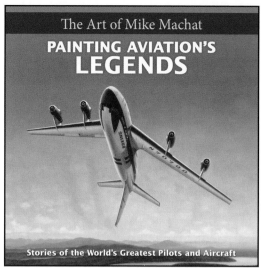
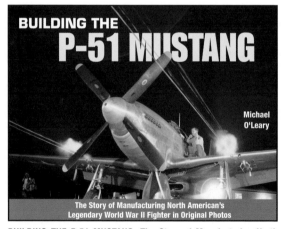
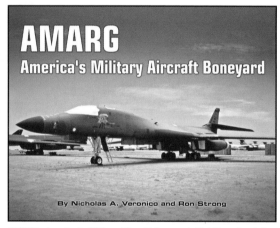